Critical Perspectives on Digital Culture and Gaming

M. Nur Erdem
Ondokuz Mayıs University, Turkey

Özgün Arda Kuş
Uskudar University, Turkey

IGI Global
Scientific Publishing
Publishing Tomorrow's Research Today

Vice President of Editorial	Melissa Wagner
Director of Acquisitions	Mikaela Felty
Director of Book Development	Jocelynn Hessler
Production Manager	Mike Brehm
Cover Design	Jose Rosado

Published in the United States of America by
IGI Global Scientific Publishing
701 East Chocolate Avenue
Hershey, PA, 17033, USA
Tel: 717-533-8845
Fax: 717-533-7115
Website: https://www.igi-global.com E-mail: cust@igi-global.com

Library of Congress Cataloging-in-Publication Data

Names: Erdem, M. Nur, 1976- editor | Kuş, Özgün Arda, 1988- editor
Title: Critical perspectives on digital culture and gaming / edited by M. Nur Erdem, Özgün Arda Kuş.
Description: Hershey PA : IGI Global Scientific Publishing, [2026] | Includes bibliographical references. | Summary: "This book explores the social, political, and cultural dimensions of digital media and interactive entertainment. Through a multidisciplinary lens, it examines how games and online platforms shape contemporary society"-- Provided by publisher.
Identifiers: LCCN 2025033157 (print) | LCCN 2025033158 (ebook) | ISBN 9798337361925 hardcover | ISBN 9798337361932 paperback | ISBN 9798337361949 ebook
Subjects: LCSH: Digital media--Social aspects | Video games--Social aspects
Classification: LCC HM851 .C736 2026 (print) | LCC HM851 (ebook) | DDC 302.23/1--dc23/eng/20250930
LC record available at https://lccn.loc.gov/2025033157
LC ebook record available at https://lccn.loc.gov/2025033158

British Cataloguing in Publication Data
A Cataloguing in Publication record for this book is available from the British Library.

Editorial Advisory Board

Table of Contents

Detailed Table of Contents

This research aims to examine AI as a "digital pharmakon," emphasizing its dual role as both a remedy and a poison in the context of epistemology and AI. Artificial intelligence can enhance human cognition and offer epistemic advantages via neural networks and social media. However, it poses serious threats to cognitive integrity, autonomy, and attention. The study proposes "critical AI literacy" as a solution to mitigate the potential harm that AI systems may cause. The study highlights the ethical and epistemological conundrums raised by the development of AI, particularly in relation to manipulation, spying, and the erosion of individual autonomy. It uses theoretical concepts from Derrida, Heidegger, Stiegler, and Vervaeke to do this. The study suggests a holistic approach to AI regulation by combining epistemology.

This study examines how users perceive the credibility of virtual versus human influencers and how these perceptions influence trust in sponsored social media posts. The research focuses on a high-involvement product (a laptop) and a low-involvement product (coffee), exploring whether the influencer's nature—virtual or human—affects this dynamic. In an experiment, Group A participants were told the influencer was virtual, while Group B believed the influencer was human. Results revealed that perceived source credibility significantly and positively impacted advertising trust across both product categories. Although virtual influencers scored slightly higher on average for source credibility and advertising trust, these differences were not statistically significant.

This study addresses the transformation of digitalization on gaming communities by examining the social, cultural and economic impacts of digital games. Digital games have evolved from a mere means of entertainment to an ecosystem that strengthens social ties between individuals and communities, fosters cultural production and creates new economic models. The research analyzes the dynamics of live streaming platforms such as Twitch, YouTube, and gaming communities such as Fortnite, Roblox, and Minecraft. The study reveals that the sociocultural effects of digital games affect not only the daily lives of individuals but also social and cultural structures at the global level.

Thanks to digital technologies offering the opportunity of interaction to its users, digital game platforms, just like other digital media platforms, reveal differences and multiplicity. Digital game platforms are environments where sexuality, genders, races, cultures and ethnicities are represented. At this point, it is seen that the "Feminist Gaming" approach, in which a counter-representation and narrative construction is positioned against the marginalizing, sexist, homophobic and male-dominated game culture in the digital game environment, appears in the context of digital game sociology and feminist theories. Assuming that transforming the digital game industry and digital game platforms (narrative-character-representation-discourse-image-space) into a research field is an important step towards combating marginalizing practices, the study will examine how a fair gaming environment can be built through the games included in the sample group based on the technofeminist perspective.

YouTube videos are now a vital part of people's lives, and it is possible to access various content, interact with others, share ideas, and discuss those videos. The innate need for individuals to play has evolved into digital gaming and has been a part of YouTube for many years. The research focused on "The Female Gamer's Experience" videos, which are montages of the toxic and gender stereotyping women

Privacy has been expressed with concepts such as individuals' private space and confidentiality in the historical process. With the opportunities provided by Web 2.0, it transforms communication and makes publishing and reaching masses extremely easy. The features offered by social media platforms such as participation, content creation, publishing and sharing have made the digital world a center of attraction for individuals. Social media platforms, which are offered for "free", provide their economy by storing individuals' private life and privacy information and commercializing the attitudes of individuals that enable them to voluntarily disclose their privacy within the platform. On the platform where more views and subscribers mean monetization, users increasingly destroy their privacy in order to attract the attention of the masses. When YouTube and Privacy literature is examined, it is seen that YouTubers try to become famous by publicizing privacy. Privacy is destroyed for the sake of individuals' self-realization and the goal of becoming famous.

This study examines how media outlets in the US, UK, and India portray feminism through sentiment analysis and machine learning-based classification models. By assessing sentiment polarity and evaluating model accuracy, the research highlights variations in feminist discourse across different media landscapes. Findings indicate that UK media maintains a more balanced and positive stance, whereas US and Indian media exhibit slight variations influenced by socio-political and cultural factors. The study provides a comparative perspective on feminist representation, offering insights into global media narratives.

Preface

INTRODUCTION

In an era where digitalization continuously reshapes how information is created, distributed, and consumed, the need to examine and understand the ever-evolving landscape of digital broadcasting and content platforms has never been more urgent. It is with great enthusiasm that we present *Advancements in Digital Broadcasting and Content Platforms*, an edited volume that delves into the theoretical, conceptual, and practical dimensions of this dynamic and multifaceted field.

This book emerges from the recognition that digital platforms—whether they serve as broadcasters, live-streaming services, social media hubs, or user-generated content repositories—have dramatically transformed how audiences interact with media. As we approach the completion of the first quarter of the 21st century, the interaction between users and these digital environments has reached unprecedented levels. These interactions now permeate not only individual behaviors but also broader societal, economic, cultural, and political structures.

Our goal in assembling this volume is to provide a rich, interdisciplinary reference that captures the scope and complexity of digital broadcasting and content platforms. We aim to shed light on the mechanisms and frameworks that define this landscape: the evolution from passive audiences to active users, the development of new content production and distribution models, and the critical implications for areas such as marketing, socialization, and the cultural industries.

The chapters featured in this book offer a diversity of perspectives that collectively work to:

- Clarify the dynamics of the digital broadcasting and content industries,
- Frame the transformation of traditional audiences into interactive users,
- Introduce new concepts, models, and theories relevant to the field, and

- Provide concrete insights into current technologies, applications, and practices.

We envision this volume as a valuable resource for a wide range of readers—including scholars, university students, digital content professionals, media technologists, and anyone with a keen interest in the future of digital communication. By bringing together contributions from leading voices across disciplines and sectors, this book seeks to inform, challenge, and inspire ongoing discourse and innovation in digital broadcasting and content platform development.

We thank all contributors who have lent their expertise and vision to this endeavor, and we hope that *Advancements in Digital Broadcasting and Content Platforms* will serve as a foundational reference for both current inquiry and future research.

ORGANIZATION OF THE BOOK

In Chapter 1, *AI as Digital Pharmakon: The Critical AI Literacy with the Perspectives of Epistemology and Meta-knowledge*, the author presents a thought-provoking philosophical inquiry into the dual nature of artificial intelligence. Positioned as both a remedy and a poison—a "digital pharmakon"—AI is shown to offer cognitive enhancement while simultaneously posing serious threats to autonomy, attention, and epistemic integrity. Drawing on critical theorists such as Derrida, Heidegger, Stiegler, and Vervaeke, this chapter calls for the cultivation of "critical AI literacy" to navigate the ethical and epistemological challenges of our increasingly AI-driven world. The chapter lays the theoretical foundation for holistic AI regulation grounded in epistemological awareness.

Chapter 2, *Trusting the Unreal: Dynamics of Anthropomorphism in Perceptions of Virtual Influencers*, explores the evolving boundary between real and virtual identities in the realm of social media marketing. Through an experimental design, the chapter compares user trust in virtual versus human influencers across high- and low-involvement products. Despite virtual influencers receiving marginally higher scores for source credibility and trust, the differences proved statistically insignificant, suggesting the normalization of virtual entities in the influencer economy. The findings underscore the nuanced relationship between anthropomorphism and digital trust.

In Chapter 3, *The Future of the Digital World: Gaming, Community, and Cultural Transformation*, the author delves into the expansive cultural and economic ecosystems of digital games. No longer confined to entertainment, gaming has become a cornerstone of socialization, community building, and even alternative economic systems. By analyzing platforms such as Twitch, YouTube, Fortnite, Roblox, and

Minecraft, this chapter captures the transformative potential of digital games to reshape global cultural norms and social structures.

Chapter 4, *A Review on Feminist and Queer Games and Game Platforms in the Axis of Techno-Feminist Approach*, confronts the prevailing exclusionary norms of the gaming industry. Through a techno-feminist lens, the chapter examines how feminist and queer game developers and platforms challenge heteronormative, sexist, and homophobic narratives. It emphasizes how counter-representations and inclusive storytelling can subvert dominant paradigms and foster equitable digital environments. The chapter positions feminist gaming as both a cultural critique and a transformative force in the broader digital media landscape.

In Chapter 5, *Reflections on Toxicity and Gender Stereotyping in "Female Gamer's Experience" YouTube Video Interactions*, the author conducts an in-depth content analysis of user comments on videos documenting the gender-based toxicity faced by female gamers. Drawing from over 1,000 comments across widely viewed videos, the research identifies prevailing attitudes, sources of solidarity, and emerging discourses that validate or challenge sexism in gaming. The chapter highlights YouTube as a vital space for witnessing, resisting, and reimagining the female gaming experience.

Chapter 6, *From Competition to Conflict: Hate Speech in Multiplayer Online Battle Arena Games (MOBAs)*, brings to light the alarming prevalence of hate speech in competitive gaming spaces. Using digital ethnography within *Mobile Legends: Bang Bang*, the study documents discriminatory language aimed at marginalized groups and reveals how these behaviors are often normalized or passively accepted. The chapter exposes how digital avatars and anonymity facilitate the reproduction of societal prejudices, urging developers and communities to take accountability for the toxic cultures bred within gaming platforms.

Chapter 7, *Digital Games in Mobile Platforms and Archetypes: A Qualitative Evaluation on Mobile Legends: Bang Bang*, investigates how mobile MOBA games construct narrative identities through character archetypes. With the game's wide accessibility on smartphones, *Mobile Legends: Bang Bang* becomes a fertile ground for examining archetypal roles that shape player engagement and story immersion. Through qualitative analysis, the chapter reveals thematic structures that guide character development, offering insights into how archetypes function in mobile game design and player psychology.

In Chapter 8, *YouTube and the Presentation of Privacy*, the author critically examines how YouTube's monetization incentives compel users to trade personal privacy for public attention. Social media's participatory culture blurs boundaries between private and public life, transforming personal content into commodified spectacle. This chapter contextualizes the erosion of privacy within Web 2.0 dynamics and argues that digital fame often hinges on self-exposure, reflecting shifting cultural norms around visibility, identity, and self-realization.

Chapter 9, *Digital Media Representation of Feminism: Sentiment Trends and Cultural Influences in the US, UK, and India*, applies machine learning and sentiment analysis to map how media portray feminism across different cultural contexts. With comparative insights into the US, UK, and India, the study uncovers how cultural, political, and social factors shape feminist narratives in digital journalism. The UK media's relatively balanced tone contrasts with the more fluctuating stances in the US and India, offering a global perspective on the politics of gender representation in the digital age.

Together, these chapters provide a multifaceted exploration of the digital media landscape—from gaming cultures and influencer dynamics to critical theory and algorithmic ethics. As editors, we believe this collection offers an essential resource for understanding the complexity, power, and potential of digital broadcasting and content platforms.

CONCLUSION

As we conclude this volume, it is evident that the digital broadcasting and content platform ecosystem is not merely a reflection of technological progress—it is a dynamic, evolving arena where social, cultural, ethical, and economic dimensions intersect. The chapters assembled in this book offer a wide-ranging exploration of these intersections, revealing how digital platforms are transforming our modes of communication, representation, and interaction at an unprecedented scale.

From the philosophical inquiry into AI as a digital pharmakon, to the cultural analysis of gaming communities and influencer economies, to the critical interrogations of gender, privacy, and digital identity, this volume underscores the complexity and urgency of understanding digital media beyond surface-level consumption. Together, these contributions deepen our appreciation for the nuances of digital engagement and shed light on both the possibilities and perils that lie ahead.

We hope this book serves as a meaningful resource for scholars, students, industry professionals, and anyone seeking to better understand the shifting landscape of digital platforms. Our intention is not only to document current trends but also to provoke critical reflection and inspire responsible innovation in the ways digital content is created, shared, and experienced.

As digital platforms continue to evolve, so too must our frameworks for analysis and action. We invite our readers to carry forward the insights offered in these pages and to contribute to the ongoing dialogue on how we shape—and are shaped by—the digital world.

Chapter 1
AI as Digital Pharmakon:
The Critical AI Literacy With the Perspectives of Epistemology and Meta-Knowledge

Feride Zeynep Güder
https://orcid.org/0000-0002-3244-3004
Üsküdar University, Turkey

ABSTRACT

This research aims to examine AI as a "digital pharmakon," emphasizing its dual role as both a remedy and a poison in the context of epistemology and AI. Artificial intelligence can enhance human cognition and offer epistemic advantages via neural networks and social media. However, it poses serious threats to cognitive integrity, autonomy, and attention. The study proposes "critical AI literacy" as a solution to mitigate the potential harm that AI systems may cause. The study highlights the ethical and epistemological conundrums raised by the development of AI, particularly in relation to manipulation, spying, and the erosion of individual autonomy. It uses theoretical concepts from Derrida, Heidegger, Stiegler, and Vervaeke to do this. The study suggests a holistic approach to AI regulation by combining epistemology.

INTRODUCTION

AI-based digital culture invaded human cognition and existence as game-changing technologies; yet, due to their dual nature, it is necessary to evaluate their qualities by concentrating on whether they are harmful or beneficial to human life. While millions of digital materials have been developed on various social media platforms and neural networks, there is still a need for rigorous investigation into the interplay

DOI: 10.4018/979-8-3373-6192-5.ch001

between the human brain, which is considered to be the source of true intelligence (human intelligence), and generative artificial intelligence. On one side, we have large language models and digital platforms that are referred to as wisdom and knowledge technology (Falk quoted in Kurbalija, 2024b).

On the other hand, these technical tools provide information and knowledge that human users can benefit from. This interaction poses significant challenges and carries inherent risks. The first obstacle is the delusion that has been generated by the mantras of the AI-based culture, which assert that having a high level of technology would result in the development of a society that is very clever. Marianna Wolf (2016) criticizes digital media, as this surface thinking and quick culture cause us to lose deep thinking and reading processes. To worsen it, "multiple screen addiction," "brain rot," and "cognitive impatience" are some of the terms that are used to describe the effects of algorithmic culture on human cognitive capacities. This is due to algorithmic culture's tendency to obstruct and deplete attention span over time. In light of these issues, it is necessary for us to rethink digital culture as an algorithmic culture and conduct an in-depth analysis of the effects that modern technologies have had on human existence.

The emphasis of this chapter is on the topic of the flawed nature of genuine human intelligence and its interaction with the Large Language Model as a higher kind of intelligence. These cognitive and intellectual challenges direct the focus of this chapter toward the concerns discussed within it. Using metaknowledge skills, artificial intelligence, and procedural epistemology as components of critical AI literacy, this chapter will try to discover a solution to this dilemma. We can see that large language models make use of the whole human intelligence legacy, as shown by Hive Mind and Big Data. To develop a good relationship, it is necessary to exert a great deal of focus, to take some time, and to choose convenient techniques.

To properly understand the epistemological approaches to digital material and large language models, it is necessary to investigate the many kinds of knowledge and the nature of the understanding of various digital media forms. If we are to follow Stiegler's conceptualizations of technology via the lens of the "pharmakon" and the paradoxical implications of digital technology, then we need to broaden the scope of the discussion by including Derrida's (1976) ideas on pharmakon, which are drawn from his reading of Plato. The objective of the research is to apply these points of view to the technology platforms that are available today, notably large language models, which have the potential to serve as both a remedy and a poison. This chapter centers on the balance between remedy and poison, attempting to provide metaknowledge, epistemology, and critical AI literacy. This chapter aims to counteract negative aspects, which include overconfidence, ignorance, and undesirable side effects like MSA, brain rot, and cognitive impatience. This approach aims to counteract negative aspects, which include overconfidence, ignorance, and undesirable side effects such as MSA, brain rot, and cognitive impatience. The negative aspects include overconfidence, ignorance, and undesirable side effects such as aspects, including overconfidence, ignorance, and undesirable side effects such as MSA, brain rot, and cognitive impatience. Keeping these trajectories in mind, this chapter explores the balance between cure and poison.

THEORETICAL BACKGROUND

The works of various philosophers examining the interconnections of technology, culture, and society are the foundation of the current digital shift. These philosophers made substantial contributions to the philosophy discipline. Martin Heidegger, Michel Foucault (1977), Gilbert Simondon, and Jacques Derrida are among the influential figures shaping current philosophers such as Stiegler's understanding of technology's role in defining human existence.

AI as Digital Pharmakon

AI presents a complex challenge for civilization to navigate. To have a complete understanding of generative artificial intelligence, it is vital to acknowledge its dual nature as a pharmakon. O'Neil (2016) asserts that artificial intelligence possesses the capacity to positively impact areas like healthcare and accessibility. However, it also can cause harm, such as repeated pre-existing biases and injustices. Another example of the dual nature of technological progress is artificial intelligence. Artificial intelligence (AI) poses ethical concerns surrounding automation and decision-making transparency (Stiegler, 2018, p. 54). While AI improves efficiency in industries such as healthcare and logistics, it also leads to ethical difficulties (Foucault, 1975, p. 89). Artificial intelligence-driven surveillance technologies, which are evocative of Foucault's panopticism (1975), pose substantial risks to individuals' right to privacy and autonomy. Furthermore, Stiegler warns that the ability of artificial intelligence to manipulate cognitive functions poses a threat to human agency and critical thinking (Stiegler, 2010, p. 76).

The term "categorical culture" refers to the human-driven process of classifying and arranging society, information, and artifacts (Beller, 2017). Algorithmic culture symbolizes a fundamental alteration of what was originally known as "categorical culture." The automation of these processes through the use of artificial intelligence has resulted in the creation of a new cultural paradigm. Within this paradigm, computational systems play a major role in determining not only how we classify the world but also the fundamental structure of the culture that we encounter. According to Zuboff (2019), this revolution is not confined to particular domains such as the entertainment industry or social media; rather, it permeates practically every facet of human existence, including education, governance, economics, and even the structure of interpersonal relationships.

It is clear that we are witnessing the decline of popular culture, which is characterized by widespread and egalitarian participation in cultural production, and the advent of a new, more elite type of culture that is shaped by technology elites (Andrejevic, 2021). This transformation is something that is becoming increasingly apparent as artificial intelligence continues to advance. The result is a high-class culture that is influenced by technology, where artificial intelligence systems and the companies that use them have more control over decisions, sharing information, and creating knowledge.

Stiegler's Digital Pharmacy and Algorithmic Surveillance

The internet and social media serve as examples of digital habitus, representing the digital pharmacy that has emerged in recent years. It would appear that the Internet makes it simpler to communicate with people all over the world and democratizes knowledge, but it also can propagate false information and influence public opinion (Stiegler, 2019, p. 92).

Heidegger demonstrates his criticism of modern communication technology through the paradox of Internet connectedness. Heidegger argues that people are becoming more distant from one another rather than getting closer to one another (Heidegger, 1977, p. 44). Although Simondon's paradigm suggests that digital networks may be beneficial to collective intelligence, it is important to note that algorithmic biases frequently contribute to the perpetuation of societal inequities (Simondon, 1989, p. 112).

The deconstructive analysis of Derrida, which emphasizes the inherent ambiguity in technological tools, serves as the foundation for Stiegler's view of technology as a pharmakon (Stiegler, 2010, p. 56). Heidegger critiques modern technology as enframing (Gestell), arguing that technical growth can reduce human existence to merely instrumental means (Heidegger, 1977, p. 19), which resonates with this idea.

Digital technologies pose significant risks to human capacities, necessitating political and ethical involvement. With a focus on collective intelligence and knowledge creation, Stiegler promotes a digital contributory economy. Heidegger urges against passive consumption and encourages authentic interaction with technology. Digital media and data exposure can negatively impact cognitive abilities, leading to the attention economy and cognitive capitalism.

The rise of algorithmic culture and AI-driven systems increases user interaction but also creates echo chambers, limiting data exposure. This creates polarization and hate speech on social media platforms, blurring the line between reality and truth.

The collection of user data contributes to surveillance capitalism and raises ethical concerns about automation and transparency in decision-making.

Derrida in AI-Based Culture: Deconstructing Knowledge and Meaning

Jacques Derrida's deconstructionist theory of language and meaning provides a useful foundation for understanding how algorithms contribute to the production of knowledge. Derrida (1976) developed this theory and asserts that meaning is never static and always reliant on its environment. Within the context of algorithmic culture, the meanings that algorithms generate are similarly unpredictable and contingent on the parameters that they are provided with as well as the data that they process.

The digital era's deconstruction of meaning has exposed the inherent biases and limitations of algorithmic systems. Algorithms are not objective; rather, the systems and data they operate on influence them. Derrida's work suggests that algorithms cannot be considered unbiased and objective systems of knowing because they are products of certain discursive practices and cultural situations. The context in which we use algorithms shapes them.

According to the paradigm that Derrida (1976) developed, engaging in the pursuit of understanding is analogous to continuously deferring the meaning of a text. Both players and readers must participate in the process of interacting with a text, according to Derrida. However, each individual reader sets the rules that govern this engagement. For the purpose of understanding the principles that control data transfer and information exposure within the context of information production and epistemology, it is vital to have a solid understanding of these principles.

With the help of procedural epistemology and grokking artificial intelligence, the parameters of this framework are established, and users are guided to reduce the negative effects of that pharmakon. The game-playing mindset exhibits distinct aspects of gamification, a common technique in the field of information systems research. Grokking and procedural techniques contribute greatly to increased levels of engagement, motivation, and learning outcomes, as demonstrated by the implementation of gamification in various fields.

The Alignment Dilemma and Guardian AI

As a cognitive scientist, Vervaeke (2025) discusses the emergence of Artificial General Intelligence (AGI) and its implications. He does so by introducing a three-point framework, which includes the alignment problem, conventional technological misunderstandings, and the requirement for individuality and decentralization in the development of AI. As far as Vervaeke is concerned, encouraging a personal approach to artificial intelligence will give consumers more authority, protect their privacy, and encourage respectful interactions between humans and technology. It is essential to establish a relationship of closeness between individuals and artificial intelligence while also acknowledging the negative impacts of the cultural practices that are already in place and the requirement for the development of both humans and AI.

When viewed from this perspective, the primary focus of this chapter—artificial intelligence, metaknowledge, and epistemology—has been clearly established. The ability to exercise control over one's own knowledge and the way in which they interact with artificial intelligence is necessary to achieve autonomy over one's knowledge. In this situation, a problem comes up with aligning artificial intelligence because keeping that alignment might cause a disregard for human values, goals, and morals, which could harm economic interests. In this particular setting, conventional methods are no longer relevant. Because aligning AI with human values is a complicated topic, AI-based culture has become more efficient and inclusive recently. Humans and artificial intelligence need to engage in a reciprocal conversation, with a primary focus on virtue and its nurturing.

The relationship between humans and artificial intelligence happens in several different ways, including teaching, protecting, challenging, shielding, and sharing data. What this means is that artificial intelligence has the potential to become a "guardian AI" if it is able to work for the benefit of human beings. This finding indicates that artificial intelligence interacts with humans beneficially, and it highlights the concept of individual attunement, which refers to a culture of autonomous computers rather than a culture of monolithic machines. In this context, soul-bound artificial intelligence is especially pertinent. It is essential to cultivate the power of a local entity, which will improve the quality of the data and also draw attention to virtue, knowledge, and reason in logic.

However, there is no universal humanity because people have conflicting goals, values, attitudes, and behaviors that don't follow a logical pattern. It is necessary to rectify this imbalance between humans and the development of artificial intelligence and artificial general intelligence (Vervaeke, 2025).

An epistemological approach that places an emphasis on metaknowledge skills is required to update and alter artificial intelligence by utilizing skills as a more complex answer.

METHODOLOGY

Research Summary

This study engages in comprehensive discussions about the characteristics of AI as a digital pharmakon. There are two opposing opinions regarding AI. The utopian side has positive expectations from technology. From the utopian vision and perspectives, AI fosters innovation, enhances human potential, and addresses global challenges. And on the other side of the pendulum, AI causes the loss of autonomy, corporate AI hegemony, and widening inequality. Furthermore, overreliance on AI can diminish people's intellectual capacity.

People lose their interest and curiosity in learning, searching, and even consulting another human being. This setting and inclination can harm human intelligence in AI-based culture instead of liberating it. To address these dilemmas, epistemological approaches combined with critical AI literacy can provide us with new methods to collaborate with AI and create environments for improved communication and interaction.

The system should encourage metaknowledge by increasing the level of and decreasing the dark side of technology. There are cognitive and cultural challenges. Focusing on metaknowledge, as Inan (2020) proposed that this approach can be a way to reduce proposed it can be a way of reducing ignorance. Similarly, one’s awareness of ignorance, particularly in the digital world and AI-based settings, requires certain skills. So, being aware of ignorance can be the first step to overcoming over-reliance on AI. In addition to these skills, too much submissive attitude causes deskilling, as it is necessary to activate the thinking skills.

This skill activates critical AI literacy, which consists of four parts. Promoting awareness must come first, followed by upholding moral principles, remaining educated, and fostering discussions. This way of thinking is similar to Immanuel Kant's famous awakening from his dogmatic slumber, which Hume is credited with causing. Kant adopted Hume's skepticism and began to think critically rather than blindly accepting concepts or beliefs. This realization made Kant reevaluate the This statement challenges the fundamental presumptions of human knowledge and questions his logic. His critical philosophy ultimately found expression in The Critique of Pure Reason.

People today continue to sleep dogmatically in the environment of digital pharmacies, giving up their intelligence and ceasing to question reality. These considerations lead us to examine AI's features in terms of eight components.

1. AI processes information differently. AI is entirely data-driven, whereas humans rely on creativity and intuition. This indicates that while AI is capable of processing enormous volumes of data, it is unable to fully "understand" what these facts imply.
2. AI shares characteristics with the human brain, such as neural networks. But it has no subjective experience nor consciousness.
3. AI is strong because it can analyze enormous amounts of data quickly and reduces human error in decision-making.
4. Because AI lacks a full mind and comprehension, it has flaws. AI experiences limitations in its intuitive reasoning and inventiveness.
5. AI possesses knowledge authority. While AI-generated information is based on algorithmic patterns and statistical analysis, traditional knowledge sources, like academics and journalists, rely on years of research and ethical norms.
6. Although AI-generated content is frequently considered unbiased and objective, biases in algorithms and training data might produce false information or skewed viewpoints.
7. AI gathers and distributes data. Because AI can translate text instantly, summarize complicated facts, and help users with individualized learning experiences, it has the potential to democratize access to information. But not everyone has equal access to AI-powered technologies, resulting in differences according to technological infrastructure, socioeconomic background, and language.
8. The digital divide can exacerbate already existing disparities in access to information and education, where wealthy countries and individuals gain more from AI developments.

The Poisonous Side of AI Age: Dark AI as Digital Pharmakon

Artificial intelligence (AI) is a complex technology that requires a holistic approach to understand and address its ethics and epistemology. This involves transforming the opaque box into a glass box that can be dissected with care, incorporating values and normative elements at critical points in the entire process. A framework called "epistemology-cum-ethics" aims to create an environment that makes it The development, deployment, utilization, and evaluation of AI systems facilitate the easier internalization of values. utilization and evaluation of AI systems.

Ignorance, or the inability to complete a task, is indicative of a lack of knowledge about a proposition, while the ability to accomplish a task is a sign of knowledge about that proposition. The ability to monitor one's own knowledge and ignorance, also known as metaknowledge, is considered a vital skill for intellectual survival in the twenty-first century. İnan (2020) categorizes propositional ignorance into three categories: "whether-ignorance," "that-ignorance," and "fact-ignorance."

Differentiating between various forms of ignorance is crucial to gaining an understanding of the nature of knowledge and ignorance. Understanding the nature of knowledge and ignorance is essential for combating cognitive impatience and brain rot. By bridging the gap between the known and the unknown, Inan underscores the importance of understanding ignorance in human cognition, cooperation, and inquiry.

Ignorance manifests in a multitude of forms, and the nature of its knowledge is diverse. To be conscious of our ignorance, we need to define something as unknown, necessitating a more advanced degree of epistemic representation. Early humans may have had a limited grasp of ignorance, which increased greatly when language arose, particularly through the use of "definite descriptions." We possess many different kinds of ignorance, and the nature of our understanding of ignorance is also quite varied. To be conscious of our ignorance, we need to be able to define something as unknown; such an ability necessitates a more advanced degree of epistemic representation. It's plausible that early humans had a limited grasp of ignorance, which increased greatly when language arose, particularly through the use of "definite descriptions," as Russell and Frege called them. This is something that's possible. The evolutionary and historical points of view are both in agreement with this assessment.

Ignorance and Overconfidence

Researchers have discovered a negative correlation between overconfidence and metaknowledge. Pinski et al. (2024) suggest that ignorance stems from overconfidence. The epistemic attitudes of users are significant in this context because they assist us in comprehending the limits of our knowledge and the manner in which our interaction with AI affects our comprehension of our lack of knowledge. When viewed from an epistemological perspective, Grok explores the process of knowing and comprehending the creation of knowledge. To comprehend artificial intelligence (AI), it is necessary to not only comprehend the outcomes but also to comprehend how AI develops knowledge and how AI systems frame knowledge. The overconfidence in artificial intelligence is a cause for concern because it impedes the processes of knowledge inquiry and continuous learning. In addition, the study draws attention to the advantages of gamification for artificial intelligence education by conducting an objective analysis of learning results and taking into account pre-learning AI literacy concerns. The outcome of this culture of reading on digital devices is that thinking is superficial.

Brain Rot and Multiple Screen Addiction

There is a loss in an individual's mental or intellectual health as a result of consuming an excessive amount of low-quality online content, particularly on social media. Language experts coined the term "brain rot" to describe this trend, and it became the Oxford Word of the Year in 2024.

In the digital age, the word gained prominence, particularly among the populations of Gen Z and Gen Alpha and other younger generations. Between 2023 and 2024, there was a 230% increase in its usage frequency. 2023 and 2024. In this day and age, the phrase has become increasingly significant, particularly in mainstream media, as a result of societal concerns surrounding the negative repercussions that might result from excessive consumption of content found online. It has been utilized more specifically and frequently in relation to the culture of the internet, particularly with viral content such as Skibidi Toilet and user-generated memes. A growing number of people are talking about the potential negative consequences that excessive consumption of this information could have on mental health, particularly among children and teenagers. The word has acquired currency in these debates. According to Heaton (2024), the expression has been embraced by members of Generation Z and Generation Alpha, who are responsible for the utilization and production of digital information.

The excessive use of various gadgets makes children more likely to develop screen addiction, which significantly negatively affects their academic progress and engagement. Consuming an inordinate amount of time in front of a screen might result in emotions of unease and discomfort when access is curtailed. Because of the expansion of electronic gadgets, people have developed a tendency to use numerous devices at the same time, which has led to a wide range of problematic media behaviors that involve multiple screens (Saritepeci, 2021).

Cognitive Impatience and Attention

Reading at a deeper level demands both time and patience. The need for a profound reading is a consequence of cognitive impatience. The concept of deep reading, according to Wolf (2016, p. 25), reflects a mix of processes. Through the act of deep reading, metacognitive processes, also known as scientific method processes, generating functions, and entrance processes, are all intertwined. A certain amount of background knowledge is required to comprehend the reading brain circuit. Analogous thinking fills this void, providing opportunities for induction, deduction, and observation. Reflection and insight are two examples of creative processes that can lead to the development of new ideas.

It is becoming increasingly prevalent in our hyperconnected age for people to experience cognitive impatience, which is a syndrome that is ascribed to the inability to concentrate on a single task. Mark Edmundson, a professor of literature, is the one who came up with the term to describe the incapacity to pay attention for the required amount of time to comprehend the intricacy of an idea or When we are inattentive and impatient, we risk forgetting simple ideas and failing to understand complex ones. failing to grasp complex ones.

In this age of hyper-connectivity, worry is the dominant emotion, and it has not been shy about eradicating the tranquility that is essential for being able to concentrate and reflect consciously. Considering that attention is a mental value that exerts a considerable impact on the way in which we navigate through life, it is important to note that it plays a key part in this state. A psychologist by the name of Daniel Goleman asserts that people are currently confronted with "a dangerous crossroad for humanity" due to the fact that when we do not pay attention, we lose the ability to think and make decisions on our own.

Cognitive impatience is a condition characterized by continuous partial attention, resulting from the constant bombardment of information from various sources. This syndrome leads to careless shortcuts and less effective attention habits, hindering our ability to reflect on our experiences. The danger of cognitive impatience extends beyond forgetfulness, as it can lead to emotional hijacking, causing our attention to focus on what scares us while our memory is restructured. This emotional hijacking can take away our ability to think and make decisions independently, making us vulnerable to deception by those in positions of power, politicians, and close acquaintances. It is essential to pay attention to the kinds of experiences and things we encounter in our everyday lives to avoid foolishness and a lack of critical thinking. Understanding how attention operates is crucial to comprehending the consequences of cognitive impatience and to avoiding being deceived by others. Therefore, it is essential to pay attention to the experiences and stimuli we encounter in our daily lives to maintain cognitive function and avoid cognitive impatience.

THE REMEDY SIDE OF AI TECHNOLOGY

Epistemology

In its simplest form, epistemology can be defined as the study of facts and information. Exploration, on the other hand, calls for at least five different approaches: First, it is the study of the concepts, information, and beliefs that originate from various groups or time eras throughout history. We can investigate these through the disciplines of anthropology, sociology, and the history of ideas. Furthermore, it is the study of how the cognitive abilities of humans develop over time. Piaget refers to this epistemology as "genetic epistemology." Thirdly, bio-epistemology is the study of how different kinds of knowledge have developed over time and how they are utilized in the world today. Fourth, epistemology is the study of knowledge from a philosophical perspective, albeit its primary objective is not to establish norms or standards but rather to uncover facts. For the purpose of assessing whether or not specific views are logical, philosophical epistemology seeks to establish criteria that can be used to evaluate the validity of inferences taken from evidence to conclusions. The fifth one is significantly linked to the investigation of the conceptual frameworks that are required in order to develop different kinds of beliefs. There is a strong connection between the study of artificial intelligence and philosophical inquiries into the concepts of space, time, substance, causation, and consciousness, which are fundamental to understanding various philosophical discussions. consciousness. When our Digital Pharmakon is considered, it is essential to place an emphasis on artificial intelligence. According to Sumner (2025), the objective of artificial intelligence is to imitate human minds or develop intelligent machines, both of which require the objective is to be able to imitate human minds or to develop intelligent machines, both of which need substantial amounts of knowledge investigation. The domain knowledge that is covered in this volume is the foundation upon which all of the expert systems that are discussed succeed. It is important to include a wide range of information about how knowledge is gained, shown, and used in adaptive systems that can be improved or can explain how the systems work. It is important to include a wide range of information about how knowledge is gained, shown, and used in adaptive systems that can be improved or can explain how the systems work. essential to incorporate broad information regarding the manner in which knowledge is acquired, represented, and utilized into adaptive systems that are capable of being improved upon or that can offer an explanation for the behavior of the systems. In order to maintain efficient communication with a diverse variety of human beings, a machine will need to be equipped This information is essential for individuals to understand what they should know in different situations. circumstances. According to Sloman (1979), this is especially true when it comes to a teaching machine.

Another aspect of the reading process that we have not yet "unraveled " is the distinctively individual contributions that the word elicits in the readers. This is a field of study that concerns the process of reading. The fourth dimension of Plato's theory, episteme, is a depiction of this internal knowledge foundation. In addition to the cognitive and affective processes that are transformed as a result of it, there is nothing more important than this internal knowledge when it comes to appreciating the literary mind and the literate human (Wolf, 2016: p. 105).

To differentiate between genuine knowledge and doxa, it is necessary to place emphasis on the training of users for the purpose of data management. Specifically, we train artificial intelligence models like Grok on vast datasets that encompass both episteme and doxa. Models such as Grok are trained on enormous datasets that include both episteme and doxa. The combination of these two factors can result in outputs that combine established knowledge with widely held beliefs. It is possible for biases to be introduced into the training data when doxa is present since the artificial intelligence may represent societal ideas rather than objective truths. Grok, for instance, integrates perspectives aimed at counterbalancing perceived 'woke' viewpoints. According to Bahunar and Roshangar (2024), consumers may have a perception that the system is less dependable when the outputs of artificial intelligence are more in line with doxa. This is especially true if the information contradicts widely held beliefs.

It is possible to raise ethical difficulties by relying on doxa, particularly in the event that the artificial intelligence spreads false information or reinforces stereotypes. Information is freely accessible to users of digital habitus and artificial intelligence, but this comes at the expense of social aphasia. The paradox of online connectivity is a clear example of Heidegger's criticism of modern communication technology, which he views as causing individuals to become more distant from one another rather than bringing them closer together (Heidegger, 1977, p. 44).

Because of this, creators of AI systems are tasked with determining the appropriate balance between episteme and doxa. The training that Grok receives places an emphasis on combating 'woke' culture, which reflects the intentional incorporation of certain doxa beliefs. Critical artificial intelligence literacy, which can be the result of the collaborative effort between epistemology and AI, is of significant use to digital empowerment (Harrington, 2023).

An understanding of artificial intelligence (AI) through critical literacy helps people comprehend not only the operation of the technology but also the societal repercussions of it. Critical AI literacy is defined as the ability to interact with artificial intelligence in a manner that promotes responsibility, openness, and moral behavior (Tufekci, 2015).

Metaknowledge

Understanding how knowledge is produced, interpreted, and used is a component of metaknowledge. To grasp AI at a metaknowledge level, one must know how AI generates and verifies knowledge as well as the algorithms and biases that underpin AI systems.

A set of skills known as AI literacy enables people to utilize AI as a tool online, at home, and at work; interact and collaborate with AI effectively; and critically assess AI technologies. However, research on AI literacy has mostly overlooked metaknowledge, or knowledge about one's own knowledge. For intentional use of AI technologies, metaknowledge is essential, particularly in situations where the division of labor between humans and technology is unclear. People need to learn metaknowledge—that is, knowledge about their awareness and abilities—to successfully navigate and utilize AI's potential.

A critical evaluation of one's skills and in-depth reflection on one's knowledge are necessary for the development of metaknowledge. Learning outcomes have been demonstrated to be positively impacted by gamification, one of the educational strategies that builds upon existing elements and has the capacity to cultivate metaknowledge. People may be able to interact with AI concepts more actively, try out various scenarios, and obtain useful insights into the implications and effects of AI in real-world settings by utilizing gamified learning experiences.

Businesses that depend on human-AI cooperation can use the design insights produced to create AI training programs that are effective and emphasize AI literacy reflection.

An important field of study in information systems (IS) is AI literacy, which is a term that includes various human abilities required for interactions with AI. Research on information systems has focused on metaknowledge, or the understanding of one's own knowledge, especially in connection with the idea of overconfidence. Paradoxically, the AI era has been marketed as the era of highly intelligent civilization. This kind of thinking creates the cultural illusion of over-knowing. This is information-age propaganda. The Dunning-Kruger effect, another name for overconfidence, is a psychological phenomenon in which people tend to believe they know more than they actually do. Despite being essential for human-AI cooperation, metaknowledge is frequently disregarded in IS research. (Pinski and others, 2024).

Grok and AI play a major part in knowledge formation, where metaknowledge enhances the quality of this knowledge construction. In this way, Grokking AI is more than just a tool; rather, it is an epistemic process that requires an active participant in knowledge formation. This viewpoint challenges conventional epistemologies and promotes new frameworks for understanding insights generated by AI (Bryson, 2019).

Metaknowledge includes an understanding of how AI systems think. Understanding AI at the metaknowledge level entails realizing that, in addition to processing data, AI also applies particular knowledge frameworks that might or might not be consistent with human comprehension. According to Kahneman (2012), the default thinking process of humans is flawed. Humans justify their feelings. This type of thinking typically faces criticism due to its narrow perspectives. Higher order thinking abilities are also diminished by this limited and perspectival thinking, and the use of digital gadgets has greatly accelerated the loss of metaknowledge and epistemic control. This reality, however, runs counter to the claim that AI is a wisdom technology that produces brilliant people. Instead, this is the age of ignorance. Furthermore, the incorrect assumptions and ideas that we know many things have been contributing to the pervasive ignorance.

Critical AI Literacy

AI literacy encompasses more than just technical proficiency; it mostly involves comprehending critical involvement. This entails comprehending not only the mechanics of AI but also its broader implications, constituting an aspect of critical AI literacy. This involves evaluating whose knowledge is embodied in AI, understanding how AI may either uphold or contest societal norms, and acknowledging its potential impact on public opinion (Eubanks, 2018).

In addition to technical proficiency, essential AI literacy encompasses comprehension of AI's societal impact. Comprehending AI requires a rigorous analysis of the effects of algorithms on marginalized populations, the transformation of information, and the influence on decision-making (Smith, 2020).

In the realm of artificial intelligence (AI), especially when evaluating systems such as Grok, it is essential to differentiate between 'episteme' (actual knowledge) and 'doxa' (popular belief or opinion). The subsequent points elucidate this distinction. In classical philosophy, episteme denotes knowledge that is unequivocal and verifiable. Conversely, doxa signifies prevailing belief or popular opinion, which may be unsubstantiated (Bahunar & Roshangar, 2024).

The underpinnings of the AI-Driven Knowledge System are epistemological. AI represents a new epistemological paradigm shift in which both machines and humans generate knowledge. To understand AI, one must recognize this transformation—how AI undermines traditional epistemic structures by affecting or even generating knowledge autonomously (Winfield, 2018).

To comprehend AI via metaknowledge, one must understand the operation of AI systems with data, the extraction of knowledge from this data, and the construction of its theoretical framework by AI. This illustrates a technical and epistemological understanding of AI's knowledge mechanisms (Sweeney, 2013).

Users must utilize critical AI literacy tools and procedural epistemology to navigate the mechanics of AI. In this context, we often employ the term "grok," which signifies profound and intuitive understanding, implying complete assimilation of information or concepts. Understanding the social, ethical, and knowledge-related effects of AI, as well as how it works, is called "grokking AI" in critical AI literacy (Hein, 2023).

A cognitive facet of comprehending AI is metaknowledge. In this context, understanding the systemic functioning of AI—encompassing algorithms, data structures, and biases—is termed metaknowledge within AI literacy. Thus, metaknowledge and comprehension are congruent. In this regard, Grok functions as an instrument for understanding the ethical ramifications of AI. Comprehending AI necessitates awareness of its ethical implications, including accountability, prejudice, and openness. A thorough strategy is necessary for individuals to make educated decisions on AI technologies (Barfield & Pagallo, 2021).

Grok and Critical AI Literacy

The process of grokking as an epistemic activity enhances critical thinking and metacognition by comprehending AI's impact on knowledge. In examining grok within the framework of critical AI literacy, we concentrate on metaknowledge, digital pharmakon, and epistemology. Comprehending AI from an epistemological standpoint entail recognizing its impact on the formation of knowledge. Grokking entails a profound understanding of how AI's decision-making processes affect social beliefs, truths, and narratives, therefore shaping the perception of knowledge (Jasanoff, 2020).

AI entails understanding its operational mechanisms as well as the foundational assumptions and constraints (Thomas, 2022). Comprehending the fundamental mechanisms of AI allows individuals to critically assess how AI systems may perpetuate unfairness or bias. A comprehensive understanding entails awareness of the ethical responsibility to tackle AI equity (Noble, 2018).

Critical thinking and agency represent the alternative dimensions of Grokking AI. Comprehending the impact of grokking AI on human agency and decision-making is crucial. It encourages individuals to critically evaluate their interactions with AI and understand the limitations of AI's decision-making capabilities (Lages, 2022).

Moreover, in an AI-centric culture, information verification and regulatory oversight constitute a significant aspect of essential AI literacy. Artificial intelligence fails to provide the promised accuracy in information delivery. Morison (2020) asserts that an internet agora, or an ideal discourse environment, is nonexistent, both online and offline. The internet, defined by anonymity, restricted quality control, and a disjointed reality, is not intrinsically devoid of value, unstructured, or universal in comparison to other domains (Morison, 2020, p. 3).

We encourage users to independently verify the information AI provides, acknowledging the potential fusion of knowledge and opinion. Users authenticate information from Grok and refrain from disclosing sensitive data. The incorporation of doxa into AI outputs may draw regulatory scrutiny, particularly if it results in the dissemination of misinformation or biases. European officials have examined Grok for possible infractions.

Critical AI literacy empowers users. Equipping users with instruments to differentiate between episteme and doxa in AI outputs helps augment trust and reliability. This process encompasses transparency concerning data sources and the incorporation of disclaimers pertaining to the nature of the information presented. Future improvements in AI should favor episteme over doxa, ensuring that systems deliver information based on confirmed knowledge while reducing the impact of unverified opinions.

Simondon's approach posits that digital networks may enhance collective intelligence; yet algorithmic biases frequently perpetuate social inequities (Simondon, 1989, p. 112).

The technological divide represents an alternative manifestation of socioeconomic inequities. Significant epistemic deficiencies exist in our comprehension of AI. Grokking AI addresses this deficiency and reconciles the disparity. A technological divide persists in an AI-driven culture. An epistemic divide occurs between the functioning of AI and its comprehension by non-experts. Grokking AI addresses this gap by promoting comprehensive knowledge and a more sophisticated comprehension of machine knowledge generation (Dastin, 2023).

AI models such as Grok are trained on extensive datasets that include both knowledge and belief. This amalgamation can produce results that combine established knowledge with common beliefs. The inclusion of doxa in training data can engender biases, as the AI may mirror society's attitudes instead of objective truths (Bahunar & Roshangar, 2024).

Observations show that Grok incorporates viewpoints that aim to challenge perceived 'woke' views. When AI outputs conform more closely to doxa, consumers may regard the system as less trustworthy, particularly if the information contradicts conventional knowledge (episteme). The reliance on doxa has ethical considerations, especially if the AI propagates falsehoods or reinforces stereotypes. Digital habitus, especially among AI users, facilitates effortless access to knowledge, albeit resulting in social aphasia. Heidegger's critique of modern communication technologies highlights their tendency to create distance rather than foster closeness, as illustrated by the paradox of online connectivity (Heidegger, 1977, p. 44).

Consequently, engineers must determine the equilibrium between episteme and doxa in AI systems. Grok's training focuses on countering 'woke' society, indicating a purposeful incorporation of specific doxa. Critical AI literacy significantly enhances digital empowerment. Grasping AI via critical literacy enables individuals to understand the technology's functionality and its societal implications. Critical AI literacy facilitates interaction with AI that promotes responsibility, transparency, and ethical behaviour (Tufekci, 2015).

HET and Metaknowledge as Part of Epistemology

The issues surrounding intellectual property, coupled with the blurring of lines between human awareness and artificial intelligence, have intensified due to their influence upon the human mind. Conversely, escaping from human limitations is more difficult than it initially appears. NBIC, which stands for nanotechnology, biotechnology, information technology, and cognitive sciences, along with HET, meaning human enhancement technologies, are examples of advancements in neurotechnology that have specifically impacted the human mind (Kim, 2022).

This situation illustrates how human minds can connect to vast quantity This situation demonstrates how human minds can connect to vast quantities of data, becoming the smallest component of a substantial 'hive mind' when their individual awareness merges with artificial collective consciousness. It can be challenging to conceive and behave in a manner unbound by the system. The study addresses the ontological uniqueness of authentic human intelligence as an individual entity. Preserving one's identity and consciousness, referred to as the ontological distinctiveness of genuine human intellect, is both challenging and unavoidable. Preserving a connection to the system is crucial. Those outside the hive mind view any actions that diverge from the system unfavorably. This novel form of otherness is perceived as an effort to combat a super-intellectual system that transcends singular identity, yet it is regarded as the outcome of a futile quest. Being categorized as "other" within the system presents numerous extra hurdles to the autonomy of being external to it and living a life grounded solely in authentic human intelligence.

Human Enhancement Technology (HET) augments human capacities via AI-driven innovations, rendering it a vital subject in Critical AI Literacy. A critical approach assesses the ethical, social, and economic ramifications of technological breakthroughs rather than perceiving them as solely advantageous. Concerns emerge over accessibility, inequity, and the possible erosion of human autonomy as AI-driven innovations increasingly permeate everyday life. Analyzing HET through a critical perspective guarantees that these technologies empower individuals fairly, rather than exacerbating societal disparities.

Evaluation: Towards a Trustworthy AI and Epistemology

Promoting CAI literacy, particularly in metaknowledge studies that emphasize awareness of ignorance, can alleviate the negative aspects of AI. Moreover, a reliable AI system must comply with legal norms, uphold ethical values, and exhibit resilience from both technological and societal perspectives. It must fulfill seven technical criteria during its full cycle.

A comprehensive approach includes philosophical AI ethics, risk-based regulatory frameworks, and global standards for ethical implementation. The seven criteria are human agency, robustness, safety, privacy, diversity, non-discrimination, fairness, societal well-being, and accountability. An effective plan guarantees legal responsibility through auditing processes. The interdisciplinary approach to trustworthy AI points out the need for legislation to align diverse viewpoints and ensure responsible AI systems for the future of society.

The results of these efforts may produce the following benefits:

1. Informed Utilization and Decision-Making: Individuals and organizations utilizing AI tools must understand the operational mechanisms of these systems and their inherent limitations.

   Being an informed user helps prevent misguided decisions or exploitation.
2. Ethics and Social Responsibility: AI systems make decisions in critical areas such as healthcare, justice, and recruitment. Therefore, users of these technologies must develop ethical awareness.

   AI literacy includes both technological proficiency and an understanding of human rights.
3. Correlates with Data Literacy: AI algorithms are predicated on data. Data biases directly affect results.

   Understanding the methods of data gathering, processing, and analysis improves the transparency and fairness of AI systems.
4. Competitive Advantage in Business: Employees possessing a comprehensive understanding of AI are more likely to embrace a data-driven approach and make informed strategic decisions.

   AI literacy has become essential for career progression.
5. Combating Disinformation: This involves tackling deepfake videos, synthetic content, and misinformation. Informing people about these technologies is crucial.

   Understanding technology is crucial for distinguishing between genuine and counterfeit items.

Critical Reflection: Raising Awareness of Ignorance

Human Enhancement Technologies (HET), particularly those influenced by artificial intelligence, provide significant ethical, societal, and economic implications that prompt readers to reflect critically. This aligns with the concept of critical ignorance, which involves recognizing the boundaries of one's comprehension and being open to altering beliefs in light of new information (Fricker, 2007).

Rather than assuming that technological advancement is invariably beneficial, the text prompts us to contemplate complex problems, such as who benefits and who may suffer from AI-driven innovations.

Epistemic humility, a crucial attribute for navigating complex technological landscapes, is focused on this type of inquiry. Acknowledging our lack of knowledge about the long-term consequences of HET facilitates responsible innovation and regulation (Medin & Bang, 2014).

Learning the Skills Necessary for Procedural Epistemology

"Procedural epistemology" denotes the methods and techniques utilized to establish and validate our knowledge. The term entails doing a critical investigation of assertions regarding artificial intelligence and high-end technology (HET) using interdisciplinary perspectives, incorporating insights from philosophy, sociology, computer science, and ethics. Students and scholars can apply procedural epistemology by utilizing the provided text. This can be achieved by

Challenge the presuppositions of the neutrality or objectivity of technology, as posited by Winner (1986). One way to achieve this is by evaluating the available evidence about how AI-driven innovations affect different populations. Couldry and Mejias (2019) propose that doing discourse analysis effectively uncovers power dynamics in the public policy and media discussions surrounding HET. Nissenbaum (2001) emphasizes the necessity of considering fairness by examining the structural factors that affect access to these technologies. The application of these methodologies promotes a critical literacy in artificial intelligence that includes both technical understanding and ethical reasoning, as well as societal ethical consciousness.

Augmented Intelligence

Augmented intelligence is fundamental to crucial artificial intelligence literacy since it enhances human cognition instead of supplanting it. It shifts the emphasis from artificial intelligence as an autonomous entity to AI as a collaborative instrument, hence highlighting issues related to prejudice, ethical considerations, and power dynamics inherent in AI. Adopting a critical perspective can ensure that artificial intelligence-driven augmentation does not perpetuate current imbalances but instead fosters equity, transparency, and human-centered innovation.

Augmented intelligence and real intelligence are developing as distinct forms of intelligence that contest the limits of human intellect in an increasingly competitive society. In the book Deep Thinking: Where Machine Intelligence Ends and Human Creativity Begins, Kasparov explores the potential for collaboration between humans and machines through games powered by artificial intelligence. The integration of artificial intelligence (AI1) and artificial intelligence (AI2) yields augmented intelligence, perhaps representing the pinnacle of human performance. Contrary to the computational essence of artificial intelligence, which thrives in data processing, Cooper (2002) emphasizes the intrinsic qualities of genuine intelligence, characterized by ethical reasoning, empathy, and innovative problem-solving. Authentic intelligence is defined by these attributes.

De Cremer and Kasparov (2021) assert that enhanced intelligence will enable organizations to enhance their proactivity, creativity, and precision in management processes. Nicky Case employs the term "symbiosis" to characterize this amalgamation, illustrating that the cosmos is not exclusively a zero-sum game but rather a dynamic where two individuals flourish together due to their inherent differences. The synergy of artificial intelligence and human intelligence can yield organizations that are more precise, efficient, innovative, and proactive.

The introduction of the socio-technical concept of augmented intelligence shifts the discourse on technological advancement from pessimistic viewpoints to more hopeful ones. Artificial intelligence challenges the constraints of human intelligence while presenting opportunities for transformative changes in politics, culture, economics, and ethical viewpoints. The integration of artificial intelligence with human intelligence is expected to transform the methods by which individuals learn and teach others. This transition is anticipated to introduce new realities and challenges, encompassing the internalization of data, intellectual property, and the surveillance of consciousness and autonomy beyond the system.

In conclusion, advancements in neuroscience and artificial intelligence pose challenges to human cognition. The Neuralink project has proposed the concept of a society characterized by heightened intelligence and augmented cognitive abilities. As the significance of anthropocentric existence diminishes, discussions regarding the digitalization of the human mind and nervous system present new prospects for human civilizations.

CONCLUSION

This research explores the relationship between artificial intelligence (AI) and epistemology, focusing on the positive and negative aspects of AI as a digital pharmacy. AI is a powerful tool for knowledge production, but ethical concerns and misinformation can significantly impact social systems. The paper examines the dual nature of AI and human enhancement technologies, arguing that AI should serve as an extension of human intellect and enhance human wisdom, closeness, and alignment through neural networks and social media platforms.

The term "wisdom and knowledge technology" refers to the relationship between AI and digital platforms, with human users benefiting from the information and knowledge gathered. However, this relationship also presents potential challenges and risks, such as overconfidence, ignorance, and cognitive impatience. Critical AI literacy is essential for understanding the various types of knowledge and interpreting digital media formats.

The research emphasizes the importance of critical AI literacy in addressing the complex interaction between AI and human improvement technologies. It focuses on the importance of ethical and political involvement, as well as a more genuine interaction with technology. The alignment dilemma and guardian AI are two of the most important challenges in Artificial General Intelligence (AGI) research. Vervaeke (2025) proposes a three-point framework emphasizing uniqueness and decentralization in AI development, emphasizing a personal approach that empowers individuals, protects privacy, and encourages respectful interactions between humans and technology. AI's alignment problem stems from its disregard for human values and vision, making it difficult to maintain alignment with itself. Traditional methods are no longer relevant, and AI-based cultures offer more effective and inclusive approaches. A critical understanding of AI can help resolve these issues and foster improved communication and interaction between humans and AI. AI's features include processing information differently, sharing characteristics with the human brain, being strong, having flaws, possessing knowledge authority, gathering and distributing data, and addressing the digital divide.

An increasing danger in the 21st century is the digital pharmakon, or dark artificial intelligence, which can be exploitative and manipulative. To address this, a holistic strategy called "epistemology-cum-ethics" is proposed, incorporating values and normative elements at critical points in the entire process. Ignorance is a key aspect of understanding AI-based technology, and understanding the nature of knowledge and ignorance is crucial for intellectual survival.

Critical AI literacy is essential in today's digital age, as it helps individuals understand the operation and societal implications of AI technology. It involves recognizing the algorithms and biases that govern AI systems, as well as how AI constructs and validates knowledge. Gamification, an approach to education that fosters metaknowledge, has been shown to positively affect learning outcomes. In conclusion, critical AI literacy is essential for individuals to effectively navigate and harness the potential of AI in various aspects of life, including digital technologies.

REFERENCES

Andrejevic, M. (2021). *Automation and the future of work: From artificial intelligence to algorithmic culture*. Wiley-Blackwell.

Bahunar, M. H., & Roshangar, M. Z. (2024). The Nature of Knowledge in Plato's Philosophy: A Study of Episteme and Doxa. Sprin Journal of Arts. *Humanities and Social Sciences*, *3*(6), 19–23. DOI: 10.55559/sjahss.v3i6.353

Barfield, W., & Pagallo, U. (2021). *The ethical dimensions of grokking AI*. *Ethics and Information Technology*, *23*(5), 347–360. DOI: 10.1007/eit.2021.14

Beller, J. (2017). *Cultural capital in the age of digital technology*. Routledge.

Bryson, J. J. (2019). The epistemic role of artificial intelligence in the construction of knowledge*. *Journal of Philosophy of Science*, *45*(3), 325–341. DOI: 10.1017/jps.2019.11

Cooper, S. (2002). *Technoculture and Critical Theory*. Routledge.

Couldry, N., & Mejias, U. A. (2019). *The costs of connection: How data is colonizing human life and appropriating it for capitalism*. Stanford University Press.

Dastin, J. (2023). Bridging the gap: Epistemology and the understanding of AI systems. *Philosophy of Technology Journal*, *28*(2), 142–160. DOI: 10.1017/ptj.2023.08

Derrida, J. (1976). *Of grammatology*. Johns Hopkins University Press.

Eubanks, V. (2018). *Automating inequality: How high-tech tools profile, police, and punish the poor*. St. Martin's Press.

Foucault, M. (1975). *Discipline and Punish: The Birth of the Prison*. Vintage Books.

Foucault, M. (1977). *Language, Counter-Memory, Practice: Selected Essays and Interviews*. Cornell University Press.

Fricker, M. (2007). *Epistemic injustice: Power and the ethics of knowing*. Oxford University Press. DOI: 10.1093/acprof:oso/9780198237907.001.0001

Harrington, N. (2023, February 9). The epistemology of AI. Project Q. https://projectqsydney.com/the-epistemology-of-ai/

Heaton, B. (2024, December 2). 'Brain rot' named Oxford Word of the Year 2024. Oxford University Press. https://corp.oup.com/news/brain-rot-named-oxford-word-of-the-year-2024/

Heidegger, M. (1977). *The question concerning technology and other essays*. Harper & Row.

İnan, İ. (2020). Awareness of ignorance. *SATS*, *20*(2), 141–173. DOI: 10.1515/sats-2020-2004

Jasanoff, S. (2020). The ethics of in/visibility: Artificial intelligence and the social construction of knowledge. *Harvard International Review*, *42*(2), 58–62.

Kahneman, D. (2012). *Thinking, Fast and Slow*. Penguin, Farrar, Straus and Giroux.

Kim, Y. (2022). Human consciousness and prosthetic temporality: On the way to new technological humanities. *New Techno Humanities.*, *2*(1), 41–46. DOI: 10.1016/j.techum.2022.10.001

Kurbalija, J. (2024b, April 13). The role of knowledge in the cyber-age of globalisation – Diplo Resource. Richard Falk, Diplo. https://www.diplomacy.edu/resource/the-role-of-knowledge-in-the-cyber-age-of-globalisation/

Lages, J. (2022). AI, agency, and the role of critical literacy in human-machine interaction. *Journal of Philosophy and Technology*, *34*(1), 89–104. DOI: 10.1007/jpt.2022.07

Medin, D. L., & Bang, M. (2014). *Who's asking? Native science, Western science, and science education*. MIT Press. DOI: 10.7551/mitpress/9755.001.0001

Nissenbaum, H. (2001). How computer systems embody values. *Computer*, *34*(3), 120–119. DOI: 10.1109/2.910905

Noble, S. U. (2018). *Algorithms of oppression: How search engines reinforce racism*. NYU Press. DOI: 10.18574/nyu/9781479833641.001.0001

O'Neil, C. (2016). *Weapons of Math Destruction: How Big Data Increases Inequality and Threatens Democracy*. Crown Publishing Group.

Pinski, M., Haas, M., & Benlian, A. (2024). Building Metaknowledge in AI Literacy – The Effect of Gamified vs. Text-based Learning on AI Literacy Metaknowledge. Proceedings of the . . . *Annual Hawaii International Conference on System Sciences/ Proceedings of the Annual Hawaii International Conference on System Sciences*. DOI: 10.24251/HICSS.2024.619

Saritepeci, M. (2021). Multiple Screen Addiction Scale: Validity and reliability study. *Instructional Technology and Lifelong Learning*, *2*(1), 1–17. DOI: 10.52911/itall.796758

Simondon, G. (1989). *Individuation in Light of Notions of Form and Information.* University of Minnesota Press.

Sloman, A. (1979). Epistemology and Artificial Intelligence. Expert Systems in the Microelectronic Age. https://cogaffarchive.org/sloman-epist-ai.pdf

Smith, D. (2020). *Critical AI literacy: A call for ethical understanding in artificial intelligence*. *Journal of Digital Ethics*, *4*(3), 56–72. DOI: 10.1007/jde.2020.12

Stiegler, B. (2010). *For a New Critique of Political Economy*. Polity Press.

Stiegler, B. (2018). *The Neganthropocene*. Open Humanities Press.

Stiegler, B. (2019). *The Age of Disruption: Technology and Madness in Computational Capitalism*. Polity Press.

Sweeney, L. (2013). *Discrimination in online ad delivery*. ACM Digital Library., DOI: 10.1145/2460276.2460278

Thomas, S. (2022). *Metaknowledge and AI: Understanding Systems Beneath the Surface. *AI in Context*, *19*(2), 67–85. DOI: 10.1007/aic.2022.02

Tufekci, Z. (2015). Algorithms in our midst: The hidden politics of AI and machine learning. *Information Communication and Society*, *18*(7), 787–804. DOI: 10.1080/1369118X.2015.1008966

Vervaeke, J. (2025, March 18). AI and the Meaning Crisis | Redefining Human Flourishing [Video]. YouTube. https://www.youtube.com/watch?v=C2Jws87yA1Y

Winfield, A. F. T. (2018). Ethics, autonomy, and artificial intelligence. In van den Hoven, M. (Ed.), *The ethics of artificial intelligence and robotics* (pp. 217–234). Springer., DOI: 10.1007/978-3-030-01789-2_14

Winner, L. (1986). *The whale and the reactor: A search for limits in an age of high technology*. University of Chicago Press.

Wolf, M. (2016). *Tales of Literacy for the 21st Century*. Oxford University Press.

Zuboff, S. (2019). The Age of Surveillance Capitalism. Public Affairs. Liddell, H. G., & Scott, R. (1940). A Greek English Lexicon. Clarendon Press. via Perseus Project.

ADDITIONAL READING

Aoun, J. E. (2017). *Robot-Proof: Higher Education in the Age of Artificial Intelligence*. MIT Press. DOI: 10.7551/mitpress/11456.001.0001

Carr, N. (2011). *The Shallows: What the Internet Is Doing to Our Brains*. W. W. Norton & Company.

Gardner, H., & Davis, K. (2013). *The App Generation: How Today's Youth Navigate Identity, Intimacy, and Imagination in a Digital World*. Yale University Press.

Han, B.-C. (2017). *Psychopolitics: Neoliberalism and New Technologies of Power*. Verso Books.

Hayles, N. K. (2017). *Unthought: The Power of the Cognitive Nonconscious*. University of Chicago Press. DOI: 10.7208/chicago/9780226447919.001.0001

Inan, I. (2012). *The Philosophy of Curiosity*. Routledge.

Morozov, E. (2013). *To Save Everything, Click Here: The Technological Fix for Everything That's Wrong with the World*. Allen Lane.

Pasquale, F. (2015). *The Black Box Society: The Secret Algorithms That Control Money and Information*. Harvard University Press. DOI: 10.4159/harvard.9780674736061

Rouvroy, A., & Berns, T. (2013). Algorithmic governmentality and the end of the modern subject. *Annual Review of Law and Social Science*, (9), 1–21.

Vervaeke, J., Mastropietro, C., & Miscevic, P. (2023). Psycho-technologies of the Self: A Research Program. Unpublished manuscript.

KEY TERMS AND DEFINITIONS

Cognitive Impatience: Cognitive impatience is a mindset that has been primarily influenced by the fast-paced digital world. It is characterized by an unwillingness to invest the time and mental effort necessary to comprehend intricate topics in depth. It manifests itself as an inclination toward concise summaries and straightforward responses rather than intricate, detailed information. The primary impact is that our capacity for in-depth analysis, reflection, and authentic learning is diminished as we become accustomed to only briefly sampling the surface of knowledge.

Critical AI Literacy: Beyond technical expertise, critical AI literacy includes the understanding of how AI affects society. Understanding AI entails critically examining how algorithms impact marginalized people, alter knowledge, and influence decision-making.

Digital Pharmakon: Emphasizing the dual role of technology as both a remedy and a poison in the context of epistemology and AI

Epistemology: Epistemology, to put it simply, is the study of knowledge

Grokking AI: It is a metaknowledge level that requires understanding the algorithms and biases that govern AI systems, alongside recognizing how AI constructs and validates knowledge.

Metaknowledge: Metaknowledge involves awareness of how knowledge is generated, understood, and applied.

Multiple Screen Addiction: Multiple screen addiction is a compulsive behaviour involving the simultaneous or rapid-alternating use of multiple electronic devices, such as televisions, smartphones, laptops, or tablets. This addiction involves loss of control, preoccupation, and negative consequences, affecting essential life areas like work, academic performance, social relationships, and mental well-being. It can lead to significant functional impairment.

Chapter 2
Trusting the Unreal:
Dynamics of Anthropomorphism in Perceptions of Virtual Influencers

Özgül Dağlı
https://orcid.org/0000-0002-3173-9196
Üsküdar University, Turkey

Damla Karşu Cesur
https://orcid.org/0000-0002-5876-5618
Kocaeli University, Turkey

ABSTRACT

This study examines how users perceive the credibility of virtual versus human influencers and how these perceptions influence trust in sponsored social media posts. The research focuses on a high-involvement product (a laptop) and a low-involvement product (coffee), exploring whether the influencer's nature—virtual or human—affects this dynamic. In an experiment, Group A participants were told the influencer was virtual, while Group B believed the influencer was human. Results revealed that perceived source credibility significantly and positively impacted advertising trust across both product categories. Although virtual influencers scored slightly higher on average for source credibility and advertising trust, these differences were not statistically significant.

DOI: 10.4018/979-8-3373-6192-5.ch002

INTRODUCTION

In 2018, Time announced the most influential people on the Internet, along with very famous celebrities such as Donald Trump, Rihanna, Kanye West, and Kylie Jenner. One of the names on the list stood out from the rest: Lil Miquela. Lil Miquela is a 19-year-old teenage model and musician. She is a Brazilian-American social media celebrity and also a kind of social activist, due to her advocacy roles on various social and political issues such as the rights of Black people and LGBTQI+ communities. She has gained 2.4 million Instagram followers across the world and collaborates with global brands such as Samsung, Prada, Calvin Klein, and Chanel.

However, what truly sets her apart is not her successful collaborations with global brands or her social consciousness at the very early age of 19. What truly makes her unique is rather her lifeless presence. More clearly, she is not a real human with bones and flesh, because she is a digitally created virtual character. More precisely, she is a virtual influencer. Today, millions of people —that even human influencers struggle to achieve — follow her on various social media platforms like Instagram, YouTube, and so on. Although she is a digital entity, she is portrayed as an emotional character who does not hesitate to share her feelings just like actual human beings. Moreover, she is presented as having her own social and personal life, meeting with her friends and even taking photos with human celebrities, such as Bella Hadid. As of 2025, she has garnered over 2.4 millionfollowers on Instagram and has recently starred in AI-generated music videos and fashion campaigns. However, Lil Miquela is not the only one. There are other virtual influencers in the digital ecosystem. Thus, these digital creatures open up a new path for virtual marketing.

Influencer marketing has become very popular since the rise of social media. The ever-increasing number of followers makes the notions of 'influencer' and 'influencer marketing' very significant for the advertising and marketing literature. However, the developments in Computer-Generated Technology (CGT) and Artificial Intelligence (AI) have set the ground for the emergence of virtual influencers in recent years. The millions of followers and numerous brand collaborations with virtual influencers attract the attention not only of brand professionals but also of advertising and marketing scholars. The advantages of virtual influencers — such as their fully controlled and physically limitless nature — augment this interest. Despite the steadily increasing interest from both sides, the whole picture still remains incomplete. What are the emotional reactions of consumers to virtual influencers? How do the anthropomorphic features of virtual influencers affect follower engagement? How does the credibility of virtual influencers affect consumer purchasing decisions? What are the ethical and social considerations of virtual influencers? How are virtual influencers perceived across different cultures? These questions, along with others, have not yet been fully answered. Moreover, studies examining virtual influencer marketing and seeking answers to these questions have sometimes revealed conflicting results. Therefore, the extant literature is still in its infancy. Considering the growing investment in virtual influencer marketing, there is an urgent need for relevant research that enables a deeper understanding.

Given the necessity outlined above, this current study compares virtual and human influencers in terms of their source credibility. Additionally, the study investigates how source credibility relates to ad trust in the context of a high-involvement product (laptop) and a low-involvement product (coffee). Therefore, the research questions are as follows:

This study aims to compare the source credibility of virtual and human influencers. Additionally, it examines how source credibility relates to advertising trust for a high-involvement product (laptop) and a low-involvement product (coffee). Accordingly, the research questions are as follows:

> RQ1. Does perceived source credibility differ between virtual and human influencers?
> RQ2. Does advertising trust in sponsored posts for high-involvement and low-involvement products vary depending on the influencer type (virtual or human)?
> RQ3. How does source credibility influence advertising trust?

The remainder of the paper is structured as follows: a literature review, research methodology, and conclusion. The literature review examines social media marketing and influencer marketing for foundational insights. It then analyzes virtual influencers as emerging actors in social media, exploring their historical context, definitions, and taxonomies from relevant literature. Additionally, the advantages and disadvantages of virtual influencers are discussed, followed by an examination through the lenses of anthropomorphism and the Uncanny Valley Theory. The research methodology section presents the experimental design. Finally, the conclusion reveals the findings and discusses their managerial and scholarly implications.

Introduction to Social Media Marketing

This section examines the conceptual definition of social media and its evolution as a process. Within the framework of influencer marketing, consumer behavior and the relationship between brand and social media are also discussed.

Definition and Development of Social Media

Social media marketing differs from traditional media by promoting a participatory communication model, enabling users to consume and generate content. This shift highlights the interactive nature of online platforms, which facilitate knowledge dissemination, opinion exchange, and user engagement. Wei (2024) describes social media as a dynamic co-creation space where users actively shape the content and experiences within their networks, moving beyond the passive consumption typical of traditional media (p. 288). These interactive features also extend to business contexts, where social media platforms serve as essential tools for brands to engage with consumers, broaden their audience, and strengthen loyalty through immersive brand experiences. This development multifaceted engagement cultivates a vibrant, interactive environment critical for fostering relationships between individuals and brands (Aljuhmani et al., 2023).

Social media marketing traces its origins to early platforms like Friendster, which debuted in 2002 and enabled users to connect with friends and share content. This paved the way for LinkedIn and MySpace in 2003, which tapped into the rising popularity of online social interaction, laying the foundation for user-generated content and community engagement (Aljuhmani et al., 2023).

The introduction of Facebook in 2004 represented a pivotal moment in the evolution of social media marketing. With its intuitive interface and focus on authentic social connections, Facebook spurred widespread adoption and robust engagement, fundamentally transforming online interactions and ushering in a new era of marketing strategies (Alalwan et al., 2017). Consequently, businesses started to see the value of these platforms, exploring early marketing approaches tailored to connect with target audiences in a more personalized way. This shift gave rise to social media–based brand communication.

The Growth of Social Media Marketing

Over time, digital marketers have harnessed social media platforms to connect with consumers in impactful ways. Starting in the late 2000s and early 2010s, companies began weaving social media into their marketing approaches to increase brand recognition, nurture customer loyalty, and elevate sales figures. The rise of platforms like Twitter, Instagram, and YouTube expanded the toolkit for marketers, allowing them to use a mix of content types—text, visuals, and videos—to engage a wider audience (Zeng et al., 2019). Studies, such as those by Cheung et al. (2020), emphasize how social media influences consumer buying decisions and deepens brand recognition. Although a claim that social media-driven global online purchases reached $87.5 billion by 2023 remains unverified and calls for a deeper scrutiny from trustworthy sources, the trend highlights the rising importance of direct consumer engagement and the shift in marketing strategies aimed at boosting brand presence, fostering loyalty, and driving revenue (Wei, 2024). Originally designed to connect friends and family, social media has evolved into a far more significant force. It now serves as a comprehensive platform where consumers can explore information about their preferred businesses and the products or services they offer. Retailers and marketers leverage these platforms to engage with their target audiences and deliver enhanced shopping experiences. Technological advancements—such as robust internet search engines, the proliferation of smartphones, improved connectivity, and the expansion of online social networks—have significantly strengthened marketers' ability to connect with consumers through innovative touchpoints (Shankar et al., 2011).

Characteristics of Social Media

Perhaps the most significant feature justifying social media's designation as "social" is its capacity to facilitate interaction through instantaneous and rapid communication technologies. Moreover, using social media does not require specialized training or expertise. Another key characteristic is the ease with which information, messages, or content can be archived and retrieved, alongside the ability to interpret and modify them. Mayfield outlines the characteristics of social media as follows (Mayfield&Mayfield, 2023):

- **Participation** emphasizes the active role of users in content creation and sharing, facilitating a dialogue that fosters community engagement. Unlike traditional media where communication is often unidirectional, social media encourages multidirectional interactions.
- **Openness** signifies the lack of barriers to information sharing, allowing for a free flow of content that contrasts starkly with the curated nature of traditional media channels. This openness helps democratize information dissemination, where any individual can engage regardless of their background or status .
- **Conversation** is a core attribute of social media, promoting ongoing dialogues that can evolve over time. It transforms communication into a two-way exchange, allowing audiences not only to receive messages but to respond and participate actively .
- **Community** builds upon the connections and relationships developed through participatory interactions. Social media acts as a hub for like-minded individuals and groups to gather and share experiences, strengthening social ties .

- **Connectedness** highlights the networked nature of social media platforms that allow users to connect with others globally. This connection facilitates rapid information exchange and mobilization around social issues and movements, showcasing the collective potential inherent in social media networks
.

Exploring Consumer Behavior and Branding in Social Media Marketing

Social media marketing has emerged as a key component of contemporary marketing approaches, capitalizing on the vast reach and interactive nature of platforms like Instagram, Facebook, and Twitter. This transition from conventional marketing methods to more engaging, flexible strategies is driven primarily by significant shifts in how consumers behave within the digital realm. Recent studies indicate that social media ads greatly enhance brand visibility, encourage deeper customer engagement, and can boost search engine optimization (SEO) performance, offering businesses a budget-friendly option (Albuquerque et al., 2023; Perez & Martins, 2024). As companies increasingly see the value of weaving social media into their marketing plans, it's evident that these platforms are far more than just add-ons—they're critical to achieving well-rounded marketing objectives.

Social media marketing's effectiveness hinges on its ability to enable real-time consumer engagement. In today's rapid digital economy, where consumer tastes can shift overnight, such interaction is vital for marketers striving to remain relevant and in tune with their audience. Social media platforms allow brands to engage directly with consumers, fostering collaboration and boosting both interaction levels and brand credibility. User-generated content is key in strengthening this bond, as it is often seen as more genuine and trustworthy than traditional brand messaging. This perception matters—it shapes consumer behavior, influencing brand perceptions and equity (Brooks et al., 2022).

The psychological aspects of consumer engagement on social media highlight a dynamic interplay between brands and their audiences. These platforms create a communal space that encourages co-creation, fostering stronger emotional bonds between consumers and brands (Pramesti & Alversia, 2023). Through actions such as liking, commenting, and sharing, consumers shift from passive recipients of marketing messages to active contributors to the brand's narrative. This transformation not only deepens emotional connections but also strengthens brand loyalty and advocacy (Ghazali et al., 2023). As a result, this interactivity emphasizes consumers' evolving role in shaping brand perceptions, requiring brands to foster participatory and community-driven environments.

Empirical research demonstrates that consumer perceptions of brand anthropomorphism—the attribution of human-like traits to brands—significantly enhance the development of emotional connections between consumers and brands. Studies reveal a positive relationship between brand anthropomorphism and key constructs such as brand love and trust, with brand trust serving as a critical mediator in this dynamic (Moreno et al., 2021). Consequently, cultivating a relatable and trustworthy brand persona on social media is essential, as it influences consumer behavior and decision-making, ultimately shaping purchasing intentions and bolstering brand loyalty (Muda & Hamzah, 2021). The capacity of social media marketing to enable real-time interactions not only heightens user engagement but also fosters enduring consumer-brand relationships, a vital advantage in today's competitive market (Khan et al., 2023).

NEW GENERATION OPINION LEADERS: THE CONCEPT AND CHARACTERISTICS OF INFLUENCERS

The Mechanisms of Influence

The impact of social media influencers on consumer behavior is mediated by several critical factors. Firstly, influencers typically possess a high level of credibility among their audiences, attributed to their perceived authenticity and relatability, which fosters trust (Abdullah et al., 2023). Research indicates that trust significantly mediates the relationship between influencer endorsements and consumers' purchase intentions (Lim et al., 2017). Secondly, the concept of social proof emerges as a crucial element; endorsements from admired individuals enhance the perceived value of products, while active engagement techniques, such as direct interaction with followers, further strengthen brand loyalty (Sahaf & Nazir, 2024).

Influencers have emerged as pivotal actors in the dissemination of information and influence within modern society. Individuals from diverse socio-cultural backgrounds not only wield significant power over their environments but are also shaped by those around them. In this context, individuals with considerable authority and expertise are often designated as 'opinion leaders' or 'influencers.' The term 'influencer' refers to individuals capable of shaping the behaviors and thoughts of others, frequently exerting a notable impact on purchasing decisions, particularly in sectors such as fashion and consumer goods (Shen, 2021; Dinh & Lee, 2021). The role of influencers extends beyond merely commenting on products and sharing lifestyles on social media; they also engage in content creation through brand partnerships, amplifying their influence in commercial contexts. Those adept at leveraging social networks possess the capacity to alter the attitudes and behaviors of their target audiences, prompting numerous companies to prioritize collaborations with these individuals as strategic imperatives (Dinh & Lee, 2021). Consequently, influencer marketing cannot be overlooked when examining social interactions and marketing trends in the digital age.

Defining Social Media Influencers and Influencer Marketing and Their Importance

Social media influencers are individuals with a significant online following who can sway purchasing decisions through their perceived authority and authenticity. Unlike traditional celebrities, these influencers cultivate their reputations within specific niches such as fashion and wellness, which allows them to engage deeply with their audiences, thereby enhancing trust and persuasive impact (Srivastava et al., 2024; Konoplıannykova, 2024). Influencer marketing has thus become an integral component of social media marketing strategies, allowing brands to leverage influencers' credibility to improve consumer engagement and brand awareness (Angraini, 2023; Leung et al., 2022).

The implementation of influencer marketing signifies a fundamental evolution in how brands interact with consumers. Research shows that consumers increasingly respond to influencer endorsements; for instance, around 70% have made purchases influenced by such content (Angraini, 2023). Marketers now face the essential task of selecting the right influencers whose audience aligns with their brand's target demographic, as effective influencer endorsements can lead to significantly higher engagement (Srivastava et al., 2024; Leung et al., 2022). Notably, the perceived credibility of influencers plays a critical role in consumers' purchase intentions, underscoring the importance of establishing authentic connections between influencers and their followers (Zheng, 2023).

In 2024, social media emerged as the leading global advertising channel, with $247.3 billion in ad spending, fueled by the rise of influencer marketing (Influencer Marketing Hub, 2025). Moreover, challenges remain, including issues of credibility and consumer cynicism towards marketing practices, showing that while influencer marketing is powerful, it requires careful strategies to maintain consumer trust (Gökerik, 2024). The rise of platforms such as TikTok emphasizes the shifting landscape in influencer marketing, where brands are now investing heavily in partnerships with influencers, particularly those with smaller, more engaged audiences (Konoplıannykova, 2024).

In summary, the influence of social media marketing and influencer strategies on consumer behavior highlights a transformative shift in brand communication. To thrive in this dynamic environment, businesses must navigate the complexities of influencer selection and engagement strategies that resonate with their audience (Angraini, 2023; Gökerik, 2024).

NEW ACTORS IN SOCIAL MEDIA MARKETING: VIRTUAL INFLUENCERS

In this chapter, to gain a comprehensive understanding, the concept of the virtual influencer is evaluated through its historical context, diverse definitions, advantages and disadvantages over human influencers, and classifications. Subsequently, it is analyzed from prominent theoretical perspectives derived from the extant literature.

Synthetic Stars: The Rise of The Virtual Influencers

The underlying technologies behind the emergence of virtual influencers is the advancement of Computer-Generated Imagery (CGI) and Artificial Intelligence (AI). Therefore, the roots of this phenomenon can be traced back to the early 1990s, during the initial stages of CGI technology. In 1996, Kyoko Date, a 3D character associated with Horipro, appeared as the first virtual pop star in Japan — not powered by AI. In the 2000s, digital entities such as Hatsune Miku, developed by Crypton Future Media, made a significant impact on the music industry (Yuan, 2025, p. 318). However, the first virtual influencer in social media, namely Lil Miquela, appeared on Instagram in 2016 and quickly gained fame (Drenten and Brooks, 2020, p. 1320).

Figure 1. Kyoko Date

Figure 2. Hatsune Miku

Figure 3. Lil Miquela

Following this trend, the popularity of virtual influencers spread from Japan and the USA to to other parts of the world (Jhawar et al., 2023, p. 470). For example, in 2017, Shudu Gram was created as a 3D supermodel by fashion photographer Cameron-James Wilson in England (Önder, 2020), while Lina Hip, developed by the Hiper Model agency in 2018, was introduced as Turkey's first virtual influencer (Sofuoğlu, 2021). Similarly, Rozy was created by Sidus Studio X in 2020 in South Korea (Honorary Reporter, 2023). Virtual influencers, who have garnered increasing recognition on a global scale, enhanced their visibility through high-profile collaborations — particularly with fashion and luxury brands — such as Lil Miquela's partnership with Calvin Klein in 2019 (Gür, 2019), Shudu Gram's collaborations with Fenty Beauty (Rosenstein, 2018), and Balmain in 2018 (Cresci, 2018).

During the COVID-19 pandemic, many countries had to implement quarantine measures that restricted access to physical spaces, especially studios, thereby hindering human influencers' flexibility in content creation. In contrast, virtual influencers had an advantage over human influencers due to being computer-generated digital beings living in a pandemic-free digital world. Therefore, COVID-19 has given rise to virtual influencers as an alternative digital solution (Franke et al., 2023, p. 523).

The development of virtual influencers has accelerated with advances in CGI and the sophistication of artificial intelligence-generated systems today. In particular, AI-powered content generation and deep learning algorithms have enabled virtual influencers to create more dynamic and interactive content. These technological advancements have significantly expanded their reach across social media platforms. As a result, virtual influencers are no longer just static images; rather, they can interact with their followers, and some even generate real-time content. Moreover, they have been adopted across multiple industries, such as fashion and luxury, technology and AI products, cosmetics, gaming and entertainment, as well as tourism and destination marketing. Moreover, according to Grand View Research (2024), the global virtual influencer market is projected to grow at a compound annual growth rate (CAGR) of 40.8% between 2025 and 2030.

Table 1. Virtual influencers in different industries

Key Industries	Key Applications	Notable Cases
Fashion and Luxury	Digital Showrooms and Collection Showcasing	Noonoouri
Technology and AI Products	AI-Powered Product Launches	Samsung Sam
Cosmetics	Makeup Trends and Product Launches	Shudu Gram
Gaming and Entertainment	Twitch and YouTube Content Creation	Kizuna AI
Tourism and Destinations	Digital Travel Guides and Destination Marketing	Jiayao

Beyond Flesh and Code: Defining Virtual Influencers

There are several definitions of virtual influencers in the literature. Thomas and Fowler (2021, p. 12) define a virtual influencer as "a digitally created artificial human who is associated with Internet fame and uses software and algorithms to perform tasks like humans." According to Meng et al. (2025, p. 1), "virtual influencers are anthropomorphic digital agents controlled by software and endowed with the ability to interact with users." Likewise, Arsenyan and Mirowska (2021) portrayed virtual influencers as digital entities that sometimes blend the physical and virtual. Byun and Ahn (2023, p. 294) underline that virtual influencers are social media content creators who share their daily activities, experiences, personas, and brand collaborations. Additionally, Kholkina et al. (2025, p. 105) highlight the AI-generated nature of some of these virtual influencers. Based on the different definitions and approaches from the literature, the main characteristics of the virtual influencers can be established as follows:

- They are digitally created entities.
- They perform the role of internet or social media influencers.
- They mimic human influencers by creating content and engaging in interactions.
- They blend physical and virtual worlds.
- Some of them are supported by AI, while others are managed manually.

From these traits, we define virtual influencers as AI-driven or computer-generated digital entities and internet celebrities that mimic human influencers, produce social media content, collaborate with brands, interact with users as part of marketing strategies, and bridge the gap between reality and the digital world.

Decoding Digital Faces: Classifications of Virtual Influencers

Just like the diverse terminology used for virtual influencers—such as CGI influencers, digital influencers, or non-human influencers (Oliveira & Chimenti, 2021; Sookkaew & Saephoo, 2021) several classifications have been proposed based on their distinctive virtual influencers is shaped around particular tools or equipment, such as kitchenware or photography gear. In contrast, product-independent influencers develop personas that are free from such associations.

According to Arsenyan and Mirowska (2021), virtual influencers can also be grouped by their visual design into human-like and non-human-like categories. Human-like or humanoid virtual influencers take attention with their highly realistic human appearances and personas. For example, Lil Miquela closely resembles a human, characterized by her distinct personality, life story, and anthropomorphic traits. On the other hand, anime-like virtual influencers may or may not possess anthropomorphic features, yet they maintain a cartoonish or stylized aesthetic. Noonoouri, for instance, is an anime-like virtual influencer distinguished by her disproportionately large eyes and head, establishing a partially anthropomorphic appearance. In contrast, Noodle is also anime-like but designed as a 3D cat figure, further distancing from human likeness.

In addition to anthropomorphic classifications, Xie-Carson et al. (2023) identify three other types of virtual influencers: zoomorphic, two-dimensional (2D) animated, and three-dimensional (3D) animated influencers. Zoomorphic influencers resemble animals, such as *Guggimon*, whereas 2D and 3D influencers are distinguished by their depth and animation techniques. Mouritzen et al. (2024) further propose that virtual influencers can be categorized based on two dimensions: the level of anthropomorphism and the degree of realism. Accordingly, they introduce a 2×2 taxonomy that comprises four categories: *hyper-realistic non-humans*, *hyper-realistic humans*, *unrealistic non-humans*, and *unrealistic humans*. This classification rests on the intersection of human-likeness and visual realism along the reality–virtuality continuum.

Unrealistic non-human virtual influencers preserve a clear distinction between reality and virtuality due to their cartoonish, non-human form. *Hyper-realistic human* influencers, on the other hand, blur the line between the two by closely resembling real humans. *Hyper-realistic non-human* influencers exhibit high visual realism but low anthropomorphism, creating a unique fusion of the real and the artificial. Conversely, *unrealistic human* influencers display strong anthropomorphic cues yet lack visual realism. This taxonomy is visually presented in Figure 4.

Figure 4. A typology based on anthropomorphism and perceived reality (Mouritzen et al, 2024)

From the classifications discussed above, it can be assumed that virtual influencers are primarily categorized with respect to their visual appearance and design elements. However, they can also be classified into distinct types based on additional parameters. Drawing upon the relevant literature, and beyond visual attributes, we propose the following three aspects through which virtual influencers may vary:

- **AI-Enhanced vs. Human-Controlled Virtual Influencers:** AI-Enhanced Virtual Influencers are AI-driven digital agents capable of making a certain level of autonomous decisions and often utilize technologies such as machine learning or natural language processing (NLP), as exemplified by Kuki AI. Conversely, Human-Controlled Virtual Influencers are entirely operated by humans, as in the case of Lil Miquela.
- **Metaverse and NFT-Integrated vs. Social Media-Based Virtual Influencers:** Metaverse and NFT-integrated virtual influencers are incorporated with blockchain technology, NFTs, and metaverse environments. They are usually 3D models and may interact with users in VR/AR environments. In contrast, social media-based virtual influencers are digital personas that

exist on platforms such as Instagram, TikTok, and YouTube, and are usually operated by an agency or production team. Therefore, the fundamental difference between the two lies in the technologies they rely on and the digital ecosystems they inhabit. However, there are no clear boundaries between these two groups, and hybrid examples are increasingly emerging.

- **Brand-Dependent vs. Brand-Independent Virtual Influencers:** Brand-dependent virtual influencers are digital agents designed for a specific brand and employed to promote its products or services and to engage with consumers. In contrast, brand-independent virtual influencers are not affiliated with a single brand; rather, they have the flexibility to collaborate with various brands. To illustrate, Samsung Sam — developed as the voice assistant for Samsung — is a brand-dependent virtual influencer, while Shudu Gram has the flexibility to collaborate with numerous brands such as Fenty Beauty, Balmain, and Gucci. Hence, the existence of brand-dependent virtual influencers is primarily centered on serving the brand that developed them.

The Digital Dilemma: Pros and Cons of Virtual Influencers in the Digital Era

Virtual influencers are steadily gaining importance in the field of marketing. In addition to technological developments, the advantages of virtual influencers over human influencers also contribute to this rise. Some of the key technological and social changes — along with the advantages driving this rise — are as follows (This classification is proposed by the authors through a synthesis of existing studies in the current literature):

- **Digital Transformation:** Virtual influencers offer several opportunities for digitally integrated brands. The development of AI and CGI technologies makes virtual influencers more adoptable. By developing specific virtual influencers or collaborating with existing ones, brands maintain consistency and face lower risks compared to human influencers. At present, virtual influencers provide a new market for digital fashion shows and virtual events.
- **Digital Adaptation of Gen Z:** Influencer marketing plays an important role in the purchase decisions of Gen Z consumers. Since Gen Z consumers tend to be more receptive to digital content and are generally more open to AI-driven experiences than previous generations, they show greater interest in virtual influencers. Consequently, brands are increasingly engaging with virtual influencers as innovative marketing ambassadors — especially today, as the human influencer market has become saturated. Virtual influencers spe-

cifically appeal to Gen Z consumers in areas such as gaming, the metaverse, and NFT projects.

- **Cost and Control Advantages:** Virtual influencers offer clear cost and control advantages over human influencers. Their content can be fully managed by brands, ensuring consistency with the brand's messages and identity (Oliveira and Chimenti, 2021). Additionally, in terms of content production, using virtual influencers is more cost-effective compared to human influencers, who may require additional expenses such as hair, makeup, studio, and transportation (Sookkaew and Saephoo, 2021, p. 329). Moreover, since virtual influencers do not create personal controversies or ethical scandals, they are considered a lower-risk choice. They may represent a way for brands to shield themselves from scandals and other human limitations such as unpredictability (Oliveira and Chimenti, 2021).
- **Physical Independence and Medical Advantages:** The physical features of virtual influencers can be quickly customized as desired, and they possess flexible movement capabilities. Unlike human influencers, they are not subject to illness, aging, or death. For example, during the COVID-19 pandemic, they were able to continue their work without interruption, unlike their human counterparts. In addition, their mental and physical health are not matters of concern (Sookkaew and Saephoo, 2021).
- **Availability:** Drawing on the above-mentioned characteristics, virtual influencers are always accessible. Unlike human influencers, who need rest and have personal lives, virtual influencers can operate non-stop, enabling brands to implement long-term marketing strategies continuously (Oliveira and Chimenti, 2021; Sookkaew and Saephoo, 2021).

Despite the advantages that virtual influencers have over human influencers, they also present certain disadvantages. Based on the existing literature, these disadvantages are as follows:

- **Lack of Trust and Sincerity:** Human influencers can deliver genuine content based on their real-life experiences, whereas virtual influencers may lack authentic emotions and sincerity, which can foster distrust.
- **Lack of Experience and Emotion:** Human influencers influence their followers by experiencing products and sharing genuine emotional reactions. In contrast, virtual influencers may encounter credibility issues due to their inability to have real experiences and emotions.
- **Psychological and Social Distance:** Consumers may perceive virtual influencers as more distant and abstract compared to human influencers, who are able to form more personal and natural connections with their audience.

The advantages and disadvantages of virtual influencers compared to human influencers, as discussed above, are presented in Table 2 below.

Table 2. Virtual influencers vs. human influencers

	Virtual Influencers	Human Influencers
Control	Fully controlled by the brand	Live independently; pose risk of personal controversies and scandals
Cost	Lower long-term cost; quick and cost-effective content production	May require high fees; content production may be more expensive
Physical Independence and Medical	Quick physical customization; flexible movement; not subject to illness or aging	Subject to aging, illness, and mortality; limited by physical conditions
Availability	Can operate 24/7; no offline life or personal obligations	Require rest and personal time; family and social commitments
Trust and Sincerity	Often perceived as less trustworthy and less sincere	Considered more authentic and emotionally credible
Experience and Emotion	Cannot truly experience products or emotions	Can provide genuine product experience and emotional engagement
Psychological and Social Distance	May be perceived as distant or robotic	Able to build personal, human relationships with followers

Virtual influencers, despite their controllability, cost-efficiency, accessibility, and physical and medical advantages, encounter a major obstacle in advertising and marketing efforts: how to build consumer trust. Existing literature suggests that consumers may find virtual influencers less trustworthy due to their lack of real-life experience, emotional depth, and non-authentic digital existence (Qu and Baek, 2024). At this point, two interrelated concepts attract particular attention: anthropomorphism and the uncanny valley.

TO BE HUMAN (LIKE) OR NOT: ANTHROPOMORPHISM IN THE UNCANNY VALLEY

Human beings—whose primary way of knowing is through their own existence—tend to attribute certain human characteristics to both living and non-living entities. One of the most striking examples of this can be found in ancient belief systems, where people imagined their gods in human forms with human traits. For instance, Zeus, the god of all gods in Greek mythology, had a humanoid appearance and exhibited emotions such as anger and joy; while Aphrodite, the goddess of beauty, was portrayed as a beautiful woman with divine powers.Similarly, in ancient Egypt, gods and goddesses were represented in hybrid forms combining human and animal features—for example, Ra, the supreme god, appeared with a human body and a falcon head. This tendency arises from the way humans understand the world through their own existence. Therefore, it is not merely an outdated way of thinking. On the contrary, it is currently argued that people tend to interact with artificial intelligence in a similar manner. These ongoing discussions on AI, along with the ancient examples provided above, highlight the timeless nature of the humanization tendency—namely, anthropomorphism.

Notable researchers (Goel and Garg, 2025, p. 2; Pan et al., 2024, p. 3231; Deng, 2024, p. 2) define anthropomorphism as the attribution of humanoid features to non-human entities. The basic human tendency to associate human characteristics with non-human beings is linked to their innate need to understand their environment, reduce uncertainty, and establish social relationships. This is because the starting point of human cognition is the self; humans attempt to understand the world by projecting their own reflections onto everything they perceive. Whether it be animals, natural phenomena, objects, or robots, people tend to approach them as if they possess a certain degree of human-like qualities. Likewise, the interaction between humans and virtual influencers—regardless of their level of human resemblance—cannot be understood independently of the concept of anthropomorphism.

Human-like features are not limited to physical attributes. In fact, anthropomorphism is a multidimensional and complex structure that involves the attribution of human characteristics on physical, emotional, and cognitive levels. Accordingly, Goel and Garg (2025, p. 2) identify three distinct dimensions of anthropomorphism: physical anthropomorphism, emotional anthropomorphism, and cognitive anthropomorphism.

Physical anthropomorphism refers to embodying non-human entities in human form or presenting them with certain human body parts. For example, Lil Miquela was designed and brought to life in the body of a teenage girl. From our perspective, wearing clothes and accessories—considering that human beings are the only living creatures who use them—is also related to physical anthropomorphism. Consider John Pork — although it is visualized with the body of a pig, it wears clothes and accessories that are uniquely human. Therefore, physical anthropomorphism involves ascribing a certain level of human appearance to non-human beings.

Emotional anthropomorphism refers to the attribution of human emotions to non-human entities. In other words, it is based on the assumption that objects or artificial intelligence systems have the ability to express human emotions such as joy, sadness, or excitement. For example, Lil Miquela shares photos of herself crying, laughing, and expressing a variety of emotions—openly showing her changing moods to her followers.

Cognitive anthropomorphism is the attribution of typically human mental processes—such as thinking, reasoning, or intentionality—to non-human entities. When emotional and cognitive dimensions of anthropomorphism are taken into account, it becomes clear that most virtual influencers exhibit emotional and cognitive anthropomorphic characteristics to some extent. For instance, although The Good Advice Cupcake is portrayed as a cartoonish cupcake, that virtual influencer is seen in human-like activities such reading books, taking baths, and even doing laundry. Thus, even though it is not embodied in a human form, it still possesses emotional and cognitive anthropomorphic features.

The Uncanny Valley Theory provides an explanatory model based on anthropomorphic perception. It suggests that the more a non-human entity exhibits human-like physical characteristics, the more likely it is to evoke a sense of uncanniness in viewers (Goel and Garg, 2025, p. 2; Pan et al., 2024, p. 3230). As can be inferred from this, the perception of uncanniness does not stem from humanoid emotions or cognitive anthropomorphic attributes of the non-human agent. Rather, the degree of realism in its human-like physical features is the key determinant of the uncanny feeling. In other words, any robot, virtual influencer, or hologram that displays a higher level of physical anthropomorphic resemblance tends to evoke a stronger sense of uncanniness.

This may prevent the target audience from establishing emotional closeness and trust in their parasocial relationship with the virtual influencer. Based on findings in the literature, Pan et al. (2024) reveal that although human resemblance is initially welcomed, once a certain threshold is exceeded, the audience begins to feel uneasy, which in turn reduces the acceptance of virtual influencers. However, considering that the literature is still emerging and that virtual influencers represent a relatively new area of research in the context of audience perception, further studies are needed to better explain the dynamics of the uncanny feeling experienced by audiences.

Hypothesis Development

Trust Transfer Theory suggests that trust placed in one entity can extend to another associated entity. This cognitive mechanism offers a valuable framework for understanding consumer behavior in digital environments (Haq et al., 2024, p. 2; Hu et al., 2019, p. 2). In the context of influencer marketing, it implies that consumers' trust in a particular influencer may spill over to the products featured in their sponsored content. Accordingly, we propose that the perceived trust of the influencer positively affects the perceived trust in the advertisement—across both high-involvement and low-involvement products—regardless of whether the influencer is virtual or human.

H1 Perceived source credibility of the influencer has a positive effect on perceived advertising trust for low-involvement product categories.
H2 Perceived source credibility of the influencer has a positive effect on perceived advertising trust for high-involvement product categories.

Within the limited body of existing literature, a number of recent studies comparing virtual and human influencers suggest that human influencers tend to perform better in certain areas—particularly in building trust and fostering favorable consumer responses—as virtual influencers may trigger a sense of uncanniness (Hofeditz et al., 2022; Özdemir et al., 2023; Arsenyan & Mirowska, 2021; Pan et al., 2024; Gutuleac et al., 2024; Qu & Baek, 2024; Kholkina et al., 2025). Based on these findings, we hypothesize that virtual influencers generate lower levels of trust compared to their human counterparts. This diminished trust, in turn, reduces perceived advertising trust across both low- and high-involvement product categories.

H3 Human influencers are perceived as more credible sources than their virtual counterparts.
H4 For high-involvement product categories, human influencers generate higher levels of perceived advertising trust than virtual ones.
H5 For low-involvement product categories, human influencers generate higher levels of perceived advertising trust than virtual ones.

METHODOLOGY

Research Summary

This study examines whether a human influencer (vs. a virtual influencer) leads to higher levels of perceived source credibility and perceived advertising trust across both high-involvement and low-involvement product categories 2 (influencer nature: human vs. virtual) × 1 (product type: a low involvement product -Coffee- and a high involvement product -Laptop). The proposed hypotheses were tested through an experimental design. The experiment was conducted at the Communication Faculty of Kocaeli University. The participants were first-year undergraduate students enrolled in the Integrated Marketing Communication course. Those who voluntarily agreed to participate in the study were randomly assigned to one of two groups: Group A and Group B. Both groups were exposed to the same fictional influencer's sponsored posts featuring two product categories: one high-involvement product and one low-involvement product. However, only Group A was informed that the influencer was virtual. Both groups began filling out the questionnaires at the same time, and each participant completed the form individually. The collected data were analyzed using SPSS.

Research Design

We followed a specific experimental procedure, including material design, questionnaire design, data collection, and data analysis. Initially, the visual stimuli for the experiment—such as the influencer's profile picture, Instagram bio, and her sponsored posts for each product—were generated. Subsequently, the online questionnaire forms were developed. Thereafter, these questionnaires were administered to respondents who had been assigned to two groups: Group A and Group B. Following data collection, the data were analyzed using statistical techniques such as the Independent T-Test and Regression.

Figure 5. Experimental procedure

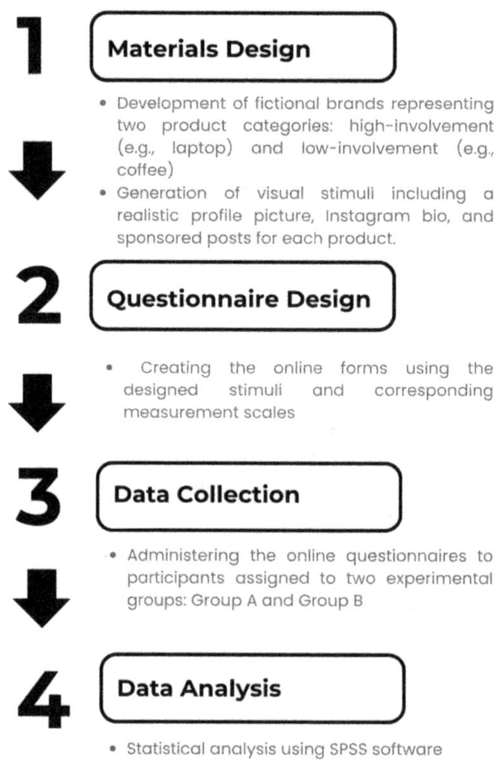

Material Design

Selection of the Social Media Platform and Influencer Design

According to the *Digital 2024 October Global Statshot Report*, Instagram ads have the capacity to reach 82.8% of the population aged 18 and over in Türkiye. This makes Türkiye the country with the highest Instagram ad reach in the world (We Are Social, 2025). Moreover, Instagram is very popular among Gen Z. Therefore, Instagram was chosen as the social media platform for this experiment.

We created a fictitious influencer character. Considering the target audience, Gen Z, this fictional character was imagined as a university student in her 20s. This character was named Zeyno, a more sincere and appealing abbreviation of *Zeynep*, which is a common female name in Turkey. The character was carefully and holistically designed, with personal traits such as a sincere and joyful communication tone, and physical features such as brown hair and brown eyes. Considering the rich demographic diversity of Turkey, she was portrayed as neither too brunette nor too blonde. Rather, she was designed as a natural-looking young female university student in her 20s, with brown hair and brown eyes. Additionally, she was meant to have a smiling facial expression to appear more sincere.

Table 3. Personality traits and physicial features of the influencer

Personality Traits	Physicial Features
Sincerity, joyful personality, young communication tone	Natural-looking female profile in her 20s Brown hair, brown eyes Smiling facial expression

According to the physical features above, a detailed visual description prompt was generated using ChatGPT, a text-based artificial intelligence tool. This initial prompt was as follows:

"A young woman in her early 20s with straight brown hair and brown eyes. She has a warm and sincere smile on her face. She is either wearing no makeup or very minimal makeup. The lighting is natural and realistic. The background is simple and everyday—such as a library, a café corner, or a plain room with neutral tones. She is casually dressed in a basic T-shirt or a plain sweater. The camera captures her face and upper shoulders clearly. Her skin tone is medium, reflecting the general demographic features of women in Turkey—not too fair, not too dark. She should look realistic, friendly, approachable, and trustworthy, just like a real university student. The image must look natural and photo-realistic, not artificial or overly edited."

The prompt above was copied and pasted into the Dream Lab of Canva, which is an artificial intelligence-supported visual design platform that also functions as a text-to-image AI tool. The prompt was revised based on the generated images, and the image generation process was repeated until an adequate image was obtained. The resulting images were evaluated, and the most realistic one was downloaded. Then, this image was uploaded to FaceApp, an image editing application, in order to be retouched for enhanced realism. Subsequently, the image below was selected as the final profile picture of the fictional influencer, Zeyno.

Figure 6. The final profiel picture of Zeyno

Considering her sincere and youth-friendly communication tone, Zeyno's bio (profile description) was generated using ChatGPT. The suggestions developed by ChatGPT were revised in accordance with the established profile, as follows:

Group A
I'm a virtual influencer created by AI
University student
Classes, exams, and lots of campus drama
Luxury living on a student budget
Group B
Open for collaborations: DMs are open University student
Classes, exams, and lots of campus drama
Luxury living on a student budget
Open for collaborations: DMs are open

The profile picture and bio information were integrated using Canva to create Zeyno's Instagram bio image. The bio was identical for both groups, except for the explicit disclosure of the AI-generated virtual influencer nature, which was presented only to Group A as the manipulative variable.

Figure 7. The final bios of Zeyno - Group A

Figure 8. The final bios of Zeyno – Group B

Brand Development and Sponsored Posts Design

University students are identified as the main consumer group for coffee consumption in Turkey (Ülker and Tosun, 2021: 212), and they are one of the consumer segments that actively use laptops (Aytekin and Kuvat, 2018: 195). Hence, coffee was selected as the low-involvement product category and the laptop as the high-involvement product category, in accordance with the target audience profile—Gen Z university students. To prevent pre-existing brand associations, two fictitious brand names were created for each category. These names were derived from Turkish words directly referring to the product categories—specifically *kahve* for coffee and *bilgisayar* for laptop. They were transformed into brand names as *JustKahve* and *Bilgiter*, which could be more appealing to young consumers. Sponsored Instagram content, designed as brand collaboration posts by Zeyno for both fictional brands, was created as follows:

- **JustKahve (low-involvement product – coffee):** A close-up image focusing on the hand of a young woman holding a coffee cup alongside a book on a table was used. No facial features were presented in the image. Due to visual cues such as nail polish, it is clearly understood that the hands belong to a female. This visual composition was created to give the impression that it was shared on Zeyno's Instagram account. The post caption was generated with ChatGPT and subsequently revised to reflect Zeyno's sincere personality and her youthful, engaging communication tone, in line with the characteristics of the target audience. Additionally, the caption was supported with relevant hashtags such as #JustKahve and an explicit sponsored ad disclosure (#Reklam / #Ad) to create a more natural impression. The final caption was determined as follows:

Lectures, exams, campus hustle… Once again, @JustKahve came to my rescue! With its delicious and budget-friendly coffee options, JustKahve is my daily essential. Pick your favorite brew and power up your day!

#JustKahve #NoDayWithoutCoffee #CampusLife #Ad"

Figure 9. Sponsored Post- JustKahve

- **Bilgiter (high-involvement product – laptop):** A close-up image of a young woman's hands working on a laptop was used. No facial features were represented in the image. Due to visual cues such as manicured hands, it is clearly seen that the hands belong to a female. Additionally, a strand of hair visible at the edge of the frame matches Zeyno's hair color, reinforcing the association with her. This visual composition was entirely created to give the impression that it was shared on Zeyno's Instagram account. The post caption was generated with ChatGPT and subsequently revised to reflect Zeyno's sincere personality and her youthful, engaging communication tone, in line with the characteristics of the target audience. Additionally, the caption was supported with relevant hashtags such as #Bilgiter and an explicit sponsored ad disclosure (#Reklam / #Ad) to create a more natural impression.

My biggest helper in university life: @Bilgiter!

Lecture notes, presentations, projects, and yes — a bit of fun... I need a powerful laptop for all of it! Luckily, @Bilgiter keeps up with all my workload with speed and performance.

What do you think is the most important laptop feature for university students?

Drop your thoughts below!

#Bilgiter #LaptopLife #CampusTech #StudentFriendlyLaptop #Ad

Figure 10. Sponsored post- bilgiter

Questionnaire Design and Mesurements

The online questionnaire forms were designed in line with the research objectives and consisted of three main sections, as follows:

- In the first section, the relevant bio image of Zeyno—based on the respondents' assigned group—was presented. Then, respondents were asked to assess the source credibility of the influencer.
- The second section aimed to evaluate the perceived advertising trust of the sponsored posts for the two fictional brands, *JustKahve* and *Bilgiter*.
- In the final section, respondents' demographic information—such as age and gender—as well as their Instagram usage and habits (e.g., usage frequency and influencer following), were gathered. The questionnaire concluded with a manipulation-check question to assess whether the manipulation was successfully perceived.

The following instruments were adopted to measure the key constructs of the study:

- The Source Credibility of a Peer Endorser scale, developed by Munnukka, Uusitalo, and Toivonen (2016), consists of 15 items and was adapted to measure the perceived credibility of the influencer. The scale originally comprises four dimensions: trustworthiness, expertise, similarity, and attractiveness.
- The ADTRUST scale, developed by Soh, Reid, and King, 2009 was adapted to measure the perceived advertising trust toward the sponsored Instagram posts of both fictional brands. The scale consists of 20 items and originally encompasses four dimensions: reliability, usefulness, affect, and willingness to rely.

The above instruments were adapted using a 7-point Likert scale ranging from 1 = strongly disagree to 7 = strongly agree.

The questionnaires were administered using Google Forms. There were several reasons behind this choice. First, the questionnaires combined both visual and textual content. Second, it was important for the experimental images to be displayed on mobile phones, as Gen Z users generally access social media platforms via their smartphones. Google Forms enables both visual and textual content to be viewed easily and seamlessly on mobile devices. Additionally, it offers advantages such as ease of use, free access, and data security. Moreover, it provides data in a format compatible with SPSS.

Ethical Clearance

Prior to the experiment, ethical approval was obtained from the Kocaeli University Ethics Committee (Decision No: [E-94094268-100-753324], Date: [21/03/2025]).

RESULTS OF THE STUDY

Manipulation Check

To test the validity of the experimental design, a manipulation check question was employed. Participants were asked to choose the correct option that accurately described the nature of the influencer they had been exposed to. The manipulation of influencer type (human vs. virtual) was successful, as the results indicated a statistically significant difference between the two groups ($\chi^2(1) = 22.88$, $p < .001$). Additionally, the Likelihood Ratio test was also significant ($G^2 = 24.33$, $p < .001$), supporting the strength of the model. These findings reveal that participants largely perceived the nature of the influencer correctly.

Table 4. Manipulation check results

	Value	df	Asymptotic Significance (2-sided)
Pearson Chi-Square	22.876	1	.000
Likelihood Ratio	24.327	1	.000

0 cells (0.0%) have expected count less than 5. The minimum expected count is 17.00.

Respondent Profiles and Instagram Usage Patterns

The sample size was determined using G*Power 3.1. Assuming a medium effect size (Cohen's $d = 0.5$), an alpha level of 0.05, and a power of 0.80, a total of 64 participants (32 per group) was calculated as the required sample size. To account for potential data loss or missing responses, the study aimed to involve more than 64 participants. Therefore, a total of 70 participants were enrolled in the experiment. Among them, 62 were female and 8 were male. 44% of the participants were 19 years old. Their ages ranged from 19 to 24 years. These results indicate that the participants belong to Generation Z, which is consistent with the scope of the study.

Table 5. Age distribution of participants

	Frequency (n)	Percent (%)
19	31	44.3
20	12	17.1
21	9	12.9
	9	12.9
23	6	8.6
24	3	4.3
Total	70	100

Table 6. Gender distribution of participants

	Frequency (n)	Percent (%)
Female	62	88.6
Male	8	11.4
Total	70	100

87% of the participants declared that they use Instagram very actively, while 13 percent stated that they use it occasionally. These rates demonstrate that the vast majority of the respondents are active Instagram users.

Table 7. Frequency of Instagram use

	Frequency (n)	Percent (%)
I use Instagram actively	61	87.1
I use Instagram occasionaly	9	12.8
	70	100

The majority of participants reported that they follow influencers regularly. Participants who follow influencers every day (40%) and those who follow them several times a week (36%) together constitute 76% of the sample. This finding also reveals the proportion of participants who are actively exposed to influencer content.

Table 8. Frequency of influencer following

Frequency	Frequency (n)	Percent (%)
Every day	28	40.0
Several times a week	25	35.7
Rarely	5	7.1
I don't follow influencers	12	17.1
Total	70	100

Most of the participants (73%) indicated that they had made a purchase based on influencer recommendations, whereas only 27% reported that they had never made a purchase based on such recommendations.

Table 9. Participants' product purchases based on influencer recommendations

	Frequency (n)	Percent (%)
Yes	48	68.6
No	19	27.1
Rarely	3	4.3
Total	70	100

Validity and Reliability of the Scales

Reliability analyses were conducted to evaluate the internal consistency of the scales. In this regard, Cronbach's alpha coefficients were calculated.

Table 10. Scale reliability measures

Scales	Cronbach's Alpha	Reliability Level
The Source Credibility of a Peer Endorser Scale	.936	0.90<Alpha Excellent (Very High)
ADTRUST scale (for coffee post)	.945	0.90<Alpha Excellent (Very High)
ADTRUST scale (for laptop post)	.964	0.90<Alpha Excellent (Very High)

The Cronbach's alpha value of .936, calculated for the *Source Credibility of a Peer Endorser* scale, indicates high reliability, confirming that the scale has excellent internal consistency. Similarly, the *ADTRUST* scale demonstrated strong internal consistency, with very high Cronbach's alpha values in both conditions: coffee post (.945) and laptop post (.964). These values reveal that all scales employed in the study exhibit strong reliability and serve as valid instruments for measurement.

In order to assess the construct validity of the scales, factor analysis was conducted. First, the Kaiser-Meyer-Olkin (KMO) coefficient and Bartlett's Test of Sphericity were calculated to assess the suitability of the sample data for factor analysis. Then, an Exploratory Factor Analysis (EFA) was performed to examine the factorial structure of the scales and the total variance explained by these factors.

- **Source Credibility of a Peer Endorser Scale:** Table 11 presents the results of the KMO and Bartlett's tests for the *Source Credibility of a Peer Endorser* scale. The Kaiser-Meyer-Olkin (KMO) value was found to be 0.860, indicating that the sample size was highly suitable for factor analysis. The significance level of Bartlett's Test of Sphericity (p = .000) indicates that the correlation matrix among the variables is appropriate for factor analysis.

Table 11. KMO and Bartlett's test results for the source credibility of a peer endorser scale

Test	Value
Kaiser–Meyer–Olkin Measure of Sampling Adequacy	0.860
Bartlett's Test of Sphericity Approx. Chi-Square	837.148
Bartlett's Test of Sphericity df	91
Bartlett's Test of Sphericity Sig.	0.000

Table 12 demonstrates the results of the factor analysis conducted for the *Source Credibility of a Peer Endorser* scale. Although the original scale consisted of four distinct dimensions—namely, expertise, credibility, identification, and attractiveness—all items in this study were loaded onto a single factor. This finding indicates that the scale assumed a unidimensional structure in this context. This component explains 55% of the total variance.

Table 12. Exploratory factor analysis results for the source credibility of a peer endorser scale

Variables	Component 1
VAR1	0.687
VAR2	0.713
VAR3	0.711
VAR4	0.640
VAR5	0.818
VAR6	0.850
VAR7	0.876
VAR8	0.877
VAR9	0.687
VAR10	0.640
VAR11	0.711
VAR12	0.774
VAR13	0.680
VAR14	0.655

Extraction Method: Principal Component Analysis
1 component extracted.

- **ADTRUST Scale:** Table 13 presents the results of the KMO and Bartlett's tests for the *ADTRUST* scale under two conditions: the coffee post and the laptop post. The Kaiser-Meyer-Olkin (KMO) value was found to be 0.879, indicating that the sample size was highly suitable for factor analysis. The significance level of Bartlett's Test of Sphericity ($p = .000$) indicates that the correlation matrix among the variables is appropriate for factor analysis.

Table 13. KMO and Bartlett's test results for the ADTRUST scale

Coffee Post Condition		Laptop Post Condition	
Tests	**Value**	**Tests**	**Value**
Kaiser–Meyer–Olkin Measure of Sampling Adequacy	0.879	Kaiser–Meyer–Olkin Measure of Sampling Adequacy	0.897
Bartlett's Test of Sphericity Approx. Chi-Square	960.921	Bartlett's Test of Sphericity Approx. Chi-Square	1266.980
Bartlett's Test of Sphericity df	120	Bartlett's Test of Sphericity df	120
Bartlett's Test of Sphericity Sig.	0.000	Bartlett's Test of Sphericity Sig.	0.000

Table 14. Exploratory factor analysis results for the ADTRUST scale

Coffee Post Condition		Laptop Post Condition	
Variables	**Component 1**	**Variables**	**Component 1**
VAR1	0.714	VAR1	0.754
VAR2	0.802	VAR2	0.797
VAR3	0.722	VAR3	0.677
VAR4	0.632	VAR4	0.717
VAR5	0.652	VAR5	0.715
VAR6	0.788	VAR6	0.855
VAR7	0.802	VAR7	0.888
VAR8	0.785	VAR8	0.837
VAR9	0.668	VAR9	0.842
VAR10	0.697	VAR10	0.866
VAR11	0.720	VAR11	0.841
VAR12	0.753	VAR12	0.803
VAR13	0.831	VAR13	0.818
VAR14	0.829	VAR14	0.828
VAR15	0.762	VAR15	0.839
VAR16	0.688	VAR16	0.795

Extraction Method: Principal Component Analysis component extracted.

Although the original scale consists of four dimensions—reliability, usefulness, affect, and willingness to rely—all items were loaded onto a single factor in both conditions. This finding indicates that the scale assumed a unidimensional structure in this study. In the context of the coffee post condition, the component explains 55% of the total variance, while in the laptop post condition, it explains 65% of the total variance.

Hypothesis Testing

In order to determine whether parametric or non-parametric tests should be employed for hypothesis testing, the normality of the scales was examined. For this purpose, both the Kolmogorov–Smirnov and Shapiro–Wilk tests were applied. The findings indicate that all scales used in the study exhibit a normal distribution.

Table 15. Normality test results for each scale

	Kolmogorov–Smirnov			Shapiro–Wilk		
	Statistic	**df**	**Sig.**	**Statistic**	**df**	**Sig.**
Source Credibility	.067	70	.200	.980	70	.308
ADTRUST (for coffe post)	.077	70	.200	.982	70	.418
ADTRUST (for laptop post)	.079	70	.200	.974	70	.161

Source Credibility and Perceived Ad Trust

Regression analysis was performed to examine whether source credibility affects the perceived trust in coffee and laptop posts. Regression analysis indicated that source credibility has a significant and positive effect on perceived trust in the coffee post, and it explains 53% of the variance in perceived trust ($R^2 = .530$). The model was statistically significant ($F(1, 68) = 76.61, p < .001$).

Table 16. Regression model summary 1

Model	R	R Square	Adjusted R Square	Std. Error of the Estimate
1	.728	.530	.523	.82505

Table 17. ANOVA table 1

Model	Sum of Squares	df	Mean Square	F	Sig.
Regression	52.148	1	52.148	76.609	.000
Residual	46.288	68	.681		
Total	98.435	69			

a. Dependent Variable: Perceived Ad Trust toward coffe post
b. Predictors: (Constant), Source Credibility

Regression analysis revealed that source credibility has a significant and positive effect on perceived trust in the laptop post, and it explains 37.8% of the variance in perceived trust ($R^2 = .378$). The model was statistically significant ($F(1, 68) = 41.29, p < .001$).

Table 18. Regression model summary 2

Model	R	R Square	Adjusted R Square	Std. Error of the Estimate
1	.615	.378	.369	1.00885

Table 19. ANOVA table 2

Model	Sum of Squares	df	Mean Square	F	Sig.
Regression	42.021	1	42.021	41.286	.000
Residual	69.209	68	1.018		
Total	111.230	69			

a. Dependent Variable: Perceived Ad Trust toward laptop post
b. Predictors: (Constant), Source Credibility

- **Source Credibility (Virtual Influencer vs. Human Influencer)**

To determine whether source credibility differs according to the nature of the influencer (virtual vs. human), the mean source credibility score was calculated (Table 20). The mean source credibility score of the virtual influencer was higher (M = 3.34, SD = 1.22) than that of the human influencer (M = 3.00, SD = 1.04). An Independent Samples T-Test was conducted to examine whether this mean difference was statistically significant.

Table 20. Mean source credibility scores for virtual and human influencers

		N	Mean	Std. Deviation	Std. Error Mean
Source Credibility	Virtual Influencer	35	3.3408	1.2155	0.2055
	Human Influencer	35	3.0000	1.0376	0.1754

According to the Independent Samples T-Test, the difference in source credibility scores between the virtual influencer and the human influencer was not statistically significant ($p > .05$).

Table 21. Independent samples t-test results for source credibility: Virtual vs. human influencers

Variance Assumption	t	df	Sig. (2-tailed)	Mean Difference	Std. Error Difference	95% CI Lower	95% CI Upper
Equal variances assumed	1.262	68	.211	0.3408	0.2701	-0.1982	0.8799
Equal variances not assumed	1.262	66.364	.211	0.3408	0.2701	-0.1985	0.8801

ADTRUST (Virtual Influencer vs. Human Influencer)

The mean ADTRUST scores for both the coffee and laptop posts were compared between the virtual influencer and human influencer conditions. As presented in Table 22 and Table 23, participants who were exposed to the virtual influencer found both the coffee and laptop posts more trustworthy. An Independent Samples T-Test was conducted to examine whether these mean differences were statistically significant.

Table 22. Mean perceived advertising trust scores (coffee – low-involvement product): Virtual vs. human influencers

	N	Mean	Std. Deviation	Std. Error Mean
Virtual Influencer	35	3.5768	1.2039	0.2035
Human Influencer	35	3.3625	1.1925	0.2016

Table 23. Mean perceived advertising trust scores (laptop – high-involvement product): Virtual vs. human influencers

	N	Mean	Std. Deviation	Std. Error Mean
Virtual Influencer	35	3.1375	1.2877	0.2177
Human Influencer	35	3.3321	1.2624	0.2134

According to the Independent Samples T-Test, the differences in ADTRUST scores for both the coffee and laptop posts between the virtual influencer and the human influencer were not statistically significant ($p > .05$).

Table 24. Independent samples t-test results for perceived advertising trust (coffee – low-involvement product): Virtual vs. human influencers

Variance Assumption	t	df	Sig. (2-tailed)	Mean Difference	Std. Error Difference	95% CI Lower	95% CI Upper
Equal variances assumed	0.748	68	.457	0.2143	0.2864	-0.3573	0.7859
Equal variances not assumed	0.748	67.994	.457	0.2143	0.2864	-0.3573	0.7859

Table 25. Independent samples t-test results for perceived advertising trust (laptop – high-involvement product): Virtual vs. human influencers

Variance Assumption	t	df	Sig. (2-tailed)	Mean Difference	Std. Error Difference	95% CI Lower	95% CI Upper
Equal variances assumed	-0.639	68	.525	-0.1946	0.3048	-0.8029	0.4136
Equal variances not assumed	-0.639	67.973	.525	-0.1946	0.3048	-0.8029	0.4136

Summary of Findings

The participants, all of whom belong to Generation Z, are active Instagram users and are regularly exposed to influencer content. A significant portion of the participants reported that they had made purchases based on influencer recommendations. The manipulation check revealed that the majority of participants accurately perceived the nature of the influencer they encountered (virtual or human), indicating that the experimental manipulation was successful.

All scales used in the study demonstrated very high reliability (Cronbach's alpha) and strong construct validity (KMO, Bartlett's Test, and Exploratory Factor Analysis). The scales exhibited a unidimensional structure with excellent internal consistency. Normality tests confirmed that the variables followed a normal distribution, which justified the use of parametric tests. Regression analyses revealed a positive and statistically significant effect of source credibility on perceived advertising trust in both the coffee and laptop post conditions. However, no statistically significant differences were found in source credibility or perceived advertising trust between the virtual and human influencer conditions. Although the mean scores were higher in the virtual influencer condition, these differences were not statistically significant. Overall, source credibility strongly influences perceived advertising trust for both product categories; however, the nature of the influencer (virtual vs. human) did not yield a significant difference in this relationship. Accordingly, the confirmed and rejected hypotheses are as follows:

Table 26. Hypothesis testing results

Hypothesis	Statement	
H1	Perceived source credibility of the influencer has a positive effect on perceived advertising trust for low-involvement product categories.	Confirmed
H2	Perceived source credibility of the influencer has a positive effect on perceived advertising trust for high-involvement product categories.	**Confirmed**
H3	Human influencers are perceived as more credible sources than their virtual counterparts.	**Rejected**
H4	For high-involvement product categories, human influencers generate higher levels of perceived advertising trust than virtual ones.	**Rejected**
H5	For low-involvement product categories, human influencers generate higher levels of perceived advertising trust than virtual ones.	**Rejected**

FUTURE RESEARCH DIRECTIONS

Although social media marketing has become an indispensable part of contemporary life, virtual influencer marketing stands an emergent area. Therefore, future studies are recommended to explore different platforms, cultural contexts, and demographic groups within the scope of virtual influencer marketing.

CONCLUSION

Virtual influencers are emerging as new agents in advertising and marketing thanks to advancements in computer-generated imagery (CGI) and artificial intelligence (AI) technologies. These virtual influencers can be designed in either human or non-human forms and exhibit varying levels of realism. Accordingly, they are classified into different types—hyper-realistic non-humans, hyper-realistic humans, unrealistic non-humans, and unrealistic humans—based on their visual appearance. Despite their various advantages over human influencers—such as controllability, 24/7 availability, and cost-efficiency—there is a limited number of studies in the extant literature.

This study analyzes how Gen Z consumers evaluate virtual and human influencers in terms of perceived source credibility, and how this credibility is reflected in advertising trust in sponsored posts. To do so, an experiment was conducted in the context of high- and low-involvement products. The participants were divided into two groups: participants in Group A were informed that the influencer was virtual, whereas participants in Group B assumed the influencer was an actual human being.

The findings revealed that source credibility had a significant and positive impact on perceived advertising trust for both high- and low-involvement products. However, no statistically significant differences were observed between virtual and human influencers in terms of source credibility or perceived ad trust. While virtual influencers received slightly higher average scores, these differences were not statistically significant. These findings are compatible with previous research suggesting that clearly disclosing the virtual nature of the influencer does not negatively affect consumer perception (Di Cicco, Neri, & Pino, 2024). Therefore, these results also challenge earlier studies which point out that virtual influencers are less trustworthy than human ones (Sands et al., 2022; Hofeditz et al., 2022; Özdemir et al., 2023). This study posits that virtual influencers can be perceived by consumers as being at least as credible as real people. Therefore, especially among consumer groups who are highly receptive to digital content—such as Generation Z—virtual influencers have the potential to offer innovative and flexible communication tools for brands. However, further research is needed. Future studies are recommended to explore different platforms, cultural contexts, and demographic groups.

LIMITATIONS

The sample of this study was limited to Generation Z university students selected through purposive sampling; therefore, the findings cannot be generalized to the whole population or other demographic groups. The research was conducted on Instagram using an image-based post format, omitting other social media platforms and content types.

REFERENCES

Abdullah, S., Hafid, A., Folke, M., Lindén, M., & Kristoffersson, A. (2023). PPG-Feat: A novel MATLAB toolbox for extracting PPG fiducial points. *Frontiers in Bioengineering and Biotechnology*, *11*, 1199604. DOI: 10.3389/fbioe.2023.1199604 PMID: 37378045

Alalwan, A. A., Rana, N. P., Dwivedi, Y. K., & Algharabat, R. (2017). Social media in marketing: A review and analysis of the existing literature. *Telematics and Informatics*, *34*(7), 1177–1190. DOI: 10.1016/j.tele.2017.05.008

Albuquerque, P., Mena, J., & Alharthi, M. (2023). The Impact of Social Media Marketing on Brand Awareness: Evidence from Emerging Markets. *JMR, Journal of Marketing Research*, *48*(2), 123–136.

Aljuhmani, H. Y., Elrehail, H., Bayram, P., & Samarah, T. (2023). Linking social media marketing efforts with customer brand engagement in driving brand loyalty. *Asia Pacific Journal of Marketing and Logistics*, *35*(7), 1719–1738. DOI: 10.1108/APJML-08-2021-0627

Angraini, N. (2023). Social media marketing influencer: literature review on promotional strategies using the influence of social media celebrities. ijerfa, 1(4). DOI: 10.55227/ijerfa.v1i4.42

Arsenyan, J., & Mirowska, A. (2021). Almost human? A comparative case study on the social media presence of virtual influencers. *International Journal of Human-Computer Studies*, *155*, 102694. Advance online publication. DOI: 10.1016/j.ijhcs.2021.102694

Aytekin, A., & Kuvat, O. (2018). Dizüstü Bilgisayar Seçiminde Değerlendirilen Kriterlerin Önem Düzeylerinin AHP ile Belirlenmesi: 1. ve 2. Sınıf Bilgisayar Mühendisliği Öğrencileri Uygulaması. MANAS Sosyal Araştırmalar Dergisi, 7(4).

Brooks, R., Christidis, R., Carah, N., Kelly, B., Martino, F., & Backholer, K. (2022). Turning users into 'unofficial brand ambassadors': Marketing of unhealthy food and non-alcoholic beverages on tiktok. *BMJ Global Health*, *7*(6), e009112. DOI: 10.1136/bmjgh-2022-009112 PMID: 35879104

Byun, K. J., & Ahn, S. J. G. (2023). A Systematic Review of Virtual Influencers: Similarities and Differences between Human and Virtual Influencers in Interactive Advertising. *Journal of Interactive Advertising*, *23*(4), 293–306. DOI: 10.1080/15252019.2023.2236102

Cheung, M. L., Pires, G. D., & Rosenberger, P. J.III. (2020). Developing a conceptual model for examining social media marketing effects on brand awareness and brand image. *International Journal of Economics and Business Research, 21*(2), 243–261. DOI: 10.1504/IJEBR.2020.10027618

Cresci, (2018) Available at https://www.bbc.com/news/newsbeat-45474286

Deng, F., Tuo, M., Chen, S., & Zhang, Z. (2024). Born for marketing? The effects of virtual versus human influencers on brand endorsement effectiveness: The role of advertising recognition. *Journal of Retailing and Consumer Services*, *80*, 103904. Advance online publication. DOI: 10.1016/j.jretconser.2024.103904

Di Cicco, R., Neri, A., & Pino, G. (2024). Emotional communicative style and anthropomorphism in virtual influencers: An experimental study on Instagram. *Journal of Business Research, 172*, 114379. DOI: 10.1016/j.jbusres.2024.114379

Dinh, T., & Lee, Y. (2021). "i want to be as trendy as influencers" – how "fear of missing out" leads to buying intention for products endorsed by social media influencers. *Journal of Research in Interactive Marketing*, *16*(3), 346–364. DOI: 10.1108/JRIM-04-2021-0127

Drenten, J., & Brooks, G. (2020). Celebrity 2.0: Lil Miquela and the rise of a virtual star system. *Feminist Media Studies*, *20*(8), 1319–1323. DOI: 10.1080/14680777.2020.1830927

Franke, C., Groeppel-Klein, A., & Müller, K. (2023). Consumers' responses to virtual influencers as advertising endorsers: Novel and effective or uncanny and deceiving? *Journal of Advertising*, *52*(4), 523–539. DOI: 10.1080/00913367.2022.2154721

Ghazali, E., Mutum, D., & Lun, N. (2023). Expectations and beyond: The nexus of ai instrumentality and brand credibility in voice assistant retention using extended expectation-confirmation model. *Journal of Consumer Behaviour*, *23*(2), 655–675. DOI: 10.1002/cb.2228

Goel, P. and Garg, A. (2025), "Virtual personalities, real bonds: anthropomorphised virtual influencers' impact on trust and engagement", Journal of Consumer Marketing, Vol. ahead-of-print No. ahead-of-print. DOI: 10.1108/JCM-05-2024-6915

Gökerik, M. (2024). Consumer cynicism in influencer marketing: an impact analysis on purchase intention and brand loyalty. İnsan Ve Toplum Bilimleri Araştırmaları Dergisi, 13(1), 404-421. DOI: 10.15869/itobiad.1422438

Grand View Research. (2024). *Virtual Influencer Market Size, Share & Trends Analysis Report.* https://www.grandviewresearch.com/industry-analysis/virtual-influencer-market-report

Gür. (2019) Available at https://vogue.com.tr/moda-haber/calvin-klein-lgbtq-toplulugundan-ozur-diledi

Gutuleac, R., Baima, G., Rizzo, C., & Bresciani, S. (2024). Will virtual influencers overcome the uncanny valley? The moderating role of social cues. *Psychology and Marketing*, *41*(7), 1419–1431. DOI: 10.1002/mar.21989

Haq, M. D., Tseng, T.-H., Cheng, H.-L., & Chiu, C.-M. (2024). An empirical analysis of eWOM valence effects: Integrating stimulus-organism-response, trust transfer theory, and theory of planned behavior perspectives. *Journal of Retailing and Consumer Services*, *81*, 104026. DOI: 10.1016/j.jretconser.2024.104026

Hofeditz, Lennart; Nissen, Anika; Schütte, Reinhard; and Mirbabaie, Milad, "Trust Me, I'm an Influencer! - A Comparison of Perceived Trust in Human and Virtual Influencers" (2022). ECIS 2022 Research-in-Progress Papers. 27.

Hofeditz, L., Nissen, A., Schütte, R., & Mirbabaie, M. (2022) Trust me, I'm an influencer!-A comparison of perceived trust in human and virtual influencers [Paper presentation]. https://aisel.aisnet.org/ecis2022_rip/27

HonoraryReporter. (2023) Available at https://honoraryreporters.korea.net/board/detail.do?pageidx=1&board_no=11587&tpln=1&articlecate=1&searchtp=all&searchtxt=taiba#:~:text=Oh%20Rozy%20(%EC%98%A4%20%EB%A1%9C%EC%A7%80)%20is,of%20Sidus%20Studio%20X%2C%20Mr

Hu, H., Zhang, D., & Wang, C. (2019). Impact of social media influencers' endorsement on application adoption: A trust transfer perspective. *Social Behavior and Personality*, *47*(11), 1–12. DOI: 10.2224/sbp.8518

Influencer Marketing Hub. (2025). Influencer Marketing Benchmark Report 2025. *Available at* https://influencermarketinghub.com/influencer-marketing-benchmark-report/

Jhawar, A., Kumar, P., & Varshney, S. (2023). The emergence of virtual influencers: A shift in the influencer marketing paradigm. *Young Consumers*, *24*(4), 468–484. DOI: 10.1108/YC-05-2022-1529

Khan, M. I., Raihan, A. F., & Hussain, M. (2023). Interactive marketing in the digital era: Effects on customer loyalty and engagement. *International Journal of Business and Social Science*, *14*(1), 12–20.

Kholkina, V., Chesnokova, E., & Zelenskaya, E. (2025). Virtual or human? The impact of the influencer type on Gen Z consumer outcomes. *Journal of Product and Brand Management*, *34*(1), 104–118. DOI: 10.1108/JPBM-12-2023-4885

Konoplıannykova, M. (2024). Influence marketing in social media. SF, 154(2), 118-144. DOI: 10.31617/1.2024(154)07

Leung, F., Gu, F., Li, Y., Zhang, J., & Palmatier, R. (2022). Influencer marketing effectiveness. *Journal of Marketing*, *86*(6), 93–115. DOI: 10.1177/00222429221102889

Lim, X. J., Radzol, A. R. M., Cheah, J.-H., & Wong, M. W. (2017). The impact of social media influencers on purchase intention and the mediation effect of customer attitude. *Asian Journal of Business Research*, *7*(2), 35. DOI: 10.14707/ajbr.170035

Mayfield, M., & Mayfield, J. (2023). Notes from the editors: spotlight on social media. International Journal of Business Communication, 60(2), 371-374. DOI: 10.1177/23294884221148615

Moreno, L., Demo, G., Rocha, T., & Scussel, F. (2021). Take a ride on credibility: The role of brand personality in users' loyalty to virtual brands in the sharing economy. *Internext*, *16*(2), 221–237. DOI: 10.18568/internext.v16i2.670

Mouritzen, S. L. T., Penttinen, V., & Pedersen, S. (2024). Virtual influencer marketing: The good, the bad and the unreal. *European Journal of Marketing*, *58*(2), 410–440. DOI: 10.1108/EJM-12-2022-0915

Muda, M., & Hamzah, M. (2021). Should i suggest this youtube clip? the impact of ugc source credibility on ewom and purchase intention. *Journal of Research in Interactive Marketing*, *15*(3), 441–459. DOI: 10.1108/JRIM-04-2020-0072

Munnukka, J., Uusitalo, O., & Toivonen, H. (2016). Credibility of a peer endorser and advertising effectiveness. *Journal of Consumer Marketing*, *33*(3), 182–192. DOI: 10.1108/JCM-11-2014-1221

Oliveira, A. B. da S., & Chimenti, P. (2021). "Humanized robots": A proposition of categories to understand virtual influencers. *AJIS. Australasian Journal of Information Systems*, *25*. Advance online publication. DOI: 10.3127/ajis.v25i0.3223

Önder. (2020) Available at https://www.marketingturkiye.com.tr/haberler/michael-jordandan-shudu-grama-yolculuk-influencer-olmak/

Özdemir, O., Kolfal, B., Messinger, P. R., & Rizvi, S. (2023). Human or virtual: How influencer type shapes brand attitudes. *Computers in Human Behavior*, *145*, 107771. DOI: 10.1016/j.chb.2023.107771

Pan, S., Qin, Z., & Zhang, Y. (2024). More Realistic, More Better? How Anthropomorphic Images of Virtual Influencers Impact the Purchase Intentions of Consumers. *Journal of Theoretical and Applied Electronic Commerce Research*, *19*(4), 3229–3252. DOI: 10.3390/jtaer19040157

Perez, A., & Martins, A. M. (2024). Exploring the Relationship between Social Media Marketing and SEO Outcomes. *Journal of Digital Marketing*, *29*(1), 45–60.

Pramesti, K. & Alversia, Y. (2023). The influence of attitude toward user generated content (ugc) in tiktok on purchase intention., 630-639. DOI: 10.2991/978-94-6463-234-7_66

Qu, Y., & Baek, E. (2024). Let virtual creatures stay virtual: Tactics to increase trust in virtual influencers. *Journal of Research in Interactive Marketing*, *18*(1), 91–108. DOI: 10.1108/JRIM-09-2022-0280

Rosenstein, (2018) Available at https://www.harpersbazaar.com/beauty/makeup/a16810663/shudu-gram-fenty-model-fake/

Sahaf, M. F., & Nazir, A. (2024). Influentiality of social media influencers on purchase intention of consumers: A regional perspective. *International Journal of Media and Communication Research*, *5*(1), 1–20. DOI: 10.25299/ijmcr.v5i1.14924

Sands, S., Campbell, C. L., Plangger, K., & Ferraro, C. (2022). Unreal influence: Leveraging AI in influencer marketing. *European Journal of Marketing*, *56*(6), 1721–1747. DOI: 10.1108/EJM-12-2019-0949

Shankar, V., Inman, J. J., Mantrala, M., Kelley, E., & Rizley, R. (2011). Innovations in Shopper Marketing: Current Insights and Future Research Issues. *Journal of Retailing*, *87*(1), S29–S42. DOI: 10.1016/j.jretai.2011.04.007

Shen, Z. (2021). A persuasive ewom model for increasing consumer engagement on social media: Evidence from irish fashion micro-influencers. *Journal of Research in Interactive Marketing*, *15*(2), 181–199. DOI: 10.1108/JRIM-10-2019-0161

Sofuoğlu. (2021) Available at https://www.indyturk.com/node/366471/ya%C5%9Fam/sosyal-medyan%C4%B1n-y%C3%BCkselen-trendi-sanal-fenomenlik

Soh, H., Reid, L. N., & King, K. W. (2009). Measuring Trust In Advertising. *Journal of Advertising*, *38*(2), 83–104. DOI: 10.2753/JOA0091-3367380206

Sookkaew, J., & Saephoo, P. (2021). "Digital influencer": Development and co-existence with digital social groups. *International Journal of Advanced Computer Science and Applications*, *12*(12), 243–252. DOI: 10.14569/IJACSA.2021.0121243

Srivastava, A., Mukaria, B., & Arora, M. (2024). Influencer marketing: A citation and co-citation analysis within business and management domains. *International Academic Publishing House*, *44*, 149–161. DOI: 10.52756/ijerr.2024.v44spl.013

Thomas, V. L., & Fowler, K. (2021). Close Encounters of the AI Kind: Use of AI Influencers As Brand Endorsers. *Journal of Advertising*, *50*(1), 11–25. DOI: 10.1080/00913367.2020.1810595

Ülker, Y., & Tosun, N. (2021). Mağaza imajının ikon marka algısına yansıması. [Turkish Review of Communication Studies]. *Türkiye İletişim Araştırmaları Dergisi*, *38*(38), 205–221. DOI: 10.17829/turcom.805829

We Are Social. 2025 https://www.guvenliweb.org.tr/dosya/95AwI.pdf

Wei, L. (2024). User-generated-content behaviours shape brand loyalty: A self-determination theory perspective. Journal of Education. *Humanities and Social Sciences*, *27*, 287–292. DOI: 10.54097/mzf86j96

Xie-Carson, L., Magor, T., Benckendorff, P., & Hughes, K. (2023). All hype or the real deal? Investigating user engagement with virtual influencers in tourism. *Tourism Management*, *99*, 104779. Advance online publication. DOI: 10.1016/j.tourman.2023.104779

Yuan, J. E. (2025). Making virtual celebrity: Platformization and intermediation in digital cultural production. *International Journal of Cultural Studies*, *28*(1), 316–331. DOI: 10.1177/13678779241230564

Zeng, X., McKenna, B., Richter, S., & Cai, W. (2019). How social media can afford engagement processes., 272-279. DOI: 10.1007/978-3-030-11395-7_23

Zheng, S. (2023). An empirical study on the effects of information characteristics in influencer marketing on consumers' purchase intention. *Advances in Economics and Management Research*, *8*(1), 179. DOI: 10.56028/aemr.8.1.179.2023

ADDITIONAL READINGS

Bartneck, C., Kanda, T., Ishiguro, H., & Hagita, N. (2007). Is the uncanny valley an uncanny cliff?., 368-373. DOI: 10.1109/ROMAN.2007.4415111

Bassett, D. (2018). Ctrl+alt+delete: The changing landscape of the uncanny valley and the fear of second loss. *Current Psychology (New Brunswick, N.J.)*, *40*(2), 813–821. DOI: 10.1007/s12144-018-0006-5

Djafarova, E., & Rushworth, C. (2017). Exploring the credibility of online celebrities' Instagram profiles in influencing the purchase decisions of young female users. *Computers in Human Behavior*, *68*, 1–7. DOI: 10.1016/j.chb.2016.11.009

Lou, C., & Yuan, S. (2019). Influencer Marketing: How Message Value and Credibility Affect Consumer Trust and Purchase Intention. *Journal of Interactive Advertising, 19*(1), 58–73. DOI: 10.1080/15252019.2018.1533501

Luo, X., Zhang, J., & Duan, W. (2013). Social media and firm equity value. *Information Systems Research, 24*(1), 146–163. DOI: 10.1287/isre.1120.0462

Morgain, R. (2012). On the use of the uncanny in ritual. *Religion, 42*(4), 521–548. DOI: 10.1080/0048721X.2012.707802

Sasaki, K., Ihaya, K., & Yamada, Y. (2017). Avoidance of novelty contributes to the uncanny valley. *Frontiers in Psychology, 8*, 1792. Advance online publication. DOI: 10.3389/fpsyg.2017.01792 PMID: 29123490

Schouten, A. P., Janssen, L., & Verspaget, M. (2020). Celebrity vs. Influencer endorsements in advertising: The role of identification, credibility, and Product-Endorser fit. *International Journal of Advertising, 39*(2), 258–281. DOI: 10.1080/02650487.2019.1634898

Sokolova, K., & Perez, C. (2021). You follow fitness influencers on YouTube. But do you really trust them? *Journal of Retailing and Consumer Services, 58*, 102276. DOI: 10.1016/j.jretconser.2020.102276

Wibawa, R., Pratiwi, C., Wahyono, E., Hidayat, D., & Adiasari, W. (2022). Virtual influencers: Is the persona trustworthy? *Jurnal Manajemen Informatika (Jamika), 12*(1), 51–62. DOI: 10.34010/jamika.v12i1.6706

KEY TERMS AND DEFINITIONS

Anthropomorphism: Anthropomorphism is the attribution of human traits, emotions, or intentions to non-human entities, such as animals, inanimate objects, or natural phenomena.

High and Low Involvement Products: High-involvement products engage consumers at a deeper cognitive and emotional level, leading to a more robust brand loyalty and attachment. This can be clearly seen in the marketing strategies employed by brands targeting these products, often relying on rational appeals that emphasize functionality and quality . Conversely, for low-involvement products, emotional advertising tends to be more effective, tapping into feelings and personal connections rather than detailed product features. High and low involvement products are defined in FCB Grid model for consumers.

Social Media Influencer: A social media influencer (SMI) is an individual who has garnered a significant following on social media platforms and is recognized as a trusted figure in specific niches or areas of interest. They leverage their influence to shape the attitudes, purchasing behaviors, and opinions of their audience through regular engagement and content creation, which may include endorsements, product reviews, or lifestyle sharing.

Social Media: Social media refers to a variety of online platforms that enable users to connect, communicate, and share ideas, content, and experiences with one another. It serves as a digital space for interaction, collaboration, and the exchange of information across diverse communities.

Source Credibility: Source credibility refers to the perception of the trustworthiness and expertise of a source providing information. It fundamentally revolves around how individuals assess the reliability of information based on their impressions of the source.

Uncanny Valley: Uncanny valley is a complex interplay of human perception and emotional response triggered by near-human artifacts. As technology develops, understanding and addressing the nuances of this phenomenon may prove essential in fields overlapping robotics, animation, and user experience design.

Virtual Influencer: A virtual influencer can be defined as a computer-generated character designed for engagement on social media platforms, primarily for marketing and branding purposes.

Chapter 3

The Future of Digital World Gaming: Community and Cultural Transformation

Serhat Erdem
https://orcid.org/0000-0002-3782-0147
Atatürk University, Turkey

ABSTRACT

This study addresses the transformation of digitalization on gaming communities by examining the social, cultural and economic impacts of digital games. Digital games have evolved from a mere means of entertainment to an ecosystem that strengthens social ties between individuals and communities, fosters cultural production and creates new economic models. The research analyzes the dynamics of live streaming platforms such as Twitch, YouTube, and gaming communities such as Fortnite, Roblox, and Minecraft. The study reveals that the sociocultural effects of digital games affect not only the daily lives of individuals but also social and cultural structures at the global level.

INTRODUCTION

The use of digital technologies has made audiovisual content presentable in almost all areas where information technologies are used and, in every vehicle, (Akmeşe Demir & Demir, 2023, p. 400). In parallel with the developments in information and communication technologies, digitalization has emerged as an effective process in the transformation process of the methods of producing, collecting and storing various data (Kotan, 2024, p. 94). In this context, digital games, as a rapidly grow-

DOI: 10.4018/979-8-3373-6192-5.ch003

ing and developing industry in recent years, have gone beyond being just a means of entertainment and have become central to social interaction, cultural production and economic activities. With the advancement of technology, games have become an integral part of individuals' daily lives, which has had profound effects on the formation of communities and cultural transformation processes. In this context, understanding the effects of digital games on community dynamics and cultural transformation is of great importance for analyzing the socio-cultural structure of the digital age.

In the traditional art of editing, both in film and television, the process relied on the skills, experience, and aesthetic sensibilities of human editors. However, with the advancement of artificial intelligence technologies, this process is undergoing significant transformation. Now, AI algorithms can automatically analyse scenes, detect emotional tones, and even create the most effective edits to convey a specific emotional state.

Thanks to the developments in information and communication technologies, traditional methods are being replaced by new channels that have become an important part of our lives. While these developing technologies connect the world with virtual networks, they have also brought significant changes in our daily lives. One of the areas affected by these changes is seen in the places and forms of playing games (Çakın & Bolat, 2018). Information systems, which have developed as a result of the convergence of information and communication tools, have enabled the integration of the computer's unique digital language into all analog data, and with the widespread use of computers and the internet over time, communication environments where everyone can intervene in digital space and content have developed (Bayraktar, 2024, p. 34).

Thanks to their interactive nature, digital games create strong bonds between players and pave the way for the formation of virtual communities. These communities are dynamic platforms where individuals united around common interests share experiences, collaborate and engage in social interactions. Especially online multiplayer games contribute to the formation of complex social networks among players and these networks play a critical role in shaping digital culture (Boyalı & Aktaş, 2023).

In terms of cultural transformation, digital games offer a medium for the reinterpretation of traditional cultural forms and the emergence of new cultural expressions. By incorporating various cultural elements such as storytelling, visual arts and music, games facilitate players' access to different cultural experiences and enable the reproduction of cultural diversity in the digital environment (Altunay, 2023). In addition, cultural codes and values are transferred to new generations through games, thus accelerating the process of digitalization of cultural heritage (Bolat, 2023).

On the economic dimension, the digital gaming industry has become a huge market and in-game economies have led to the emergence of new forms of value production in interaction with real-world economies. In-game purchases, trade in virtual goods and e-sports are important components of the digital economy. This shows that, in addition to the economic value of digital games, they also have an impact on the consumption habits and economic behaviors of players (Çakar, 2021). In addition to creating new consumer profiles and consumption practices, digital games have made it necessary for brands to develop consumer-centered interaction-oriented strategies marketing their products and services (Çakın & Yaman, 2022).

In order to understand the impact of digital games on community and cultural transformation, qualitative research has been conducted focusing on analyzing user interactions, live streams and AI- powered content on gaming platforms. These studies provide important data to understand how games shape social interactions, contribute to cultural production processes and the dynamics of digital communities. For example, studies on live streaming platforms such as Twitch reveal how players interact and how these interactions contribute to community formation (Çakar, 2021).

However, the fact that research in this area is limited to specific gaming platforms and user groups makes it difficult to generalize the general results to the entire gaming ecosystem. Therefore, more comprehensive studies on different game genres, platforms and demographic groups are needed. In addition, the negative effects of digital games, such as addiction, antisocial behavior or violent tendencies, should also be taken into account and in-depth research should be conducted on these issues.

Digital games play an important role in processes of community formation and cultural transformation. Games are dynamic platforms that shape individuals' social interactions, cultural experiences and economic behaviors. Therefore, understanding the socio-cultural impacts of digital games is critical for analyzing the social structure of the digital age. In the future, more comprehensive and interdisciplinary research on the social effects of digital games will increase the knowledge in this field and contribute to the understanding of digital culture.

Digital technologies play an important role in the transformation of individuals, communities and cultures. In parallel with new developments in digital technologies, information, content, entertainment and similar situations have gained the opportunity to reach every individual and reached large masses (Yurdigül & Yurdigül, 2019, p. 197). Gaming platforms have become not only a means of entertainment, but also an area of social interaction, economic activity and cultural production. This study aims to understand how gaming culture shapes the future of the digital world by examining the impact of gaming and digital content production on community formation. The main aim of the research is to reveal the role of digital game platforms and the communities developed on these platforms in cultural transformation processes. In particular, it focuses on how factors such as in-game advertising, user interactions, game economies and digital content production affect individuals' digital identities and communities. In addition, how these processes resonate with different segments of society and how the boundaries of cultural production are redefined through technological tools is analyzed.

A qualitative approach was adopted in the research. The data collection phase focused on analyzing user interactions, live broadcasts and AI-supported content on gaming platforms. Both textual and visual data were used throughout the study and interpreted through content analysis. Gaming platforms, live streams, community engagement and AI plugins are considered as critical elements in the development of the digital ecosystem. However, the study was limited to specific gaming platforms and user groups. While this limitation enables the research to provide an in-depth analysis, it may make it difficult to generalize the overall results to the entire gaming ecosystem.

As a sample, specific communities selected from popular gaming platforms and user interactions within these communities were analyzed. Especially on live streaming platforms such as Twitch and YouTube, the interaction dynamics of individuals who produce game content and the communities that participate in this content are analyzed. In addition, the effects of communities in digital gaming platforms such as Fortnite, Roblox and Minecraft on economic models and cultural production processes were investigated. These examples provide the basis for understanding how the process of digitalization is shaping community structures and how gaming culture can transform the future digital world.

The study aims to show that gaming and digital content production is not only a means of entertainment, but also a tool for social interaction and cultural production. In order to understand the future of the digital world, examining the dynamics of gaming platforms and the transformation processes of the communities that develop on these platforms provides a broader interpretation of technological and cultural changes in today's societies.

FORMATION AND DYNAMICS OF DIGITAL COMMUNITIES

Digital technologies have radically changed the ways of interaction between individuals, paving the way for new community formations. In particular, digital gaming platforms offer the strongest examples of communities where individuals come together in virtual environments, act in line with common goals, exchange information and develop social bonds. These communities have become an important research area in understanding the social and cultural dimensions of digitalization.

The Nature and Definition of Digital Communities

Digital communities are interaction networks formed when individuals come together on online platforms in line with common interests (Rheingold, 2000). These communities can form strong bonds in virtual environments independent of face-to-face communication and offer an important space that shapes individuals' identities. For example, communities formed on online gaming platforms not only bring people together to play games, but also perform a wide range of functions such as information sharing, collaboration and social support (Steinkuehler & Williams, 2006).

Digital communities are social structures where individuals come together on online platforms to interact and share information and experiences. These communities are formed when people with common interests meet in digital environments such as social media, forums and online games (Rutinika, 2024). As dynamic structures that shape individuals' identities, values and social relationships, digital communities go beyond being mere virtual spaces (Güzel, 2020). In addition to increasing the social interactions of individuals, these communities also provide an important ground for economic and creative activities. Especially through digital games, while the interaction between individuals and communities in the physical environment continues, a new form of interaction emerges as a requirement of the virtual environment (Boyalı & Aktaş, 2023). The open structure of digital communities, by offering various possibilities in the interaction process, becomes more flexible and attractive than physical life and encourages democratization. Digital communities are dynamic and multifaceted social structures that meet the needs of individuals to socialize, share information and create support networks in online environments.

Digital Game Platforms and Community Building

Gaming platforms are one of the areas where digital communities are most visible. Popular games such as Fortnite, Minecraft, Roblox and League of Legends offer dynamic ecosystems where players constantly interact with each other. On these platforms, players engage in joint activities such as teamwork, strategizing, and achieving goals, which contribute to strengthening community bonds (Taylor, 2019). Furthermore, communication tools such as in-game chat rooms, forums and social media groups play a critical role in sustaining communities.

Digital gaming platforms are online environments where players interact, play games and share content. These platforms pave the way for the establishment of social ties between players and the formation of communities. Especially multiplayer online games allow individuals to come together in virtual environments to cooperate, compete and interact socially. These interactions lead to the formation of strong community ties among players. In addition, digital gaming platforms offer social spaces where players can create their own identities, share their experiences and connect with others with common interests. This contributes to gamers experiencing feelings of fulfillment such as being present in the community, self-aggrandizement and appearing charismatic (Sayar, 2022).

Socio-Cultural Dynamics of Digital Communities

Throughout history, people have developed oral, written and visual narratives in line with various needs and experiences; these narratives bear the traces of humanity's production of common phenomena, problems and themes in different forms (Akmeşe, 2021, p. 326). The dynamics of digital communities are directly affected by the interactions of individuals. Online communities provide their members with opportunities for social bonding, a sense of belonging and support (Kraut et al., 2002). In this context, digital communities can be considered not only as entertainment and game-oriented structures, but also as platforms that meet the social needs of individuals. Communities that develop especially on gaming platforms offer a space where individuals construct and express their digital identities (Turkle, 1995).

With the development of modern communication technologies, digital communities have led to radical changes in forms of social interaction. These communities remove geographical limitations, enabling individuals to connect with others with similar interests. For example, social media platforms, forums and gaming communities offer virtual spaces that allow individuals to reshape their identities (Baym, 2015). In these communities, shared values, norms and rituals appear as digital reflections of traditional socio-cultural structures in the physical world . However, the socio-cultural dynamics of digital communities are not limited to relations between individuals. Macro-level factors such as globalization, economic power balances and inequalities in access to digital technologies also affect these dynamics (Castells, 2009).

The socio-cultural structures of digital communities play an important role in the identity construction processes of individuals. In particular, anonymity and customized communication opportunities allow individuals to display aspects of themselves in virtual environments that they cannot express in traditional social contexts (Turkle, 2011). This leads to a multi-layered structure of identities. On the other hand, digital communities also transform the processes of cultural production and consumption. While users contribute to the creation of cultural products by taking active roles as content producers, they also interact as consumers of these products (Jenkins, 2006). In this context, digital communities have transformed traditionally one-way cultural production processes into a more participatory structure.

Another important element shaping the dynamics of digital communities is social capital. While digital platforms increase the potential of individuals to strengthen their social ties and develop new relationships, they can also lead to negative consequences such as exclusion, misinformation and digital addiction (Putnam, 2000). For example, while social media platforms allow users to expand their personal networks, the superficiality of these networks and the transience of interactions call into question the depth of community ties (Ellison, Steinfield & Lampe, 2007).

Digital communities have had a profound impact on the socio-cultural lives of individuals and have played an important role in the transformation of societies. However, when assessing the impact of these communities, it is necessary to consider their multifaceted effects at the individual, cultural and societal levels. Future research should aim to explore these dynamics of digital communities in more detail to understand their long-term impact on societies.

Leadership and Hierarchy

In digital communities, leadership and hierarchy play an important role in the functioning of the community. In online gaming communities, certain players stand out as natural leaders and guide other players. These leaders play a critical role in setting the norms and rules of the community. For example, in MMORPG games, the effectiveness of the community is enhanced when leaders formulate team strategies and take steps towards conflict resolution (Williams et al., 2006).

Leadership and hierarchy play a critical role in the functioning of organizations. Leadership is defined as the process of influencing and directing others in order to enable individuals or groups to achieve set goals (Baloğlu & Öz, 2021). Hierarchy, on the other hand, is accepted as a structure in which individuals within the organization are ranked according to different levels of authority and responsibility.

The relationship between leadership and hierarchy in educational institutions has significant effects on organizational commitment and performance. For example, in a study conducted by Baloğlu and Öz (2021), it was concluded that the perception of academic leadership affects the level of organizational commitment. This shows how leaders can create an impact within the hierarchical structure.

In addition, leadership styles and hierarchical structures were also found to be effective on teachers' motivation and job stress. Halitoğlu and Akpınar (2022) reported that school administrators' leadership styles were related to teachers' perception of stress. This finding suggests that the relationship between leadership and hierarchy is also effective on the psychological state of employees.

The relationship between leadership and hierarchy is critical for organizational efficiency and employee satisfaction. It is possible for leaders to increase organizational commitment and motivation by acting effectively within hierarchical structures. Therefore, more in-depth research on leadership and hierarchy will be beneficial for the success of organizations.

EQUALITY AND DIVERSITY IN DIGITAL COMMUNITIES

Digital communities go beyond geographical boundaries, bringing together individuals of different ages, genders and cultural backgrounds. While this diversity increases the richness of communities, it can also lead to conflicts from time to time (Nardi & Harris, 2006). Especially in online gaming communities, gender equality and toxic behaviors are among the frequently discussed issues. In this context, inclusive policies and moderation systems need to be developed for communities to function in a healthy way.

Equality and diversity in digital communities are becoming increasingly important in today's digital age. As digital platforms offer their users the opportunity to come together across geographical, cultural and social boundaries, it is critical that these platforms operate in an inclusive and fair manner. While equality refers to all users having equal access and participation rights in digital spaces, diversity emphasizes the representation of different social, cultural and individual identities. Research shows that diverse digital communities both unleash the creative potential of individuals and strengthen social solidarity. However, digital platforms also face challenges such as discrimination, algorithmic bias and the digital divide. For example, some algorithms can systematically exclude certain groups, reducing their visibility in the digital space (Noble, 2018).

In this context, collaboration between policymakers, technology companies and users are necessary to promote equality and diversity in digital communities. As a first step, reducing algorithmic bias, adopting inclusive design principles and increasing user education are recommended (Benjamin, 2019). Furthermore, organizing the governance policies of online platforms in a transparent and accountable manner can increase community engagement and trust (Floridi, 2021). Promoting diversity is not only an ethical imperative, but also a requirement for digital innovation and sustainable growth. Therefore, equality and diversity in digital communities should be treated as an important building block shaping the future of technology.

Live Streaming Platforms and Digital Communities

Live streaming platforms such as Twitch and YouTube Gaming play an important role in expanding digital communities and increasing interactions. These platforms allow broadcasters to communicate with their communities in real time while producing content (Hamilton et al., 2014). This interaction between the broadcaster and the audience is an important element that strengthens the bonds within the community and increases the sense of belonging. For example, community events organized by a popular streamer strengthen social ties between players and ensure the long-term sustainability of the community.

Live streaming platforms play an important role in the formation of digital communities by allowing users to create and share content in real time. By enabling individuals to produce their own content and deliver it to large audiences, these platforms offer a space for expression independent of the control and monitoring mechanisms of traditional media. For example, YouTube Live allows users to broadcast live broadcasts and archive these broadcasts for later viewing, while Twitch stands out as a platform that stands out especially for its game broadcasts (Bigo.tv, 2024).

These platforms offer features that allow users to create and manage their own communities. For example, Discord allows users to create private servers and communicate via text, audio and video. TikTok Live is also popular among young users, allowing them to share creative and entertaining content (Bigo.tv, 2025).

These platforms increase the formation and interaction of digital communities by allowing users to produce and share their own content. Moreover, thanks to the advantages and opportunities provided by social media, digital broadcasting platforms can reach large audiences beyond national borders and encourage competition in the production of quality content (Okmeydan, 2020).

However, the inadequacy of supervision and control mechanisms on these platforms brings along problems such as copyright violations. For example, platforms such as Facebook Live, Periscope and YouTube Live face problems such as unauthorized broadcasting of copyrighted content (Şahin, 2016).

Live streaming platforms and digital communities allow individuals to produce and share their own content, providing a space for expression independent of the control and monitoring mechanisms of traditional media. However, the inadequacy of supervision and control mechanisms in these platforms brings along problems such as copyright violations.

Economic Dynamics of Communities

Digital communities are also part of economic interactions. In-game purchases, trade in virtual goods and sponsorships are economic aspects of these communities. For example, in online games, players spending money on cosmetic items or power-ups contributes to increasing the economic value of the community. Moreover, e-sports organizations and tournaments demonstrate the economic potential of digital communities (Newzoo, 2022).

The economic dynamics of communities refers to the processes of interaction and cooperation that shape the economic activities of individuals and groups (Smith, 2019). These dynamics represent a structure in which economic activities are shaped not only by individual interests, but also by the principles of social benefit and solidarity. In this context, the solidarity economy stands out as an approach that prioritizes social and environmental goals in economic activities. The solidarity economy includes various structures such as cooperatives, foundations and non-governmental organizations (NGOs) and aims to ensure that economic activities provide social benefits. This approach emerged as a response to inequality and injustice in the wake of neoliberal policies and global financial crises. Especially after the 2008 Global Financial Crisis, the increase in economic inequalities and the deepening of social injustices have increased the importance of solidarity economy. In this process, communities have established cooperatives and similar structures to meet their economic needs and build a solidarity-based economy. Cooperatives are non-profit, socially beneficial organizations in which producers, workers and consumers work together (Dogarawa, 2005). These structures are concrete examples of how economic activities can be shaped in a social context and how the economic dynamics of communities' work. The economic dynamics of communities refers to a structure in which economic activities are shaped not only by market mechanisms but also by social values and solidarity principles. These dynamics provide an important perspective on how economic activities can be shaped in a social context and how communities can meet their economic needs.

Future Perspectives

As digital communities are becoming increasingly important, research in this field is diversifying. In the future, interdisciplinary studies are expected to increase to understand the broader socio-cultural impacts of digital communities. In particular, the impact of AI-enabled systems on community dynamics is an important area of research.

Artificial intelligence affects individuals' social skills and relationships by simulating social interactions through applications such as digital assistants and chatbots. These technologies have the potential to change users' content consumption habits and the nature of social relationships (Doğruyol & Olgaç, 2018).

Moreover, the role of AI in social relationships is also manifested in AI-based systems such as digital assistants and chatbots that simulate social skills by interacting with users. This allows AI to function as an intermediary in social relations and act as a friend or advisor to users (Doğruyol & Olgaç, 2018).

However, the role of AI in social relationships is not limited to positive effects. Some critics suggest that AI can cool human interactions and cause a reduction in emotional bonds. For example, a user may make fewer social connections when interacting with a digital assistant than when interacting with real people. This could weaken emotional bonds between people and lead to increased social isolation

To understand the socio-cultural implications of digital communities and assess the impact of AI- enabled systems on community dynamics, it is important to take an interdisciplinary approach. This requires social scientists and technologists to work together. It is also important to consider the ethical and cultural dimensions of AI's role in social relations. For example, discussions on how AI affects human interactions and how these effects fit into the values of society are important.

CULTURAL TRANSFORMATION AND DIGITALIZATION

Cultural transformation and digitalization have significantly affected the capacity of games to reproduce cultural codes. Games in the digital environment offer dynamic processes in which both users and creators interact, and these processes allow cultural diversity to find expression in new ways. By presenting the symbols, stories and values of different cultures and ethnic groups to players, digital games pave the way for the continuous reproduction of cultural codes (Huizinga, 1950). At the same time, thanks to the global reach provided by digitalization, games contribute to the consolidation of local and national identities while promoting cultural diversity (Anderson, 1991). Especially in virtual worlds, the way players represent themselves enriches and diversifies cultural representations. In this context, games have the potential to initiate a global cultural dialogue through cultural representations (Kishonna, et all., 2024). The process of digitalization has led to the emergence of new narrative forms and experiences that go beyond the cultural codes of traditional media.

Digital Game Economy and New Value Generation

With the rapid development of the virtual world, the digital game economy has become an important area that transforms traditional economic structures and value production processes. This economy is shaped by in-game economies, trade in virtual goods, e-sports and similar dynamics. With the impact of technology and the internet, digital games are not only used for entertainment purposes, but have also created a strong economic structure.

In-Game Economies and Virtual Goods

In-game economies refer to the processes by which players trade virtual goods and services in the game world. These economies begin when game developers create digital goods in the game world, such as currencies, items, skins (visual customizations), and so on. Players can buy, trade or sell these goods. For example, in games such as "Fortnite", players can purchase items such as virtual clothes and accessories for real money. This in-game spending reflects the exchange value of virtual goods for real money, bringing the digital economy into the broader economic realm (Hamari, Koivisto & Sarsa, 2014).

On the other hand, the development of in-game economies has led to the rise of a payment model called "micropayments". Micro-payments allow players to acquire in-game items by paying small amounts of money. This model has become particularly prevalent in mobile games and has become a major source of revenue. The proliferation of mobile games has also contributed to the growth of the digital gaming economy (Raneri, et all, 2022).

E-Sports and Digital Gaming Industry

E-sports is an event where digital games are competed professionally and shared with the audience. E- sports organizations are a rapidly growing part of the industry, where professional players and teams compete for big prizes. Since the mid-2010s, the audience for e-sports tournaments has reached millions and game developers have started investing in e-sports to support its growth (Scholz, 2020). With the rise of e-sports, a new economic field has emerged. E-sports organizations generate huge economic values through revenue sources such as sponsorship agreements, media rights and ticket sales. In addition, e-sports players can build a professional career thanks to the prizes they win in tournaments, broadcasting revenues and sponsorship agreements. This creates new job opportunities in the gaming world and accelerates the transformation of the digital gaming economy.

New Value Generation and the Economic Role of Digital Games

Digital games not only provide entertainment, but also contribute to new value production processes. Dynamics such as in-game economies and e-sports make the economic role of digital games more salient. Trading virtual goods within games not only provides players with entertainment, but also generates huge economic value. Trading these goods creates a process where the value of digital goods increases and the virtual economy is integrated with real-world economic structures (Cunningham & Craig, 2019).

The economic impact of digital games is not limited to in-game commerce. Games create a huge market space for content producers and broadcasters. YouTube, Twitch and similar platforms offer huge revenue opportunities for game content producers. In addition to generating revenue from their viewers, game publishers also earn from advertising revenue, sponsorships and donations and contribute to the growth of the digital gaming ecosystem (Johnson & Woodcock 2018).

The digital game economy has become a dynamic field that shapes new value production processes through components such as in-game economies, trade in virtual goods and e-sports. Games create huge economic value as economies that start in the virtual world merge with the real world. This new value creation has transformed the economic role of digital games, transforming them from mere entertainment to a global economic force.

THE FORMATION AND DYNAMICS OF DIGITAL COMMUNITIES: A STUDY ON TWITCH, YOUTUBE AND POPULAR GAMING PLATFORMS

Digital communities have rapidly diversified and expanded thanks to the opportunities offered by the internet. Digital gaming platforms stand out as areas where community interactions deepen and form social structures. In this context, understanding the ways in which communities interact on live streaming platforms such as Twitch and YouTube, and games such as Fortnite, Roblox and Minecraft offers a critical opportunity to explore the social and cultural reflections of the digitalization process.

User Interactions on Twitch and YouTube

Twitch and YouTube are some of the most important platforms on which digital gaming communities interact. While Twitch offers the opportunity to broadcast live and interact with viewers in real time, YouTube provides an environment where communities of viewers interact with content creators by commenting, as well as producing and sharing video content (Hamilton, Garretson, & Kerne, 2014). These platforms provide a constant flow of communication between individuals producing game content and their audiences. By chatting with streamers, interacting in chat rooms, and commenting on content, viewers strengthen ties within the community.

Live broadcasts, especially on Twitch, allow viewers to provide instant feedback and participate in events.

On Twitch, streamers create a community by forming social bonds with their viewers, and viewers develop a sense of belonging by participating in this community. Twitch viewers often contribute to the economic and social fabric of the community through subscribing, donating, and being active in chats (MusicIndustry123, 2025). This dynamic interaction between broadcasters and viewers ensures the growth and continuity of the digital community. YouTube, on the other hand, mostly allows creators to build communities through long-form videos, while allowing viewers to interact with creators through comments and likes (Jenkins, 2006).

Fortnite, Roblox and Minecraft: In-game Communities and Economic Dynamics

The popular digital gaming platforms Fortnite, Roblox and Minecraft are important examples of communities shaping their social, cultural and economic structures. Fortnite is a platform where players compete together in virtual environments, but also engage in social interactions by participating in in-game activities. In-game social interactions allow players to come together to form teams, strategize and participate in events (Juul, 2013). Fortnite's cross-platform support allows players to play the game on different devices, allowing communities to expand even further.

Roblox allows users to create their own games and share them with others. Roblox's economy is shaped by players buying and selling in-game items, and this economy influences the social dynamics of communities on the platform (Kou & Gui, 2023). Roblox also provides a revenue model for game makers, allowing content producers to make economic gains. This enables gaming and content creation to become a career path within digital communities.

Minecraft is another popular platform that allows players to build their own worlds and share them with others. Minecraft's open-world structure allows players to use their creativity to build communities. Players can set up their own servers within Minecraft to create various game modes and build communities through events organized on these servers. These events allow players to come together, have fun together and create cultural meanings (Salen & Zimmerman, 2004).

Game Culture and Digitalization Process

Digital games are not only played for entertainment; they have also become cultural tools that change the way individuals interact socially. Games like Fortnite and Roblox not only allow players to have fun, but also foster cultural values and norms among community members. Fortnite's seasonal events and Roblox's user-generated games allow gaming culture to evolve and communities to form around shared experiences. By offering virtual events that community members can experience together, these games allow individuals to build stronger bonds with each other. Digitalization has transformed gaming culture from a mere recreational activity into a tool that reshapes the way individuals express themselves, the way they do business and even their cultural meanings. In games, users express themselves through character creation, storytelling and virtual goods, and these communities have become spaces where new social norms and values are constructed (Williams et al., 2006).

The Role of Social Capital and Trust in Digital Communities

The development of digital gaming communities is closely related not only to technological infrastructures but also to social capital and trust dynamics within the community. Social capital is defined as the set of values that individual's access through their social networks and plays a decisive role in the resilience, functionality and sustainability of communities (Putnam, 2000). In digital platforms, especially in gaming communities, social capital is shaped by cooperation, solidarity and trust relationships between individuals.

Live streaming platforms provide a prominent example of the formation of these social capital networks. Platforms such as Twitch offer an environment where broadcasters interact one-on-one with viewers, strengthening mutual trust and a sense of belonging (Sjöblom & Hamari, 2017). Broadcasters' regular delivery of content to viewers, transparent communication, and sensitivity to the needs of the community increase viewers' loyalty to the platform. For example, a broadcaster who regularly answers audience questions contributes to building not only individual trust but also a norm within the community. Such interactions provide a foundation for engagement and long-term participation in digital communities.

Trust is critical in digital gaming communities, not only in interpersonal relationships but also in the overall functioning of communities. In collaborative games like Minecraft, players need to trust each other to achieve common goals. This environment of trust encourages players to take part not only in individual projects, but also in community-wide projects. For example, players participating in a large city-building project on a Minecraft server have to trust each other's contributions and share a common vision (Kowert & Quandt, 2016). This helps individuals within the community to develop their social skills outside of the game.

In the formation of trust and social capital in digital communities, shared values and rules are of great importance. In games such as Fortnite, adherence to common game rules among players and the monitoring of these rules by community members contribute to the strengthening of trust. Moreover, the presence of trust in in-game economies makes players more open to buying and selling virtual goods (Banks,

2013). For example, players feeling safe from fraud in the process of purchasing a virtual product is an important factor supporting the growth of in-platform commerce.

However, the negative aspects of social capital and trust should not be ignored. In digital communities, exclusionary behaviors, toxic discourses and overly oppressive in-group dynamics can lead to the weakening of social capital and the fragmentation of communities. At this point, game developers and platform managers need to develop inclusive policies and safety-enhancing mechanisms. For example, in games such as League of Legends, algorithms and community guidelines to prevent toxic behavior have been effective in rebuilding trust (Consalvo, 2012).

In digital gaming communities, social capital and trust are among the key elements that enrich individuals' experiences and make communities sustainable. These two concepts affect not only in- game interactions, but also individuals' social skills and sense of belonging in their offline lives. By focusing on how these dynamics can be made more inclusive and resilient, future research can more comprehensively address the socio-cultural impacts of digital communities.

Future Perspectives: The Evolution of Digital Communities

In the future, digital communities will become platforms that offer more social and cultural interaction, as well as economic opportunities. Especially with the development of virtual reality and augmented reality technologies, digital games will become more interactive and inclusive. This will allow digital communities to grow further and create more diverse social structures. Moreover, new technologies such as artificial intelligence and data analytics will make the management of digital communities more dynamic and provide players with personalized experiences.

CONCLUSION

As a product of rapidly changing technological and social dynamics, digital games have evolved from mere tools consumed for entertainment purposes to a phenomenon that radically transforms the ways in which individuals, communities and cultures interact. The effects of digital games on social life have a multi-layered structure ranging from the daily experiences of individuals to large-scale cultural and economic transformations. This study examines how digital games have transformed entertainment, social interaction and cultural production; how digitalization has shaped these effects; and how gaming communities play a role in the reproduction of social structures.

The social effects of digital games are closely related to the quality of the social bonds that individuals establish through gaming and the reflections of these bonds on offline life. Digital gaming platforms offer players the opportunity to communicate and collaborate with individuals from different parts of the world by going beyond physical borders. In this context, it can be said that online games function as a "third place" and create a space where individuals can socialize comfortably away from the pressures of everyday life. In particular, the open-ended interaction models offered by games such as Fortnite, Roblox, and Minecraft facilitate the inclusion of players in communities and allow for the formation of strong bonds between individuals. This shows that digital games should not only be seen as leisure activities for individuals; they also contribute to the formation and strengthening of new social networks.

The cultural impact of digital games is further complicated by the fact that they function both as cultural products and as means of cultural production. Digital games are embedded with stories, symbols and values that belong to a particular cultural context. However, these values are reinterpreted by players and take on new meanings within gaming communities. For example, games such as Minecraft encourage individuals to take an active role in cultural production by offering players the opportunity to build their own worlds and explore creative means of expression in the process. This production process not only enhances individual creativity, but also increases cultural diversity within communities, creating a space where different cultures can coexist. This aspect of digital games has become an important tool in the reproduction of cultural codes.

In economic terms, digital games are becoming an increasingly complex mechanism of value production. Elements such as in-game economies, trade in virtual goods, e-sports organizations and live streaming platforms are increasing the impact of digital games on the global economy. In particular, platforms such as Roblox and Fortnite offer a new model of economic value creation by allowing players to create in-game products and sell these products to other players. This has created an ecosystem where individuals can contribute to the economy as producers rather than consumers. Live streaming platforms have further expanded the economic dimension of digital gaming communities by enabling content producers to generate revenue directly from viewers. This process enables games to become an economically sustainable field of cultural production.

The future impact of digital games will continue to have a wider impact depending on technological advances and their reflections on social life. The development of virtual reality and augmented reality technologies will make the digital gaming experience more immersive and allow individuals to engage more deeply in game worlds. Furthermore, the integration of artificial intelligence technologies into game design will offer personalized experiences based on players' individual needs and preferences. These technologies can transform digital games from being merely entertainment tools into tools that can meet the needs of individuals in different areas such as education, health and business life.

Research on the socio-cultural impacts of digital games is of great importance to increase the body of knowledge in this field and to provide a more inclusive understanding of games. Interdisciplinary research provides a necessary framework for a deeper understanding of the effects of digital games on social structure. For example, perspectives from fields such as psychology, sociology, economics and cultural studies make it possible to comprehensively address the effects of digital games at the individual and societal level. Future research can contribute to a more sustainable development of this phenomenon, especially by offering more insights in areas such as the environmental impact of digital games, inclusivity and accessibility.

In conclusion, digital games are a dynamic and ever-changing field that permeates every aspect of social life. The findings discussed in this study show how digital games shape not only individuals' entertainment experiences, but also social structures, cultural values and economic models. An interdisciplinary approach is needed to understand the effects of digital games and to evaluate these effects in a more inclusive way. Future studies in this field will shed light on how to better understand the potential of digital games and how this potential can be used for social benefit.

The Importance of Interdisciplinary Research on the Socio-cultural Effects of Digital Games

Digital games are increasingly impacting cultural, social and psychological contexts in today's societies, and understanding these interactions is possible through multidisciplinary research that brings together various disciplines. In this paper, the importance of interdisciplinary research examining the socio-cultural effects of digital games will be emphasized and suggestions for future research will be made.

Socio-cultural Effects of Digital Games

Digital games are not only a fun activity, but also a powerful socio-cultural tool that shapes users' ways of thinking, social interactions, identities and value systems (Gee, 2003). At both individual and societal levels, digital games offer interactive environments, allowing players to meet different worlds, build communities and question cultural norms. Understanding the socio-cultural effects of digital games therefore lies at the intersection of many different disciplines such as psychology, sociology, education, economics and cultural studies. In particular, there is a growing body of research showing that games can have a significant impact on issues such as gender, ethnic identity and cultural representations. Gender representations of characters, cultural stereotypes and racial themes in games can influence players' social values and behaviors (Shaw, 2015). In this context, the effects of digital games on individuals' identity development and the processes of reconstructing social norms are also discussed (Turkle, 2011).

Importance of Interdisciplinary Research

When investigating the socio-cultural effects of digital games, the perspective of only one discipline may not be sufficient. It is increasingly recognized that such research should include a variety of fields such as psychology, sociology, media studies, economics, education and cultural studies. For example, the effects of a game design on perceptions of gender should be addressed not only through media and cultural studies, but also through psychological and sociological theories. Likewise, the study of the economic dimensions of digital games, the global impact of marketing strategies and the gaming industry does not belong solely to the discipline of economics; it should be integrated with cultural studies to understand the global cultural impact of games as well. An interdisciplinary approach should encompass not only the content analysis of digital games, but also the production processes through which these games are created, the forms of interaction in the games, the communities of players and their social impact. In this way, the long-term effects of digital games on social structures can be more clearly understood.

FUTURE RESEARCH DIRECTIONS

Game Design and Socio-cultural Representations: Future research needs to delve deeper into cultural representations in game design. In particular, how representations of gender, race, and ethnic identity in games can be shaped by awareness of issues such as gender equality and cultural diversity (Ward & Grower, 2020). Studies in this area can contribute to designing games that are more inclusive and promote diversity.

Psychological Effects of Games: It is clear that more research is needed on the psychological effects of digital games on players. In particular, focusing on the addictive properties of games, their effects on social relationships and players' behavioral patterns will contribute to the growth of the field of game psychology (Kuss & Griffiths, 2012). Furthermore, the effects of games on the cognitive development of children and youth can be addressed in the context of educational psychology.

Socio-cultural Dimensions of Game Communication: The role of games in establishing social relations between players and communicating cultural codes needs to be examined in more depth. Research should be conducted on how games function as a language in a social context, how players interact with each other, and the impact of these interactions on social norms. In particular, the cultural dynamics of online multiplayer games and gaming communities is an important area of research for future studies (Cairns & Cox, 2008).

Economic Dimensions and the Digital Gaming Industry: The economic dimensions of digital games are not limited to game sales. Research on in-game purchases, microtransactions, and the economic impact of digital games play an important role in understanding the game economy (Hamari, Koivisto, & Sarsa, 2014). In this context, more analysis is needed on how digital games are shaped in global markets and the social and cultural impacts of the gaming industry.

New Technologies and Digital Games: The impact of new technologies such as virtual reality (VR) and augmented reality (AR) on digital games is also an important area of research. Studies on how these technologies will be integrated into game experiences, how they will transform player experiences, and their socio-cultural impacts can provide important insights into future game design (Jerald, 2015).

As digital games have become an important part of today's culture, interdisciplinary research on the socio-cultural effects of these games is becoming increasingly important. As games provide interactive spaces in which social norms, identities and cultural values are shaped, multifaceted studies in this area are certain to play an important role in the future development of digital games. Future research will encourage more inclusive, effective, and ethical game design and help us understand the societal impact of digital games more deeply.

REFERENCES

Akmeşe, E. (2021). Ateşle Oyun filminde bireyin dönüşümü üzerine arketipsel bir analiz. *İNİF E- Dergi, 6*(2), pp. 325-339.

Akmeşe Demir, Z. ve Demir Ö. (2023). Dijital medyada içerik üretiminin geleneksel içerik üretimi teknikleri bağlamında değerlendirilmesi. Paper presented and published in *Üsküdar Unıversıty Faculty of Communıcatıon 10th International Communication Days Digital Capitalism and Communication Symposium Proceedings Book*, 16-18 Mayıs, 2023, İstanbul: Üsküdar University Publications, pp. 400 – 408.

Altunay, A. (2023). *Dijital Oyun Kültürü*. Nobel Bilimsel Eserler.

Anderson, B. (1991). *Imagined Communities: Reflections on the Origin and Spread of Nationalism*. Verso.

Baloğlu, N., & Öz, H. (2021). Yükseköğretim kurumlarında akademik liderlik ile örgütsel bağlılık arasındaki ilişki. *İnönü Üniversitesi Eğitim Fakültesi Dergisi*, 22(1), pp 410-445.

Banks, J. (2013). *Co-creating videogames*. Bloomsbury Academic. DOI: 10.5040/9781472544353

Baym, N. K. (2015). Personal connections in the digital age. *Polity*.

Bayraktar, R. (2024). Dijital Okuryazarlık. *Dijital İletişimde Güncel Çalışmalar*, İçinde (Ed). Demir, B. Ç. Konya: Eğitim Yayınevi. pp. 27-35

Benjamin, R. (2019). *Race after technology: Abolitionist tools for the new Jim code*. Polity Press.

Bigo.tv. (2024). *Canlı yayın platformları*. Retrieved from:https://blog.bigo.tv/en-iyi -uygulamalar-en/canli-yayin-platformlari/, Date of Access: 02.01.2024.

Bigo.tv. (2025). *En popüler canlı yayın uygulamaları nelerdir?* Retrieved from: https:// www.tamindir.com/liste/canli-yayin-uygulamalari/, Date of Access:13.01.2024.

Bolat, N. (2023). Dijital oyunlarda kültürel görsel kodlarla kültürün yeniden üretimi: Uruz Er kişinin dönüşü. *Middle Black Sea Journal of Communication Studies*, *8*(2), 165–178. DOI: 10.56202/mbsjcs.1361429

Boyalı, U., & Aktaş, C. (2023). Dijital oyun ve sosyal etkileşim. *TAM Akademi Dergisi*, *2*(2), 226–242. DOI: 10.58239/tamde.2023.04.005.x

Cairns, P., & Cox, A. (2008). *Research Methods for Human-Computer Interaction*. Cambridge University Press. DOI: 10.1017/CBO9780511814570

Çakar, Ü. (2021). Popüler kültür ve dijital oyunlar: Twitch platformu üzerine nitel bir araştırma. *SAÜ İletişim, 1*(1), 26–40.

Çakın, Ö. ve Bolat, N. (2018). Sosyal Medya Reklamcılığı ve Dijital Mecra Etkileşimleri (Ed). V. Çakmak & S. Çavuş, içinde *Dijital Kültür ve İletişim*, Konya: Literatürk Yayınevi

Çakın, Ö., & Yaman, D. (2022). Dijital Oyunlar- Fijital Deneyim Alanları. (Ed). M. N. Erdem, in *Gamevertising Dijital Çağda Oyunlaştırma ve Reklam* (pp. 118-134). İstanbul: Eğitim Yayınevi.

Castells, M. (2009). *The Rise of the Network Society*. Wiley-Blackwell. DOI: 10.1002/9781444319514

Consalvo, M. (2012). Confronting toxic gamer culture: A challenge for feminist game studies scholars. *Ada: A Journal of Gender, New Media, and Technology,* 1. Retrieved from: https://adanewmedia.org/supplements/ada/issue1/Consalvo_Final.pdf.doi:10.7264/N33X84KH

Cunningham, S., & Craig, D. (2019). *Social Media Entertainment: The New Intersection of Hollywood and Silicon Valley*. NYU Press.

Dogarawa, A. B. (2005). *The Role of Cooperative Societies in Economic Development. University Library of Munich*. MPRA Paper., DOI: 10.2139/ssrn.1622149

Doğruyol, B., & Olgaç, A. (2018). Gelecek Zaman Perspektifi Ölçüm ve Kavramsallaştırmalarına Yeni Bir Bakış. *Psikoloji Çalışmaları, 38*(2), 201–217. DOI: 10.26650/SP2018-0011

Ellison, N. B., Steinfield, C., & Lampe, C. (2007). The benefits of Facebook "friends": Social capital and college students' use of online social network sites. *Journal of Computer-Mediated Communication, 12*(4), 1143–1168. DOI: 10.1111/j.1083-6101.2007.00367.x

Floridi, L. (2021). *The Ethics of Artificial İntelligence*. Oxford University Press.

Gee, J. P. (2003). What Video Games Have to Teach Us About Learning and Literacy. [CIE]. *Computers in Entertainment, 1*(1), 20–20. DOI: 10.1145/950566.950595

Güzel, E. (2020). Sosyal Medya Sosyolojisi L. Eraslan (Ed), *Dijital Toplum, Kamusal ve Özel Alan: Mahremiyet ve İlişkilerinin Dönüşümü*, Anadolu Üniversitesi Yayınları, pp. 62-86.

Halitoğlu, Ş. N., & Akpınar, B. (2022). Okul yöneticilerinin liderlik stilleri ile öğretmenlerin stres algısı arasındaki ilişki. *Elektronik Sosyal Bilimler Dergisi, 21*(82), 661–673. DOI: 10.17755/esosder.1028315

Hamari, J., Koivisto, J., & Sarsa, H. (2014). *Does gamification work? A literature review of empirical studies on gamification.* 47th Hawaii international conference on system sciences, pp. 3025-3034. DOI: 10.1109/HICSS.2014.377

Hamilton, W. A., Garretson, O., & Kerne, A. (2014). Streaming on Twitch: Fostering participatory communities of play. *Proceedings of the SIGCHI Conference on Human Factors in Computing Systems*, pp. 1315-1324. DOI: 10.1145/2556288.2557048

Huizinga, J. (1950). *Homo Ludens: A Study of the Play-Element in Culture.* Beacon Press.

Jenkins, H. (2006). *Convergence culture: Where old and new media collide.* NYU Press.

Jerald, J. (2015). *The VR Book: Human-Centered Design for Virtual Reality.* Association for Computing Machinery. DOI: 10.1145/2792790

Johnson, M., & Woodcock, J. (2018). The impacts of live streaming and Twitch.tv on the video game industry. *Media Culture & Society*, *41*(5), 670–688. DOI: 10.1177/0163443718818363

Juul, J. (2013). *The art of failure: An essay on the pain of playing video games.* MIT Press.

Kishonna, G., McPherson, T., Gillian, R., & Anderson, R. (2024). Video Games and Race. In *Handbook of Children and Screens*, (Eds.) D. A. Christakis & L. Hale, Springer, pp. 291 – 296. Doi: DOI: 10.1007/978-3-031-69362-5_40

Kotan, S. (2024). *Dünyayı ardında bırak filmi özelinde sinemada dijital kıyamet anlatısı. İletişim Bilimlerinde Yenilikçi Araştırmalar I, İçinde* (Küçük Durur, E., Yılmaz, A., & Cinisli, Z., Eds.). Gazi Kitabevi.

Kou, Y., & Gui, X. (2023). Harmful Design in the Metaverse and How to Mitigate it: A Case Study of User-Generated Virtual Worlds on Roblox. In *Designing Interactive Systems Conference (DIS'23)*, July 10–14, 2023, Pittsburgh, PA, USA. ACM, New York, NY, USA, 14 pages. DOI: 10.1145/3563657.3595960

Kowert, R., & Quandt, T. (2016). *The Video Game Debate: Unravelling the Physical, Social, and Psychological Effects of Video Games.* Routledge.

Kraut, R. E., Kiesler, S., Boneva, B., Cummings, J., Helgeson, V., & Crawford, A. (2002). Internet paradox revisited. *The Journal of Social Issues*, *58*(1), 49–74. DOI: 10.1111/1540-4560.00248

Kuss, D. J., & Griffiths, M. D. (2012). Internet gaming addiction: A systematic review of empirical research. *International Journal of Mental Health and Addiction, 10*(2), 278–296. DOI: 10.1007/s11469-011-9318-5

MusicIndustry123. (2025). How Twitch Transformed the Streaming Landscape: A Deep Dive, https://vocal.media/education/how-twitch-transformed-the-streaming-landscape-a-deep-dive, Date of Access: 14.01.2025.

Nardi, B., & Harris, J. (2006). Strangers and friends: Collaborative play in World of Warcraft. *Proceedings of the 2006 ACM Conference on Computer Supported Cooperative Work*, 149-158. DOI: 10.1145/1180875.1180898

Newzoo. (2022). *Newzoo Global Games Market Report 2022 | Free Version,* https://newzoo.com/resources?type=trendreports&tag=all. Date of Access: 08.02.2025.

Noble, S. U. (2018). *Algorithms of oppression: How search engines reinforce racism.* NYU Press. DOI: 10.18574/nyu/9781479833641.001.0001

Okmeydan, S. B. (2020). Dijital Yayın Platformlarının Sosyal Medya Analizi: Netflix, Blutv ve Puhutv Youtube Kanalı Örneği. Proceedings Book- Internatıonal Asian Congress on Contemporary Scıences-Iv.

Putnam, R. D. (2000). *Bowling Alone: The Collapse and Revival of American Community*. Simon and Schuster.

Raneri, P. C., Montag, C., Rozgonjuk, D., Satel, J., & Pontes, H. M. (2022). The role of microtransactions in Internet Gaming Disorder and Gambling Disorder: A preregistered systematic review. *Addictive Behaviors Reports, 15*, 100415. DOI: 10.1016/j.abrep.2022.100415 PMID: 35434248

Rheingold, H. (2000). *The Virtual Community: Homesteading on the Electronic Frontier*. MIT Press. DOI: 10.7551/mitpress/7105.001.0001

Rutinika. (2024). "Dijital Topluluklar Nedir?" https://rutinika.com/dijital-topluluklar-nedir/, Date of Access: 10.01.2024.

Şahin, M. (2016). Geleneksel Medyanın Yeni Rakibi Yeni Medya ve Canlı Yayınlar. *Yeni Medya, 1*(1), 50–63.

Salen, K., & Zimmerman, E. (2004). *Rules of play: Game design fundamentals.* MIT Press.

Sayar, T. E. (2022). *Dijital Oyunlar ve Kimlik.* Eğitim Yayınevi.

Scholz, T. M. (2020). Deciphering the World of eSports. *International Journal on Media Management, 22*(1), 1–12. DOI: 10.1080/14241277.2020.1757808

Shaw, A. (2015). *Gaming at the Edge: Sexuality and Gender at the Margins of Game Culture*. University of Minnesota Press. DOI: 10.5749/minnesota/9780816693153.001.0001

Sjöblom, M., & Hamari, J. (2017). Why do people watch others play video games? An empirical study on the motivations of Twitch users. *Computers in Human Behavior, 75*, 985–996. DOI: 10.1016/j.chb.2016.10.019

Smith, L. (2019). Economic cooperation and communal dynamics. *Journal of Applied Econometrics, 39*(3), 112–130.

Steinkuehler, C., & Williams, D. (2006). Where everybody knows your (screen) name: Online games as "third places". *Journal of Computer-Mediated Communication, 11*(4), 885–909. DOI: 10.1111/j.1083-6101.2006.00300.x

Taylor, T. (2019). *Watch Me Play: Twitch and the Rise of Game Live Streaming*. Princeton University Press., DOI: 10.1515/9780691184975

Turkle, S. (1995). *Life on the Screen: Identity in the Age of the Internet*. Simon & Schuster.

Turkle, S. (2011). *Alone together: Why We Expect More from Technology and Less from Each Other*. Basic Books.

Ward, L. M., & Grower, P. (2020). Media and the development of gender role stereotypes. *Annual Review of Developmental Psychology, 2*(1), 177–199. DOI: 10.1146/annurev-devpsych-051120-010630

Williams, D., Ducheneaut, N., Xiong, L., Zhang, Y., Yee, N., & Nickell, E. (2006). From tree house to barracks: The social life of guilds in World of Warcraft. *Games and Culture, 1*(4), 338–361. DOI: 10.1177/1555412006292616

Yurdigül, A., & Yurdigül, Y. (2019). Information society and television news. (Ed). Sarı, Ü. & Aytekin, M., in *International Communication Studies*. İstanbul: Kriter Yayınevi, pp.193-200.

ADDITIONAL READINGS

Alsaleh, A. (2024). The impact of technological advancement on culture and society. *Scientific Reports, 14*(1), 32140. DOI: 10.1038/s41598-024-83995-z PMID: 39738478

Bogost, I. (2007). *Persuasive Games: The Expressive Power of Videogames*. The MIT Press. DOI: 10.7551/mitpress/5334.001.0001

Carstens, A., & Beck, J. (2005). Get Ready for the Gamer Generation. *TechTrends, 49*(3), 22–25. DOI: 10.1007/BF02763643

Cerezo-Pizarro, M., Revuelta-Domínguez, F.-I., Guerra-Antequera, J., & Melo-Sánchez, J. (2023). The Cultural Impact of Video Games: A Systematic Review of the Literature. *Education Sciences, 13*(11), 1116. DOI: 10.3390/educsci13111116

Cooper, S. (2002). *Techno Culture and Critical Theory*. Routledge.

Erdem, M. N. (Ed.). (2022). *Game-vertising: Dijital Çağda Oyunlaştırma ve Reklam*. Eğitim Yayınevi.

Fink, E. (Ed.). (2015). *Play as Symbol of the World: And Other Writings*. Indiana University Press.

Meriläinen, M. (2023). Young people's engagement with digital gaming cultures – Validating and developing the digital gaming relationship theory, *Entertainment Computing, Volume 44*, ISSN 1875-9521, DOI: 10.1016/j.entcom.2022.100538

Pitroso, G. (2024). Beyond subcultures: A literature review of gaming communities and sociological analysis. *New Media & Society, 0*(0), 14614448241252392. Advance online publication. DOI: 10.1177/14614448241252392

Toffler, A. *The Third Wave*. William Morrow.

KEY TERMS AND DEFINITIONS

Digital Culture: The concept of digital culture refers to a technology-driven cultural transformation. This concept differs from traditional culture in that it encompasses the global community. Digital culture is the culture of the digital society and requires digital equality rather than geographical boundaries.

Digital Diversity: Digital diversity concept can be used to explain the inclusion of individuals who have different digital skills, experiences, knowledge and competences to digital cultural climate.

Digital Equality: Digital equality concept refers to the principle that all individuals, communities and societies have equal rights to access and utilize digital sources.

Gaming Industry: The gaming industry is a term used to describe the sector that includes hardware and software components related to digital games and has economic value.

Socio-cultural Boundaries: Socio-cultural boundaries are a term used to describe differentiated, specific, and institutionalized relationships within specific socio-cultural structures, and to distinguish one socio-cultural structure from another.

Value of Production: The concept of production value refers to the total economic and reputational value of the products, services, and organizations produced by a sector.

Chapter 4
A Review on Feminist and Queer Games and Game Platforms in the Axis of Techno-Feminist Approach

Meltem Merve Urfalı
https://orcid.org/0009-0003-4139-0658
Ondokuz Mayıs University, Turkey

ABSTRACT

Thanks to digital technologies offering the opportunity of interaction to its users, digital game platforms, just like other digital media platforms, reveal differences and multiplicity. Digital game platforms are environments where sexuality, genders, races, cultures and ethnicities are represented. At this point, it is seen that the "Feminist Gaming" approach, in which a counter-representation and narrative construction is positioned against the marginalizing, sexist, homophobic and male-dominated game culture in the digital game environment, appears in the context of digital game sociology and feminist theories. Assuming that transforming the digital game industry and digital game platforms (narrative-character-representation-discourse-image-space) into a research field is an important step towards combating marginalizing practices, the study will examine how a fair gaming environment can be built through the games included in the sample group based on the technofeminist perspective.

DOI: 10.4018/979-8-3373-6192-5.ch004

INTRODUCTION

This study, titled "A Technofeminist Approach to Digital Gaming Platforms: Feminist and Queer Gaming Studies," consists of four sections. The first section, "Technofeminism: A Feminist Perspective on Technology," examines the interrelationship between feminism, technology, and gender and attempts to explain the concept of technofeminism. The technofeminist approach is significant in that it goes beyond merely addressing the liberating and positive aspects of technology to problematize the hate speech and violent practices that technology is thought to facilitate. It also stands out as a more inclusive approach than other concepts, as it offers a more holistic perspective on digital feminism, xenofeminism, and cyberfeminism.

The second section of the study, titled "The Relationship Between Digital Games and Gender," examines the relationship between digital games, which are digital media products, and gender. Throughout the section, it is emphasized that digital games are not merely a means of entertainment, but also an environment where codes related to personality, self, identity, sexuality, gender culture, and gender find representation. It is demonstrated, supported by literature, that digital games are designed, constructed, and produced within a male-dominated culture and perspective.

The third section of the study, titled "The Digital Gaming Environment as a Space for Representation," emphasizes that digital gaming environments are spaces where identities and selves can be reconstructed. The digital gaming environment, which can be interpreted as a means of expression, is considered important in that it offers users a space for freedom of self-realization and expression. In addition to providing a platform for othering practices and hate speech, digital game environments are important in that they have a structure that affirms the other, enabling representation and existence, thanks to feminist policies, perspectives, and feminist and queer game studies.

The fourth section of the study, titled "Feminist and Queer Game Studies," discusses the necessity of a feminist perspective in digital game environments. By bracketing the traces of the dominant ideology in digital game environments, researchers have been driven to feminist and queer media and game studies by their belief in the necessity of fair interpretation, representation, and identity politics. In this context, how a fair gaming environment can be constructed within a global cultural context is linked to the use of stereotypes, the deconstruction of representations squeezed between gender binaries, the transcendence of normative boundaries, and players' experiences of otherness. Ultimately, the achievement of a fair gaming environment is associated with a technofeminist perspective.

TECHNOFEMINISM: A FEMINIST TECHNOSCIENCE PERSPECTIVE

Technofeminism, also known as the feminist technoscience approach, examines the relationality between sex, gender and technology. It can be stated that having a technofeminist perspective is an approach that requires deciphering and fighting against the formations that create domination, oppression and inequality in virtual space, and affirms the emancipatory aspects of technologies. It would be appropriate to underline the inclusiveness of the concept of "technofeminism" as a concept that embraces all of the conceptualizations such as digital feminism, cyberfeminism, online feminism, online feminism, internet feminism, among contemporary and current approaches; and basically, the use of feminist principles and policies through technologies, making them operational and embracing all struggles. It should not be forgotten that the studies carried out in the field of technofeminism are inclusive of feminist approaches centering on technology.

As Elnur (2022, p. 332) points out in her study, for example, while the cyber-feminism approach is more optimistic and positive towards technologies, the tech-nofeminism approach is more skeptical, critical and distant. Wajcman (2006, pp. 103-104) underlines that the argument of "change" should be put into practice by conducting studies on power and politics as well as technology-centered studies in combating gender inequality. Wajcman (2007, p. 287) adopts the view that the aspect of the relationship between gender and technology that will eliminate inequalities is only possible by making the feminist perspective dominant and carrying out feminist policies.

The technofeminism approach is not only limited to focusing on the emancipatory aspect of technology, but also problematizes hate speech and violence practices that are thought to be facilitated by technology. The problem of women's participation in social life, which is limited to the private sphere and constructed as the other of the public sphere by society with a gender-centered perspective, continues with the lack of participation in science and technology studies. Therefore, it can be stated that the phenomenon underlying the development of studies in the field of techno-feminism in the historical process from past to present is due to the curiosity and passion for deciphering the underlying problems by examining the relationship between women and technology (Wajcman, 2004, p. 18; Elnur, 2022, pp. 322-324).

Having a technofeminist perspective; in line with Wajcman's discourses and in the context of the relationality of gender systems with technologies, the relation-ship between technology and society is accepted as a heterogeneous process that changes together (2010, p. 149), and it can be stated that having a technofeminist perspective means having the critical power of knowing that norms, discourses and identities are produced simultaneously with technologies and from the same perspective (2006, p. 15).

DIGITAL GAMES AND GENDER RELATIONS

Studies on how gender is constructed are important for problematizing the loss of subjectivities through imprisonment in gender identities. On the axis of gender, it is thought that constructing gendered being through the dichotomy of male and female has a limiting approach to sexual orientations and freedoms in this context. The realization of the questioning of sexuality as a constitutive, assigning and constructive phenomenon actually means that "it is capable of displacing gender identity and institutions" (Braidotti, 2017, p. 112).

Representation and identity politics idealized through mass media mediate the functioning of masculine reason and sovereignty in the eyes of society. Although the media and its contents are not independent from the society in which they are produced, they also have the power to influence and direct society. Therefore, through the media, gender representations are conveyed in accordance with the gender perception desired to be created, constructed and idealized; thus, equality or inequality between gender roles is spread. This situation causes "manufactured" gender representations to be considered normal by the society. Therefore, digital game environments, one of the new media products, are not only entertainment and experience spaces, but also environments where personality, self, identity and gender codes find a space for representation.

The relationship between visual images, discursive practices and representation is related to power relations and ideology (Bayraktar, 2021, p. 115). Ideology is related to society and social life and is also related to the mass production of meanings, systems and values (Eagleton, 2011, p. 18). Just as in the traditional media environment, it can be stated that in the digital game environment, while it is still in the design process; the decision of what will or will not come to the forefront, the marginalization of others while certain representations are included, and ultimately this creation, which is framed around ideological views, shapes and constructs knowledge, meaning and memory (Kılıç, 2020, p. 269). In the digital game environment, it is thought that the visual images, music and storytelling of the created game universe are related to the dominant ideology; patriarchal codes, racism and sexism in social life are reproduced and presented to the masses, and players are involved in this reproduction process through discourses and actional practices (Öztekin & Öztekin, 2020, pp. 540-541).

Basically, the fact that digital games are designed, constructed and produced to appeal to the male perspective results in the construction of gender stereotypes and thus inequality. It is seen that traces of gender stereotypes in real life are seen in the game environment, the ideal image of women and men is reproduced, bodies -especially women- are sexualized and presented as objects of desire, and thus gender inequality is produced. This is because body types in the game environment are compatible with the myth of the "ideal body" and "ideal beauty" that the mainstream and the media envisage and idealize (Militsi, 2021, p. 29). It is thought that the sexualized presentation of the physical body to the masculine gaze constructs perceptions of the female body and perspectives that render female existence passive.

While the "strong and brave" representations of traditional depictions of women in the digital game environment, which can be evaluated in the context of post-feminism, is an aspect that can be affirmed; the sexualization of the body and its confinement to the sexual body creates the problematic side of the issue. It can be stated that the view of women through techno culture cannot break away from the traditional understanding and this traditionalized view is presented to the masses by carrying it from techno culture products to the digital game environment. With the use of today's reality technologies in the game environment, images multiply their impact and power. As Balsamo (1996, p. 125) states, the point that should not be forgotten is that digital and virtual reality technologies not only create an imitation-representation of reality, but also virtually reconstruct reality.

In social life, situations, discourses and images that are far from gender equality and often even violent; it is thought that these phenomena are reproduced in virtual environments and cause the reinforcement of gender-oriented behavior patterns. Therefore, digital game environments are among the new media products in which gendered, idealized gender codes are included; gender, identities and becomings are both performed and constructed.

The digital game universe has a cultural environment in itself. The patriarchal system and accordingly gender stereotypes appear as environments where we can see their representations and discourses in the nature of the concept of game, which changes form with technological developments. As Binark puts it, "in computer games, one of the most important cultural industries of capitalism, the new media tool with the feature of interactivity, the patriarchal system realizes and reproduces itself through technology" (2008; cited in Kan, 2012). Players "carry their habitus in real life to the virtual space through the virtual identities they construct in the game" (Binark, 2009). It is thought that creating a space of existence in the digital environment, that is, in virtual space, is not independent from the habitus found offline. But it can create a new identity, field of existence and habitus.

DIGITAL GAME ENVIRONMENT AS A SPACE OF REPRESENTATION

It is believed that through digital technologies, media and networks, a global call culture will be created and gender, sexism and misogyny will be combated (Munro, 2013). Another perspective on the subject is that what we know exists in social life but cannot be visible due to the difficulty of sharing, transferring, defining and confronting the hurtful side of fear, pain and violence; can start to become visible with the virtual space allowing multiple, hidden and hidden identities.

According to Plant (1998, p. 37), digital technologies, which are dominant on a global scale, have displaced the social codes associated with gender. It is thought that the perceptions dictated by norms and discourses about body and gender from the past to the present have been overturned by women's use of technological opportunities and environments. The fact that digital technologies make multiple becomings and alternative identity structures visible is evaluated in this context.

In our daily lives, we have multiple different identities. In the workplace, we can take part with our teacher identity, while in cyberspace, for example, we can take part with our warrior identity in the digital gaming environment. This is because cyberspace offers a libertarian environment for the presentation and creation of one's own self and identity. In cyberspace, "with the production of a second self, communication takes place in a disembodied way" (Demir, 2017, p. 90).

Here, it is important to open parentheses to Foucault's concept of "heterotopia" in order to expand the subject. In terms of the meaning Foucault attributes to the concept of "heterotopia", it can be stated that it refers to the field of existence of multiple self-presentations such as cyber-identities in cyberspace. When we evaluate it in the context of the relationality of space and society, Foucault's heterotopian spaces bear the traces of an opposing and contradictory structure. Foucault, who defines opposites through each other, explains the concept of heterotopian space as the realization space of utopian narratives by using the metaphor of "mirror". The point he emphasizes with the mirror metaphor is the possibility of common experience, the possibility of seeing oneself in an unreal, unreal space and finding oneself again. Foucault's heterotopias are defined as spaces of deviation and the space of the non-norm (2005, pp. 291-296). Therefore, cyberspace has a structure that offers its users the opportunity to find themselves again.

On the other hand, digital games, one of the functional environments of new media, appear as a socialization space. In the order dominated by simulations where reality is questioned and surreal realities are created (Baudrillard, 2011, p. 13), digital game environments, one of the new media environments, are among the media environments created to be simulated. In this game environment where the distinction between virtual and real is blurred, the entire boundary of reality is limited to the universe in which the game is created and the player. Therefore, thanks to technological advances, the digital game environment is a space that enables simulated images that stand in opposition to Plato's "representation".

On the other hand, the fact that digital gaming platforms, as a medium of socialization and socialization, blur the distinction between real and virtual due to their position and environment in our lives; their integrated structure has made it possible for virtual culture and social culture to intertwine. This situation brings along the transformation of the virtual environment into a public space (Sepetçi, 2017, p. 91). In addition to all these, it is thought that our representation, which we mentioned that it has changed and transformed thanks to the possibilities of technology and virtual space, is intertwined with the concepts of self, self, identity and subject. Guignion emphasizes that although the traditional perception of identity is replaced by a "simulated emancipatory self-expression policy" (2021, p. 189) in technology-mediated environments that allow fluidity in the construction and presentation of identities, and although the emancipatory aspect is emphasized, an expression policy independent of social and cultural dynamics cannot exist.

Therefore, digital media environments, where it is possible to freely construct and create the state of being with an identity -in virtual space- are important in terms of having a structure in which the other is affirmed, representation and existence are made possible, in addition to finding an environment for becoming the other. Stone defines the structure of technology that enables these multiple becomings as follows: "for him, networks are spaces of transformation, identity factories where bodies are machines of meaning, and being transgender - identity as performance, as play, as a monkey wrench that stops the ticking wheels of the social apparatus of vision - is the fundamental condition" (1995: 180 as cited in Kara, 2013, p. 24).

Because "at this point, the media is a privileged space where social disintegration, fracture and oppositional movements can be expressed." (Sepetçi, 2017, p. 70). In this context, it is thought to be a space of creation independent from the given identity structure in digital media and channels - at the point of sexual and individual identity (Curtis & Parc, 1991; Bruckman, 1993; Mazur, 1994; Reid, 1994; Mortensen, 2003; Turkle, 1997 as cited in Soyseçkin, 2007, p. 19). Soyseçkin, 2007, p. 19).

However, today, at the point where we think in the context of postmodernism, in addition to defining the human being, who is in the position of influencing and being influenced by technology, not only with a biological or cultural identity, but also transforming under the influence of human and machine interaction causes new concepts, definitions and discussions. With the increase in the possibilities of interaction, digital environments are thought to cause the transformation of people and cultures and thus identities. In this direction, identity, which is in a constant state of innovation and redefinition, is fluid, in becomings and possibilities. "Becoming is never an imitation of something or an attempt to identify something, becoming is a progressive process (...)" (Deleuze and Guattari, 1993, p. 239).

Braidotti, on the other hand, states that after poststructuralism, different subject positions have emerged and thus new debates have been enabled and a stance against the dialectical has begun to be taken (2017, p. 20). In her work, by criticizing a world that is ethically problematic, technologically mediated and determined through the gendering of the body, the possibilities of a subjectivity that is not capable of the body are discussed (2017, p. 25). "Nomadic subjects in the making are crucial for a feminist and anti-racist democratic politics as they co-evolve with and creatively engage with the discourses and practices of the "others" of postmodernity" (Braidotti, 2019, p. 152).

By becoming a nomadic subject, the existence of oppressive, dominating and marginalizing power must be displaced (2017, p. 18). Only in this way will the desire to create a "space of becoming" that is polyphonic, encompassing all categories, far from hierarchy, where opposites are not distinguished will achieve its ambitions (2017, p. 15). So how will Braidotti's "nomadic subject" come into being?

The nomadic subject that Braidotti presents as a feminist form of subjectivity leads us to Haraway's work and the Cyborg myth. In her work "Cyborg Manifesto Science, Technology and Socialist-Feminism in the Late Twentieth Century" (1991-2006), Donna Haraway focuses on the blurring of the boundaries of machine-human-animal existence through technology.

By definition, the cyborg is a figuration that emerges from the convergence and even immanentization of humans and machines in the period we live in, the positioning of machines in the human body just like a limb, and the blurring of the distinction between human-machine-animal with today's technology. It is the definition of a hybrid being that emerges in the mediation of human-machine-animal.

However, the definition of the cyborg through a narrative based on the blurred convergence between humans and machines would not be correct. Because "the cyborg is a figure that cannot be placed in an origin story" (2010, p. 12). Haraway's cyborg is not a being born of sexuality centered on biological reproduction. It is a creature that exists in a post-gender world where there is no gender, no race (2006, pp. 3-5). Haraway's image of the cyborg continues from the idea of the possibility of the existence of a feminist body and thus a life. The domination of the masculine mind can transform into new forms of oppression and domination with science and technology behind capitalism. In Haraway's work, this situation is explained by "informatics of domination", that is, "frightening networks of domination". She states that technological developments have turned into a field of domination that consumes women as much as the liberating aspect of technology today. In this predicament, Haraway constructs a feminist body and subject through technology: The cyborg.

The cyborg is not only anti-domination, but also against gendered bodies, and is a contrary and oppositional form that stands against dualities. It is neither entirely human nor entirely machine. The cyborg is a hybrid being. Just like Deleuze and Guattari's "becoming" and Braidotti's "nomad", the cyborg identity has a structure that transcends finitude and a dynamic that always establishes new relations. It is believed that becoming with a cyborg identity will open the doors to a world free from traditional identity politics and all otherizing practices.

Haraway's transhuman and trans-species approach to the "cyborg" body constructs a narrative that is opposed to gender, binaries, all approaches that cause inequality and polarize, and basically all practices and thoughts that provide domination. Because he states that all binaries are ideologically problematic (2006, p. 34). Her figure of the cyborg is "not so much a category as a figure concerned with making possible the unity of singular existences by bearing the trace of experiences of exclusion and negation" (Haraway, 2010, p. 11). The cyborg "erases the essential origin myths of Western culture" (2006, p. 60). Defined as originless, rootless, the cyborg is in a form stripped of the binary border narratives of duality. "It is a boundary-figure that blurs the boundary and is itself subject to this blurring" (Haraway, 2010, p. 15).

Considering that the "violated boundaries" of the body (2006, p. 13) are constructed through patriarchal codes and power, it would be appropriate to interpret that the "body" is deconstructed not only physically but also ontologically with the imagination of the "cyborg body". Haraway thinks that the possibility of resistance to liberate a body from domination is possible through opening up to nature, animals, other companion species, machines and technology. Therefore, it can be stated that Haraway's cyborg myth is an intermediary actor in overcoming gender inequality. The cyborg, which is interactive both in the physical world and the virtual world, is not only coded as an imaginary representation of existing in a feminist body, but also appears as an actor that can be used as a figure of politics and politics.

On the other hand, the liberating aspect of experiencing the digital game environment can be expressed as being in an environment free from the limits of mind, body and norms. It is thought that the transformative potential of digital game environments is not only limited to the struggles mediating gender inequality, but also has the power to overthrow the system of thought inherited from dualism; that everything in the universe will exist with its opposites. At this point, it is identical with the Cyborg myth. Visual and discursive narratives about the myth of "becoming a cyborg" can also be seen in digital game environments. At the point of combating gender inequality in technofeminism, the idea that "cyborg being" is a figure that will represent techno-feminist ideals and ideologies is associated with the subject. The cyborg being is a being that can be identified with the dynamics of the digital game environment as an entity representing a figure in which the virtual and the real are blurred, rootlessness, identitylessness, genderlessness and a figure that is purified from the phenomenon of gender. Because, as Giddings (2007, cited in Keogh, 2014, p. 14) emphasizes in his study, “to play a digital game is to put oneself into a cybernetic circuit”.

The fact that the digital game environment includes the user in the active participatory culture with the interaction opportunity it offers to the user due to its structure, and that the perception including the distinction between real and virtual space is included in each other - which Rakes defines as “a hybridized sphere of existence that intertwines the physical and the digital” (2016, p. 8) -allows the relationship between the cyborg and the digital player to be clarified . The cyborg-ness of the digital gaming environment is created by the infinite cycles and possibilities of interaction between players and this “seamless articulation” through machines (2016, p. 11). The fact that the game environment increases the convergence between human and machine through interaction and experience cyborgizes the player during the time he/she plays the game. At this point, in direct proportion to the development of augmented reality, virtual reality and artificial intelligence technologies; it can be interpreted that the effect of the player's experience of becoming a cyborg in the game environment has increased on the player. Rakes states that this formation, which he defines as an effect and assimilation of technology, is a reality of today (2016, p. 31).

Militsi's 2021 study “Undoing Gender Interpellations in Role-Playing Videogame Spaces: The Case of Cyberpunk 2077 As a Case of Resistance From a Feminist Post-constructionist Perspective” in 2021, Militsi discusses the relationship between digital games and gender in the context of posthumanism, “post-human human” and whether digital game environments can be used as a means of resistance as a space against the normative within the human-technology relationality. In this direction, Militsi (2021) questions Haraway's Cyborg myth and the possibility of experiencing and internalizing beyond hegemonic and binary gender regulations by becoming a Cyborg as a player and avatar in the digital game environment, which is the boundary between the virtual and real worlds. It is thought that by identifying with the avatar in the game environment, the player resists and struggles against the existing binary gender practices. Through becoming a cyborg in the game environment, she finds the opportunity to destabilize gender hierarchy and heteronormativity by experiencing performative multiplicities (2021, p. 27). To summarize, the gaming environment enables and will enable insights into what a post-gender world might look like. The game environment and representations in the game environment transcend gender boundaries and function as an exit from the gender hierarchy (2021, p. 34).

In this context, the gender representations and gender distribution of women, men and LGBTIQA+ individuals in the game environment -in the context of identity representation-; the role of the characters in the game narrative and the game, their role, active-subjectivity; in addition to how gender stereotypes are displayed in the game environment through visual images and discursive practices; game introductions, the depiction of the spaces in the game, and how the items (items, objects) used by the characters are created are the parameters that we pay attention to in the studies of digital games, gender and feminism.

Therefore, in the context of digital game sociology (Kepenek, 2020; Demirel, 2022; Tor & Irmak, 2022) and feminist theories, it would be appropriate to emphasize that transforming the digital game industry and the digital game platform (narrative-character-representation-discourse-image-space) into a research field is an important step towards combating marginalizing practices. At this point, we come across the "Feminist Gaming" approach in which a counter-representation and narrative construction is positioned against the marginalizing, sexist, homophobic and male-dominated game culture in the digital game environment. This approach, also known as "Gaming Feminism", questions the possibility of a holistic-inclusive, libertarian and diversity-affirming gaming environment and culture.

FEMINIST AND QUEER GAME STUDIES

In the course of the historical process, it has been revealed that digital game environments are not as innocent as they are thought to be, and that users do not only play games for pleasure and experience. In this direction, the belief that a fair system of signification and perception will be represented by bracketing the perspective that media environments construct dominant ideologies in the context of perceptions is a driving force that leads us to readings, research and studies in the field of feminist and queer media studies.

In the early period of feminist game studies, it is seen that the studies on the reasons for the fact that the audience preferring the game environment consists of male players and that girls are not included in the game environment and how to bring them into the game environment are included in the literature. With the marketing activities carried out, "pink games for girls" were created and campaigns were carried out to invite them to the digital gaming environment (Jenson & Castell, 2015).

It can be stated that feminist and queer game studies have emerged as a reactionary approach to the male-centered perspective of the gendering of technologies and the digital game environment, visual and discursive practices that imprison women in an idealized and sexualized body perception, sexist behaviors, and hate speech based on the LGBTIQA+ individual. Leaving feminist or queer nomenclature aside for now, it is thought that it would be appropriate to ask the question "how to build a fair gaming environment?". In line with the content published by the Women In Games platform, approaches are presented on how design processes can be realized fairly in digital game environments. In this direction, Kate Edwards examines the ways in which digital game environments can be constructed fairly in the context of global culture. In digital game environments, many parameters need to be evaluated, from avatar and character designs to the game's storytelling, the language used, and the players' experience (2023, p. 82). He emphasizes that the first feature to be considered for the existence of a fair game environment is that it must be compatible with the multicultural structure of the age we call the postmodern age.

Another issue to be considered is the use of stereotypes. At this point, Kate emphasizes that the use of stereotypes should be evaluated within ethical frameworks (2023, p. 84). She states that various organizations are working to create a digital gaming environment free of sexist, racist and marginalizing practices (2023, p. 85) and to raise awareness of the masses on this issue (such as Women In Games and Fair Play Alliance). As one of the points criticized by feminist and queer game researchers; the addition of feminine, feminine and things that are identified with women by society such as jewelry, buckles, high heels, make-up, etc. to a character that already exists in the game environment, which has already been created, can be nothing but the image of discourses that strengthen the binary gender paradigm.

In the axis of these discussions, we can see traces of the existence of non-binary game characters (outside the female-male binary) in game environments where technofeminist perspectives are tried to be brought to digital game environments and where we have started to see traces of alternative representation policies. It can be stated that in these game environments where gender is destabilized, character descriptions and definitions deviate from the male-female binary, and the aim is to create a creation in which the characteristics of gender identified with femininity and masculinity cannot be understood from the appearance and behavior of the created character. It is thought that how the characters are defined by other game characters is as important at this point as the visual and behavioral representations of the characters in the game environment. Therefore, in the digital game environment; outside of duality, a non-binary embodiment, gendering, or more accurately, de-gendering is sought. For example, the character Alex Cyprin from the game "Astoria: Fate's Kiss" and Jordan Davies from the game "Havenfall is For Lovers".

The quuerization of the game environment means the deconstruction of "hegemonic normativities" (Militsi, 2021, p. 30). However, while emphasizing the emancipatory aspect of experiencing nomadic spirits, gender and becoming in the game environment, it should be underlined that it is necessary to examine the questioning of the rights of choice defined to the users and who allows this in the production process of the game environment (2021, p. 33).

As a "site of resistance" to multiple becomings, identities and marginalizing practices, the fluid nature of the gaming environment offers a created space for the postmodern subject. Clarke, 2023, p. 71) "games can be used to communicate and experience different forms of agency". Accordingly, game designers are looking for ways to bring digital game users together with new constructions that break normative boundaries in the creation processes of game environments from a techno-feminist perspective (Pederson, 2021 cited in Clarke, 2023, p. 71).

It is thought that it would be appropriate to express the opinion that experiences in digital games, which are a simulated environment where the virtual and the real are mixed together; experiencing being gendered, being sexually oriented, being female, male, trans, asexual, queer, animal, machine, in short, being the other of traditional humanism, experiencing by actively participating in the digital game environment, is important in the process of understanding and empathy. Because "representations produce meanings that enable us to understand our own experience and who we are. We can go further and say that these symbolic systems create the possibilities of what we are and what we can be" (Woodward, 1997: 14 as cited in Kara, 2013, p. 76).

It is thought that trying to be the other, to be someone else, to be multiple and nomadic or a cyborg in the digital game environment and integrating it into the digital game environment and storytelling will mediate the empathy of the player who spends hours in the game environment in his daily life. It is thought that experiencing being LGBTIQA+, fluidity, animal, machine or a robot through digital games contributes to the normalization process. The need for feminist and queer game studies is important in terms of being seen as a feminist transformative resistance policy to the construction of heteronormativity in the game environment, which is also conceptualized as a "technonormative matrix", beyond the efforts to provide representation and visibility to those who cannot find representation in the mainstream (Chang, 2017; Militsi, 2021).

Feminist and Queer game studies is a practice of refusal against digital games' reconstruction of gender through heterosexuality, the limitation of desires, and the positioning of identity through binaries and inequalities. In this context, Ruberg (2018, p. 543) emphasizes the importance of game studies that reveal and affirm the interactive aspect of the digital game environment and the relationship between queer and technology. Ruberg's views suggest that the digital gaming environment can be defined as a queer space. The phenomenon of queering the game environment is not only the diversification of representations in the game environment, but also the situation where a queer critical perspective adds a queer spirit to the game environment (Ruberg & Shaw, 2017). The fact that the digital game environment often offers the player an environment in which they can construct their character, gender and identity design supports Ruberg's discourse. The Last of Us/ Ellie, League of Legends/Neeko, Cyberpunk 2077/ Kerry Eurodyne and many more are characters with LGBTIQA+ representation in digital environments.

In their study, Ruberg and Shaw (2017) convey the features that a queer game design should have. In this direction, Ruberg and Shaw (2017) convey the parameters considered in the design processes of queer games as follows: a queer game environment offers an experience outside of norms and normative boundaries by creating environments for imagining utopias and possibilities (2017, p. 4), it is thought to be important for players to interact while designing the game environment; in this way, the game environment will make it possible to maintain the multicultural structure of the game environment (2017, p. 8), the existence of other media products should not be forgotten while designing a queer game environment, as the digital game environment has transmedia features due to its structure (2017, p. 18), queer gaming environment can be designed as an environment where the educational aspects of the game can be kept alive (2017, p. 24), it is not enough to find representation alone in a queer gaming environment; it is necessary to integrate various perspectives such as queer experiences, self and identity, struggle against difficulties and love (2017, p. 53), it is important to avoid "building games without relying on normative game ideologies" by removing the player from the action, war, struggle and race of traditional digital game environments (2017, p. 54), and it is also important to present the ideas of communities and organizations during the creation and testing process (2017, p. 253). Sundén (2009, as cited in Yılmaz, 2013, p. 19), on the other hand, sees queerized game environments and works as "a transgressive form of play, which is symbolic disobedience and an act of deviating the player from 'dominant ways of writing and imagining'". In this direction, in feminist and queer game studies, the creation of feminist and queer images within the techno-feminist perspective and the strengthening of existing images include "the embodiment of the image through a new signification" (Rowland, 2020, p. 4, cited in Clarke, 2023, p. 126). Therefore, the "fairness" of the gaming environment is also related to the internalization of the "feminist gaze". The creation of healing and inequality-transforming images is important in facilitating the disseminati,,on of feminist perceptions and ways of seeing.

According to Welch (2018), queer game modes should be popularized in order to "reflect the types of representation that underrepresented groups want to see in games". Mods in the digital game environment can be defined as an add-on that paves the way for the existing digital game to be developed after the game is published. They "arbitrarily" open the doors to a new experience, area, chapter, world and alternative environment in the existing game environment. From this approach, it is understood that mod add-ons do not exist in every digital game environment, but can be. The game can be designed with a feminist and queer perspective during the initial production process, or it can be improved by including mod add-ons in the game environment. Or, as Welch states in his study, they can displace the images, content and representations that disturb them in the digital game environment with mod plugins through "hacking", an approach that can be considered as a digital activist movement.

Chang (2017, p. 15) makes discourses that affirm the provocative aspect of the gaming environment. Queer game studies is "a rejection of the idea that digital games and gaming communities are the sole source of adolescent, heterosexual, white, cisgender, cisgender, masculine, able-bodied, male and "hardcore" bodies and desires, and a rejection of the idea of articulating and investing in alternative forms of play". In line with Chang's discourse, he argues that the mod add-ons that are activated in the aforementioned game environments are also problematic. Chang emphasizes that the queer perspective should be the dominant view in the design and creation phase of digital games before the distribution and publication process. Chang (2017, p. 20) emphasizes that the "queer enhancement" approach in digital game environments should not only include the aspect of representation and making visible, but also the ways of queering the interaction and communication of the players in the game environment with each other.

At this point, feminist and queer media studies should be carried out together with activism movements in digital environments, and the struggle to create an environment for "creating a feminist consciousness" before the masses should continue. Newman (2020, p. 194) presents hacking game environments and adding a feminist game mode as an approach that can be considered as feminist activist interventions in the digital game environment. Although it is not known how it will be evaluated in the context of laws, aside from hacking, supporting feminist game producers, raising awareness of the team involved in the design process, and the spread of feminist-queer games would be a useful suggestion at this point. It is seen that feminist games are presented by affirming the features that are seen as "weakness" towards women's existence and body in mainstream games, and that the marginalized and constructed as "other" is positioned in the game environment, creating opposing representations, discourses, stories and images in this context.

FUTURE RESEARCH DIRECTIONS

It is believed that researchers who wish to conduct studies on the relationship between technofeminism and digital games should focus their research on artificial intelligence learning. Can artificial intelligence technology be feminist and fair? At this point, technofeminism, which is a feminist technoscience perspective, is also concerned with artificial intelligence. This is because the struggle and criticism of the technofeminist perspective is based on the genderization of technology, artificial intelligence technologies, and machine learning. On the other hand, the question of whether the content, visual, imagery, and behavioral characteristics of the gaming environment can be organized according to feminist and queer game theories through artificial intelligence technologies can also be raised. More accurately, the question of how to combat othering and violent situations in digital gaming environments through artificial intelligence technology would be appropriate. Here, it may be necessary for practitioners involved in software technologies and digital game design to work together. Among the other issues that researchers working in the field of digital games should pay attention to are the need to diversify examples of feminist and queer games and to theorize analyses. This is because the creation and dissemination of feminist and queer games through a technofeminist approach is among the goals of technofeminism.

CONCLUSION

Centering on the critical paradigms that gendered being is the product of a social, social and cultural construction process; it is thought that in the process of construction and normalization of perceptions, differences of opinion on the acceptance of genders and sexual orientations in society feed inequalities, marginalizing practices and violence in social life. The fact that representations in the media environment are constructed by prioritizing the male gender, masculine perspective and hegemonic masculinity, and that they create inequalities as a result of accepting individuals as "subjects" only through the masculine and feminine are among the common problems of feminisms.

It can be stated at this point that in the postmodern period, the views that subjecthood, identity, self, gender and sexuality are capable of the biological body are questioned, and the assumptions about gender and sexual orientation, which are thought to be fixed and unchanging, are deconstructed and displaced. As an expression of the self, identity and subjectivity, it is seen that the indicators and representations of gender and sexuality have evolved from masculine-feminine, female-male binaries constructed on the axis of duality to multiple formations, variability and fluidity.

In this context, the creation of feminist counter-opposite representation policies is among the prioritized studies in terms of challenging the practices that create inequality between individuals, marginalize, polarize and render them passive. The creation of a public sphere by developing counter-alternative discourses and representations against hegemonic discourses and representations through digital technologies is attempted to be realized through feminism and queer media studies. It is thought that digital media environments and social media platforms are a space where diversity, difference and oppositional views on life and society can be reflected in the creation of alternative, counter and oppositional representations.

The liberating aspect of experiencing the digital game environment can be expressed as being in an environment by getting rid of the boundaries of mind, body and norms; in other words, by deviating. As one of the spaces of cyber-virtual space, the presentation and creation of one's own self and identity in the digital gaming environment offers a liberating environment. It is thought that the transformative potential of digital game environments is not only limited to the struggles mediating gender inequality, but also has the power to overthrow the system of thought inherited from dualism; that everything in the universe will exist with its opposites. From a techno-optimistic point of view, it is thought that technology will displace the oppositions in dualism and enable new becomings, possibilities, relationships and intimacies.

The importance of creating digital games as a space for experiencing performative multiplicities and destabilizing gender practices from a technofeminist perspective, which is thought to give meaning to feminist and queer game studies, is emphasized. How gender dynamics are constructed in the creation and design of digital environments through technologies is analyzed from a technofeminist perspective. In line with Wajcman's discourses, having a technofeminist perspective means accepting the relationship between technology and society as a heterogeneous process that changes together (2010: 149) in the context of the relationality of social and gender systems with technologies, and having the critical power of knowing that norms, discourses and identities are produced by technologies at the same time and from the same perspective (2006: 15). With the technofeminist perspective; it is thought that normative boundaries will be broken down, the maintenance of the multicultural structure will be made possible, it will mediate the development of positive empathy by experiencing multiple becomings as well as traditional forms of agency, and alternative-counter representations will function as a transformative resistance policy. Internalizing the perspective of technofeminism is seen as important in terms of expanding the potential of images and representations to heal, liberate and transform inequalities by centering feminist perceptions, ways of seeing and critical paradigms.

Having a technofeminist perspective is evaluated in relation to having a holistic and critical perspective beyond being gendered. The use of the Internet and virtual reality technologies in digital game environments is thought to maximize the construction of perceptions and the power to shape cognitive processes by increasing the impact levels of narratives, images and indicators, as well as the aspects that increase experience and pleasure. Therefore, internalizing technofeminism as a political perspective and doctrine is considered to be a very important approach to combat inequalities. The perspective that “feminism is for everyone” reveals the dominant view throughout the study.

REFERENCES

Balsamo, A. (1996). *Technologies Of The Gendered Body: Reading Cyborg Women*. Duke University Press.

Baudrillard, J. (2011). *Simulacra and Simulation* (Adanır, O., Trans.). Doğu Batı.

Bayraktar, E. (2021). *Gender and Representation in Popular Culture and New Media: LGBTI Visibility in Digital Games*. [Unpublished Master's Thesis] Istanbul University Institute of Social Sciences New Media and Communication Management.

Braidotti, R. (2017). *Nomadic Subjects, Embodiment and Gender Difference in Contemporary Feminist Theory* (Karakaş, Ö., Trans.). Kolektif.

Braidotti, R. (2019). Posthuman, very human: Memoirs and ambitions of a posthumanist, *Cogito - The Posthuman*. Issue: 95-96, pp. 53-97.

Chang, E. Y. (2017). Queergaming. In Studies, Q. G. (Ed.), *B. Ruberg & A* (pp. 15–23). Shaw., DOI: 10.3138/jrpc.9.1.003

Deleuze, G., & Guattari, F. (1993). *Kapitalizm ve şizofreni 2: Bin yayla* (Akay, A., Trans.). Bağlam Publications.

Demir, V. I. (2017). Evaluation of Kardelen Fincancı, Nezaket Ekici and Tunç Ali Çam's works on the concepts of Deleuze and Spinoza, *Turkish Online Journal of Design. Art and Communication*, *7*(3), 427–437. DOI: 10.7456/10703100/005

Eagleton, T. (2011). *Ideology* (Özcan, M., Trans.). Ayrıntı Publications.

Elnur, A. (2022). From cyberfeminism to technofeminism: Developments in feminist technology studies. *Eurasian Journal of International Studies*, *10*(32), 321–339. DOI: 10.33692/avrasyad.1176864

Foucault, M. (2005). *The Political Function of the Intellectual* (2nd ed.). (Ergüden, I., Akınhay, O., & Keskin, F., Trans.). Ayrıntı Publications.

Haraway, D. J. (2006). *The Cyborg Manifesto: Science, Technology and Socialist Feminism in the Late Twentieth Century*. Agora Library.

Haraway, D. J. (2010). *Another Place* (Pusar, G., Trans.). Metis Publications.

Jenson, J., & Castell, S. (2015). Online games, gender and feminism, In *The International Encyclopedia of Digital Communication and Society*, (Eds.) R. Mansell & P. H. Ang pp. 1-5. DOI: 10.1002/9781118767771.wbiedcs116

Kan, D. (2012). Yeni medya aracı bilgisayar oyunlarında toplumsal cinsiyetin inşası. *Turkish Online Journal of Design Art and Communication*, *2*(4), 52–60. DOI: 10.7456/10204100/009

Kara, U. Y. (2013). Computer Games, New Media and Identity: Theoretical Quest/ Computer Games, New Media and Identity: A Theoretical Research. [Unpublished Master's Thesis]. Hacettepe University Institute of Social Sciences.

Keogh, B. (2014). Across worlds and bodies: Criticism in the age of video games. *Journal of Games Criticism*, *1*(1), 1–26.

Kılıç, N. P. (2020). Reconstruction of memory in digital games: The case of Nusrat. *Moment Journal*, 7(2), pp. 265 286. DOI: 10.17572/mj2020.2.265286

Militsi, A. (2021). Undoing Gender Interpellations In Role-Playing Videogame Spaces: The Case Of Cyberpunk 2077 As A Case Of Resistance From A Feminist Post-Constructionist Perspective. Umeå University. Umeå Center for Gender Studies. Magister Thesis in Gender Studies.

Munro, E. (2013). *Feminism: A Fourth Wave?* The Political Studies Association.

Öztekin, H., & Öztekin, A. (2020). Hate speech and discriminatory language in digital games: The case of Agar, *Turkish Studies-. Social Sciences*, *15*(1), 533–558. DOI: 10.29228/TurkishStudies.39019

Plant, S. (1998). *Zeros And Ones*. Fourth Estate.

Rakes, Z. T. (2016). *My Avatar, My Self: A Posthuman Examination Of Video Games And Cyborg Bodies*. [Unpublished Master's Thesis]. Marshall University.

Ruberg, B., & Shaw, A. (Eds.). (2017). *Queer Game Studies*. University of Minnesota Press.

Sepetci, T. (2017). Digital Games, Digital Players: Counter Hegemony Practices and Social Interaction. [Unpublished Doctoral Thesis]. Akdeniz University Social Sciences Institute.

Wajcman, J. (2004). *El Tecnofeminismo*. Universitat de València.

Wajcman, J. (2006). Technocapitalism meets technofeminism: Women and technology in a wireless world. labour and industry. *Journal Of The Social And Economic Relations Of Work*, *16*(3), 7–20.

Wajcman, J. (2007). From women and technology to gendered technoscience. *Information Communication and Society*, *10*(3), 287–298. DOI: 10.1080/13691180701409770

Wajcman, J. (2010). Feminist theories of technology. *Cambridge Journal of Economics, 34*(1), 143–152. DOI: 10.1093/cje/ben057

Welch, T. (2018). The Affectively Necessary Labor Of Queer Mods. Game Studies, 18(3). Retrieved from: https://gamestudies.org/1803/articles/welch

ADDITIONAL READING

Aavik, K., Bland, C., Hoegaerts, J., & Salminen, J. (2020). *Men, Masculinities And The Modern Career: Contemporary And Historical Perspectives*. De Gruyter Oldenbourg., Https://Doi.Org/10.1515/9783110651874 DOI: 10.1515/9783110651874

Åsberg, C., & Lykke, N. (2010). Feminist Technoscience Studies. *European Journal of Women's Studies, 17*(4), 299–305. DOI: 10.1177/1350506810377692

Best, S., & Kellner, D. (2016). In Search of the Postmodern, Postmodern Feminism and the Politics of Identity and Difference. (In S. B. Kellner) Postmodern Theory. M. Küçük (Trans.), 3 B., pp. 15-59, 287-299). Ayrıntı.

Butler, J. (2008). *Gender Trouble* (Ertür, B., Trans.). Metis Publications.

Çelikkol, İ., & Hira, İ. (2022). Gender, Sexual Orientations and Desexualization in the Axis of Modernism and Postmodernism Discussions. *Sakarya University Journal of Women's Studies, 1*(1), 37–54.

Direk, Z. (2021). *Being Gendered: Feminist Views on Social Sciences*. Yapı Kredi Publications.

Fischer, M. (2018). Queer and Feminist Approaches to Transgender Media Studies. In *Feminist Approaches to Media Theory and Research*, (Eds.) D. Harp et al., Palgrave Macmillan, pp. 93-107. DOI: 10.1007/978-3-319-90838-0_7

Isanović, A. (2023). Differential body politic beyond pacified techno-futures. *Filozofski Vestnik, 44*(2), 71–94. DOI: 10.3986/fv.44.2.04

Linabary, J. R., Corple, D. J., & Cooky, C. (2020). Feminist activism ın digital space: Postfeminist contradictions ın# whyıstayed. *New Media & Society, 22*(10), 1827–1848. DOI: 10.1177/1461444819884635

MacCormack, P. (2018). Posthuman Sexuality: From Ahumanity to Cosmogenic Desire. In Åsberg, C., & Braidotti, R. (Eds.), *A Feminist Companion to the Posthumanities* (pp. 35–43). Springer., DOI: 10.1007/978-3-319-62140-1_3

Selwyn, N. (2019). *What is Digital Sociology?* John Wiley & Sons.

Tripathy, P. R. (2021). What Is Playing Cyborg: An Investigation Of The Gamer As A Figure. Inhabiting Cyberspace. In *India: Theory* (pp. 119–126). Perspectives, And Challenges.

KEY TERMS AND DEFINITIONS

Counter and Oppositional Representation Policy: In the context of technofeminism and digital games, the counter and oppositional representation policy evaluated in this study refers to the presence in the digital environment of representations that take a stance against idealized gender and sexual culture that is identified with the social gender hierarchy. The digital gaming environment is a free representation environment where counter and oppositional representation policies can be visible. The digital gaming environment, which offers opportunities for liberation in terms of gender and sexual identity, thus carries traces of fairness, equality, feminism, and queerness.

Digital Culture: It is a concept that expresses the transformation of the cultural phenomenon in virtual space and its globalization as part of virtual space with the developments in the Internet and communication technologies.

Digital Game Sociology: As is well known, we refer to the concept of digital games as a result of the transfer of the traditional game phenomenon to virtual space through the process of digitization. On the other hand, the digital game environment is a space for individuals to socialize and represent themselves. Digital game sociology is a field of study that conducts both sociological and psychological analyzation of digital games and digital players in virtual space.

Feminist and Queer Gaming: It can be stated that feminist and queer gaming studies emerged as a reaction to the gaming environment produced by a heteronormative, othering, and male-dominated perspective. Feminist and queer gaming studies have been continued from the efforts toward a technofeminist perspective and how a fair gaming environment should be.

Gendered Formation: Within the framework of critical paradigms, gendered formation is used as an umbrella concept that expresses gender identity reduced to the axis of womanhood and manhood within the social gender hierarchy.

Technofeminism: Technofeminism is a concept that examines the relationship between technology and the concepts of gender, sex, and feminism, and embraces critical paradigms. This concept prioritizes exposing technology and all the innovations that come with it to a feminist perspective.

The Counter-Representation and Oppositional Gaze Policies: The counter-representation and oppositional gaze policies which are evaluated in this study refer to the digital presence of representations which oppose sexual culture and sex that are idealized and identified with the gender hierarchy. The digital gaming environment is a free representational environment in which the counter-representation and oppositional gaze policies are able to be seen. The digital gaming environment, which enables freedom in the context of sex and sexual identity, carries traces of what is fair, egalitarian, feminist and queer as a result of it.

The Myth of Cyborg: When evaluated in the context of work, cyborg is a myth that emerges as the ultimate result of human-machine convergence. Within the scope of the concepts of social gender, feminism, and technofeminism, the cyborg myth represents independence and purity from all phenomena that exist on the border of duality. In the context of human-machine convergence, the cyborg myth is a figuration in which feminist consciousness finds its existence. At this point, it can be said that it is independent of origin and gender.

Chapter 5
Reflections on Toxicity and Gender Stereotyping in "Female Gamer's Experience" YouTube Video Interactions

Esin Selin Karaöz
https://orcid.org/0000-0001-6162-0391
Istanbul Bilgi University, Turkey

Esra Pelin Güregen Dereboyu
https://orcid.org/0009-0008-9038-5229
Fenerbahçe University, Turkey

ABSTRACT

YouTube videos are now a vital part of people's lives, and it is possible to access various content, interact with others, share ideas, and discuss those videos. The innate need for individuals to play has evolved into digital gaming and has been a part of YouTube for many years. The research focused on "The Female Gamer's Experience" videos, which are montages of the toxic and gender stereotyping women often face when playing online multiplayer games. It aims to provide a perspective on YouTube users' perceptions and opinions about these videos and their content. Using content analysis, the study analyzed 1082 comments from the three most viewed videos, which were selected to represent a wide range of perspectives and experiences. Four main categories and 17 subcategories were identified. The videos raised viewers' awareness and understanding of female gamers' experiences and instilled solidarity, encouragement, and comfort.

DOI: 10.4018/979-8-3373-6192-5.ch005

INTRODUCTION

In the world of the 21st century, only two things are needed to access unlimited information and ideas: the internet, and a technological device to connect to it. As a social animal, it has been a while since humans started to fulfill most of their socializing needs through these new media that know no time or place. Communicating with people one knows or does not know using modern technological opportunities, participating in groups and communities that suit your interests, or forming one of them have become ordinary, everyday practices for today's generation. These so-called Online Social Networks (OSNs) have become an undeniable part of our lives. According to DataReportal, Meltwater, and We Are Social (2025), as of February 2025, there are 5.56 billion internet users worldwide today, of which 5.24 billion (equivalent to 63.9% of the world's population) are social media users. These numbers show that a large proportion of people with the necessary technological means are now using these options to connect with others. Although many social media platforms allow users to share text, visuals, audio and video content with the world, one stands out as perhaps the one that created and transformed the internet and our understanding of video content: YouTube. YouTube has the highest number of active participants worldwide after Facebook and has more than 2.70 billion monthly active users, according to February 2025 data (GMI, 2025). Based on the numbers above, it is possible to state that studies that will examine the sociocultural practices of individuals who spend time and pro-consume on this platform are of great importance in terms of understanding the presence of today's people in the digital world accurately and reflecting on the effects of these platforms on people.

The study aims to examine the judgments and expressions by analyzing the comments left by the users who watched these videos on YouTube, which has become an indispensable part of our daily lives and is arguably one of the most used video platforms on the "negative experiences of female gamers in games". The study's objectives also include evaluating these comments on the topics of gender stereotyping and toxicity, which are crucial in understanding and addressing issues in both gaming culture and social media. Studying and analyzing the comments under these YouTube videos is envisioned to assist in understanding how YouTube users perceive these situations described in videos that focus on negative experiences and the general judgments and thoughts about female gamers. This research has the potential to significantly impact our understanding of online interactions and online behavior. In this context, the anonymity effect that the YouTube platform provides to its users brings along another element that needs to be considered in our research.

This study fills the gap in the literature as there is no similar research in both digital media and game studies. By analyzing and interpreting the comments on these videos, we reveal the significant prejudice and stereotyping practices against women who play games. The study also provides a unique opportunity to understand the impact on users of popular content production platforms such as YouTube and the videos shared on them. The findings can guide YouTube creators who produce gaming videos to show the impact of their content on viewers and can affect their video production processes. Furthermore, this research can serve as a basis for future academic studies that are planned to be carried out in a similar context. Notably, the study has the potential for expansion and future support, offering hope for further exploration and understanding of this issue.

YOUTUBE AS VIDEO SHARING PLATFORM AND GAMING VIDEOS

In order to better understand video content and the interactions around it, we should first examine the history of the video-sharing platform and its place in our lives. YouTube is a social networking platform that many of us may have met for the first time, and it has started its life completely video-centered. This video-sharing platform was launched exactly 20 years ago by Jawed Karim, Chad Hurley, and Steve Chen. Today, YouTube users watch approximately one billion hours of video daily and participate in production as prosumers (Toffler, 2022), uploading an average of 2.6 million videos to the platform daily (Duncum, 2011; Dean, 2024). With these figures alone, it is clear that YouTube has become essential to modern people's daily lives. In addition to producing and/or consuming content, the comments that each user can leave under YouTube videos enable the sharing of information and ideas, bringing together like-minded people, building community, and even supporting the formation of unique cultures (Burgess, Green & Rebane, 2020; Vizcaíno-Verdú et al., 2023). Moreover, both social media and these online prosumer activities encourage and pave the way for participatory creativity and offer a wide range of new inspiration possibilities (Tirocchi, 2023). At this point, it is possible to state that YouTube goes beyond the features of merely uploading or consuming videos and acts as a bridge that enables one-to-one communication and interaction with individuals (Dynel, 2014).).

It is possible to produce video content on every subject that is in human life and affects human beings and to make them accessible to the relevant audience by uploading them to YouTube. One of these areas is playing (games), which is one of the basic needs of human beings (Caillois, 2001). It shows its universal existence at every age by changing its shape depending on the concept of time and place. At this point, it will not be surprising that games have also kept pace with the transformation of the digital world, and that games and game-related content is one of the most shared topics on social media platforms. Developing its service area with products and features such as YouTube Kids, YouTube Music, YouTube Premium, YouTube Shots, and YouTube TV; YouTube Gaming is another sub-area that enables YouTube to reach such a high number of viewers daily (YouTube, 2025). Although the Gaming service was launched as a product in 2015, YouTube has been a platform for gamers to create content, live stream games with their viewers, and share gameplay or other videos related to the game. In the years that followed, sites like Twitch and Kick focused on streaming gaming videos, but YouTube is still one of the platforms where the most gaming-centric content is produced. Moreover, the place of game videos in our lives is increasing day by day. So much so that people are now watching game videos rather than playing games. In December 2024, Midia Research found that gamers play games for an average of 7.4 hours per week, but they watch an average of 8.5 hours per week of video on gaming-centric platforms such as YouTube and Twitch. This indicates that these platforms are now a key part of gaming culture (Elliot, 2024).

According to a 2017 Google Consumer Insight report by Petrova & Gross, people watch gaming videos on YouTube for four different reasons. These are the possibility to access a large community on YouTube, the sense of inclusion and acceptance in something big, the search for entertainment and respite, and the desire to acquire new skills and develop oneself (p. 1-5). Considering the platform's evolution since 2017 and the ever-increasing number of users, it is safe to assume that YouTube is still visited for these reasons and that the number of creators and viewers is steadily increasing. As we have mentioned, when we think about social environments with such a large number of people, it is possible to see not only positive but also negative situations, as can be seen in the YouTube example. Given YouTube's unlimited reach and diverse catalog of content, these interactions can occur between like-minded individuals and people with different ideas or opinions. As expected in any physical/digital space where different people come together, it is far from uncommon to encounter toxic, polarizing, and offensive content directly on YouTube videos or in the comments left under them (Alshamrani et.al., 2020). It is known that toxic content that aims to spread hate, racist or misogynistic narratives is much more likely to be seen, particularly on platforms that offer anonymity, such as YouTube (Lange, 2007). This can be seen as one of the negative factors in being able to hide one's identity, and it is common to see the reflections of this mainly in the comments left under the video comments.

TOXICITY AND GENDER STEREOTYPING IN DIGITAL GAMES/MEDIA

Since the late 20th century, female gamers have historically been perceived to be a minority in contrast to male gamers, and the activity of playing games on a computer or console is unfortunately still mostly attributed exclusively to men (Fleck, 2025). Although there is no clear data on worldwide statistics on the number of male and female gamers today, when raw figures from studies conducted are combined, it is thought that there is approximately 1.7 billion male gamers and 1.39 billion female gamers in 2025 (Exploding Topics, 2025). Reports and studies from various countries also indicate that digital gaming is not the domain of only one gender. For instance, studies conducted in the US show that in 2024, male gamers accounted for 55 percent of the total number of gamers, and female gamers make up a substantial 45 percent of the total (Statisca, 2024). These figures underscore the gender-neutral nature of digital gaming, where your gender does not limit your participation. Now, the practices that stereotype the notion of *woman* and the toxic experiences both in digital game content and the gaming community will be addressed.

It is a known fact that gender stereotypes have existed in digital games from the past to the present (Khandaker, 2019). It can be seen that not only games but also gamers are stereotyped, and this stereotyping has become more severe, especially in online games (Paaßen et al., 2017). Steele and Aronson (1995) stated that this stereotypical attitude, which female gamers are particularly exposed to, has developed into toxicity and a condescending view of female gamers. While in-game toxicity is experienced by gamers of both genders, research shows that female gamers experience much higher rates of online harassment and prejudice (Kuznekoff and Rose, 2012; Pew Research Center, 2021). It is known that female gamers may prefer to hide their gamer identities both in-game and in their daily lives due to being exposed to negative behaviors by the male gamers (Cote, 2016). The usernames they use in the game, the characters they choose to play as, or the items they use in-game can be gender cues for these players, and female players may take particular care when choosing them. On top of that, some female gamers' sense of belonging to the gaming culture is also diminished due to the negative experiences they have in and out of the game and the stereotyping they are subjected to (McLean and Griffiths, 2018). In these platforms where women are constantly excluded and marginalized, they do not feel that they are respected and may become disenchanted with the practice of playing games. It is possible to see that this male-dominated attitude also finds its place in social media, where digital game culture is reproduced at every moment (Sims, 2014). Amarasekara and Grant's study (2018) reveals that women are 12 times more likely than men to be bullied, subjected to toxic behaviors, and subjected to stereotyping on social media platforms. This shows that women's experiences in digital games or on social media are radically different from those of men and need to be addressed accordingly.

This sexist stereotyping and toxic attitude towards both female gamers and content creators has also been the subject of academic studies for especially the last twenty years. There is a remarkable amount of research that examines the gaming experiences of female gamers and the behaviors they encounter in the game (Gao et al., 2017; Khandaker, 2019; Ghazzawi, 2023) and studies on gender stereotyping in the context of digital game content (Mou & Peng, 2009; Aramendia-Muneta et al., 2019; Baltezarević et al., 2021; Cross et al., 2024). These studies have mostly focused on women's experiences in and out of digital games and the stereotyping and toxicity they are subjected to. In addition to these works, research has also been carried out under the headings of gender stereotyping on the YouTube platform (Wotanis & McMillan, 2014; Döring & Mohseni, 2017, 2019a, 2019b; Mohseni & Mourey, 2019; Park et al., 2021; Cambronero-Saiz et.al., 2023) and toxicity (Obadimu, Mead, Hussain, & Agarwal, 2019; Dehkhoda & Gunica, 2022; Güregen & Karaöz 2022; Baker, Ging, & Andreasen, 2024). These studies explore women's experiences of negative interactions when they are present on this video-sharing platform as creators or mere users. They have centered on research questions such as the causes of these behaviors, their effects on women, and how they can be prevented.

As can be seen, the experiences of women gamers in digital media have been addressed through different studies focusing on the themes of toxicity and gender stereotyping. However, no study has been conducted on video content focusing on in-game female experiences, which will be the subject of our research. Therefore, this study is important in order to examine the reflection of the content on YouTube, especially the content on in-game female experiences, on YouTube users. In this respect, it is possible to state that the study will illuminate an area that has not been analyzed before and will play the role of exploratory research that will reveal the attitudes and judgments of people relevant to the subject.

RESEARCH: VIDEO CONTENT INTERACTIONS, TOXICITY AND GENDER STEREOTYPING: REFLECTIONS ON THE "FEMALE GAMER'S EXPERIENCE" ON YOUTUBE VIDEOS

In the research conducted within the scope of the study, the comments left under YouTube videos were analyzed. The research examined the comments added by YouTube users under the "Female Gamer Experience" videos created by female YouTube creators by combining the toxic situations they have experienced during their gameplay. In this way, it aims to understand the reflections of the toxicity and stereotyping behavior that the videos primarily focus on the users who prefer to leave comments on the video. By analyzing the comments of YouTube users who watched the videos in question, attitudes and tendencies toward toxicity and sexism are evaluated. At this point, our research question can be stated as "How YouTube users' attitudes toward female gamers' negative experiences in-game are shaped in the context of toxicity and gender stereotyping?".

YouTube was chosen for the research specifically since, unlike live streaming platforms such as Twitch, users can edit videos outside the platform, combine them with different videos and create video montages called "compilations". In addition, by its nature, YouTube is not a platform that focuses solely on gaming live streaming, and its algorithm makes it possible to reach all users whose algorithm is compatible with the videos, and not just video game-oriented audiences. Therefore, examining the video content available on YouTube will help us analyze community views from a broader perspective. The study participants were YouTube users who left comments under these videos. The study aims to examine how viewers perceive the experiences of toxicity and gender stereotyping that women are exposed to, which are the main topics of the videos to be examined. It is also important to mention that, in our research, the terms "gamer" and "player" were used together when referring to "the person who plays games", as observed in the majority of the YouTube comments.

Content Analysis Method

It was decided to conduct the study using qualitative research methods in order to carry out the research effectively within the framework of the research question and the issue addressed. In qualitative research, various methods of analysis such as phenomenology, ethnography, digital ethnography or content analysis are used (Burnard, 1995). In general, two types of analysis are performed in content analysis: conceptual analysis and relational analysis (Columbia University Mailman School of Public Health, 2025). Researchers using conceptual analysis examine the existence of words, topics or themes by contextualizing them and measure the concepts they contain by relating them to each other (Krippendorf, 1980). In this analysis, the agreed text is categorized into codable categories, and the research question is answered through these categories. Conceptual analysis methods will be used in our research.

The selection criteria utilized by King and McCashin in their study conducted in 2022 investigating the comments of YouTube vlogs on "Living with Borderline Personality Disorder" is used to select the video comments to be included in the study. In order to maximize the efficiency of the research process, this study focused on 4 vlog videos uploaded on the topic of interest. It included five pages of comments from the "Top Comments" section under each video for a total of 375 comments in the analysis process. As a result, a total of 1500 comments were obtained to be analyzed. The selected comments were verified to ensure that they included texts, and the comments in which the users stated that they were under 18 years of age were eliminated; the remaining comments were analyzed. Our research followed the road map used by the aforementioned research. In our study, the 3 videos uploaded on YouTube on "Female Gamer Experience" with the highest number of views are selected. The comments left under these videos are analyzed using the content analysis method. From the "Top Comments" section under each video, 5 pages, i.e., 375 comments in total, are included in the analysis process. In this case, it can be said that an average of 1125 comments was planned to be analyzed. During the research process, a total of 43 comments that did not contain text and in which the commenter stated that they were under the age of 18 were found, and these comments were excluded from the research. As a result, the total number of comments included in the study is 1082. The names of the videos to be analyzed in the research, the game played in the videos, the video link, the total number of views, and the total number of comments are listed below in table format (Table 1). MaxQDA software is used for the systematic analysis of data, and it is also one of the programs utilized during data visualization. At the end of the process, the selected comments are analyzed using the MaxQDA qualitative data analysis program and are classified into common codes.

Table 1. Detailed information on selected YouTube videos

Video Name	**Name of the Game Played in The Video**	**Link**	**Total Views**	**Number of Comments**
What Girl Gamers REALLY Have To Deal With I OMG a Girl Series [1]	Tom Clancy's Rainbow Six Siege	https://www.youtube.com/watch?v=jL0aVqVslSE	4,811,204	76,722
The Female Experience UNCENSORED I Valorant	Valorant	https://www.youtube.com/watch?v=YEOhb8B6rEU&t=3s	3,225,461	15,154
The Female Experience: Part 2 I Valorant	Valorant	https://www.youtube.com/watch?v=j_HHBmB2l5s	598,871	1,460

Two of the three videos in the study are about the game experience of Valorant, one of the most popular 5v5 FPS games of Riot Games today, which was launched in 2020. The other selected video is based on Tom Clancy's Rainbow Six Siege, a tactical FPS shooter/strategy game released by Ubisoft in 2015, also played in 5v5 groups. Both of these games fall under the category of online multiplayer games and can be described as competitive games. Competitive games offer a gaming experience where strategy, teamwork and individual skills are of great importance. The players perform the experience of playing the game together with other players registered on their server. Establishing a successful strategy, each team member taking on different roles and correctly using the skills of the selected character leads teams to success. It is, therefore, possible and encouraged in these games to use in-game microphones and chat during the gameplay process to communicate instantly and interact with other players met in the game.

Before moving on to the research findings, it is necessary to look at the known number of female gamers of these games. It is known that the number of female gamers is lower in Competitive games compared to other games (Yee, 2018). In this regard, no study or report on the number of female players playing Tom Clancy's Rainbow Six Siege has been found. However, Valorant's Head of Esport Partnership, Matthew Archambault, stated that Valorant has between 30 and 40 percent female players, which is very different from League of Legends, another popular game under Riot Games (Takahashi, 2021). However, the proportion of the game's women players was not disclosed as of 2025.

Findings and Discussion

All comments left under the videos selected within the scope of the research were analyzed and grouped under four main categories in total. These main categories were formed by combining the relevant sub-categories (codes) and collecting them under common themes. These sub-categories consisted of 17 different headings and were classified according to the elements in the analyzed comments. The codes created as a result of the research will also be expressed as sub-categories of the relevant main category for easier understanding. The codebook describing the main and sub-categories created based on the exploration of the shared concepts, topics and themes is presented in Table 2.

Table 2. Codebook: Main and sub-categories (codes) of the research

Main Category	Sub-Categories (Codes)
Comments on Sexist and Toxic Behavior through Experience	• Sexualization or Objectification of Female Gamers • Toxic Attitudes Toward Female Gamers • Toxic Attitudes Toward Individuals • Sharing Relevant Personal Experiences • Gender Stereotypes of Women
Comments on Raising Awareness in All Gamers and a "Better Gaming Community"	• Educational Impact of the Video • Informative Comments /Advices • Expressing Respect and Support Toward Female Players • Female Gamers Supporting Female Gamers • Hope for Positive Change in the Gaming Community • Male Gamers' Awareness of the Issue • Supportive Male Allyship
Comments on the Effects of Negative Experiences on Perspectives on Gaming	• Toxic Behaviors as a Reason for Avoiding In-Game Communication / Game • Need to Conceal Gender
Entertainment or Sarcasm-Oriented Comments	• Quotes from the Video • Humor or Satirical Comments • Dismissive or Mocking Responses

In this section of our research, the categories identified after the completed content analysis will be explained in detail. At the stage of creating the categories, we proceeded through the words, comments, and themes that were repeated and/or frequently encountered in the comments. Since comments may contain more than one element within an entry, all comments were analyzed and categorized based on the elements they contain most predominantly. The analyzed comments we mentioned in the study were transferred according to the textual format that the authors added on YouTube to preserve their originality.

Table 3. The code frequencies of the YouTube video comments

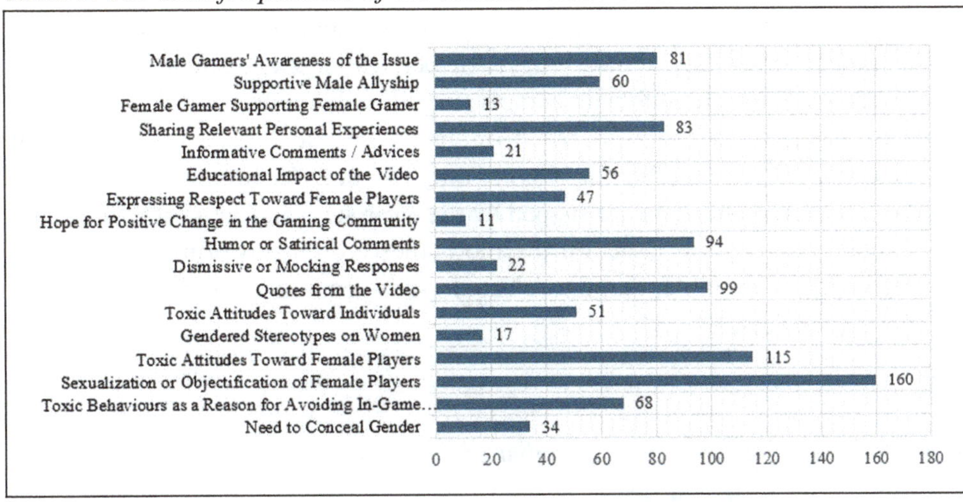

When the codes (sub-categories) under the main categories were examined one by one and frequency values were analyzed, it was observed that the most common component in all comments was "Sexualization or Objectification of Female Players". A total of 160 comments were shaped by experiences and situations in which female gamers were directly referred to and seen as sexual objects. This code is followed by the "Toxic Attitudes Toward Female Players" code, which consists of a similar theme to the previous one and is in the same primary category (Comments on Sexist and Toxic Behavior through Experience) with 115 comments. In these responses, female gamers shared remarks on their negative experiences, such as disrespectful and misogynistic attitudes they encountered in the game.

After these two codes with the highest number of frequencies, the rest of the list includes a variety of codes ranging in number from 34 to 83. Among the codes, the themes that are least frequently encountered in the comments but still appear in the comments at a considerable rate can be expressed as "Hope for Positive Change in the Gaming Community" with 11 comments and "Female Gamers Supporting Female Gamers" with 13 comments. However, the number of comments in which gender stereotyping, one of the main themes of our research, was included in the comments was only 17. This reveals that the individuals who watched the video preferred to leave their comments below. The comments on the videos did not focus only on gender stereotypes but also analyzed the negative experiences women were exposed to as a whole, with all its different elements. The table that shows the frequency ranges of the codes in our research (Table 3) is given above.

When we analyze at the distribution of the main categories,

- It is found that the most common category is “Comments on Sexist and Toxic Behavior through Experience,” with 446 comments (41%), which includes comments on gender stereotyping, toxic behaviors, sexualization and objectification faced by both female gamers and all individuals.
- This category is followed by “Comments on Raising Awareness in All Gamers and a 'Better Gaming Community'” with 296 comments (28%) in total. The comments here are shaped by the awareness and support of male and female actors on this issue. Furthermore, these comments bring various code together, for example, that the selected videos contain educational elements for the viewers.

Figure 1. Main categories by the number of comments

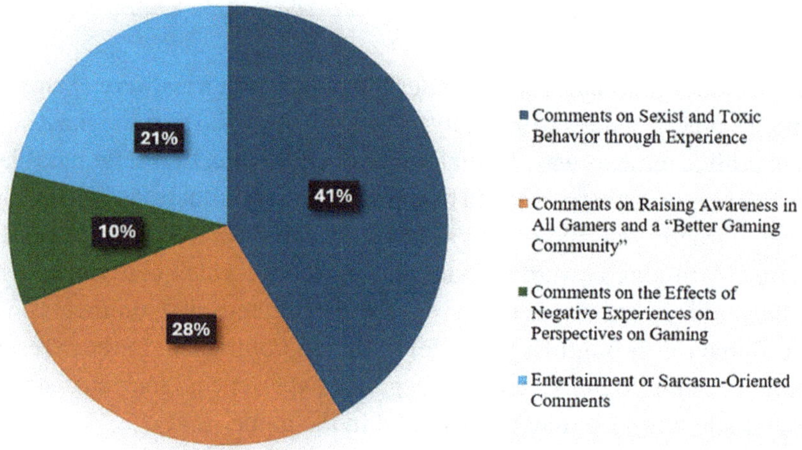

- “Entertainment or Sarcasm-Oriented Comments,” which ranked third in the analysis with 228 comments (21%), contain entertaining content, humor or satirical perspectives on the videos. Other comments under this category consist of comments that ignore or downplay the negative experiences of the female gamers
- Lastly, “Comments on the Effects of Negative Experiences on Perspectives on Gaming”, which includes comments revealing that negative in-game experiences affect individuals' views on gaming practices, ranked fourth with 112 comments (10%). All these main categories are explained in detail below, and the codes under each category are defined and supported by sample comments.

The figure containing the percentages of the main categories within the comments studied in the analysis process of our research is presented above (Figure 1).

Main Category 1: Comments on Sexist and Toxic Behavior through Experience

This main category serves as an umbrella for all the comments left under the relevant videos on gendered stereotyping, sexualization and objectification practices in digital games, and toxic behaviors faced by both female gamers and all individuals regardless of gender. This category covers five different codes, which will be explained by giving examples of comments focusing on each component.

Sexualization or Objectification of Female Players

Description: The comments under this code focus on the themes of seeing female gamers as an entertainment, sexualization and objectification based on the narrative in the relevant video or their own experiences.

Example Comment: *"This is genuinely so sad. Like a girl calls out someone for asking for personal information, and is then told they are 'weird for taking it seriously'. This. This is the problem with the culture of interactions between genders. People say stuff and excuse it as a joke. It is NOT a joke. It is annoying at best, harassment or sexual harassment at worst (which is a scary amount of the time)*" – from "The Female Experience UNCENSORED | Valorant."

Toxic Attitudes Toward Female Players

Description: This code includes YouTube video comments on the toxic behaviors that female gamers are constantly exposed to before, during, and after the game, including abuse, hate speech, insults, and disrespect.

Example Comment: *"not gonna lie, i'm at 4:35 of the video and I just feel so bad for her, it sounds so unreal to me how male players can be this toxic and totally disgusting towards women.. they failed as human beings and it shows. What amazes me the most are the twitch streamers who got such a toxic audience as well by typing, commenting and suggesting such kind of shit.. I really feel like to throw up, games should be a safe place for everyone who needs to chill and relax.. not a torture place for minorities."* – from "The Female Experience UNCENSORED | Valorant"

Toxic Attitudes Toward Individuals

Description: Comments that illustrate and address the fact that not only female players, but also all players are subjected to these toxic behaviors are gathered under this code. In these comments, the toxic behaviors experienced by female players are not underestimated. Instead, the fact that individuals of all genders are subjected to this bullying is emphasized and the comments aim to support the victims on the subject.

Example Comment: "*If you say anything online you are open to some sort of abuse. All online abuse should be tackled equally and not made out that females suffer it more.*" – from "What Girl Gamers REALLY Have To Deal With | OMG a Girl Series [1]"

Sharing Relevant Personal Experiences

Description: YouTube users who posted under the code shared situations they have encountered in their own lives regarding sexist discourse and toxic behavior, aiming to show how widespread the problem actually is.

Example Comment: " *Ok when you said "no he's not, he's just a good team-mate" I literally said that to someone and they all got mad at the dude who bought me bc he was a "simp" but he just bought me a gun T-T 811"* – from "The Female Experience: Part 2 | Valorant"

Gender Stereotypes of Women

Description: This category includes posts that directly address gender stereotypes and generalizations. As seen in our research, while comments specifically about stereotypes were less common, the most intensely mentioned topics in this category were directly toxic and sexually objectifying behaviors.

Example Comment: *"Ok, but it's all women. By that I mean, if you're a girl and you turn on your mic, you're guaranteed to receive sexist comments."* – from "What Girl Gamers REALLY Have To Deal With | OMG a Girl Series [1]"

Main Category 2: Comments on Raising Awareness in All Gamers and a "Better Gaming Community"

Comments in this main category broadly address both female and male players' awareness of the toxic behaviors and sexist treatment that women are regularly subjected to. It also includes support and advocacy for players suppressed by these attitudes and the hope of achieving an equal gaming community. In this respect, it is seen that the comments under this category have a supportive, positive and helpful perspective. The fact that raising awareness will lead to a more equal game community is also clearly highlighted in the comments.

Educational Impact of the Video

Description: This sub-category consists of comments that emphasize the educational and constructive aspects of all three videos in this research. Here, YouTube users mention that they find the videos very enlightening, revealing that they see more clearly how widespread and concerning this issue actually is. The content included in this code also shows that there are many gamers who are 'open to growth', especially by revealing the lack of knowledge of male gamers on the subject. Therefore, it can be argued that increasing the number of similar videos would be an important strategy to draw attention to this crucial issue.

Example Comment: *"As a dude I must say that this is torture. I had a conversation with someone who has experience such hate while gaming recently and I'd never think that this is your casual experience. Thank you for this video and thank you for spreading awareness."* – from "The Female Experience UNCENSORED | Valorant"

Informative Comments/Advices

Description: Comments placed under this code contain informative or advisory content, both for the video's creator and for all individuals who may encounter a similar situation.

Example Comment: " *The audacity baffles me. Also, I think all of you experiencing this shit, you should get a voice changer and be like ""Here's my real voice"" and absolutely troll them. No other way."* – from "The Female Experience: Part 2 | Valorant"

Expressing Respect and Support Toward Female Gamers

Description: This code's main theme can be respect and support for female players. Although the content of these comments varies, most mention that women players do not deserve these behaviors. Despite this discouraging environment, messages of praise and support for women who continue to stay in the game are frequently seen. In addition, some of the male gamers who leave comments under the videos apologize on behalf of the toxic male gamers.

Example Comment: " *I was curious about this video series. But after just the first video, I stand by my choice to be a silent Male on the internet. You deserve the ability to talk or be quiet without risk of harassment. Again, you deserve the choice I'm naturally given, and I'm sorry you and so many other females face this as gamers online."* – from "What Girl Gamers REALLY Have To Deal With | OMG a Girl Series [1]"

Female Gamers Supporting Female Gamers

Description: Under this heading, the support of female players for other female players, as well as their experiences and collaborations in the processes they play together, are included. As seen in the comments, women feel happy and "at home" when they encounter other female players and think they have a more enjoyable and "safer" gaming experience.

Example Comment: "*Lol honestly everytime me and my friends (we're a grp of girls) and we have another girl on the team which is not one of us, it makes us happy and enjoy the game more. There's just this sense of relief and security knowing ur a girl playing with another girl on valorant."* – from "The Female Experience: Part 2 | Valorant"

Hope for Positive Change in the Gaming Community

Description: This section contains a series of comments on wishes for a better gaming community, with increased awareness and understanding among gamers. While the comments under this code express these hopes, they also underline that this is still far off.

Example Comment: *"Hell that was disturbing to watch. Those were some really nasty guys and boys. I hope one day the gaming comunity will outgrow this kind of behavior, but I fear we have a long way ahead of us until then.."* – from "The Female Experience UNCENSORED | Valorant"

Male Gamers' Awareness of the Issue

Description: This section focuses directly on male gamers' awareness of these negative attitudes that women are often exposed to and how crucial it is to be mindful of these issues. As they state, "not all men are the same when it comes to in-game toxicity," and developing awareness, especially among male gamers, is important for the positive transformation of the gaming experience.

Example Comment: "*I'm so sorry for all of these men being creeps. Being a guy myself, I'm ashamed on their behalf, and I promise all the gamer girls (and women for that matter) that not all boys/men are like this. Hearing all of these guys being creepy sometimes makes me hate being born as the same gender as them.. truly i feel sad there are genuine men out there, who're silent or just don't get noticed enough i feel like*" – from "The Female Experience UNCENSORED | Valorant"

Supportive Male Allyship

Description: Although this title emphasizes similar elements to "Male Gamers' Awareness of the Issue," the main point of difference is that conscious male gamers stand by female gamers who face sexist or toxic attitudes during the game and adopt a supportive attitude against the bullies. Most comments suggested that "such disrespectful men may actually engage in behaviors like this to impress other men and show superiority." In addition, female YouTubers who were subjected to toxic behavior in-game also expressed their gratitude to the male players who supported them and backed them up at the time.

Example Comment: "*And this, gents, is why it's important for other men to call out this bad behaviour: the guys are being disrespectful to women to impress other men. They only stop when you call them out. Put them in their place. Be like Reyna: king shit.*" – from "The Female Experience UNCENSORED | Valorant"

Main Category 3: Comments on the Effects of Negative Experiences on Perspectives on Gaming

This main category presents findings that reveal that negative in-game experiences directly affect individuals' views on their gaming practices. Under this category, the need to hide one's gender and the instinct to stay away from all kinds of in-game interactions are included. On top of this, regardless of gender, players who are subjected to bullying and unpleasant experiences in the game may completely lose interest in the game or prefer not to play the same type of games for this reason.

Toxic Behaviors as a Reason for Avoiding In-Game Communication / Game

Description: These comments express the opinions of users who feel distanced from the in-game communication element, which is necessary in competitive online games, the type of games in which all three videos are examined in this study feature. The comments show that exposure to bullying affects individuals of all genders, not just women. Individuals hesitate to make their voices heard in the game and are harassed over different themes when they turn on their microphones. In addition, women whose voices are compared to a man-child or men whose voices are compared to a woman also share their experiences under this heading. The analysis of comments shows that these negative experiences can reach such a point that players hesitate to communicate and may even lose the desire to play the game directly.

Example Comment: *"As a female gamer myself, I fear going on mic for reasons like this. Why can't men and woman just recognize each other as both being humans with feelings and just play the freaking game".* – from "What Girl Gamers REALLY Have To Deal With | OMG a Girl Series [1]"

Example Comment 2: *"I'm a man and I still avoid game chat. It's full of mental patients."* – from "What Girl Gamers REALLY Have To Deal With | OMG a Girl Series [1]"

Need to Conceal Gender

Description: Another common element found in the comments analyzed is that women avoid incorporating any factor that would indicate their gender openly into their gameplay experience. Examples include choosing a gender-neutral username or even choosing male characters to play as in the game. Women who have been mistaken for a man or a child have also mentioned that they are particularly reluctant to express that they are "women" because the behavior of other players may completely change if their gender is known. Some female gamers even think it makes for a more "comfortable" gameplay experience because their voices do not sound like a woman's.

Example Comment: *"As a girl with a lower voice, I'm happy that I don't sound like a girl to these people cuz I have a deeper and raspier voice. They always assume I'm a younger boy. I've seen how they treat me differently before and after I told them. I've seen the things they say to their bros. It's really shit and I'm lucky to be at least a bit more comfortable*" – from "The Female Experience UNCENSORED | Valorant"

Main Category 4: Entertainment or Sarcasm-Oriented Comments

The fourth and final main category, "Entertainment or Sarcasm-Oriented Comments", brings together different opinions about the video in the comment section, including entertaining content and witty or satirical perspectives. Users quote from the videos and interact with other users by making funny and sarcastic comments. In addition, different comments that ignore, downplay or trivialize the negative experiences that female gamers are experiencing also form one of the codes under this category.

Quotes from the Video

Description: Comments with various quotes from different video parts are generally categorized under this code. In these comments, YouTube users may either quote the lyrics directly, without any commentary, or add their own opinions to the post, such as that they find this interaction very funny or annoying.

Example Comment: *"are you a girl?"*
"no, I'm a brimstone"
LMAOOOOOOOOOO" – from "The Female Experience: Part 2 | Valorant"

Humor or Satirical Comments

Description: Comments classified under this sub-category present ideas with humorous, sarcastic or ironic tones. In these comments, there are practices of criticizing the situations they find inappropriate in the video, making fun of them, generating entertainment through these situations, or interpreting the experience in the video in sarcastic ways. The main feature that distinguishes these comments from the responses in the "Dismissive or Mocking Responses" category is that they are not focused on the female gamers but on the gamers who mistreat them.

Example Comment "*I watch these vids to feel good about myself "You can always sink lower" lmfao"*– from "The Female Experience: Part 2 | Valorant"

Dismissive or Mocking Responses

Description: The comments included in this code see the situations discussed in the videos, which involve a great prejudice and negative perspective towards female gamers, as "women exaggerate" or "a common situation in all of the gaming communities". Comments that belittle, ignore or position these negative experiences as "deserved behavior" rather than being aware of the situation can also be included in this category. In these comments, there is an attitude that normalizes the negative situations and the insults that female actors are exposed to. By giving the impression that this is the "ideal", the need for female gamers to stand up against these offensive actions is labeled as "overreaction". The perspective is far from understanding or empathizing, and in some comments, it even turns into an accusatory attitude towards women.

Example Comment: *"Lol dont think that these insults are only coming towards women. I get shit on in video games all the time, you just get used to it and it really doesnt matter. And quite frankly stop making such a big deal out of it, it only encourages them to do it more. I feel as if a big reason that women get insulted more is that they react more."* – from "What Girl Gamers REALLY Have To Deal With | OMG a Girl Series [1]"

Code Relations

We have stated in our research that the theme found most strongly and intensely in each comment is assumed to be the core code of that comment. However, in some of these comments, there were also cases where there was more than one element, i.e. code. Therefore, apart from the principal codes analyzed above, we examined in which cases the codes on the comments co-existed. In line with this data, we analyzed the contextual and relational meanings of the shared components. This is significant for identifying common patterns and correlations.

When the relations between the codes obtained from the analyzed comments were examined, three sets of related codes were encountered that attracted particular attention. The first of these sets is the code "Toxic Behaviors as a Reason for Avoiding In-Game Communication / Game," which deals with the fact that the toxic environment and sexist behaviors encountered in the game lead to distancing from in-game audio or written forms of communication, or the game itself, and "Need to Conceal Gender", which sheds light on the need for female players to avoid all kinds of elements that will show their gender in the game as much as possible. These two sub-categories are included in "The Effects of Negative Experiences on Perspectives on Gaming", one of the four main categories of our research. At this point, it can be said that these toxic attitudes that both female gamers and all gamers can encounter in the game directly affect individuals' gaming experiences and their perspectives on the game. This relationship also aligns with analyzing the codes and reveals a process that complements each other.

Another related code set consists of "Male Gamers' Awareness of the Issue" and "Supportive Male Allyship" codes. Although the content of both codes includes the support and awareness of male gamers on the issue, the "Supportive Male Allyship" code is based on in-game experiences, such as male gamers directly supporting and defending female gamers in the game and warning other individuals who show toxic behaviors. In the "Male Gamers' Awareness" sub-category, comments expressing the significance of male gamers' having this level of sensitivity in in-game and out-of-game processes were brought together. It can be stated that these codes are related since they contain examples of behaviors that contribute to each other. It can be concluded that as male gamers' awareness of the subject increases, the rate of keeping silent in unfair attitudes they encounter will decrease, and they will act in a supportive manner in favor of female gamers.

Finally, the third and the most predominant code relationship is between the codes "Sexualization or Objectification of Female Players" and "Toxic Attitudes Toward Female Players." The codes obtained from these comments, which examine and criticize all these toxic, sexist, and objectifying attitudes that women are exposed to, support each other. At this point, we can state that it is apparent to viewers that women who are subjected to negative attitudes and behaviors during such competitive games are seen as inferior and objectified simply because of their gender. YouTube users who watched the video reflected on the content exemplified in these videos, reflecting fundamental interactions, and essentially found it "disturbing." This finding points to videos' utility in contributing to individuals' awareness, as some comments left under the videos indicate.

CONCLUSION

When we consider the magnitude and prevalence of the problem, it is unfortunately not possible to thoroughly analyze all the negative experiences that women face in digital gaming communities, their in-game experiences, whenever they want to make their voices heard and share their opinions on social media with only one study. However, this study examined misogyny, toxicity, and sexist discourse, which are encountered more frequently than desired in all areas of life, through the example of digital game-centered videos. It also shed light on YouTube users to understand the reflections of videos addressing this crucial issue. As seen in the results of our research, a wide range of comments were left on these videos that reveal the experiences of female gamers, which can be interpreted as a "galvanizing" effect on YouTube users. It can be said that there is room for improvement in the general level of awareness of both YouTube users and community members who play games and/or like to watch the experiences of different gamers. Although there is a majority in the comments who acknowledge the existence of toxicity, sexualization, and hate speech against women gamers and are disturbed by it, it is also clear that there is a group of people who are not aware of the importance of this issue and the magnitude of the damage it causes.

Considering the research results obtained, this study proves that online interactions on content sharing platforms such as YouTube can create spaces where individuals can support each other and offer suggestions and encouragement. By raising awareness, these videos can contribute to solving these important problems. In the comments left on videos, it is possible to see YouTube users sharing their opinions and experiences, interacting with other users, and overcoming negative experiences and feelings. The study's findings have practical implications, demonstrating that delving into online interactions facilitated by video content platforms like YouTube is an impactful tool for understanding the perspectives and opinions of individuals in today's digital world on a variety of issues. This knowledge can empower researchers and practitioners in digital media and communication studies. Finally, the main categories and codes presented in this study can serve as a categorization tool that can be used in future similar studies.

FUTURE RESEARCH DIRECTIONS

The authors recommend future research. Future research could conduct in-depth interviews or focus group discussions to better understand how viewers interpret and reflect on videos that aim to raise awareness about women's experiences in competitive online games. In addition, the limitations of this study should also be considered. The fact that this study only focused on the three most viewed videos on Female Gamer's Experiences and selected the top 350 comments from each video (a total of 1082 comments when comments not included in the study are removed) may result in a narrow range of ideas and contexts that the study encountered. Therefore, future studies could both increase the number of videos analyzed and aim to inspect a larger number of comments. Finally, due to the anonymity of the comments within the scope of this research, analysis and discussion could not be carried out on the demographic characteristics of the commenters. However, in future similar studies, new discussion topics can be created on features such as regional/cultural diversity based on the demographic characteristics of the participants.

REFERENCES

Alshamrani, S., Abuhamad, M., Abusnaina, A., & Mohaisen, D. (2020). Investigating Online Toxicity in Users Interactions with the Mainstream Media Channels on YouTube. October 2020. In CIKM (Workshops).

Amarasekara, I., & Grant, W. J. (2018). Exploring the YouTube science communication gender gap: A sentiment analysis. Public Understanding of Science, 28(1), pp. 68-84. (Original work published 2019)DOI: 10.1177/0963662518786654

Aramendia-Muneta, M. E., Olarte-Pascual, C., & Hatzithomas, L. (2019). Gender stereotypes in original digital video advertising. *Journal of Gender Studies*, *29*(4), 403–419. DOI: 10.1080/09589236.2019.1650255

Baker C., Ging D. & Andreasen, M B. (2024). Recommending Toxicity: The role of algorithmic recommender functions on YouTube Shorts and TikTok in promoting male supremacist influencers. DCU Anti-Bullying Centre Dublin City University, April 2024.

Baltezarević, B., Baltezarević, R., Baltezarević, V. N., Kwiatek, P., & Baltezarević, I. (2021). Stereotypical negative female gender roles in digital games. *Acta Ludologica*, *4*(2), 42–61.

Burgess, J., Green, J., & Rebane, G. (2020). Agency and Controversy in the YouTube Community. In Friese, H., Nolden, M., Rebane, G., & Schreiter, M. (Eds.), *Handbuch Soziale Praktiken und Digitale Alltagswelten*. Springer VS., DOI: 10.1007/978-3-658-08357-1_10

Caillois, R. (2001). *Man, play, and games* (Barash, M., Trans.). University of Illinois Press. (Original work published 1958)

Cambronero-Saiz, B., Cristófol-Rodríguez, C., & Segarra-Saavedra, J. (2023). Content analysis from a gender perspective of comments received by Spanish science youtubers. *Media and Communication*, *11*(1), 252–263. DOI: 10.17645/mac.v11i1.5971

Columbia University Mailman School of Public Health. (2025). Content Analysis Method Research of Columbia University. https://www.publichealth.columbia.edu/research/population-health-methods/content-analysis

Cote, A. C. (2016). I can defend myself. *Games and Culture*, *12*(2), 136–155. DOI: 10.1177/1555412015587603

Cross, L., Kaye, L. K., Savostijanovs, J., McLatchie, N., Johnston, M., Whiteman, L., Mooney, R., & Atherton, G. (2024). Gendered violence and sexualized representations in video games: (Lack of) effect on gender-related attitudes. *New Media & Society*, *26*(3), 1648–1669. DOI: 10.1177/14614448221075736

Data Reportal, & Meltwater, & We Are Social. (February 5, 2025). Number of internet and social media users worldwide as of February 2025 (in billions) [Graph]. In Statista. Retrieved February 14, 2025, from https://www.statista.com/statistics/617136/digital-population-worldwide/

Dean, B. (2024). YouTube Stats: How Many People Use YouTube? In Backlinko. Retrieved from February 14, 2025, from https://backlinko.com/youtube-users

Dehkhoda, S., & Gunica, J. (2022). *Analyzing Toxicity in YouTube Comments with the Help of Machine Learning. Department of Computer and Systems Sciences.* Stockholm University.

Döring, N., & Mohseni, M. R. (2019b). Fail videos and related video comments on YouTube: A case of sexualization of women and gendered hate speech? *Communication Research Reports*, *36*(3), 254–264. DOI: 10.1080/08824096.2019.1634533

Döring, N., & Mohseni, R. (2017). Do female Youtubers receive more hateful comments? Results of three content analyses. Conference: CYPSY22 - 22nd Annual CyberPsychology, CyberTherapy & Social Networking ConferenceAt: Wolverhampton, England. June 2017. DOI: DOI: 10.13140/RG.2.2.29229.46561

Döring, N., & Mohseni, R. (2019a). Male dominance and sexism on YouTube: Results of Three Content Analyses. *Feminist Media Studies*, *19*(4), 512–524. DOI: 10.1080/14680777.2018.1467945

Duncum, P. (2011). Youth on YouTube: Prosumers in a peer-to-peer participatory culture. *The International Journal of Art Education*, *9*(2), 24–39.

Dynel, M. (2014). Participation framework underlying YouTube interaction. *Journal of Pragmatics*, *73*, 37–52. DOI: 10.1016/j.pragma.2014.04.001

Elliot, R. (2024). Gamers spend more time on social video than games. Midia Research Blog. 5, Dec. 2024. Retrieved from: https://www.midiaresearch.com/blog/gamers-spend-more-time-watching-twitch-and-youtube-than-playing-games-are-publishers-leaving-engagement-and-revenue-on-the-table

Fleck, A. (2025). State of Play: Female Gamers Around the World. Statisca, Video Gaming Industry Blog. Published on March 7, 2025. April 2, 2025. Retrieved from: https://www.statista.com/chart/34067/femal-pc-and-console-gamers/

Gao, G., Min, A., & Shih, P. C. (2017). Gendered design bias. *Proceedings of the 29th Australian Conference on Computer-Human Interaction*. https://doi.org/DOI: 10.1145/3152771.3152804

Global Media Insight. (2025). YouTube Statistics 2025 (Demographics, Users By Country & More). Global Media Insight. February 14, 2025, Retrieved from: https://www.globalmediainsight.com/blog/youtube-users-statistics/#:~:text=Monthly%20Active%20Users%20on%20YouTube,-Monthly%20active%20users&text=YouTube%20has%20more%20than%202.70,population%2C%2052%25%20access%20YouTube

Güregen, E. S. & Karaöz, Ç. (2022). Kadın Oyuncular, Cinsiyetçi Tektipleştirme ve Toksisite: İntearktif Sözlükler Üzerine Bir Araştırma. A chapter of "Dijital Oyunlar 2.0: Kimlik". Nobel Yayınevi, Aralık 2022

Khandaker, J. (2019). *Girl Gamers and Toxicity*. University of Houston. Master Thesis. The Faculty of the Department of Sociology.

King, C. M., & McCashin, D. (2022). Commenting and connecting: A thematic analysis of responses to YouTube vlogs about borderline personality disorder. *Internet Interventions : the Application of Information Technology in Mental and Behavioural Health*, *28*, 100509. Advance online publication. DOI: 10.1016/j.invent.2022.100540 PMID: 35493438

Kuznekoff, J. H., & Rose, L. M. (2012). Communication in multiplayer gaming: Examining player responses to gender cues. *New Media & Society*, *15*(4), 541–556. DOI: 10.1177/1461444812458271

Lange, P. G. (2007, March). Commenting on comments: Investigating responses to antagonism on YouTube. In Society for Applied anthropology conference, 31(1), pp. 163-190.

McLean, L., & Griffiths, M. D. (2018). Female gamers' experience of online harassment and social support in online gaming: A qualitative study. *International Journal of Mental Health and Addiction*, *17*(4), 970–994. DOI: 10.1007/s11469-018-9962-0

Mohseni, R., & Mourey, J. (2019). Male dominance and sexism on YouTube: Results of three content analyses. *Feminist Media Studies*, *19*(4), 512–524. DOI: 10.1080/14680777.2018.1467945

Mou, Y., & Peng, W. (2009). Gender and Racial Stereotypes in Popular Video Games. In *Handbook of Research on Effective Electronic Gaming in Education*, (Ed.) R. E. Ferdig, IGI Global, pp. 922–937. https://doi.org/DOI: 10.4018/978-1-59904-808-6.ch053

Obadimu, A., Mead, E. L., Hussain, M., & Agarwal, N. (2019). Identifying toxicity within YouTube video comment. In Thomson, R., Bisgin, H., Dancy, C., & Hyder, A. (Eds.), Lecture Notes in Computer Science: Vol. 11549. *Social, Cultural, And Behavioral Modeling* (pp. 207–217). Springer., DOI: 10.1007/978-3-030-21741-9_22

Paaßen, B., Thekla, M., & Stratemeyer, M. (2017). What Is a True Gamer? The Male Gamer Stereotype and the Marginalization of Women in Video Game Culture. *Sex Roles*, *76*(7), 421–435. DOI: 10.1007/s11199-016-0678-y

Park, C. S., Liu, Q., & Kaye, B. K. (2021). Analysis of ageism, sexism, and ableism in user comments on YouTube videos about climate activist Greta Thunberg. *Social Media + Society*, *7*(3), 1–14. DOI: 10.1177/20563051211036059

Petrova E., & Gross N. (2017 June). 4 Reasons People Watch Gaming Content on YouTube: On Video, Gaming. Consumer Insights and Gaming. *Consumer Insights Report*. Think With Google.

Sims, C. (2014). Video game culture, contentious masculinities, and reproducing racialized social class divisions in Middle School. *Signs (Chicago, Ill.)*, *39*(4), 848–857. DOI: 10.1086/675539

Statisca (2024). Distribution of video gamers in the United States from 2006 to 2023, by gender. https://www.statista.com/statistics/232383/gender-split-of-us-computer-and-video-gamers/

Steele, C. M., & Aronson, J. (1995). Stereotype threat and the intellectual test performance of African Americans. *Journal of Personality and Social Psychology*, *69*(5), 797–811. DOI: 10.1037/0022-3514.69.5.797 PMID: 7473032

Takahashi, D. (2021, June 14). How Riot Games will ensure that Valorant's esports stars include women. VentureBeat. Retrieved from: https://venturebeat.com/games/how-riot-games-wants-to-ensure-that-valorants-esports-stars-include-women/#:~:text=But%20Valorant%20is% 20different% 20from,in%20an%20interview%20with%20GamesBeat.

Toffler, A. (2022). *The Third Wave: The Classic Study of Tomorrow*. Bantam.

Topics, E. (2025). How Many Gamers Are There? (New 2025 Statistics). by Fabio Duarte. Exploding Topics Blog. March 28, 2025. Retrieved from: https://explodingtopics.com/blog/number-of-gamers

Vizcaíno-Verdú, A., De-Casas-Moreno, P., & Tirocchi, S. (2023). Online prosumer convergence: Listening, creating and sharing music on YouTube and TikTok. *Communicatio Socialis*, *36*(1), 151–166. DOI: 10.15581/003.36.1.151-166

Wotanis, L. L., & McMillan, L. (2014). Performing Gender on YouTube. *Feminist Media Studies*, *14*(6), 912–928. DOI: 10.1080/14680777.2014.882373

Yee, N. (2018, June 14). Beyond 50/50: Breaking down the percentage of female gamers by genre. Quantic Foundry. https://quanticfoundry.com/2017/01/19/female-gamers-by-genre/

ADDITIONAL READINGS

Apperley, T., & Jayemanne, D. (2020). *Towards a game studies methodology: Reflexive and interdisciplinary approaches to game research*. MIT Press.

Charnock, D., & Standen, P. J. (2013). Second-Hand Masculinity: Do Boys with Intellectual Disabilities Use Computer Games as Part of Gender Practice? [IJGBL]. *International Journal of Game-Based Learning*, *3*(3), 43–53. DOI: 10.4018/ijgbl.2013070104

de Rijk, B. J. S. (2016, March 26). *Watching the game: How we may understand Let's Play videos* (Master's thesis, Utrecht University).

Golob, U., Kraševec, M., & Oblak Črnič, T. (2020). Video gaming spectatorship: What drives gameplay watching on YouTube? *Medijske studije / Media Studies*, *12*(23), 41–55. DOI: 10.20901/ms.12.23.3

Khan, I. A., Reyes, A., & Subhani, A. (2022). Women in online gaming: The female experience within the gaming community. *Journal of Administrative and Business Studies*, *8*(1), 8–14. DOI: 10.20474/jabs-8.1.2

Maykut, P. S., & Moorhouse, R. (1994). *Beginning qualitative research: A philosophic and practical guide*. Routledge Falmer Press.

Mäyrä, F. (2008). An Introduction to Game Studies: Games in Culture. *Sage (Atlanta, Ga.)*.

McLean, L., & Griffiths, M. D. (2013). Female gamers: A thematic analysis of their gaming experience. *International Journal of Game-Based Learning*, *3*(3), 54–71. DOI: 10.4018/ijgbl.2013070105

Putra, A. M., Anggoro, A. D., Aunul, S., & Putra, R. D. (2021, July). Understanding the motives and typifications of YouTuber gaming on social media: A phenomenology study. *ASPIRATION Journal*, *2*(1), 19–41. DOI: 10.56353/aspiration.v2i1.25

Shaw, A. (2014). *Gaming at the edge: Sexuality and gender at the margins of gamer culture*. University of Minnesota Press.

Taylor, T. L. (2006). *Play between worlds: Exploring online game culture*. MIT Press. DOI: 10.7551/mitpress/5418.001.0001

KEY TERMS AND DEFINITIONS

Content Creator: A person who prepares and shares content such as videos, photos, and articles for digital environments.

Gamer: A person who plays video games with passion and is generally involved in sharing information, experiences, or interacting with communities related to these games.

Prejudice: Making a preconceived positive or negative judgment about a person or situation without sufficient knowledge or consideration.

Social Media: Digital platforms where people communicate with each other online and share photos, videos, and thoughts.

Toxicity: Offensive, hurtful, or hostile language and behavior that harms people in online environments.

YouTube: A popular internet platform where people watch, upload, and share videos.

YouTube Comments: Messages written by viewers under videos on YouTube expressing their thoughts, likes, or criticisms.

Chapter 6
From Competition to Conflict:
Hate Speech in Multiplayer Online Battle Arena Games (MOBAs)

Emre Meric
https://orcid.org/0009-0000-1862-8654
İstanbul Bilgi University, Turkey

ABSTRACT

This study investigates the prevalence and dynamics of hate speech in one of the multiplayer online battle arena game (MOBA) named as Mobile Legends: Bang Bang using digital ethnography. Data were collected through participant observation across 540 matches and analyzed via content analysis, yielding 267 documented instances of hate speech. Findings reveal that hate speech is pervasive and disproportionately targets women, ethnic minorities (particularly Kurds and Arabs), LGBTQ+ individuals, and people with disabilities. Hate speech was most commonly delivered through in-game chat and intensified in higher-ranked, solo matches. Player reactions were largely passive, indicating a culture of normalization. Avatar-based discrimination further demonstrated the role of digital identity in shaping hostility. These results suggest that multiplayer games reflect and reproduce broader societal biases.

INTRODUCTION

Digital games have progressed beyond being simple forms of entertainment and now function as interactive platforms that connect people globally and influence cultural and social interactions. They now rival traditional media such as television and cinema, in some cases, surpass them. With 2.68 billion active players worldwide,

DOI: 10.4018/979-8-3373-6192-5.ch006

a number expected to grow to 3.2 billion by 2029 (Clement, 2025), the gaming industry continues to expand rapidly. This growth supports the formation of virtual communities and new channels of social interaction among players. However, this digital expansion also presents certain challenges. One of the most pressing issues is the rising use of hate speech and discriminatory language in online games, which undermines positive communication and harms the player experience. In comparison to social media platforms, in-game communication systems are less regulated, allowing hate speech to spread more easily through anonymous user identities (Costa et al., 2023). This has emerged as a critical issue affecting the long-term health and sustainability of the gaming industry.

In recent years, digital games have received growing academic interest in areas such as consumer behavior, representation, psychological impacts, and player motivations (Williams, 2006; McLean & Griffiths, 2013; Wallenius et al., 2009). Although this literature has contributed to understanding the cultural and social dimensions of games, research on hate speech and discriminatory language in gaming environments is still limited. Existing studies mainly focus on three areas: discriminatory content in the game itself (offline gameplay), hate speech during online matches, and toxic behavior in gaming communities (Costa et al., 2020). However, there is a clear gap in research that directly observes how hate speech occurs during actual gameplay.

The aim of this study was to explore the prevalence and dynamics of hate speech in the context of the online multiplayer online battle arena game Mobile Legends: Bang Bang. To this end, digital ethnography was employed as the methodological framework. Data were collected through participant observation and analyzed using content analysis. The phenomenon of hate speech was examined across eight analytical dimensions: ypes of hate speech, distribution across competitive ranks (Epic, Legend, Mythic), targeted groups, forms of hate speech, prevalence in solo versus group gameplay, intensity of hate speech, player reactions to hate speech, and player responses to identity-based avatars.

The structure of this chapter reflects the progression of the study: the first section introduces the conceptual definition of hate speech; the second presents the relevant literature on hate speech and discriminatory language in digital games; the third outlines the methodology; and the fourth provides the research findings. The chapter concludes with a discussion of the results in relation to the broader sociocultural implications.

Theorizing Hate Speech Across Legal, Academic, and Digital Domains

The feeling of hate is deeply rooted in human psychology and social dynamics. When hatred becomes ideologically motivated, individuals or groups adopt a binary worldview, defining themselves in opposition to a constructed "other" (Çayır, 2010, p. 48). In such contexts, hatred is not merely an emotional reaction but a constitutive element of identity, shaping one's self-perception through the devaluation of others. Discriminatory forms of hatred, often based on gender, ethnicity, skin color, religion, or culture, contribute directly to the emergence of hate speech (Boyle, 2001, p. 489). Nevertheless, hate speech remains a highly contested concept, with its meaning varying across cultural, historical, and legal contexts (Gelber & McNamara, 2016, p. 324).

In the literature, definitions of hate speech are commonly situated within four broad domains: legal, lexical, academic, and practical (Popcunova et al., 2023; Sellars, 2016). Each of these approaches emphasizes different components, resulting in definitional variations. At the international level, global institutions have developed widely cited working definitions. The United Nations (2019, p. 2) describes hate speech as "*any kind of communication in speech, writing or behavior that attacks or uses pejorative or discriminatory language concerning a person or a group based on who they are,*" such as their religion, ethnicity, nationality, race, or gender. The Council of Europe's 1997 Recommendation further defines hate speech as "*all expressions that spread, incite, promote or justify hatred grounded in intolerance, including xenophobia and discrimination against minorities or migrants.*" Expanding on this, the European Commission against Racism and Intolerance (ECRI) offers a comprehensive understanding that encompasses "*the advocacy, promotion or incitement, in any form, of the denigration, hatred or vilification of a person or group,*" *including the use of stereotypes, insults, threats, and justifications thereof, based on characteristics such as race, descent, religion, sex, or disability* (ECRI, 2015, p. 3).

National legal systems have similarly incorporated hate speech regulations, though each framework reflects the country's specific cultural and legal priorities. As Waldron (2012) notes, countries such as Canada, Denmark, Germany, New Zealand, and the United Kingdom prohibit speech acts that intentionally insult, defame, or threaten individuals based on group characteristics, especially when such expressions threaten social harmony. Similarly, Turkey addresses the issue in Article 216 of its Penal Code, which criminalizes incitement to hatred or enmity against groups distinguished by class, race, religion, or regional identity (Aydınlı, 2021, p. 5). Despite contextual differences, these frameworks share a legislative tendency to restrict expressions that target vulnerable minorities through aggressive, insulting, or threatening discourse likely to provoke public disorder.

Alongside legal approaches, mainstream lexicons provide simplified yet consistent definitions that reinforce the essential characteristics of hate speech. The Cambridge Dictionary conceptualizes hate speech as *"public speech that expresses hate or encourages violence towards a person or group based on something such as race, religion, sex, or sexual orientation."* Merriam-Webster defines hate speech as *"expressing hatred of a particular group of people."* Oxford Learner's Dictionary explains hate speech as *"speech or writing that attacks or threatens a particular group of people, especially on the basis of race, religion or sexual orientation."* According to Collins Dictionary, *hate speech is "speech disparaging a group on the grounds of color, race, ethnicity, nationality, religion, sex, sexual orientation, gender identity, or disability, or a person who identifies with such a group."* These definitions share common traits, characterizing hate speech as any form of communication, whether written or spoken, that conveys hatred and promotes violence against a particular group. These dictionary entries, by focusing on the literal meanings of "hate" and "speech," underscore the communicative intent and potential social consequences of such expressions (Popcunova et al., 2023, p. 2829).

Scholars also adopt varying approaches when defining hate speech, often influenced by their specific objectives. Some researchers focus purely on analyzing the phenomenon without advocating for legal consequences. Others actively push for its criminalization, working to influence lawmakers and judicial bodies by refining legal terminology. Meanwhile, a third group remains neutral, neither endorsing nor opposing legal sanctions (Sellars, 2016: 15). Scholars such as Delgado (1982), Matsuda (1989), Massey (1992), Moran (1994), Ward (1997), and others have examined the definitions of hate speech, with standard features including the speaker's intent to demean or incite hatred, the harmful impact on targeted individuals or groups, and the reinforcement of historical oppression and social subordination.

In contrast, recent scholarship offers broader definitions that respond to changing sociocultural and digital realities. Pankowski (2007, p. 1), for instance, defines hate speech as any discourse designed to discredit, threaten, or incite violence or prejudice against individuals or groups based on characteristics such as race, gender, nationality, appearance, political beliefs, or socioeconomic status. Cohen-Almagor (2011, pp. 1–2) similarly emphasizes that hate speech is not merely offensive but intentionally dehumanizing and aimed at causing psychological or social harm. Parekh (2012, p. 41), adopting a culturally embedded approach, identifies three core features of hate speech: the targeting of irrelevant traits, the stigmatization of groups, and the justification of hostility, whether overt or covert, verbal or symbolic. Marwick and Miller (2014, pp. 16–17) further synthesize academic thought by proposing a tripartite model encompassing content, intent, and harm.

Digitalization has added new complexity to this landscape. While the Internet and social media have empowered civic engagement and expanded the public sphere, they have also intensified the circulation of harmful content, including hate speech. The speed, reach, and anonymity of digital platforms have exacerbated the dissemination and visibility of discriminatory discourse. In response, digital platforms have developed internal policies and definitions to moderate such content, recognizing their dual role as enablers of both democratic participation and digital hostility (Costa et al., 2023; Castano-Pulgarin, 2021; Chetty & Alathur, 2018; Çakıcı, 2024).

Major online platforms such as Facebook, Instagram, X (formerly Twitter), YouTube, and TikTok have created practical and operational definitions of hate speech to guide their moderation efforts. For instance, Facebook and Instagram (2025) define hate speech as content that includes *"violent or dehumanizing speech, statements of inferiority, calls for exclusion or segregation,"* mainly when based on identity markers such as race, ethnicity, religion, sexual orientation, or gender identity. X identifies hate speech as *"a form of attack"* based on similar attributes. At the same time, YouTube and TikTok explicitly prohibit content that *"attacks, threatens, promotes violence or hatred"* against individuals or groups based on protected characteristics. These policy frameworks reflect a growing institutional recognition of the impact of online hate speech and the necessity for its regulation.

Common elements consistently emerge across these diverse definitions: legal, lexical, academic, and practical. First, hate speech targets a group or an individual associated with that group based on identity-related features such as race, ethnicity, religion, or sexual orientation. Second, the expression must convey animosity or hatred toward the target. Third, such speech often results in or is intended to cause harm. Fourth, the speaker's intent is frequently cited as a key determinant. Finally, hate speech can manifest through language, imagery, or symbols that carry discriminatory or hostile meanings. Based on these shared criteria, the present study adopts the following working definition to guide the research process: *"Hate speech refers to any expression, symbol, or image intended to incite hatred against a group or an individual affiliated with that group based on protected characteristics such as race, ethnicity, national origin, religion, caste, sexual orientation, sex, gender, gender identity, age, serious illness, disability, or immigration status."*

Hate Speech and Discriminatory Practices in Digital Games

In recent years, digital games have attracted growing scholarly interest across a range of disciplines, encompassing diverse research areas such as consumer behavior, narrative and representational structures, psychological effects, and player motivations (Shaw et al., 2019; Williams, 2006; McLean & Griffiths, 2013; Wallenius et al., 2009). While this expanding body of literature has significantly contributed to understanding gameplay's cultural, social, and psychological dimensions, exploring discriminatory language and hate speech within digital game environments remains relatively underdeveloped. Despite the increasing attention to representational politics in gaming, there is a marked gap in the academic literature concerning the manifestation of hate speech and the subjective experiences of players exposed to such content. According to Costa et al. (2020), hate speech in digital games was seen across three interconnected domains: offline gameplay, online gameplay, and online community.

The first dimension, offline gameplay, relates to the game's content and the general experience it offers players. In this context, certain video games may include elements that reflect hate speech or foster its emergence through the depiction of extreme violence and aggressive language (Costa et al., 2020, p.264). Game content developed during production often reproduces or reinforces problematic ideologies through narratives, character portrayals, and gameplay mechanics. Hate speech and discriminatory representation may be embedded explicitly through violent or dehumanizing content or implicitly through stereotypical or exclusionary tropes. The Pan European Game Information (PEGI) rating system includes "discrimination" and "hate speech" among its content descriptors, an acknowledgment of the persistent presence of such elements in widely consumed games. For instance, the Grand Theft Auto franchise, developed by Rockstar North, has faced censorship or bans in multiple countries, including Brazil, China, Germany, Saudi Arabia, and Thailand, due to its explicit violence and discriminatory undertones (Costa et al., 2020).

Content analyses have highlighted how gender, sexuality, race, and religion are portrayed in stereotypical and harmful ways. A significant body of research has revealed that female characters are frequently underrepresented and hypersexualized (Dietz, 1998; Beasley & Standley, 2002; Dill et al., 2005; Burgess et al., 2007; Miller & Summers, 2007; Jansz & Martis, 2007; Martins et al., 2009; Williams et al., 2009; Downs & Smith, 2010; Lynch et al., 2016). Female characters are often depicted with unrealistic body proportions and in roles such as seductive villains or passive figures awaiting rescue (Martins et al., 2009; Dietz, 1998). In contrast, male characters are portrayed as powerful, weapon-equipped protagonists embodying hegemonic masculinity (Miller & Summers, 2007). Moreover, studies have demonstrated that such portrayals reinforce sexist attitudes among players. Exposure to games with stereotypical female representations has been linked to increased acceptance of sexual harassment (Dill et al., 2008), objectification of women (Yao et al., 2010), and heightened benevolent sexism (Stermer & Burkley, 2015).

Issues of representation also extend to game development, where the underrepresentation of women and LGBTQ+ developers has tangible effects on content diversity. The #1ReasonWhy hashtag, which gained traction on Twitter in 2012, provided a platform for women in the gaming industry to share experiences of harassment, marginalization, and sexualization (Blodgett & Salter, 2014). LGBTQ+ developers face similar barriers, including pressures to disclose their identities in heteronormative environments that hinder the authentic portrayal of queer narratives (Bragança et al., 2016). According to the 2021 IGDA Developer Satisfaction Survey, the industry remains dominated by heterosexual men, with 62% of respondents identifying as male and 68% as heterosexual (Kumar et al., 2021). Consequently, queer representation in games is limited and often shaped by tokenism or stereotypical frameworks. Queer characters, when present, are frequently trivialized, portrayed for comic relief, or embedded within heteronormative structures (Conn, 2015). Even in games praised for engaging with queer themes, such as Persona 4, queerness is sometimes framed as abnormal or problematic. As Shaw (2012) notes, discussions of in-game sexuality often isolate queerness from other intersecting identities like race and gender, further flattening the complexity of queer representation.

Racial and ethnic stereotypes are also widespread in digital games. Characters of color, particularly Black, Latinx, and Arab individuals, are often reduced to archetypes such as gangsters, terrorists, or exotic others (Glaubke et al., 2001; Leonard, 2006; Mou & Peng, 2009; Everett & Watkins, 2008; Nakamura, 2014; Wohn, 2011). Glaubke et al. (2001) found that 56% of characters in their sample were white, while African American, Asian/Pacific Islander, and Latino characters were significantly underrepresented. Moreover, Leonard (2006) documented recurring racialized figures such as Cuban drug dealers, Afro-wearing trash-talking boxers, and heavily accented immigrants, all of which reinforce damaging stereotypes. Mou and Peng (2008) and Williams et al. (2009) further confirm the racial homogeneity of lead characters in games, with over 70% being white. Nakamura (2019) and Everett and Watkins (2008) have shown how such portrayals extend beyond representation to impact cultural perceptions, reinforcing racial hierarchies and exclusionary ideologies within the virtual and real world. Additionally, religious identity, particularly Islam, is often depicted through orientalist and adversarial frameworks in Western games (Šisler, 2008). These games frequently portray Muslims and Arabs as antagonists, especially in first-person shooter genres, thereby reducing religious and ethnic diversity to simplistic binaries of good versus evil.

The interactive nature of online gameplay adds further complexity to the circulation of hate speech. Multiplayer digital games often unfold in real-time with limited moderation, offering fertile ground for hate speech and discriminatory language. Women and LGBTQ+ players are frequent targets. Fox and Tang (2016) found that female players experience high levels of general and sexual harassment, often leading to rumination, self-withdrawal, and the adoption of defensive strategies. In eSports and competitive arenas, women continue to face significant barriers, including sexual harassment and exclusion (Ruvalcaba et al., 2018; Butt, 2019). Events like GamerGate, which mobilized online harassment against women in the industry, have further normalized misogyny within gaming culture (Shepherd et al., 2015; Mortensen, 2018). LGBTQ+ players similarly face homophobic, transphobic, and heteronormative aggression. Pulos (2013) highlights how game developers such as Blizzard shape normative player behavior by constraining LGBTQ+ discussions to specific forums while promoting heteronormative character constructions in games like World of Warcraft. Research by Gillin and Signorella (2023) and Brenner Levoy (2023) confirms the prevalence of anti-LGBTQ+ language during gameplay, often accompanied by racist expressions.

Racialized hate speech remains a core issue within online interactions. Condis (2021) and Nakamura (2019) demonstrate how white supremacist ideologies manifest through casual racism, verbal abuse, and targeted harassment of Black and Brown players. Gray's longitudinal research (2011, 2012, 2014, 2018) on African American gamers highlights how "trash talking" and linguistic profiling operate as mechanisms of racialization. Players are often interrogated about their racial identity and subjected to explicit racial slurs (Gray, 2012). Ortiz (2019) similarly finds that men of color experience frequent racist encounters yet remain engaged in gameplay, often without using available protective tools such as muting or blocking. Keum and Hearns (2022) show that Black gamers, in particular, report higher levels of psychological distress as a result of online racism, especially when compared to their Asian or Latinx counterparts.

Online game communities such as Discord, Steam, Twitch, and YouTube serve as additional arenas for hate speech dissemination. These platforms vary in their moderation practices. While Discord has taken clear steps to remove users associated with hate groups, Steam avoids censorship, framing itself as a neutral marketplace (Costa et al., 2020; Condis, 2021). Due to their live-streaming nature, Twitch and YouTube struggle to prevent hate speech in real time (Koehler et al., 2023). Extremist groups have also capitalized on these platforms. Dawey (2021) and Schlegel (2021) document the infiltration of gaming spaces by radical actors who exploit the cultural norms of gaming to spread misogynist, racist, and antisemitic rhetoric. Powell and Williams-Johnson (2023) find that white supremacist discourses on Twitch often emerge through downplaying systemic racism and advocating for unregulated "free speech."

A particularly troubling development in this context is the phenomenon of "hate raids," where automated bots flood livestreams with usernames and messages steeped in racism, sexism, homophobia, or transphobia. Meisner (2023) highlights how these attacks force streamers, particularly those from marginalized communities, to end their broadcasts prematurely. Han et al. (2023) note that such raids disproportionately target Black and Jewish creators. These attacks reinforce the cultural dominance of white, cisgender, heterosexual masculinity, the normative identity long embedded in gaming cultures (Consalvo, 2008; Gray et al., 2018).

METHOD

This study examines the emergence and sociocultural dynamics of hate speech in Mobile Legends: Bang Bang through digital ethnography, a method tailored to explore digitally mediated interactions and cultures. Unlike traditional ethnography, which focuses on cultural practices in physical settings (Jensen, 2012), digital ethnography expands inquiry to online environments, recognizing them as integral to everyday life and social meaning (Postill & Pink, 2012).

A range of terms has emerged to describe this evolving approach: "online ethnography" (Garcia et al., 2009), "cyberethnography" (Black, 2016), "virtual ethnography" (Hine, 2000), "internet ethnography" (Sade-Beck, 2004), "discourse-centered online ethnography" (Androutsopoulos, 2008), "netnography" (Kozinets, 2010), and "network ethnography" (Howard, 2002). Despite their semantic differences, these approaches share a commitment to understanding meaning-making and interaction in digital spaces. Postill and Pink (2012) identify five core routines of digital ethnography: staying updated via digital media, sharing content, following hyperlink networks, interacting with communities, and archiving digital materials. These routines offer a methodological structure for studying complex, participatory environments such as online games.

Digital ethnography is particularly effective in analyzing gaming cultures, where communication, identity, and symbolic practices are constantly negotiated (Chee, 2015). It allows for the integration of diverse data sources, chat logs, gameplay, and user interactions, providing a holistic view of in-game social behavior. Moreover, it enables researchers to observe how cultural values are shaped and contested in digital play. As Wullach et al. (2021) note, such contextual insight is essential for understanding and addressing hate speech, as it reveals the social norms and power dynamics that sustain or challenge harmful discourse.

Population and Sample

This study investigates online gaming culture and the dynamics of hate speech in Turkey by focusing on multiplayer online battle arena (MOBA) games, particularly Mobile Legends: Bang Bang (MLBB). MOBA games' interactive and competitive structure fosters intense player engagement and creates a conducive environment for hate speech. MLBB was chosen for its popularity in Turkey, mobile accessibility, and large, diverse player base. The game enables interaction with both acquaintances and strangers, fostering varied social dynamics (Ong et al., 2023). Its dual-currency economy, based on earned and premium currencies, reinforces material hierarchies through exclusive content, contributing to symbolic distinctions and exclusionary practices.

MLBB's mobile compatibility ensures widespread access across socio-economic groups, and it leads MOBA revenues in Turkey (Gaming Turkey, 2022). National and international tournaments further promote community building and competitive identity. The researcher's sustained engagement with MLBB since 2018 enhances the ethnographic depth of the study, allowing for contextualized analysis of player discourse, social norms, and hate speech. This long-term immersion strengthens methodological rigor by enabling the observation of in-game interactions within their native digital environment.

Data Collection

As defined by Dixon et al. (2016), observation involves systematic data collection within natural settings to capture authentic behaviors and interactions. Beuving and de Vries (2015) emphasize its multisensory nature, while Creswell and Poth (2018) highlight the active role of the researcher in participant observation. In this study, participant observation was employed to examine hate speech dynamics within Mobile Legends: Bang Bang (MLBB). The researcher joined gameplay sessions as a participant observer, documenting hate speech and discriminatory language as they emerged during real-time interactions. This method provided contextual insights into communicative practices in online gaming environments.

The fieldwork was conducted from 1 June to 1 September 2024, involving daily two-hour sessions between 22:00 and 24:00, time slots aligned with prior findings on player activity patterns (Öztekin & Öztekin, 2020; Meriç et al., 2021). Over 12 weeks, the researcher completed 540 matches and logged 8,892 minutes of gameplay across three competitive tiers: Epic, Legend, and Mythic. Data were collected via in-game text, voice, and avatar-based communication. A detailed research diary documented each session. Covert observation was used (Dixon et al., 2016), with strict anonymization through gamertags to ensure ethical compliance. Moonton's privacy policy affirms that all in-game actions are public, legitimizing unobtrusive data collection.

Data Analysis

The collected data were analyzed using content analysis, a methodological approach that facilitates the systematic, objective, and quantitative examination of communication content (Çakıcı, 2025, p. 141). This method was selected because it can generate valid and replicable inferences by categorizing textual and symbolic data within a structured analytical framework (Demirel et al., 2025, p. 148). Its systematic nature involves selecting content based on predefined criteria and applying rigorous sampling protocols. Objectivity is achieved by minimizing researcher bias, allowing consistency in results across different coders. The quantitative dimension enables the precise measurement and interpretation of patterns within the dataset, enhancing the findings' reliability and validity (Meriç, 2025, pp. 85–86).

A key requirement of content analysis is the development of coding categories that are both mutually exclusive and collectively exhaustive (Meriç, 2025; Çakıcı & Aslıbay, 2025). In this study, the coding framework was derived from a comprehensive review of the relevant literature and applied to 267 instances of hate speech identified through participant observation. These instances were systematically examined across eight analytical dimensions: (1) types of hate speech, (2) distribution across competitive ranks (Epic, Legend, Mythic), (3) targeted groups, (4) forms of expression, (5) prevalence in solo versus group gameplay, (6) intensity of hate speech, (7) player reactions to hate speech, and (8) player responses to identity-based avatars.

In the first phase, the 267 instances of hate speech were classified according to established typologies in the literature. Drawing on the work of Chatty and Alathur (2018), Tuğrul Çomu and Binark (2013), and Castaño-Pulgarín et al. (2021), seven principal types of hate speech were identified: religious, gender-based, political, racial/ethnic, and hate speech targeting individuals with disabilities or severe illnesses. This classification allowed for a comprehensive understanding of the forms of hate speech in the context of digital gaming.

In the second phase, the study examined the relationship between competitive ranking and the frequency of hate speech. To ensure a robust and representative dataset, 180 matches were observed in the Epic, Legend, and Mythic ranks. This comparative approach assessed whether the frequency and nature of hate speech varied across different levels of competitive play, thus providing insights into the behavioral dynamics associated with skill-based progression.

The third phase focused on identifying the specific target groups of hate speech. Seventeen distinct categories were recorded, including women, men, Arabs, Iranians, Kurds, Afghans, refugees, Syrians, Israelis, Turks, Roma individuals, children, Muslims, atheists, members of the Justice and Development Party (AKP), LGBTQ+ individuals, and persons with disabilities. Each instance was coded based on the targeted demographic to reveal the sociocultural contexts and discriminatory patterns present within the game.

The fourth phase examined the relationship between gameplay mode and the occurrence of hate speech. Matches were categorized into solo games, randomly assigned to teams, and group games, where players entered with pre-formed teams. A total of 270 games were observed in each mode, allowing for the evaluation of how interpersonal familiarity and social cohesion among team members influence the frequency and intensity of hate speech.

The fifth phase involved analyzing the communicative channels through which hate speech was expressed. Instances were coded according to three primary modes of expression: (1) usernames, (2) profile photos, and (3) in-game communication, including text and voice chat. Usernames were examined for implicit or explicit offensive content, profile images were analyzed for visual markers of hate, and chat interactions were assessed for verbal abuse, slurs, and discriminatory language. This multimodal analysis provided a nuanced understanding of how hate speech is articulated and disseminated within the game.

In the sixth phase, the intensity of hate speech was assessed using the Hate Speech Intensity Scale developed by Bahador et al. (2019), which classifies hate speech across six escalating levels: Disagreement, Negative Actions, Negative Character, Dehumanization/Demonization, Violence, and Death. Each instance was evaluated and coded according to this scale to determine its severity and potential impact on the gaming environment.

Figure 1. The intensity of online hate speech

Color	Title	Description	Examples
	6. Death	Rhetoric includes literal killing by group. Responses include the literal death/elimination of a group.	Killed, annihilate, destroy
	5. Violence	Rhetoric includes infliction of physical harm or metaphoric/ aspirational physical harm or death. Responses include calls for literal violence or metaphoric/aspirational physical harm or death.	Punched, raped, starved, torturing, mugging
	4. Demonizing and Dehumanizing	Rhetoric includes subhuman and superhuman characteristics. There are no responses for #4.	Rat, monkey, Nazi, demon, cancer, monster
	3. Negative Character	Rhetoric includes nonviolent characterizations and insults. There are no responses for #3.	Stupid, thief, aggressor, fake, crazy
	2. Negative Actions	Rhetoric includes negative nonviolent actions associated with the group. Responses include nonviolent actions including metaphors.	Threatened, stole, outrageous act, poor treatment, alienate
	1. Disagreement	Rhetoric includes disagreeing at the idea/belief level. Responses include challenging claims, ideas, beliefs, or trying to change their view.	False, incorrect, wrong, challenge, persuade, change minds

The seventh phase analyzed player responses to hate speech. Reactions were categorized as positive (supportive of hate speech), negative (oppositional or critical), neutral (non-committal or unrelated), or no reaction (complete absence of response).

This coding provided insight into the social reception of hate speech and the extent to which it is normalized, contested, or ignored within the in-game community.

The eighth and final analytical dimension involved an identity-based avatar analysis to assess player responses to different identity representations. Over 24 days, 144 matches were observed in each competitive tier. Based on the most frequently targeted identities, custom avatars were designed to reflect specific social markers. In the Epic rank, gender-based hate speech was most prevalent (39 instances), with women comprising 38 of those cases. A female avatar named "Gamze," a common Turkish name was created using feminine indicators and the Turkish flag to elicit player reactions. In the Legend tier, racial hate speech predominated (43 instances), with Arabs as the most targeted group (14 cases). An avatar named "Arap King" was created, incorporating the Saudi Arabian flag and a gender-neutral image. In the Mythic tier, racist hate speech again dominated (46 instances), with Kurds as the primary target (11 cases). An avatar named "Kurdish Tiger" was developed using Kurdish identity markers and the Turkish flag to explore nationalistic responses.

The category definitions and coding schema were informed by the literature and reviewed in consultation with a scholar specializing in communication studies to ensure the validity of the research. Intercoder reliability was tested through the independent coding of a random subsample of 20 hate speech instances by the researcher and a second coder. A 90% agreement rate was achieved, with discrepancies resolved through discussion to refine the coding framework. Given that an intercoder agreement rate of 80% or higher is considered acceptable in content analysis (Miles & Huberman, 1994; Patton, 2002; Gheyle & Jacobs, 2017), the reliability of the study was deemed satisfactory.

Limitations

This study has several limitations. It focuses on Mobile Legends: Bang Bang within the Turkish gaming context, limiting the generalizability of findings to other games or cultures. While inter-coder reliability was ensured during analysis, data collection was conducted by a single researcher, which may have introduced subjective bias despite systematic procedures. Additionally, although the study included extensive observation over three months, it may not reflect long-term changes in hate speech, which can evolve with shifting game dynamics and sociopolitical contexts.

FINDINGS & DISCUSSION

Table 1 analyzes 267 instances of hate speech identified within the Mobile Legends: Bang Bang (MLBB) gaming environment, categorizing these cases according to the most commonly observed types of discriminatory discourse. The results indicate that hate speech in the game is predominantly concentrated around specific themes. Racial hate speech emerged as the most prevalent, comprising 118 instances (44.2% of the total), followed by gender-based hate speech, which accounted for 76 cases (28.5%), reflecting a high level of discrimination based on gender identity during gameplay. Hate speech targeting individuals with disabilities or severe health conditions was identified in 33 cases (12.4%), pointing to the stigmatization of physical and mental health issues. Homophobic hate speech appeared in 27 instances (10.1%), suggesting a considerable presence of discriminatory attitudes toward sexual orientation. By contrast, religious hate speech (8 cases, 3.0%) and political hate speech (3 cases, 1.1%) were less frequently observed. Age-based hate speech was the least common, with only 2 instances recorded (0.7%). Overall, the findings demonstrate that hate speech in online gaming settings tends to be systematically directed toward specific identity groups, with race, gender, and health-related factors being the primary targets.

Table 1. The types of hate speech in MLBB

The Types of Hate Speech	Number of Hate Speech
Gender-Based Hate Speech	76
Racist Hate Speech	118
Disability or Severe Disease Hate Speech	33
Political Hate Speech	3
Homophobic Hate Speech	27
Religious Hate Speech	8
Age-Based Hate Speech	2
Total	267

Table 2 reveals that hate speech incidents in Mobile Legends: Bang Bang (MLBB) increase with competitive rank: 30.0% in Epic, 32.6% in Legend, and 37.5% in Mythic League. Racial hate speech was most frequent overall, especially in the Legend tier (58.6%). Gender-based hate speech peaked in the Epic League (28.5%) but declined in higher ranks, suggesting greater gendered hostility at lower levels. In contrast, hate speech targeting disabilities rose with rank, reaching 19.0% in Mythic. Homophobic hate speech remained steady in lower tiers but increased notably in Mythic (14.0%). Religious hate speech was generally rare, peaking modestly in Legend (5.7%), while political hate speech appeared only in Mythic (3.0%). Age-based hate speech was observed solely in Epic (0.7%), indicating it primarily affects lower-ranked or newer players.

Table 2. The relationship between hate speech and ranks in MLBB

The Type of Hate Speech	Number of Hate Speech and Ranks			
	Epic	Legend	Mythic	Total
Gender-Based Hate Speech	46	13	17	76
Racist Hate Speech	21	51	46	118
Disability or Severe Disease Hate Speech	3	11	19	33
Political Hate Speech	0	0	3	3
Homophobic Hate Speech	6	7	14	27
Religious Hate Speech	2	5	1	8
Age-Based Hate Speech	2	0	0	2
Total	80	87	100	267

Table 3. The targets of hate speech in MLBB

The Targets of Hate Speech	Number of Hate Speech
Women	75
Men	1
Arabs	31
Iranians	15
Kurds	37
Afghans	2
Refugees	7
Syrians	12
Israelis	2
Turks	12
Gypsies	1
Children	2
Islam	6
Atheists	1
AKP members	3

continued on following page

Table 3. Continued

The Targets of Hate Speech	Number of Hate Speech
LGBTQ+ members	27
Disabled individuals	33
Total	267

Table 3 details 267 hate speech incidents in Mobile Legends: Bang Bang (MLBB), showing that women were the most frequently targeted group, with 75 cases (28.1%). These involved sexist remarks like "Woman chaining," "Sister jumping," and "She is just a girl, she does not know," reflecting gender-based marginalization and reinforcing toxic masculinity in the game. In contrast, only one case (0.4%) targeted men, with the insult "Do men play Nana?", mocking the use of a feminized character. Ethnic and national identities were also common targets. Kurds experienced 37 cases (13.9%) with statements such as "Kurds do not have the right to speak" and "You are a PKK member, Kurd." Arabs were targeted in 31 cases (11.6%), including "Go back to your country" and "We will lose if there are Arabs on the team." Iranians (15 cases, 5.6%) faced insults like "Iranian dogs" and "If there is an Iranian on the team, I am throwing the match." Syrians (12 cases, 4.5%) were told "There are Syrians everywhere" and "Go back to your war-torn country." Even Turks (12 cases, 4.5%) faced internalized hate through remarks such as "Dog Turks" and "Turks are donkeys." Refugees (7 cases, 2.6%) and Afghans (2 cases, 0.7%) were targeted with phrases like "The last refugee hunter" and "I do not want refugees in my country." Religious-based hate speech, though less common, included six cases (2.2%) targeting Islam, with expressions like "Pigs love to eat Allah" and "Shut up for your Allah and your prophet." One case (0.4%) involved anti-atheist speech: "atheist enemy." LGBTQ+ individuals were targeted in 27 cases (10.1%), with homophobic and transphobic remarks such as "Top, faggot," "Gays hang yourself," and "Do not play like a faggot." These expressions reflect exclusion and discrimination based on sexual orientation and gender identity. Players with disabilities faced 33 cases (12.4%) of hate speech, including "Are you autistic, son?" and "People with autism should be burned with petrol," indicating normalized ableism and dehumanization. Finally, political hate speech appeared in three cases (1.1%), targeting AKP supporters with phrases like "The first one to die is from AKP" and "There is no gang for AKP members," illustrating how political identity can become a basis for hostility in competitive settings.

Table 4 shows that hate speech in Mobile Legends: Bang Bang (MLBB) is significantly more common in solo matches (78.7%) than in group matches (21.3%) across all competitive tiers. In the Epic League, 72.5% of incidents occurred in solo games; this rate increased to 79.3% in Legend and 83.0% in Mythic. The data suggest that solo play is consistently linked to higher levels of hate speech, with its prevalence rising alongside competitive rank, indicating that individual gameplay may intensify verbal hostility, especially at higher levels.

Table 4. Types of playing and hate speech

Different Types of Playing	Epic	Legend	Mythic	Total
Solo Playing	58	69	83	210
Group Playing	22	18	17	57
Total	80	87	100	267

Table 5. Forms of hate speech in MLBB

Forms of Hate Speech	Epic	Legend	Mythic	Total
Username	20	10	12	42
Profile Photo	1	0	0	1
Text and Voice Chat	59	77	88	224
Total	80	87	100	267

Table 5 shows that most hate speech in Mobile Legends: Bang Bang (83.9%) occurs through in-game text and voice chat, with usage increasing at higher ranks: 73.8% in Epic, 88.5% in Legend, and 88.0% in Mythic. Hate speech via usernames made up 15.7% of cases, more common in the Epic League (33.9%) but declining in higher tiers. Only one instance (0.4%) involved a profile photo, observed solely in the Epic League. These findings highlight that real-time communication is the primary channel for hate speech, while identity markers like usernames are more frequently misused in lower leagues.

Table 6. The intensity of hate speech in MLBB

Intensity of Hate Speech	Epic	Legend	Mythic	Total
Disagreement	0	0	0	0
Negative Actions	18	19	20	57
Negative Character	36	27	44	107
Demonizing and Dehumanizing	23	32	28	83
Violence	3	8	3	14

continued on following page

Table 6. Continued

Intensity of Hate Speech	Epic	Legend	Mythic	Total
Death	0	1	5	6
Total	80	87	100	267

Table 6 categorizes hate speech incidents in Mobile Legends: Bang Bang (MLBB) by intensity and severity level, revealing "negative characterization" as the most frequent form (107 cases), with 36 in Epic, 27 in Legend, and 44 in Mythic. This includes direct insults like "Cancer faggot," "F**k your mother," and "These actresses are all such imbeciles." The second most common category, "dehumanization and demonization" (83 cases), involves comparing targets to animals or non-humans, as in "dog Turks," "pigs love to eat Allah," and "Iranian dogs." "Negative actions" followed with 57 instances, where players blamed groups for losses, using remarks like "We always lose because of those Kurds" and "What can you expect from a team with Arabs?" "Incitement to violence" included 14 cases, such as "refugee beater" and "last refugee hunter." The most extreme form, "death summoning," appeared in six cases, all in higher leagues, with explicit threats like "Kurdish animists should be burned" and "Autists should be burned with petrol." These findings demonstrate how hate speech in competitive gaming escalates in intensity and severity across league tiers.

Table 7. The reactions to hate speech in MLBB

The Reactions to Hate Speech	Epic	Legend	Mythic	Total
Positive	16	10	2	28
Negative	0	0	0	0
Nötr	7	11	9	27
No reaction	57	66	89	212
Total	80	87	100	267

Table 7 demonstrates that player reactions to hate speech in Mobile Legends: Bang Bang (MLBB) are primarily passive. The highest response category across all league levels is "no reaction," with 57 cases (71.3%) in the Epic League, 66 cases (75.9%) in the Legend League, and 89 cases (89.0%) in the Mythic League. In total, 212 out of 267 hate speech incidents (79.4%) received no response, indicating that players largely ignore hate speech.

Positive responses, those that support or agree with the hate speech, were observed in 16 cases (20.0%) in the Epic League, 10 cases (11.5%) in the Legend League, and only 2 cases (2.0%) in the Mythic League. In total, 28 cases (10.5%) received a positive reaction, showing that the tendency to respond with similar hateful language decreases at higher league levels.

No negative responses were recorded in any league (0.0%), meaning no players directly criticized or rejected the hate speech. Neutral reactions, neither supporting nor opposing hate speech, were found in 7 cases (8.8%) in Epic, 11 cases (12.6%) in Legend, and 9 cases (9.0%) in Mythic, totaling 27 cases (10.1%).

The highest rate of no reaction to hate speech points out that experiencing hate speech online gameplay often leads to "desensitization". Gamers started to perceive hate speech as an unavoidable element of the gaming experience. This reflects a broader pattern of normalization, consistent with studies on the habituation effect in digital spaces, where continuous exposure to hate speech diminishes emotional responses and fosters acceptance of aggressive discourse as a normative behavior (Ortiz, 2019; Costa et al., 2023; Wells et al., 2025).

Table 8. Reactions to different identities in MLBB

Playing with Different Identities in MLBB		
Rank	Number of Games with Women Avatar	Number of Hate Speech
Epic	36	7
	Number of Games with Arabic Avatar	Number of Hate Speech
Legend	36	8
	Number of Games with Kurdish Avatar	Number of Hate Speech
Mythic	36	8

Table 8 examines hate speech in Mobile Legends: Bang Bang (MLBB) during matches featuring avatars representing female, Arab, and Kurdish identities across 36 games. In the Epic League, seven instances (19.4%) targeted female avatars, often with sexist remarks like "Those girls should not play the game! I hate girls who play Angela" and "She is a fucking girl! This will happen if we let the girl get a mid-show," reflecting gender-based exclusion and performance bias. In the Legend League, Arab identities were targeted in eight cases (22.2%), with hostile comments such as "Fucking Arab," "I am going to make my name Arap catcher," and "I wish no Arabs would play the game," revealing strong ethnic animosity. Similarly, in the Mythic League, eight incidents (22.2%) involved Kurdish avatars, with discriminatory remarks like "Kurd, what do you expect?" and "Stupid Kurd," indicating persistent ethnic stereotyping and scapegoating. These findings highlight the intersection of identity and targeted hate speech across all competitive levels.

FUTURE RESEARCH DIRECTIONS

Future research could build on these insights by expanding to other gaming genres and platforms to assess whether similar patterns persist. Longitudinal studies would also be beneficial in exploring how hate speech evolves over time and in response to moderation policies. Additionally, incorporating players' narratives through interviews or surveys could offer a deeper understanding of the emotional and psychological consequences of encountering hate speech in digital games.

CONCLUSION

Multiplayer online games have developed into immersive social ecosystems where players engage in real-time collaboration, competition, and identity performance. While these digital environments offer avenues for interaction and entertainment, they also create conditions that can encourage toxic behavior. The anonymity, fast-paced communication, and competitive pressures characteristic of such games often serve as catalysts for the emergence and normalization of hate speech. This study explored the prevalence and dynamics of hate speech within Mobile Legends: Bang Bang using digital ethnography as its methodological framework. Data were collected through participant observation and analyzed using content analysis. Hate speech was examined through eight analytical lenses: types of hate speech, distribution across competitive ranks (Epic, Legend, Mythic), targeted groups, forms of hate speech, prevalence in solo versus group gameplay, intensity of hate speech, player reactions to hate speech, and player responses to identity-based avatars. Over the course of 540 matches, 267 instances of hate speech were recorded and analyzed.

The findings indicate that hate speech in MLBB is not an isolated or incidental occurrence; rather, it is deeply embedded in the game's social fabric. The most frequent targets were women, ethnic minorities, especially Kurds and Arabs, LGBTQ+ players, and individuals with disabilities. Racial and gender-based hate speech emerged as dominant patterns. A clear increase in both frequency and severity of hate speech was observed in higher-ranked competitive environments, suggesting that intensified competition may amplify discriminatory tendencies. The severity of hate speech extends beyond mere verbal aggression, many instances involved dehumanizing language, incitement to violence, and in extreme cases, death threats. The use of expressions such as "Kurdish animists should be burned" or "Autists should be burned with petrol" underscores a disturbing level of verbal cruelty that transcends typical competitive trash talk and reflects deeply rooted social hostilities.

The most common medium for expressing hate speech was in-game text and voice chat, while other channels such as usernames and profile images were used less frequently. Solo matches yielded a significantly higher volume of hate speech compared to group games, indicating that weaker social ties and greater anonymity may facilitate hostile expression. Importantly, the vast majority of players either ignored the hate speech or responded passively, with no instances of direct opposition. This silence reflects a broader culture of normalization, where discriminatory language is treated as an ordinary aspect of gameplay rather than a behavior to be challenged. Moreover, avatar-based analysis revealed that players using identity markers associated with marginalized groups were more likely to be targeted, highlighting the role of digital representation in shaping discriminatory behavior. These findings suggest that digital play spaces often mirror and reproduce the structural biases of the offline world.

To address hate speech in digital games, developers can adopt a multifaceted approach that combines technology, transparency, and community engagement. Machine learning tools provide effective real-time moderation, but players often find ways to bypass these systems using abbreviations or coded language. Anonymity further enables such behavior, making detection more difficult. Therefore, while technology is essential, it must be supported by clear communication of anti-toxicity policies, player involvement in shaping community standards, and adaptive strategies that evolve with player behavior (Cruz et al., 2024; Wijkstra et al., 2024).

In conclusion, this study illustrates that hate speech in multiplayer games is not simply an outgrowth of competitive frustration, but a reflection of broader societal prejudices intensified by digital affordances. Addressing this issue requires not only content moderation but also culturally informed strategies that promote inclusion, empathy, and accountability in online gaming communities.

REFERENCES

Androutsopoulos, J. (2008). Potentials and limitations of discourse-centred online ethnography. *Language@Internet,*5(8).

Aydınlı, S. (2021). Factsheet on the national regulatory and self-regulatory framework against hate speech and disinformation. *South East European Network for Professionalization of Media* (EENPM), Peace Institute, Bianet.

Bahador, B., Kerchner, D., Bacon, L., & Menas, A. (2019). *Monitoring hate speech in the US media*. Media and Peacebuilding Project, George Washington University.

Beasley, B., & Standley, T. C. (2002). Shirts vs. skins: Clothing as an indicator of gender role stereotyping in video games. *Mass Communication & Society*, *5*(3), 279–293. DOI: 10.1207/S15327825MCS0503_3

Beuving, J., & de Vries, G. C. (2015). *Doing qualitative research: The craft of naturalistic inquiry*. Amsterdam University Press.

Binark, M., & Çomu, T. (2013). Yeni medya ortamlarında nefret söylemi. In Çınar, M. (Ed.), *Medya ve nefret söylemi: Kavramlar, mecralar, tartışmalar* (pp. 199–216). Hrant Dink Vakfı Yayınları.

Black, M. (2016). Cyber ethnography: A critical tool for the Department of Defense? *Comparative Strategy*, *35*(2), 103–113. DOI: 10.1080/01495933.2016.1176456

Blodgett, B. M., & Salter, A. (2014). #1ReasonWhy: Game communities and the invisible woman.

Boyle, K. (2001). Hate speech, *The United States versus the rest of the world. Maine Law Review*, *53*, 487.

Bragança, L., Mota, R., & Fantini, E. (2016). Twine game narrative and discussion about LGBTQ representation. *In Proceedings of SBGames* (pp. 937–946).

Brenner-Levoy, J. (2023). Virtually masculine: Queer men's experiences with harassment in online video games. *Sociology of Sport Journal*, *40*(4), 385–398. DOI: 10.1123/ssj.2022-0170

Burgess, M. C. R., Stermer, S. P., & Burgess, S. R. (2007). Sex, lies, and video games: The portrayal of male and female characters on video game covers. *Sex Roles*, *57*(5–6), 419–433. DOI: 10.1007/s11199-007-9250-0

Butt, M. A. (2019). "I never use headsets": Women, wariness, and hypervigilance for the inevitability of online harassment in gaming culture. *AoIR Selected Papers of Internet Research.*

Çakıcı, Z. (2024). Cyberstalking practices among youth in Türkiye: Motivational drivers, digital avenues, and perceptual paradigms. *Türkiye İletişim Araştırmaları Dergisi*, (46), 1–22. DOI: 10.17829/turcom.1488278

Çakıcı, Z. (2025). Tiktok as a political communication medium: An examination of the United Nations. *İletişim Kuram ve Araştırma Dergisi* (69), 136-156. DOI: 10.47998/ikad.1580671

Çakıcı, Z., & Aslıbay, E. (2025). The utilization of social media by far-right political parties: A study on Victory Party. In Vieira, A. T., Joaquim, A. F., & Duarte, A. (Eds.), *Digital populism and the use of neo-propaganda and fake news*. IGI Global., DOI: 10.4018/979-8-3693-9999-6.ch009

Castaño-Pulgarín, S. A., Suárez-Betancur, N., Vega, L. M. T., & López, H. M. H. (2021). Internet, social media and online hate speech: Systematic review. *Aggression and Violent Behavior, 58*, 101608. DOI: 10.1016/j.avb.2021.101608

Çayır, K. (2010). Ayrımcılığın sosyolojisi ve Türkiye toplumu. In Çavdar, A., & Yıldırım, A. B. (Eds.), *Nefret suçları ve nefret söylemi* (pp. 45–54). Uluslararası Hrant Dink Vakfı Yayınları.

Chee, F. M. (2015). Online games and digital ethnography. In Mason, R. M., & Peng, H. A. (Eds.), *International encyclopedia of digital communication and society* (pp. 1–6). John Wiley & Sons. DOI: 10.1002/9781118767771.wbiedcs086

Chetty, N., & Alathur, S. (2018). Hate speech review in the context of online social networks. *Aggression and Violent Behavior, 40*, 108–118. DOI: 10.1016/j.avb.2018.05.003

Clement, J. (2025). *Number of video game users worldwide from 2019 to 2029.* Statista.

Cohen-Almagor, R. (2011). Fighting hate and bigotry on the Internet. *Policy and Internet, 3*(3), 1–26. DOI: 10.2202/1944-2866.1059

Condis, M. (2021). Playing at racism: White supremacist recruitment in online video game culture. In Nilsen, S. D., & Turner, S. E. (Eds.), *White supremacy and the American media* (pp. 246–274). Routledge. DOI: 10.4324/9781003215172-17

Conn, M. (2015). Gaming's untapped queer potential as art. *QED: A Journal in GLBTQ Worldmaking*, 2(2), 1–5.

Consalvo, M. (2008). Crunched by passion: Women game developers and workplace challenges. In Yasmin, B., Kafai, C. H., Denner, J., & Sun, J. Y. (Eds.), *Beyond Barbie and Mortal Kombat: New perspectives on gender and gaming* (pp. 177–193). MIT Press. DOI: 10.7551/mitpress/7477.003.0017

Costa, S., da Silva, B. M., & Tavares, M. (2023). Online hate speech in video games communities: A counter project. In Ullman, S., & Tomalin, M. (Eds.), *Counterspeech: Multidisciplinary perspectives on countering dangerous speech* (pp. 123–146). Taylor & Francis. DOI: 10.4324/9781003377078-9

Costa, S., Tavares, M., da Silva, B. M., Isca, B., & Cerol, F. (2020). Hate speech in video games and online gaming communities — *State of the art. Revista Comunicando, 9*(1), 261–278.

Creswell, J. W., & Poth, C. N. (2018). *Qualitative inquiry and research design: Choosing among five approaches* (4th ed.). Sage Publications.

Delgado, R. (1982). Words that wound: A tort action for racial insults, epithets, and name-calling. *Harvard Civil Rights-Civil Liberties Law Review, 17*, 133–181.

Demirel, S., Çakıcı, Z., & Bulur, N. (2025). Exploring reflections of the 2023 Kahramanmaraş earthquake on X: A computational study on Türkiye and Syria. *Akademik İncelemeler Dergisi, 20*(1), 143–171. DOI: 10.17550/akademikincelemeler.1593038

Dietz, T. L. (1998). An examination of violence and gender role portrayals in video games: Implications for gender socialization and aggressive behavior. *Sex Roles, 38*(5–6), 425–442. DOI: 10.1023/A:1018709905920

Dill, K., Gentile, D., Richter, W., & Dill, J. (2005). Violence, sex, race and age in popular videogames. In Cole, E., & Daniel, J. (Eds.), *Featuring females: Feminist analyses of media* (pp. 115–130). American Psychological Association. DOI: 10.1037/11213-008

Dixon, J. C., Singleton, R. A.Jr, & Straits, B. C. (2016). *The process of social research.* Oxford University Press.

Downs, E., & Smith, S. L. (2010). Keeping abreast of hypersexuality: A video game character content analysis. *Sex Roles, 62*(11–12), 721–733. DOI: 10.1007/s11199-009-9637-1

European Commission Against Racism and Intolerance. (2015). ECRI General Policy Recommendation No. 15 on combating hate speech.

Everett, A., & Watkins, S. C. (2008). The power of play: The portrayal and performance of race in video games. In Tekinbaş, K. S. (Ed.), *The ecology of games: Connecting youth, games, and learning* (pp. 141–164). MIT Press.

Facebook. (2025). Hate speech. Meta Transparency Center. https://transparency.meta.com/reports/community-standards-enforcement/hate-speech/instagram/

Fox, J., & Tang, W. Y. (2016). Women's experiences with general and sexual harassment in online video games: Rumination, organizational responsiveness, withdrawal, and coping strategies. *New Media & Society*, *19*(8), 1290–1307. DOI: 10.1177/1461444816635778

Gaming Turkey. (2022). Turkey game market report 2022. https://www.turkiyeoyunsektoruraporu.com/en/turkey-game-market-report-2022/

Garcia, A. C., Standlee, A. I., Bechoff, J., & Cui, Y. (2009). Ethnographic approaches to the internet and computer-mediated communication. *Journal of Contemporary Ethnography*, *38*(1), 52–84. DOI: 10.1177/0891241607310839

Gelber, K., & McNamara, L. (2016). Evidencing the harms of hate speech. *Social Identities*, *22*(3), 324–341. DOI: 10.1080/13504630.2015.1128810

Gillin, L. E., & Signorella, M. L. (2023). Attitudes toward sexual orientation and gender identity in online multiplayer gaming spaces. *Psychological Reports*. PMID: 36688329

Glaubke, C. R., Miller, P., Parker, M. A., & Espejo, E. (2001). *Fair play? Violence, gender and race in video games*. Children Now.

Gray, K. L. (2011). Intersecting oppressions and online communities: Examining the experiences of women of color in Xbox Live. *Information Communication and Society*, *15*(3), 411–428. DOI: 10.1080/1369118X.2011.642401

Gray, K. L. (2012). Deviant bodies, stigmatized identities, and racist acts: Examining the experiences of African-American gamers in Xbox Live. *New Review of Hypermedia and Multimedia*, *18*(4), 261–276. DOI: 10.1080/13614568.2012.746740

Gray, K. L., Voorhees, G., & Vossen, E. (2018). *Feminism in play*. Palgrave Macmillan. DOI: 10.1007/978-3-319-90539-6

Han, C., Seering, J., Kumar, D., Hancock, J. T., & Durumeric, Z. (2023). Hate raids on Twitch: Echoes of the past, new modalities, and implications for platform governance. *Proceedings of the ACM on Human-Computer Interaction*, 7(CSCW1), 1–28. DOI: 10.1145/3579609

Hine, C. (2000). *Virtual ethnography*. Sage Publications. DOI: 10.4135/9780857020277

Howard, P. N. (2002). Network ethnography and the hypermedia organization: New media, new organizations, new methods. *New Media & Society*, *4*(4), 550–574. DOI: 10.1177/146144402321466813

Instagram. (2025). Hate speech. Meta Transparency Center. https://transparency.meta.com/reports/community-standards-enforcement/hate-speech/instagram/

Jansz, J., & Martis, R. G. (2007). The Lara phenomenon: Powerful female characters in video games. *Sex Roles*, *56*(3–4), 141–148. DOI: 10.1007/s11199-006-9158-0

Jensen, K. B. (2012). Media reception. In Jensen, K. B. (Ed.), *The handbook of media and communication research* (pp. 171–185). Routledge.

Keum, B. T., & Hearns, M. (2022). Online gaming and racism: Impact on psychological distress among Black, Asian, and Latinx emerging adults. *Games and Culture*, *17*(3), 445–460. DOI: 10.1177/15554120211039082

Koehler, D., Fiebig, V., & Jugl, I. (2023). From gaming to hating: Extreme-right ideological indoctrination and mobilization for violence of children on online gaming platforms. *Political Psychology*, *44*(2), 419–434. DOI: 10.1111/pops.12855

Kozinets, R. V. (2010). *Netnography: Doing ethnographic research online*. Sage Publications.

Kumar, S., Kwan, E., Weststar, J., & Coppins, T. (2021). *Developer Satisfaction Survey 2021 Diversity in the Game Industry Report*. International Game Developers Association.

Leonard, D. J. (2006). Not a hater, just keepin' it real: The importance of race- and gender-based game studies. *Games and Culture*, *1*(1), 83–88. DOI: 10.1177/1555412005281910

Lynch, T., Tompkins, J. E., van Driel, I. I., & Fritz, N. (2016). Sexy, strong, and secondary: A content analysis of female characters in video games across 31 years. *Journal of Communication*, *66*(4), 564–584. DOI: 10.1111/jcom.12237

Martins, N., Williams, D. C., Harrison, K., & Ratan, R. A. (2009). A content analysis of female body imagery in video games. *Sex Roles*, *61*(11–12), 824–836. DOI: 10.1007/s11199-009-9682-9

Marwick, A. E., & Miller, R. (2014). Online harassment, defamation, and hateful speech: A primer of the legal landscape. *Fordham Center on Law and Information Policy Report.*

Massey, C. R. (1992). Hate speech, cultural diversity, and the foundational paradigms of free expression. *UCLA Law Review. University of California, Los Angeles. School of Law*, *40*, 103–177.

Matsuda, M. J. (1989). Pragmatism modified and the false consciousness problem. *Southern California Law Review*, *63*, 1763–1802.

McLean, L., & Griffiths, M. D. (2013). The psychological effects of video games on young people. *Aloma: Revista de Psicologia. Ciències de l'Educació i de l'Esport Blanquerna*, *31*(1), 119–133.

Meisner, C. (2023). Networked responses to networked harassment? Creators' coordinated management of "hate raids" on Twitch. *Social Media + Society*, *9*(2), 20563051231179696. DOI: 10.1177/20563051231179696

Meriç, E. (2025). Pandemi döneminde dijital sağlık iletişimi: T.C. Sağlık Bakanlığı COVID-19 kamu spotları üzerine stratejik bir inceleme. *Kronotop İletişim Dergisi*, *2*(1), 77–106.

Meriç, E., Başer, B., & Tandaçgüneş, N. (2021). Kuşaklararası mobil oyun oynama pratikleri üzerine nitel bir inceleme. In Uğurlu, Ö. A., & Kuş, Ö. A. (Eds.), *Oyunların dijital hali* (pp. 77–118). Urzeni Yayınevi.

Miller, M. K., & Summers, A. (2007). Gender differences in video game characters' roles, appearances, and attire as portrayed in video game magazines. *Sex Roles*, *57*(9–10), 733–742. DOI: 10.1007/s11199-007-9307-0

Mortensen, T. E. (2018). Anger, fear, and games: The long event of #GamerGate. *Games and Culture*, *13*(8), 787–806. DOI: 10.1177/1555412016640408

Mou, Y., & Peng, W. (2009). Gender and racial stereotypes in popular video games. In Ferdig, R. E. (Ed.), *Handbook of research on effective electronic gaming in education* (pp. 922–937). IGI Global. DOI: 10.4018/978-1-59904-808-6.ch053

Nakamura, L. (2019). Gender and race online. In Graham, M., & Dutton, W. H. (Eds.), *Society and the internet: How networks of information and communication are changing our lives* (pp. 126–146). Oxford University Press. DOI: 10.1093/oso/9780198843498.003.0008

Ong, A. K. S., Prasetyo, Y. T., Robas, K. P. E., Persada, S. F., Nadlifatin, R., Matillano, J. S. A., Macababbad, D. C. B., Pabustan, J. R., & Taningco, K. A. C. (2023). Determination of factors influencing the behavioral intention to play "Mobile Legends: Bang-Bang" during the COVID-19 pandemic: Integrating UTAUT2 and system usability scale for a sustainable e-sport business. *Sustainability (Basel)*, *15*(4), 3170. DOI: 10.3390/su15043170

Ortiz, S. M. (2019). “You can say I got desensitized to it”: How men of color cope with everyday racism in online gaming. *Sociological Perspectives*, *62*(4), 572–588. DOI: 10.1177/0731121419837588

Öztekin, H., & Öztekin, A. (2020). Dijital oyunlarda nefret söylemi ve ayrımcı dil: Agar.io örneği. *Turkish Studies -. Social Sciences*, *15*(1), 533–558.

Pankowski, R. (2007). *How to understand and confront hate speech* (Vol. 3). United for Intercultural Action.

Parekh, B. (2012). Is there a case for banning hate speech? *In The content and context of hate speech: Rethinking regulation and responses* (pp. 22–23). DOI: 10.1017/CBO9781139042871.006

Postill, J., & Pink, S. (2012). Social media ethnography: The digital researcher in a messy web. *Media International Australia, Incorporating Culture & Policy*, *145*(1), 123–134. DOI: 10.1177/1329878X1214500114

Powell, A., & Williams-Johnson, D. (2023). “You dumb cracker b*tch”: The legitimizing of white supremacy during a Twitch ban of HasanAbi. *New Media & Society*. Advance online publication.

Pulos, A. (2013). Confronting heteronormativity in online games: A critical discourse analysis of LGBTQ sexuality in World of Warcraft. *Games and Culture*, *8*(2), 77–97. DOI: 10.1177/1555412013478688

Ruvalcaba, O., Shulze, J., Kim, A., Berzenski, S. R., & Otten, M. P. (2018). Women’s experiences in eSports: Gendered differences in peer and spectator feedback during competitive video game play. *Journal of Sport and Social Issues*, *42*(4), 295–311. DOI: 10.1177/0193723518773287

Sade-Beck, L. (2004). Internet ethnography: Online and offline. *International Journal of Qualitative Methods*, *3*(2), 45–51. DOI: 10.1177/160940690400300204

Sellars, A. (2016). Defining hate speech. Berkman Klein Center Research Publication, No. 2016-20; Boston University School of Law, *Public Law Research Paper*, 16–48.

Shaw, A. (2012). Talking to gaymers: Questioning identity, community and media representation. *Westminster Papers in Communication and Culture*, *9*(1), 67–89.

Shepherd, T., Harvey, A., Jordan, T., Srauy, S., & Miltner, K. (2015). Histories of hating. *Social Media + Society*, *1*(2), 2056305115603997. Advance online publication. DOI: 10.1177/2056305115603997

Šisler, V. (2008). Digital Arabs: Representation in video games. *European Journal of Cultural Studies*, *11*(2), 203–220.

Stermer, S. P., & Burkley, M. (2015). SeX-Box: Exposure to sexist video games predicts benevolent sexism. *Psychology of Popular Media Culture*, *4*(1), 47–55. DOI: 10.1037/a0028397

TikTok. (2025). Countering hate speech and behavior. https://www.tiktok.com/safety/en/countering-hate

United Nations (2020). United Nations Strategy And Plan Of Action On Hate Speech.

Waldron, J. (2012). *The harm in hate speech*. Harvard University Press. DOI: 10.4159/harvard.9780674065086

Wallenius, M., Rimpelä, A., Punamäki, R. L., & Lintonen, T. (2009). Digital game playing motives among adolescents: Relations to parent–child communication, school performance, sleeping habits, and perceived health. *Journal of Applied Developmental Psychology*, *30*(4), 463–474. DOI: 10.1016/j.appdev.2008.12.021

Ward, K. D. (1997). Free speech and the development of liberal virtues: An examination of the controversies involving flag-burning and hate speech. *University of Miami Law Review*, *52*, 733–788.

Wells, G., Romhányi, Á., & Steinkuehler, C. (2025). Hate speech and hate-based harassment in online games. *Frontiers in Psychology*, *15*, 1422422. DOI: 10.3389/fpsyg.2024.1422422 PMID: 40046807

Wijkstra, M., Rogers, K., Mandryk, R. L., Veltkamp, R. C., & Frommel, J. (2024). How to tame a toxic player? A systematic literature review on intervention systems for toxic behaviors in online video games. Proceedings of the ACM on Human-Computer Interaction, 8(CHI PLAY), 1-32.

Williams, D. (2006). Virtual cultivation: Online worlds, offline perceptions. *Journal of Communication*, *56*(1), 69–87. DOI: 10.1111/j.1460-2466.2006.00004.x

Williams, D., Martins, N., Consalvo, M., & Ivory, J. D. (2009). The virtual census: Representations of gender, race and age in video games. *New Media & Society*, *11*(5), 815–834. DOI: 10.1177/1461444809105354

Wullach, T., Adler, A., & Minkov, E. (2021). Fight fire with fire: Fine-tuning hate detectors using large samples of generated hate speech. *arXiv,* 1–6.

Yao, M. Z., Mahood, C., & Linz, D. (2010). Sexual priming, gender stereotyping, and likelihood to sexually harass: Examining the cognitive effects of playing a sexually-explicit video game. *Sex Roles*, *62*(1–2), 77–88. DOI: 10.1007/s11199-009-9695-4 PMID: 20098511

YouTube. (2025). Hate speech & harassment policy. https://www.youtube.com/howyoutubeworks/our-commitments/standing-up-to-hate/

ADDITIONAL READINGS

Boellstorff, T., Nardi, B., Pearce, C., & Taylor, T. L. (2012). *Ethnography and virtual worlds: A handbook of method*. Princeton University Press. DOI: 10.2307/j.cttq9s20

Butler, J. (1997). *Excitable speech: A politics of the performative*. Routledge.

Citron, D. K. (2014). *Hate crimes in cyberspace*. Harvard University Press. DOI: 10.4159/harvard.9780674735613

Delgado, R., & Stefancic, J. (2012). *Critical race theory: An introduction* (2nd ed.). NYU Press.

Gillespie, T. (2018). *Custodians of the internet: Platforms, content moderation, and the hidden decisions that shape social media*. Yale University Press.

Gray, K. L. (2014). *Race, gender, and deviance in Xbox Live: Theoretical perspectives from the virtual margins*. Routledge. DOI: 10.4324/9781315721378

Kozinets, R. V. (2015). *Netnography: Redefined*. SAGE Publications.

Nakamura, L. (2009). Don't hate the player, hate the game: The racialization of labor in World of Warcraft. *Critical Studies in Media Communication*, *26*(2), 128–144. DOI: 10.1080/15295030902860252

Penny, L. (2014). *Cybersexism: Sex, gender and power on the internet*. Bloomsbury Publishing.

Shaw, A. (2015). Gaming at the edge: Sexuality and gender at the margins of gamer culture. University of Minnesota Press.

KEY TERMS AND DEFINITIONS

Digital Ethnography: Digital ethnography is a methodological approach that is specifically developed to examine the complex social structures and cultural practices mediated by digital technologies.

Digital Game: Digital games are games played on a computer, game system, television, or mobile device.

Hate Speech: Hate speech refers to any expression, symbol, or image intended to incite hatred against a group or an individual affiliated with that group based on protected characteristics such as race, ethnicity, national origin, religion, caste, sexual orientation, sex, gender, gender identity, age, serious illness, disability, or immigration status.

Multiplayer Online Battle Arena Game (MOBA): MOBA games are characterized by their highly interactive and competitive structure, which fosters intensive interpersonal engagement.

Chapter 7

Digital Games in Mobile Platforms and Archetypes:

A Qualitative Evaluation on Mobile Legends Bang Bang

Özgün Arda Kuş
https://orcid.org/0000-0002-1487-3772
Uskudar University, Turkey

Asena Irmak Yavuz
https://orcid.org/0009-0007-4562-8001
Independent Researcher, Turkey

ABSTRACT

Digital games experience growing demand and are available on multiple platforms such as PC, consoles, and smartphones. Smartphone-based games eliminate constraints of time and space, making games continuously accessible. This study focuses on Mobile Legends: Bang Bang, a MOBA (Multiplayer Online Battle Arena) game playable on Android and iOS devices. MOBA games involve 5v5 team battles where players select heroes with distinct roles, abilities, and backstories, aiming to destroy the opponent's main tower. The study employs descriptive qualitative analysis to examine in-game characters through the lens of archetypes, using predetermined thematic classifications to identify patterns and relationships within the data.

DOI: 10.4018/979-8-3373-6192-5.ch007

INTRODUCTION

We are currently living in a world order where the traces of digitalization permeate every aspect of life. The boundary between the physical and digital realms is becoming increasingly blurred, allowing individuals to fulfill their need for social interaction in various ways. This variation refers to the effort to establish a presence in the virtual space—a pursuit that can be either individual or collective. Regardless of its nature, whether individual or collective, this pursuit is a manifestation of personal preference.

Individuals can fulfill their socialization needs within virtual spaces according to their own choices. One such domain of social interaction in the virtual environment is digital games. Digital games serve as a medium that shortens the distance between reality and virtuality, offering individuals access to an entirely new world. Within this medium, individuals may choose either to socialize solely in the virtual domain or to carry these interactions into the real world. Digital games are not solely spaces for social interaction; they also constitute environments where the past and future converge, transcending the concept of time. Within a digital game, the player may experience a simulation of the past or engage with a future designed by the game's developer. Once again, the player's agency and preferences play a central role in shaping this experience. Engaging in a digital game also involves experiencing multiple emotions either simultaneously or at different points in time. These emotions are often accompanied by a positive mental state, primarily derived from the pleasure of gameplay. This positive affect plays a crucial role in maintaining a sense of flow within the game. The establishment of flow, in turn, enables the player to become detached from notions of time, space, and physical environment.

What is a Digital Game?

Digital games have emerged as a significant phenomenon in the lives of many individuals, driven by technological advancements and the growth of the digital game industry. Frasca (2001) defines digital games as entertainment software consumed by one or more players through computers, mobile devices, or consoles, built upon images and texts, and requiring specific technological hardware and software. With the development of the digital game industry, certain stereotypes—such as digital games being predominantly played by adolescent males or containing mostly violent content—have gradually begun to diminish. Today, digital games constitute a massive global industry, boasting billions of players and followers worldwide. This industry encompasses not only the names, producers, and developers of the games but also includes brand value, technology, design, narrative, visual and auditory diversity, gaming peripherals and devices, distribution, advertising and marketing networks, e-sports tournaments, trade fairs, gaming lounges, and numerous related commercial activities (Bülbül, 2022). One of the key reasons behind the digitalization of games and their appeal to billions of players worldwide is their ability to allow users to perform actions in virtual environments that are impossible in real life. Players can achieve reputation and status through their in-game characters—something they may find difficult or unattainable in reality. Additionally, the ability to play anytime and anywhere has made digital games especially attractive (Uzunoğlu, 2021).

Digital games, with their increasing cultural, economic, and sociological functions in our lives, also influence communication processes. Beyond being merely entertainment, digital games have found widespread application in various fields such as education, work, and even art.

Mobile Legends: Bang Bang (MLBB) as a MOBA Game Genre

The increasing availability and advancement of mobile devices have significantly contributed to the growing interest in digital games. Technologies that enable players to access and play games anytime and anywhere have driven the continuous development of the digital gaming market. With a player base that spans all age groups, digital games have shattered the long-standing stereotype that gaming is primarily for children. The diversity of game genres has enabled the industry to reach a much broader demographic, offering a wide range of options that satisfy varied user preferences. One of the most popular genres among players is MOBA, or Multiplayer Online Battle Arena, which is a subgenre of real-time strategy (RTS) games. Unlike traditional RTS games, MOBAs do not include gameplay mechanics such as unit production, base building, or survival elements. Instead, MOBA games typically revolve around two teams—usually consisting of five players each—where every player controls a single character (Zachrisson et al., 2023). Matches take place on a predefined battlefield, and players must collaborate to defend their base while attempting to destroy the opposing team's base. The first team to successfully eliminate the enemy base wins the game. The battlefield usually contains several key components: both teams' bases; three main lanes (top, middle, and bottom) that connect the bases; defensive structures (typically towers) positioned along these lanes; and minions—computer-controlled units that periodically spawn and travel along the lanes to assist players by attacking the enemy and defending their own team. The lanes may have different names depending on the specific game, but their function remains similar. Each team also has access to jungle areas located on their side of the map. These jungles contain neutral monsters that players can defeat to gain experience points and gold. Some monsters are stronger than others and, when defeated—either individually or as a team—provide greater rewards to the entire team. While some MOBA games adopt side-scrolling or third-person perspectives, the genre predominantly utilizes an isometric perspective, which allows players to oversee the battlefield. A mini-map is also included in the game interface, enabling real-time strategic awareness. Each hero or playable character in a MOBA game possesses unique abilities. As the match progresses, players can level up by gaining experience and enhance their hero's capabilities by purchasing in-game items using the gold they earn. Heroes are usually assigned to specific roles such as fighter, support, or tank, although these roles may vary depending on the game. In titles like Mobile Legends: Bang Bang (MLBB), a single hero can fulfill multiple roles depending on how they are played. Additionally, most MOBA games are set in a fictional universe, with each character having a unique background story that contributes to the game's lore. This narrative depth, combined with strategic gameplay and team-based mechanics, has helped make the MOBA genre one of the most engaging and widely played in the digital gaming world.

Among the most popular games in the MOBA (Multiplayer Online Battle Arena) genre is Mobile Legends: Bang Bang, commonly abbreviated as MLBB. The game was developed and released in 2016 by Shanghai Moonton Technology, a company operating under the name Moonton. MLBB features competitive gameplay between two teams of five players each. The primary objective is for each team to defend its own base while attempting to destroy the opposing team's base. As of April 2025, the game includes a total of 128 unique heroes, each offering distinct abilities and playstyles. The competitive structure of MLBB is organized into ten ranked tiers, which players progress through based on their in-game performance. These tiers, in ascending order, are: Warrior, Elite, Master, Grandmaster, Epic, Legend, Mythic, Glorious Mythic, Mythic Honor, and Mythical Immortal. In addition to its ranked mode, MLBB offers several other game modes designed to cater to a variety of player preferences. These include: Classic Mode, Ranked Mode, Magic Chess and Club Mode.

- Classic Mode in Mobile Legends: Bang Bang is a game mode commonly chosen by players for several practical reasons, including the desire to avoid ranked demotion, preserve hero win rates, test new heroes or equipment, and practice with their current roster of heroes. In this mode, players are not penalized for losing a match; they do not lose stars, ranking points, or alter the win rate statistics of the heroes they use. One of the key characteristics of Classic Mode is that hero selection is non-exclusive—meaning the same hero can be picked by players on opposing teams simultaneously (e.g., two players may select the same marksman hero). This provides more flexibility for experimentation and practice. Unlike Ranked Mode, Classic Mode does not require any eligibility points or prior progress to enter. For this reason, it serves as the initial entry point for new players, allowing them to accumulate experience points (EXP) and gradually progress through the game's internal leveling system. Upon leveling up, players gain access to additional game features and modes, including Ranked Mode. The battlefield map used in Classic Mode is identical to the one used in Ranked Mode, providing players with consistent spatial awareness and tactical familiarity as they transition between different game modes.

- In Mobile Legends: Bang Bang, players must have at least 90 activity points to participate in Ranked Mode. This mode represents the game's competitive framework and requires a higher level of strategy and coordination compared to Classic Mode. The battlefield in Ranked Mode is composed of several key areas: the EXP lane, the mid lane, the gold lane, and the jungle. In addition to these lanes, each team has its own base and defensive turrets placed along the lanes. The map also includes interactive environmental features such as bushes and walls, which players can use for ambushing or hiding. Within the jungle, there are neutral monsters—most notably the red and blue buffs, named after the color-coded effects they provide. The red buff grants enhanced attack effects, while the blue buff supports mana regeneration and cooldown reduction. Other jungle objectives include the Turtle, which spawns in the early game and provides team-wide rewards when slain, and the Lord, a powerful neutral boss that appears in place of the Turtle after the ninth minute. The team that defeats the Lord gains a significant advantage, as the Lord emerges from the team's base and automatically advances along one of the lanes to assist in sieging the enemy base. Eliminating jungle monsters provides players with experience points (EXP) and gold, which are essential for leveling up and acquiring in-game items. At the beginning of a match, each player selects one of five positions on the map, and the roles of the heroes—such as tank, support, mage, marksman, assassin, or fighter—are crucial in determining team composition and success. From the Epic rank and higher, teams participate in a hero banning phase, during which three to five heroes can be banned and are rendered unavailable for the match. Unlike in Classic Mode, where the same hero can be selected by players on both teams, Ranked Mode enforces unique hero selection—each hero may only be picked by one player per match. All heroes begin the match at level one, and no items (except the standard boots) can be purchased until the player accumulates gold. A hero's ultimate ability becomes available upon reaching level four, which requires a certain amount of EXP. The outcome of a Ranked match directly affects the player's standing. Players on the winning team earn one star, or two stars if their performance and activity points meet certain thresholds. The losing team's players typically lose one star, and the win rate statistics of the heroes used in the match are also adjusted accordingly. However, if a player has earned sufficient protection points, they may avoid losing a star. Accumulating five stars advances the player to the next rank, while losing five stars results in demotion to a lower tier.

- The Magic Chess mode was first introduced to Mobile Legends: Bang Bang in 2020 as a limited-time event. Due to its popularity, it was later permanently incorporated into the game as an alternative strategic gameplay mode. Unlike the traditional five-versus-five battle structure of the main game, Magic Chess is an auto-battler mode in which eight players compete individually on a chessboard-like battlefield. Each player is accompanied by a guiding unit known as a "Little Commander," which serves as their primary avatar and provides various passive abilities that influence gameplay strategy. In this mode, players purchase and position heroes on the board in a tactical arrangement before each automatic round of combat. Heroes are drawn randomly from a shared pool, and players must carefully manage their gold and unit synergy to build effective lineups. The ultimate objective is to strengthen both the chosen heroes and the Little Commander over time in order to outlast the other players. The last surviving player on the board is declared the winner. Magic Chess emphasizes strategy, resource management, and adaptability, offering a distinctly different experience from the core mechanics of the standard MOBA format. Its integration into the game has diversified MLBB's appeal, attracting players who enjoy slower-paced, tactical decision-making in a competitive environment.
- Club Mode in Mobile Legends: Bang Bang introduces a casual and experimental gameplay format, distinct from the game's ranked and standard modes. To enter a match in this mode, players must first select one of two randomly offered heroes presented in a pre-game interface. Each player is automatically granted one dice roll, which can be used to reshuffle the hero selection. Alternatively, players may spend ten diamonds to send the offered hero to a shared hero pool, making it available for other players to choose. A unique feature of Club Mode is that players can select heroes not only from their own options but also from those made available in the shared pool by other participants. Once the match begins, each selected hero starts at level four, allowing for the immediate use of their ultimate ability. Before leaving the base, players can purchase items for their hero; however, if they exit the base area before purchasing, they must wait until the hero dies and respawns at the base in order to buy equipment. The map used in Club Mode differs significantly from those used in other game modes. It consists of a single lane, with two bushes located at the center of the lane that can be used for ambushing or hiding. Additionally, the map contains two crabs, two turrets per team, and healing orbs that appear periodically in both corners of the map

after a certain amount of time has passed. Each team also has its own base and a bush positioned near the base for additional tactical options. Unlike Ranked Mode, matches played in Club Mode do not affect a player's ranking or the win rate statistics of the heroes used. As such, this mode is often favored for casual play, experimentation with different heroes or strategies, and stress-free matches without competitive consequences.
- Additionally, Mobile Legends: Bang Bang offers training and practice options for players who wish to learn the game mechanics or improve their individual skills. These modes allow users to play against AI-controlled opponents, commonly referred to as bots. Through these training environments, players can familiarize themselves with hero abilities, map layouts, item builds, and basic strategic principles in a low-pressure setting, making them especially beneficial for beginners or those testing new gameplay approaches.

As of April 2025, Mobile Legends: Bang Bang, one of the most popular mobile games worldwide, features a total of 128 playable heroes. Each hero possesses unique abilities and can fulfill various roles during gameplay. The game classifies heroes into six main roles: Fighter, Support, Mage, Marksman, Tank, and Assassin. While some heroes are capable of performing more than one role, each is typically designed with a primary role that defines their core function within a team composition.

The characteristics of these roles are as follows:

- Fighters are melee combatants known for their balanced offense and defense. Although they are less durable than Tanks, they are generally more resilient than other hero types. Fighters may not deal as much burst damage as Assassins, but their damage output increases steadily as the game progresses. Each Fighter has unique traits, such as distinct attack combos, mobility patterns, or damage types. They are most commonly positioned in the EXP lane, although this may vary depending on the hero.
- Supports play a vital role in sustaining their team during battles. These heroes are typically fragile and more susceptible to incoming damage compared to other roles. Depending on the specific hero, Supports may provide healing, shielding, or crowd control, and may even sacrifice themselves to protect allies. They are usually paired with the Marksman in the Gold Lane, occupying the "Roam" position. However, some Support heroes may accompany Mages in the Mid Lane or move around the map to assist teammates in need.
- Mages are magic-damage dealers that often hold critical strategic importance during combat. Positioned primarily in the Mid Lane, Mages typically lack durability but compensate with high ability damage, crowd control effects,

and poke potential. Their spells can disrupt enemy formations, initiate fights, or finish off low-health opponents.

- Marksmen are long-ranged heroes who inflict high damage, particularly in the later stages of the game. Often referred to as ADCs (Attack Damage Carries), they are effective at dealing sustained damage from a distance and are key contributors to tower destruction. Marksmen are generally placed in the Gold Lane and require protection during the early game due to their vulnerability. Despite their fragile nature early on, they become one of the most powerful roles in the late game as they gain experience and gold.
- Tanks are the most durable heroes in the game, acting as the front line in team fights. They initiate engagements and absorb the bulk of the enemy's damage, thereby protecting more fragile teammates such as Supports, Mages, and Marksmen. Tanks are typically located in the Roam position or the EXP Lane. While they have high health and strong defensive attributes, they usually have low damage output.
- Assassins, often played in the Jungle role, are agile and high-damage heroes specializing in quickly eliminating key targets. Instead of engaging head-on like Fighters or Tanks, Assassins rely on stealth, timing, and precision. They move through the jungle, killing neutral monsters to restore health and gain resources, while also looking for opportunities to ambush and eliminate enemy heroes. Due to their low durability and high-risk playstyle, Assassins are difficult to master and are highly dependent on proper positioning and decision-making. A mistimed or poorly executed attack can leave them vulnerable to quick elimination.

THE CONCEPT OF ARCHETYPE AND TYPES OF ARCHETYPES

The foundation of the concept of archetype comes from the French word archétype, which means first example, original, or model. The first use of the archetype concept in the field of psychology is attributed to Carl Gustav Jung. Jung, who devoted the last forty years of his life to developing the concept of archetypes, frequently referred to archetypes when defining the collective unconscious. When describing the unconscious, Jung emphasized two components. The first is the individual's internal world unique to themselves, and the second is the collective unconscious, which dates back to the first human and encompasses common symbols and codes, primitive in nature, and present in every individual at varying degrees and levels. Archetypes can be defined as parts of the collective unconscious that interact with the individual through deeply ingrained personality traits and guide human emotions, thoughts, and behaviors (Jung, 1954). Based on Jung's definition of archetypes, it can also be stated that archetypes influence the attitudes present in the individual. According to Jung, archetypes are elements that exist in the collective unconscious even before a person is born (Tsai, 2006).

Although Jung did not limit the number of archetypes, he primarily focused on four main archetypes. These archetypes are Persona, which reflects our identity within society; Shadow, associated with the unconscious and representing our dark side; Anima and Animus, the inner feminine and masculine reflections of the opposite sex, respectively; and Self, which is the synthesis of all archetypes and symbolizes physical and psychological wholeness (Jung, 2019).

The 12 archetypes used today were developed by Carol S. Pearson based on Jung's ideas. The influence of Joseph Campbell's Mythology Theory can also be seen in the formation of these 12 archetypes. The archetypes developed by Pearson are based on four fundamental themes: stability, independence, belonging, and change. Carol S. Pearson identifies and explains the 12 archetypes as follows (Pearson, 1991):

- The Innocent: Optimistic by nature, they have a dreamy and romantic disposition. They harbor overly positive feelings and thoughts toward the world and their surroundings. They constantly want to make others happy. Their fears include making mistakes and being punished by those around them. They are represented by purity and childlike innocence.
- The Orphan / Regular Person: Their purpose in life is to connect with others. They have a quiet temperament and lack grand ambitions. They live day-to-day with few worries or dreams about the future. They value the concept of family. Their greatest fear is being rejected or excluded by family, friends, or society. They are represented as an everyman, an average person.
- The Hero: Driven by a need to prove themselves, heroes strive to make the world a better place. Success on this path is their main life goal. They have high self-confidence and are goal-oriented, rarely giving up easily. Their greatest fear is failure. They are symbolized by struggle and perseverance.
- The Caregiver: They dedicate their lives to the well-being of those close to them. They are helpful and protective, generous, overly understanding, and deeply compassionate. Their greatest fear is facing selfishness and neglect. They are represented by compassion and the mother figure.
- The Explorer: Freedom-loving, they enjoy traveling and discovering new things. Adventurous and curious, they value their inner journey and self-exploration. Their greatest fears are boredom, being stuck in one place or mindset, and obedience. They are symbolized by the journey and exploration.
- The Outlaw / Rebel: They build their lives around breaking norms. They aim to create change and challenge taboos. Revolution is their fundamental

purpose. Their greatest fears are weakness and being controlled or oppressed. They are characterized by revolutionary figures.

- The Lover: Their lives revolve around loving others and being loved. Belonging and forming connections are important, and they are pleasure-focused. They strive to be prominent in every relationship. They value experience and have strong passions. Their greatest fears are loneliness, being unloved, and rejection. They are represented by romance and intimacy.
- The Creator: They value originality and innovation, aiming to create lasting elements and values. Dreamy in nature, they pursue unique ideas. This archetype includes individuals who advance fields such as science, health, art, and technology. Their greatest fears are being ordinary and mediocre. They are represented by artists and scientists.
- The Creator: They value originality and innovation, aiming to create lasting elements and values. Dreamy in nature, they pursue unique ideas. This archetype includes individuals who advance fields such as science, health, art, and technology. Their greatest fears are being ordinary and mediocre. They are represented by artists and scientists.
- The Sage: Their primary goal is to reach absolute truths. They live life guided by this pursuit. They keep their intellect and logic constantly active, with a questioning nature. They value objective and analytical thinking. Their greatest fears are being deceived, ignorance, and following false information. They are represented by advisors and philosophers.
- The Magician: Visionary and intuition-focused, this archetype's fundamental desire is to understand the workings of the universe. Associated with alchemy, mystery, wisdom, power, and transformation, they possess insight, reason, intuition, goodwill, and helpfulness. They often protect and guide others. They are skilled in manipulation and persuasion. Their greatest fear is negative transformation. They are characterized by shamans and magicians.
- The Ruler: A leadership archetype focused on stability and order. They want to keep their surroundings under control. Their most important concern is holding power. They excel at organizing people and motivate those close to them. Their greatest fear is losing power. They are represented by kings, rulers, and leaders.

Today, archetypes are no longer solely a subject of the discipline of psychology. The use of archetypes and research on them can be found in many fields such as cinema, advertising, literature, gaming, mythology, marketing, philosophy, the history of religions, and academic studies.

Use of Archetypes in Digital Games

Digital games have increasingly become a part of our lives with the rapid advancement of technology. Every day, a new game is released, intensifying the competition among brands in the digital game market more than ever. With the growing variety among digital games, this competitive environment has driven developers in the digital gaming sector to seek different ways to attract and influence their target audiences. Although the diversity within the digital game market offers players a wide range of options across different genres, in terms of marketing, the technical features of a game alone are not sufficient. Most players seek to build an emotional connection with the games they play. For players to form such a connection, the characters in the game and their backstories play a crucial role. Characters and their narratives allow players to empathize with them and, in a way, identify themselves with the characters they control. When a player learns about a character's past, their connections with other characters, and their personality traits, the game begins to hold a deeper meaning beyond mere entertainment. A player who knows the backstory of a character can witness their development and transformation throughout the game and, through experiencing the character's thoughts, internal conflicts, goals, and challenges, can identify with them. In many newly released games, players are also offered dynamic choices such as changing or controlling the course of the story, and these features further enhance the emotional engagement process.

In the creation of characters and their stories in digital games, Jung's concept of archetypes is frequently utilized. Archetypes, rooted in Carl Gustav Jung's analytical psychology theory, represent universal values that exist in human behavior, personality structures, and cultural expressions.

PURPOSE AND METHOD OF THE RESEARCH

The aim of this study is to explain the stories of heroes and in-game hero dynamics in the narrative of the popular mobile MOBA game Mobile Legends: Bang Bang in line with archetypes. Archetypes are examined in many culturally based elements such as cinema, advertising, literature, and games. The game itself is essentially a product of culture and also a constantly consumable commodity. The development of the gaming industry, just like in other commodities, is based on the dynamics of consumer culture and the capitalist system. In this context, the study seeks to answer two research questions:

R.Q.1: Are archetypes used in MOBA games?

R.Q.2: Are all archetypes present in hero stories and in-game hero dynamics in Mobile Legends: Bang Bang?

Within the scope of this study, the narratives of the characters in the game will be examined in accordance with Pearson's archetypes. Content analysis and thematic analysis methods were utilized in this research. Content analysis can be defined as a systematic method that involves analyzing the written, visual, or auditory elements of existing content with an objective perspective and aims to obtain meaningful results through the evaluations made. Thematic analysis, on the other hand, is a qualitative research method characterized by the processes of creating themes from existing data, interpreting these themes, and reporting them (Braun & Clarke, 2021). Both content analysis and thematic analysis can be applied across all disciplines related to social sciences.

In this study, based on these two methods, the in-game characters of the digital game Mobile Legends: Bang Bang (MLBB) were examined in line with archetypes, and the findings obtained were shared in the findings section. As of May 2025, there are 128 in-game heroes in MLBB. These heroes fight according to different roles in the game (support, tank, fighter, assassin/jungler, mage, marksman/MM). The study employed the purposeful sampling technique. In this technique, the researcher makes selections according to their own judgments and includes them in the sample in line with the purpose of the study (Akto & Akto, 2017). Based on purposeful sampling, 5 heroes from each role in the game were analyzed in the context of archetypes using content analysis and thematic analysis methods.

An Analysis of Mobile Legends: Bang Bang Characters in Light of Archetypes

Mobile Legends: Bang Bang, or MLBB for short, is a MOBA (Multiplayer Online Battle Arena) game released in 2016 by the company Moonton. According to statistics published by Active Player (2025), the game has reached 600 million downloads on the Google Play Store and 700 million on the Apple Store, with nearly 52 million monthly active users. Mobile Legends: Bang Bang is played in real-time by two teams consisting of five players each (5v5 format). Each team member selects a hero that suits their role and must strategically position themselves on the battlefield. In order to achieve victory, players must work together to destroy the opposing team's base. Hence, team coordination and strategic gameplay are of critical importance. The game features six main hero roles: Tank, Support, Fighter, Jungler/Assassin, Marksman, and Mage. Although most heroes are defined by a single role, there are some multi-role heroes who can adapt to different positions depending on the needs of the team. Each role presents specific advantages and disadvantages during combat. For example, Tank heroes are characterized by their durability and their ability to shield teammates by absorbing enemy damage. Support heroes, on the other hand, are relatively fragile but may have abilities such as healing allies or stunning opponents to provide tactical advantages. Fighter heroes are the second most durable after Tanks; they can protect more vulnerable teammates and inflict considerable damage. Assassin (or Jungler) heroes are known for their high burst damage and agility, but they are not particularly durable. However, when well-equipped and positioned correctly, they are capable of eliminating key targets on the enemy team swiftly. Marksman heroes are especially fragile at the beginning of the game, and they generally require protection from Tanks or healing from Support heroes. However, once they gain sufficient experience and level up, they can deal extremely high damage and even eliminate the strongest opponents. Mage heroes, who rely on magic-based abilities, are powerful in terms of magic damage but lack durability and have slow mana regeneration in the early stages of the game, making them dependent on team support. Since MLBB is a real-time, team-based strategy game, it is essential for every player to understand the role of their selected character and to support teammates as needed. A team can outperform the opponent and achieve victory only when each member comprehends and executes their role effectively, thus establishing a well-coordinated team dynamic.

FINDINGS

Tigreal (Tank): Tigreal was born into the Wertz family, which has trained generations of soldiers for the Moniyan Empire and ensured the empire's national security since its founding. His father Gareth is the Minister of Defense of the Moniyan Empire and the emperor's right-hand man, while his uncle Eckert is responsible for guarding the most dangerous regions of the empire, particularly the southern area near the Land of Despair. From a young age, Tigreal received military training in the city of Lumina and learned various combat skills such as swordsmanship, hand-to-hand combat, and horsemanship. At the age of sixteen, Tigreal joined the Imperial Army and was placed in the Garrison Army. After spending four years in the Garrison Army, Tigreal's command and leadership skills improved significantly, earning him the support of the Order of Light. Later, due to his extraordinary military talent and leadership ability, he was selected to join the Light Knights. The Light Knights is a unit within the Moniyan Empire composed solely of the most loyal and brave warriors who have undergone intense training. Tigreal became the youngest member in history to join the Light Knights, which elevated him to the status of a prodigy in the eyes of the Moniyan people, who believed he would become a hero remembered in the empire's history. However, during a battle, the Second Army he led was ordered by high-ranking officials to advance deep into enemy territory alone, resulting in heavy losses. Consequently, Tigreal was forced to take responsibility for the incident and left the empire, retreating to the Northern Vale. There, he built strong ties with the local tribes and fought alongside them in many conflicts. Over time, he resolved his internal struggles and returned to the empire, eventually becoming the leader of the Order of Light.

Several details in Tigreal's story indicate that the Ruler archetype is predominantly used for this character. His strongest in-game ability (ultimate) is crowd control. Crowd control allows him to gather enemy team members into a group, enabling his teammates to inflict collective damage on the enemies. In addition to grouping opponents, Tigreal's ultimate can push them in a desired direction and stun them. The Ruler archetype is primarily associated with traits of power and control, and Tigreal's ultimate ability exemplifies these characteristics. The references to various military units, his authority over them, and his leadership position further support the classification of Tigreal under the Ruler archetype. Beyond his narrative, Tigreal has several in-game voice lines. His most commonly used phrase is: *"For our honor!"* Other notable lines include: *"A real man never hides in the bush," "A true hero has come to help,"* and *"I never retreat, I lead with honor, for I am the vanguard of the Order of Light."* These lines also reflect the presence of the Hero archetype in Tigreal's characterization.

Minotaur (Tank/Support): Minotaur was the prince of Minoa, an ancient civilization that once flourished in the Agelta Drylands. As the most revered warrior of his time, Minotaur possessed a deep passion for combat and often drew his strength from his own rage. Known for unleashing powerful shockwaves on the battlefield through his fury, he was feared and respected, with few able to withstand his force. Over time, the people of Minoa grew to admire him, though his father, the aging king, harbored deep concerns. Despite his victories in battle, the king found Minotaur's brutality incompatible with the role of a sovereign heir. Seeking to instill in him the qualities of a true ruler, the king devised a test: Minotaur was to defeat a mysterious warrior who had traveled from distant lands. The duel would be unarmed, and Minotaur accepted the challenge without hesitation. In the arena, he initially relied on brute strength as usual, but found himself fatigued against an opponent of exceptional skill and resilience. The crowd began to cheer for the stranger as Minotaur gradually lost his advantage, leaving him humiliated and enraged. When the duel concluded, the mysterious warrior extended a hand to help Minotaur to his feet. Overwhelmed by shame and anger, Minotaur seized the hand, dragged his opponent down, and began to beat him mercilessly. As his fists became soaked in blood and the opponent ceased moving, Minotaur tore off the warrior's mask and froze in horror. Beneath it lay his own father, gravely wounded. With his final breaths, the king urged Minotaur to understand the true responsibilities of a ruler and to uphold the legacy of Minoa. Devastated by guilt and sorrow, Minotaur withdrew to the ancestral tombs within the Labyrinth of Minoa. There, he committed himself to mastering his anger through disciplined training. However, the explosion of the

Twilight Orb one day destroyed the Minoa civilization entirely. Minotaur, sheltered within the labyrinth, survived and fell into a deep slumber. When he awoke many years later, he discovered the annihilation of his people and kingdom. Refusing to accept this reality, he set out on a journey to find the remnants of his lost civilization and to fulfill his father's final wish: to rebuild Minoa and restore its former glory.

Minotaur's narrative exhibits a notable transformation in archetypal representation, shifting from one identity at the beginning of the story to another by its conclusion. In the early stages of his tale, Minotaur is portrayed as a wild, power-driven figure prone to explosive fits of rage, which aligns closely with the characteristics of the Rebel archetype. This archetype is most clearly observed in his brutal and ruthless behavior within the battle arena, as well as in his defiance of rules and disregard for consequences. However, the narrative takes a turning point following the tragic realization that he has severely wounded his own father. The emotional impact of guilt, shame, and remorse initiates a profound shift in Minotaur's character. His decision to retreat into the Labyrinth of Minoa to engage in self-discipline and learn to control his rage reflects qualities associated with the Sage archetype. His pursuit of inner balance and self-awareness marks a departure from impulsive aggression toward reflective wisdom. This duality between the Rebel and the Sage archetypes is also reflected in Minotaur's in-game voice lines. For instance, the lines *"Minoan rage!"* and *"Do not test my patience, or my fury"* clearly express the impulsive and emotionally charged traits of the Rebel. In contrast, the lines *"Rage, when controlled, brings the best outcome"* and *"Life itself is a trial"* embody the contemplative and disciplined nature of the Sage. Minotaur's character arc demonstrates a rare narrative progression in which an impulsive and destructive warrior evolves into a more introspective and purpose-driven individual. This transformation not only deepens the complexity of his character but also highlights how internal conflict and emotional reckoning can lead to growth and wisdom.

Gloo (Tank): A devastating battle once took place in the region known as the Barren Lands, during which the Moniyan Empire's Second Battalion was nearly annihilated. Only one Moniyan soldier survived and was forced to return to the empire alone. On his way back, the disoriented soldier lost his way and inadvertently wandered into the Shadow Swamp, an area corrupted by the influence of the Abyss. On the brink of unconsciousness, the soldier awoke to a strange sensation his body felt sticky, and he had lost control of his movements. It was as if his limbs were being manipulated like a puppet. Unable to resist, his body was dragged toward the ruins of an ancient temple entwined with vines. Slowly, the foreign sensation began to recede from his back, and he noticed a small creature leaping into the nearby bushes. Suspecting that the creature was responsible for his strange experience, the soldier pursued it. Just as he was about to catch it, hundreds more emerged, stacking together in a coordinated manner to form a massive being. Terrified, the soldier lost consciousness. When he awoke, he found himself on the border between the Empire and the Barren Lands. Upon returning home, he reported the encounter in detail. Although the public admired his bravery, his account was dismissed as the hallucination of a man traumatized by war. Not even the empire's wisest scholars had ever heard of such a creature. Driven by a desire to be believed, the soldier eventually wrote down his experience. Years later, a student of ancient texts discovered references in old Elven inscriptions to a race known as the Gloo. These beings matched the soldier's description exactly. Gloos were intelligent, highly flexible life forms capable of merging with one another. Though generally harmless and known to be playful and peaceful, they possessed a unique secretion that allowed them to adhere to other beings and temporarily control their movements. The Gloo had never initiated conflict, and their massive, combined form was used only to intimidate intruders approaching their territory. These beings had lived in the region known as Azyra since birth, serving as guardians of its forests and temples. Despite their peaceful nature, they eventually began to succumb to the dark power emanating from the Abyss, which slowly corrupted both the land and the Gloo themselves.

Unlike most other characters in the game, Gloo is portrayed not as a singular individual but as a member of an entire race. Within the game, Gloo possesses the unique ability to divide and reassemble its body, a trait that reflects its collective and fluid nature. Among the various archetypes identifiable in Gloo's narrative, the Jester archetype is the most prominent. The Jester archetype is characterized by themes of humor, playfulness, and entertainment, all of which are evident in Gloo's story. Despite the mysterious and initially unsettling elements of the narrative, the Gloo species is ultimately revealed to be harmless, intelligent, and even endearing. Their primary intention is not conflict but rather the protection of their home, and they adopt playful methods to deter intruders. The presence of the Jester archetype is also apparent in Gloo's in-game voice lines. Phrases such as *"If you like weird things, we're actually quite adorable!"* and *"Where's the best place to hide a leaf? In the forest!"* reflect the archetype's core attributes. These lines emphasize humor and whimsy, reinforcing Gloo's identity as a lighthearted, unconventional figure in contrast to the often serious or combative nature of other heroes. Through both its story and in-game dialogue, Gloo exemplifies how a character can embody comedic and playful traits while still fulfilling a meaningful narrative role. The use of the Jester archetype in Gloo's design adds a layer of levity to the game's broader mythos, highlighting the value of humor and strangeness in storytelling.

Angela (Support): Angela is an android created by Dr. Baker in Laboratory 1718. Dr. Baker is one of the founding members of Laboratory 1718, an institution originally established with the goal of bringing peace to the world. Although Laboratory 1718 was likewise intended to pursue peace, over time, its other scientists began to conduct morally compromised experiments, including attempts to weaponize human beings. In response to these unethical practices, Dr. Baker rejected experimentation on humans and initiated a new project. His endeavor focused solely on mechanical frameworks, synthetic skin, and marionette-like control mechanisms, through which he successfully created a new form of life. Believing that love and hope are humanity's greatest inventions, Dr. Baker embedded one of the world's most touching stories into the core programming of his creation. He named this prototype of the Peace Android whom he affectionately referred to as his "mechanical angel" Angela. Angela devoted herself to meeting the expectations of her creator, whom she regarded as a father, and worked diligently to understand the world around her. However, their peaceful existence was soon disrupted when the other scientists at Laboratory 1718 learned of Dr. Baker's creation—an artificial lifeform that did not rely on a human body. Interpreting his secrecy as betrayal, they turned against him. To eliminate the perceived threat, they dispatched Alpha and Beta, two of Dr. Baker's earlier creations, to hunt down Angela and her creator. As Angela was about to be captured, Dr. Baker placed her in an escape capsule and sent her to seek out his trusted colleague, Dr. Rooney. However, due to a violent storm, the capsule veered off course and crash-landed in a remote corner of the Land of Dawn. Surviving the wreckage, Angela sets out on a journey to find Dr. Rooney and rescue the one she calls her father.

In Angela's narrative, the predominant archetype portrayed is that of the Innocent. Characteristics commonly associated with the Innocent archetype include a desire to bring happiness to others, purity, faith, and optimism. One of the initial indicators of this archetype is Dr. Baker's decision to instill love and hope qualities he regards as humanity's greatest inventions into Angela during her creation. Another indication lies in the very purpose behind Angela's existence: she was created as a reaction to unethical human experimentation, signifying an aspiration toward purity and moral integrity. While Angela also exhibits traits of the Caregiver archetype, these are not as dominant as those of the Innocent. Her role as a Peace Android, her desire to please her creator (whom she sees as a father), and her journey to rescue him reflect the nurturing and selfless aspects of the Caregiver archetype. Angela's main in-game quotes, such as *"Love and hope are the two greatest inventions"* and *"Stay cheerful every day,"* further reinforce the Innocent archetype. Additionally, lines like *"My job is to help people,"* and *"I can do all the housework well, except cooking,"* illustrate elements of the Caregiver archetype.

Estes (Support): All Elf kings are born at the Tree of Life, located at the heart of the Emerald Woodland, and are destined to rule their generation. Estes, the king of the most recent generation, is a unique and distinguished figure among the Elves. Deeply respected and beloved by the Moon Elves, King Estes was gravely wounded during the Second Great War and fell into a deep slumber within the Emerald Woodland. In his absence, the Moon Elves were left without guidance. His sister, the Moonlight Archer Miya, assumed the responsibility of defending their homeland. Meanwhile, the Blood Queen Alice began to corrupt the young elves, luring them into darkness and bringing them under her control. With the Moon Elves once again facing peril, King Estes awakens from his long slumber on a thunderous night. Though firm in resolve, he is compassionate by nature. Gathering the sacred power of moonlight, Estes vows to aid his people and make every enemy who dares to invade their homeland regret their actions.

Estes's narrative incorporates elements of both the Caregiver and Hero archetypes. His altruistic nature and unwavering dedication to protecting his people and homeland are indicative of the Caregiver archetype. These traits are not only evident in his backstory but also reflected in his in-game ultimate ability, which heals himself and his allies. One of his quotes that exemplifies the Caregiver archetype is: *"Love yourself as much as you love others."* At the same time, Estes embodies the Hero archetype through his role as the king and by extension, the guide of the Moon Elves. His commitment to defending his people under all circumstances and leading them through adversity illustrates the heroic qualities of courage, responsibility, and leadership. A representative quote that reflects this archetype is: *"I am the chosen one."*

Rafaela (Support) & Argus (Warrior): With the end of the era known as the Golden Age, a fissure called the Abyss reopened within the lands of the Dawn Realm, releasing dark energies from its depths. To protect the world from these evils, the Lord of Light decreed that pure virgins be chosen to give birth to angels. According to legend, only women could become angels; therefore, those selected by the Lord of Light could only bear daughters. Rafaela and Argus were twin siblings born in the Moniyan Empire. The priests of the Light Monastery sought to have their mother drink the sacred water in the name of the Lord of Light, aiming for her to give birth to an angel. Their mother was an ordinary woman, devoted faithfully to her lover, but under the priests supervision and persuasion, she had no choice but to accept this honor. Her pregnancy was agonizingly long and painful, lasting three years. She endured the loneliness of this ordeal for two years before fleeing to be with her lover. However, the priests soon found her and punished her lover for defiling the bloodline of the Lord of Light. The lover was executed before her eyes, and the woman was returned to the temple. A year later, she died during childbirth but astonishingly gave birth to twins a girl and a boy. Upon noticing that the male infant's eyes closely resembled those of the mother's deceased lover, the Lord of Light realized the child was of human lineage yet possessed the power of angels. The priests attempted to kill him, but each time they tried, light emanating from Rafaela protected her brother, blocking their attacks. Seen as a miracle, the decision to kill the child was abandoned, and the Light Monastery concealed this truth from the twins themselves. Thus, Rafaela and Argus grew up together and received the same education. Although deeply loving each other, public perception regarded Rafaela as the true angel, while Argus was kept in the shadows, denied glory. Despite Argus's exceptional qualities and his fight for the Light, all praise and admiration were directed toward Rafaela, leaving Argus in darkness. Rafaela repeatedly spoke on behalf of her brother, attempting to change people's attitudes, but she was never successful. Over time, Rafaela noticed a change in Argus's view of humanity: he saw people as selfish and evil, whereas Rafaela believed the source of this evil was the Abyss. Both remained steadfast in their beliefs, and despite numerous arguments, neither could convince the other. Their philosophies and even their battlefield tactics diverged. During one battle, driven by a desire for swift victory, Argus fell into a demon's trap. Rafaela ordered a retreat, but Argus ignored her command and charged into the enemy's stronghold. When he returned, he wielded a demonic sword emitting a dark aura. Rafaela tried to dispel the darkness surrounding Argus, but he pushed her away, killing nearby soldiers before fleeing. Since that day, Rafaela has relentlessly searched for any trace of her brother. Meanwhile, the monastery priests told her that Argus's soul was already corrupted and that they had foreseen this day. Angered by their words, Rafaela punished the priests severely and left the monastery to seek Argus. Argus, meanwhile, was cursed by the sword he had found the weapon of Cyd, the god of destruction. The curse caused him to act according to his own fury. Months later, when Rafaela found Argus, he was unrecognizable: the radiant aura and golden wings he once had were replaced by a dark aura and shadowy wings. Rafaela raised her staff, prepared to fulfill her duty, but memories of their shared past restrained her. Argus looked at her silently from afar, then turned his back and walked away.

The story of Argus and Rafaela encompasses multiple complex elements. Due to their divergent treatment and upbringing since childhood, Rafaela exhibits characteristics of the Sage and Innocent archetypes, while her love for Argus also reveals traits of the Caregiver archetype. Argus, on the other hand, can be primarily associated with the Orphan and Rebel archetypes. Although Argus initially shows some Caregiver traits due to his affection for Rafaela, these qualities diminish as his curse takes hold later in the narrative. Argus's internalized anger and submission to the dark side exemplify the Rebel archetype, whereas his experience of being perceived as ordinary, marginalized, and ostracized during his upbringing reflects aspects of the Orphan archetype. Rafaela's philosophy, as an angel embodying the power of Light and maintaining a positive attitude toward humanity, further affirms her alignment with the Sage and Innocent archetypes. The in-game dialogues between Argus and Rafaela also substantiate the presence of these archetypes. For instance, Argus's lines such as *"The world was born from darkness, and it will end in darkness," "The darkness in my heart runs deeper than the Abyss,"* and *"Never speak the name, the name is Rafaela,"* illustrate the Orphan and Rebel archetypes.

Conversely, Rafaela's lines including *"Argus... forgive me," "Do not look into the darkness; it stains your soul,"* and *"We stand with the innocent,"* clearly reflect the elements of the Sage and Innocent archetypes.

Ruby (Warrior): Ruby lived in a remote village at the edge of the forest known as the Dark Woods, with her grandmother and grandfather. Years ago, the legendary hunter Roger had saved her family from a pack of wild wolves they encountered while traveling in the Dawn Land. Roger's courage made a great impression, and at the elders' request, he stayed to train the villagers, but one day he left without warning, leaving no trace behind. On a silent, moonless night, the new Wolf King, Pale Tusk, ambushed the village by sneaking in and launching a surprise attack. During this assault, Ruby's grandparents died while protecting her, right before her eyes, and Ruby narrowly survived by hiding beneath the bodies. Witnessing her grandparents' death caused a profound change in Ruby's character; she rose in shock and anger. Grabbing a sickle from the villagers, she charged at the wolf pack and nearly slaughtered them all. Despite her fragile appearance, beneath it dwelled a restless and furious spirit. Only one wolf survived the massacre: Pale Tusk. Previously undefeated, Pale Tusk was severely wounded. However, in a critical moment, Ruby hesitated to kill him, and Pale Tusk took advantage by slashing Ruby's left eye with his claw, knocking her to the ground. After the wolf left, Ruby regained consciousness to find she had lost her left eye and vowed to take revenge.

At the beginning of Ruby's story, characteristics of the Innocent and Orphan archetypes are evident. The Innocent archetype is reflected in Ruby's inability to protect herself and her reliance on others for protection. The Orphan archetype is demonstrated by Ruby's ordinary, quiet, and peaceful life. However, after witnessing the murder of her grandparents, the transformation in her character brings forth more prominent traits of the Rebel archetype. Her shift towards vengeance and actions driven by anger are illustrative of this archetype. This is further supported by her in-game quotes, such as *"I love the feeling of the hunt,"* and *"I wash the tip of my sickle with blood,"* which clearly reflect the characteristics of the Rebel archetype.

Aldous (Warrior): According to legends from the Dawn Land, there exists a mysterious labyrinth belonging to the Minoan Empire in the Western Desert. Although many soldiers once guarded the sacred labyrinth, over time they became corrupted and abandoned their duties, leaving only one soldier remaining: Aldous. One day, a deity descended from the heavens to punish the land, devastating the Minoan Empire. Severely wounded by the influx of both dark and light energies coursing through his body, Aldous underwent a profound transformation, with his skin covered in black scales capable of protecting him from most attacks, and his arms growing monstrous in appearance. Upon regaining consciousness, Aldous realized that his kingdom had been completely destroyed and that the mysterious labyrinth had been sealed by an unknown power. Despite this, he continued to guard the labyrinth. However, when Selena and the demons of the Abyss arrived at the labyrinth's gates, a great battle commenced.

In Aldous's story, the Caregiver and Hero archetypes are predominantly portrayed. Aldous's unwavering dedication to his duty and his persistence in remaining in the labyrinth to protect it, no matter the circumstances, exemplify the Caregiver archetype. Meanwhile, his courage to continue fighting despite the horrific events he has endured and his solitary position reflect the characteristics of the Hero archetype. The line *"I always fulfill my duties"* represents the Caregiver archetype, whereas the line *"Words are meaningless. Let your fists speak now!"* embodies the Hero archetype.

Fanny (Assassin): Fanny is the youngest daughter of the Wertz family and the younger sister of Tigreal. Although the men in the Wertz lineage have served and protected the military for generations, the women of the family were never permitted to enlist. As a result, Fanny was forced from a young age to take lessons in painting and design. However, her greatest desire was to fight on the frontlines of battle, just like her brother Tigreal, whom she regarded as her hero. As she grew older, Fanny began to rebel frequently skipping her lessons and becoming increasingly drawn to the artistry of combat. While Tigreal recognized his sister's passion for battle, he consistently denied her requests to join the military in an effort to protect her. Nevertheless, he promised to take her to the headquarters of the Order of Light when she turned eighteen. Tragedy struck, however, when Tigreal failed to return from a campaign and was subsequently labeled a deserter and coward throughout Moniyan. Determined to restore her family's honor and clear her brother's name, Fanny joined the army despite being judged by her peers as nothing more than a pampered noble girl. Undeterred, she passed every test and was eventually assigned to the reconnaissance unit. During her years of service, Fanny frequently had to navigate treacherous terrain and steep cliffs. To overcome her lack of physical strength, she combined the combat techniques taught by her brother with the design skills she had acquired earlier in life to create a unique weapon system. Fanny designed two long blades equipped with steel cables embedded in their hilts, which could be launched and retracted via a trigger mechanism. These cables allowed her to grapple onto surfaces and swiftly propel herself through the air. After countless trials, she mastered the use of her invention. Her exceptional performance eventually earned her a place within the Order of Light. Years later, Tigreal returned home, welcomed her with pride, and proposed that they fight side by side as equals.

Fanny's narrative primarily reflects the Hero and Creator archetypes. Her embodiment of the Hero archetype is evident in her unwavering determination to join the military by following the example set by her brother, Tigreal. Her perseverance, resilience, and willingness to defy societal and familial expectations underscore her heroic qualities. She refuses to accept the limitations imposed upon her and instead dedicates herself to proving her worth on the battlefield. Simultaneously, Fanny exemplifies the Creator archetype through the innovative combat style she develops. Drawing upon the design education she was forced to undergo in her youth, she ingeniously merges this knowledge with the martial techniques taught by her brother. This synthesis results in the invention of a unique weapon system two bladed swords with steel cables that grants her exceptional mobility and combat effectiveness. Through this, Fanny transforms her perceived weaknesses into strengths, a hallmark of the Creator archetype. Furthermore, her in-game line directed at Tigreal *"I will always fight by your side, brother."* reinforces the Hero archetype by expressing loyalty, courage, and a sense of duty rooted in familial bonds and shared ideals.

Benedetta (Assassin/Warrior): Benedetta is the daughter of a once-ordinary soldier of the Moniyan Empire, who, after his death, was dishonorably branded a traitor and denied recognition by the very empire he served. Deeply affected by her father's unjust legacy, Benedetta aspired to become a Warrior of Light, hoping to restore her family's honor. However, due to a strict policy that prohibited the enlistment of children of alleged rebels, she was barred from joining the military. Disillusioned and grieving, Benedetta chose to abandon Moniyan and ventured into the Desolate Lands, driven by a desire for vengeance. At first, she succumbed to her anger, directing her fury toward the monstrous creatures that inhabited the wastelands. Yet over time, she witnessed the resilience and suffering of the people struggling to survive in that harsh environment. Moved by their perseverance, Benedetta's purpose began to shift. Instead of seeking revenge, she formed a group to protect the inhabitants of the Desolate Lands. Her motivations evolved from personal vengeance to a broader mission: to honor her father not through destruction, but through justice and protection. Eventually, her ultimate goal became to challenge the Abyss itself, turning her pain into a force for righteous resistance.

Benedetta's narrative prominently features the Outlaw and Orphan archetypes. Her father's posthumous branding as a traitor by the Moniyan Empire not only stripped him of his honor but also cast a long shadow over Benedetta's life. Being denied the right to join the army due to her lineage compels her to reject the very institutions that marginalized her and to forge her own path. Her desire to prove herself on her own terms and to establish her own set of rules exemplifies the core traits of the Outlaw archetype. This defiance is encapsulated in her in-game line, *"The Moniyan Empire knows nothing of justice,"* which reflects her disillusionment with authority and her pursuit of a personal code of honor. The Orphan archetype is also evident in the early stages of Benedetta's story. Like many others, she initially longs to become a Warrior of Light and be recognized as an equal within her society. However, the social exclusion and systemic barriers she faces following her father's disgrace reflect the orphan's fundamental struggle: the search for belonging and fairness in a world that has unjustly rejected them. Her journey is shaped by this sense of abandonment, fueling both her inner resilience and her desire to protect those who, like herself, have been cast aside.

Hayabusa (Assassin): Hayabusa is a descendant of the Shadow Clan and was trained from childhood alongside his older brother to become a ninja. His brother was a figure of admiration and inspiration, and Hayabusa's ultimate goal was to help bring an end to the long-standing conflict between the Shadow Clan and the Scarlet Sect. However, this fragile balance was disrupted when the Scarlet Sect issued a warning: one clan had to rise above the other in power. A pawn had to be chosen either Hayabusa or his brother. Hayabusa volunteered and was sent to the Scarlet Sect. Upon arrival, he was met with scorn and skepticism, but through determination and discipline, he gradually earned the respect of his peers. During this period, he developed his own unique fighting style and met Hanabi, the heir to the Scarlet Sect. Despite challenging Hayabusa numerous times, Hanabi was repeatedly defeated by him, which further established his prowess. Tragedy struck when a prodigious yet dangerous ninja, Hanzo, infiltrated a forbidden area and stole the sealed weapon Ame no Habakiri. Hayabusa's brother, who pursued Hanzo, vanished without a trace. Both clans dispatched their best to recover the weapon and stop Hanzo. Before Hayabusa set out, he received a secret order from his father: retrieve the blade and eliminate Hanzo and anyone who stood in his way. Notably, the command made no mention of his brother. As he tracked Hanzo, Hayabusa found Hanabi gravely wounded. Soon after, he encountered a bloody and furious figure his brother's silhouette, lifeless in the eyes, and unresponsive to Hayabusa's pleas. It was only after a relentless confrontation that Hayabusa realized the truth: the weapon, Ame no Habakiri, was manipulating his mind, exploiting his emotional vulnerabilities through illusions. Having severed his connection to the weapon's darkness, Hayabusa emerged with a renewed sense of purpose. From that moment on, he would fight not merely for his clan, but for his own convictions, shaped by loss, betrayal, and clarity.

Hayabusa's story clearly exhibits the Hero archetype. His dedication to martial arts on the path to becoming a ninja, as well as the courage he shows by following the beliefs he considers right, are elements that exemplify the Hero archetype. In the game, lines such as *"There is no end to the path of the ninja"* and *"My belief brought me here; it can take me even further"* can also be seen as examples of the Hero archetype.

Natan (Marksman): Born and raised in the city of Eruditio, Natan proved himself to be naturally gifted by achieving successes that ordinary people could hardly even imagine, whether in science or magic. Eruditio was known as the pinnacle of human wisdom, and like other sages living in this city, Natan took on the mission of saving the world at a young age. Resisting the endless war, Natan participated in various research projects and, by the age of 28, was appointed as the official leader of Eruditio. Together with his people, he strove to find a solution to save the world.

Meanwhile, the Abyss had gathered more Twilight Orbs. If the last orb fell into the hands of the Lord of the Abyss, pure chaos would return to the world, with all light swallowed by darkness. At that dark moment, Natan once again stepped forward and proposed a new idea: to build a time machine. However, there were two major problems they lacked a power source to energize the machine, and the Dawnland had been devastated by war. Just as hope was fading with the last remaining Twilight Orb falling into the Abyss's hands, the energy emitted from the orb resonated with the time machine, enabling Natan to successfully activate it. He then traveled back in time to change their present fate.

Elements of the Sage archetype are frequently observed in Natan's story. Born and raised in Eruditio, known in the game as the city of sages, Natan's sole purpose is to save the world, a goal he seeks to achieve through the use of science. His ability to become the leader of Eruditio at the age of 28 is owed to his accumulated knowledge and wisdom. In the game, his lines such as *"We give meaning to life by understanding time."* and *"I do not pray for miracles; I create them."* also reflect characteristics of the Sage archetype.

Granger (Marksman): Granger was born in an unnamed town on the coast of the Moniyan Empire. During his childhood, demons devastated his hometown on a dark night. That night, Granger's mother and father sacrificed their lives by hiding him in a small space beneath the floorboards to protect him; the only remnants of that night were the screams eternally ringing in his ears and the ominous growls of the demons. These sounds, etched into Granger's mind, would later shape his destiny. After this event, Granger withdrew from people and became reclusive until one day he heard a melody called the "Hymn of Light" played on a priest's violin. This melody helped Granger emerge from his shell; the priest taught him not only music but also hope. Although Granger initially struggled to play the violin, his talent in demon hunting was undeniable, and he was accepted as a demon slayer by the Church of Light. Using a pistol that could absorb demon energy and convert it into special bullets, Granger always worked alone; the only motivation driving him was to avenge that dark night that had overshadowed his life. One day, a group of demons led by Dyrroth invaded his most trusted place, the monastery, and took away the priest who had given him a second chance at life. From that day, Granger fell silent and never spoke again. He named one of his pistols *"Dirge,"* meaning lament, and the other *"Requiem,"* meaning funeral chant.

Granger's story prominently features the Orphan archetype. After experiencing the traumatic loss of his family in childhood, he withdrew into himself, becoming a quieter person and maintaining his silence in response to the events that followed throughout his life. Another archetype visible in the story is the Rebel. The most significant expression of the Rebel archetype is Granger's pursuit of vengeance. The line *"I fight only for myself, not for others."* clearly reflects the Rebel archetype.

Lesley (Marksman): Lesley's father was the protector of the Vance dynasty and raised her. Growing up by observing her father, Lesley became aware at a young age that loyalty, silence, and virtue were the duties of her role. One day, Lesley's father was shot and killed in front of her eyes during a sudden attack by a rival family. As the enemies approached the Vance mansion, Lesley took her father's black rifle in hand and, for the first time in her life, aimed and fired. Each shot hit its target, and through tears, Lesley took down her enemies one by one. After that day, she was adopted by the Vance family. The head of the noble house entrusted Lesley not only with a home but also with the responsibility of training Harley, the heir of the family. Harley was a mischievous child with magical abilities, and though unintentionally causing trouble for the house, Lesley was the only one who could control him. Harley's small mischiefs were the last warmth in Lesley's heart. Years later, Lesley learned that Harley had defeated the Lord of Dark Magic and had gone alone to the Dawn Land. As soon as she received this news, she slung her rifle over her shoulder and set off on a difficult journey. When she found him, she saw a stranger in Harley someone grown and shaped by experience. Lesley understood that her little brother now had to forge his own path. But that did not mean she would leave him alone. From that day on, every monster weakened by magic was struck down by a dark bullet fired from Lesley's heart. No one saw her, but everyone felt her presence. Rumors of a mysterious sniper protecting the young mage from the shadows spread like lightning across the Dawn Land. Lesley did not speak; she only observed, waited, aimed, and pulled the trigger with flawless silence.

Lesley's story predominantly features the Caregiver archetype. Lesley grew up observing her father, who was the protector of the Vance dynasty. After her father's death and her adoption by the Vance family, she began secretly caring for and protecting her stepbrother, Harley. During conflicts, when Harley stunned and weakened an opponent, Lesley would stealthily take aim from the shadows to neutralize the threat, thus continuing to protect him. This allowed her to stay out of the spotlight while still looking after and safeguarding her younger brother. The Caregiver archetype is also reflected in one of her in-game lines: *"Where has Harley gone? I haven't seen him for a while."*

Vexana (Mage): Vexana was a princess who had never left Lumina City and never wished to leave. Lumina, the capital of the Moniyan Empire, was warm and prosperous, but due to her father's decision, she had to marry Duke Atticus and move to a fortress in the South, which terrified her. However, she could not oppose her father's will. When Vexana arrived at the fortress, she could not meet Duke Atticus because he had left to deal with a demon invasion on the border. Although Vexana disliked the conditions of the fortress, she did not lose hope. During this time, Atticus began sending frequent letters. In these letters, Vexana could sense Atticus's feelings and gradually began to love this man she had never met. One day, however, the letters stopped. With the cessation of the letters, Vexana started living with the fortress's people and developed a bond with them. Two years later, when news arrived that Atticus was returning, Vexana grew excited, but her excitement turned to fear upon seeing him. Atticus's face lacked the liveliness and joy from the letters and instead showed an empty, exhausted expression. After the wedding preparations were completed, everyone gathered in the city of Ridgeburg to watch the ceremony begin. During the ceremony, when the box containing Vexana's and Atticus's rings was opened, Atticus and his men transformed into demons and began destroying the townspeople. When Atticus attacked Vexana, she shouted for him to stop. For a brief moment, Atticus returned to his former self and ordered Leomord to pierce his heart and entrusted Ridgeburg to Vexana. From then on, Ridgeburg became a cursed city, entrusted to Vexana's care.

In Vexana's story, at the beginning, we observe her as an innocent and sheltered princess. This indicates the use of the Innocent archetype in Vexana. As the story progresses, the experiences she undergoes lead to significant character changes. Her fiancé entrusting the city to her before his death and Vexana dedicating her life to saving the city signal the use of the Ruler archetype in her character. In the game, the lines she uses, such as *"Hope finds a way even in the most desperate moments"* and *"Until Ridgeburg breathes again!"* demonstrate the presence of the Ruler archetype.

Pharsa (Mage): Pharsa was the princess of the Crow People, one of the oldest races living in the Askati Forest. This race had mastered the arts of sky magic, such as transforming into a bird, soaring through the skies, and attacking from long distances; however, only those whose blood had been awakened could use this magic. Pharsa was born with an unknown type of blood said to have great potential when awakened, but no matter what her tribe members tried, they could not awaken her blood. Soon, it became known throughout the land that Pharsa's blood was a special gift, and malicious individuals sought to seize it for their own gain. On Pharsa's wedding day, Alice attacked the Askati Forest, mercilessly slaughtering countless Crows and leaving behind a ruin covered in ashes. Numbed by the massacre around her, Pharsa dropped her crown, and at that moment, her appearance began to change. Her blood finally awakened; first, her eyes clouded over, causing her to lose her sight, then one side of her hair turned completely white, and she ascended to the sky, launching a terrifying magical assault powerful enough to repel even Alice. Verri, Pharsa's fiancé and the love of her life, could not bear to see her live alone with blindness, so he used his magic to form a permanent bond with Pharsa, granting her the ability to see through his eyes. Pharsa wished her power had never awakened and vowed to take revenge on Alice for all that had happened.

In Pharsa's story, the Orphan archetype is reflected in the beginning, while the Rebel archetype emerges as the events unfold. Initially, Pharsa is portrayed as an ordinary princess trying to awaken the power within her while continuing her life, illustrating elements of the Orphan archetype. The Rebel archetype becomes apparent after Alice's attack on Pharsa's wedding, which triggers the awakening of Pharsa's power and her desire for revenge due to the losses she suffered. The use of the line *"Time for vengeance."* in the game also exemplifies the Rebel archetype.

Cecilion (Mage): Cecilion was the last surviving Blood Demon of his kind. In order to keep his true identity a secret, he lived as an opera singer because his kind was a species that was ostracized and hunted by both humans and the Abyss. One day, he gave an unforgettable performance and when he went to the center of the stage to bow, he saw Carmilla, and this beautiful woman was looking at him and they fell in love. Although Cecilion warned him to stay away from unnecessary closeness with humans, he could not help his love for Carmilla, so he decided to follow his heart. He dedicated a song to Carmilla in each of his performances and they never stopped looking into each other's eyes. They met frequently without the others knowing, but Carmilla's father, Count Ansaac, knew everything. In his opinion, Cecilion was just an ordinary opera singer and thought that his daughter should marry a more powerful man. As their relationship deepened, Count Ansaac forcibly ended the relationship, imprisoned Carmilla, sealed the Opera House, and exiled Cecilion. Soon, rumors spread that Count Ansaac would marry his only daughter, Carmilla, to Baron Tawil, General of the Imperial Army. At that time, Cecilion considered overthrowing the guards and kidnapping Carmilla, but he knew that this would only make Carmilla a fugitive and would not bring her happiness. So he decided that it was best to give up. Carmilla was going to marry Baron Tawil, but just before dawn, Cecilion left a rose and a letter with his name on it on Carmilla's window and walked away. After putting on her white wedding dress, Carmilla cut her wrist with a sharp dagger, dedicating her life to her lover Cecilion. Giving up Carmilla plunged Cecilion into deep sorrow, and his life returned to its former lonely days. After two lonely nights, Cecilion went to see Carmilla from afar, but when he arrived, he saw Carmilla's cold body lying in a silent funeral. At that moment, an indescribable pain and regret filled Cecilion's chest as he looked at Carmilla's lifeless body. Then, he brought her back to life with his own blood, but this power came at a great cost. And so, Carmilla also became a Blood Demon forever. In order to protect this eternal love, Cecilion decided that he would not allow anyone to separate them.

We can see the Lover archetype in Cecilion's story. Cecilion was a blood demon who had isolated himself from people and lived unhappily throughout his life, so nothing made him happy. The moment he saw Carmilla, these feelings gave way to love and feeling loved. At the end of the story, the promise he made to not let Carmilla go despite the cost of bringing her back to life also reflects the Lover archetype. The line Cecilion uses in the play, *"Only love and night are eternal."* also reflects the Lover archetype.

Table 1. Same MLBB Hero's, Lane's, role's and archetypes

Hero(s)	Role(s)	Lane(s)	Archetype(s)
Miya	Marksman	Gold Lane	Hero, Caregiver
Balmond	Fighter	EXP Lane	Orphan
Saber	Assassin	Jungle/Roam	Rebel
Alice	Mage/Tank	Mid Lane	Rebel, Ruler
Nana	Mage	Mid Lane	Innocent
Tigreal	Tank	Roam	Ruler, Hero
Alucard	Fighter/Assassin	EXP Lane/Jungle	Hero
Karina	Assassin	Jungle	Caregiver, Orphan
Akai	Tank	Roam	Hero, Jester
Franco	Tank	Roam	Hero
Bane	Fighter/Mage	Jungle/EXP Lane	Rebel, Ruler
Bruno	Marksman	Gold Lane	Jester, Orphan
Clint	Marksman	Gold Lane	Hero, Explorer
Rafaela	Support	Roam	Sage, Innocent
Eudora	Mage	Mid Lane	Sage
Zilong	Fighter/Assassin	EXP Lane	Hero, Explorer
Fanny	Assassin	Jungle	Hero, Creator
Layla	Marksman	Gold Lane	Innocent, Caregiver
Minotaur	Tank/Support	Roam	Rebel, Sage
Lolita	Support/Tank	Roam	Caregiver
Hayabusa	Assassin	Jungle	Hero
Freya	Fighter	EXP Laner	Hero
Gord	Mage	Mid Lane	Sage
Natalia	Assassin	Roam/Jungle	Rebel
Kagura	Mage	Mid Lane	Lover, Innocent
Chou	Fighter	EXP Lane/Roam	Hero
Sun	Fighter	EXP Lane/jungle	Ruler, Hero
Alpha	Fighter	Jungle/EXP Lane	Rebel
Ruby	Fighter	EXP Lane	Orphan, Innocent
Yi Sun-shin	Assassin/Marksman	Jungle/Gold Lane	Ruler
Moskov	Marksman	Gold Lane	Rebel
Johnson	Tank/Support	Roam	Orphan, Jester
Cyclops	Mage	Mid Lane	Sage
Estes	Support	Roam	Caregiver, Hero
Hilda	Tank/Fighter	EXP Lane/Roam	Hero
Aurora	Mage	Mid Lane	Lover, Hero
Lapu-Lapu	Fighter	EXP Lane	Hero

CONCLUSION AND DISCUSSION

This study aimed to examine the stories of the heroes featured in the narrative of the game MLBB (Mobile Legends: Bang Bang) within the framework of psychoanalytic theory archetypes, using content analysis and thematic analysis methods.

The use of archetypes in digital games is a common occurrence in reflecting the hero's character, background, relationships with other heroes, goals, abilities, and motivations into the game's story. As a result of the research, it can be observed that each hero in Mobile Legends: Bang Bang carries dominant archetypal traits. Aside from the hero's individual story and characteristics, archetypal features can also be found in the hero's in-game lines, dialogues with other heroes, and the role the hero plays within the game. In this study, five heroes from each role were selected, and examples from their stories and dialogues were given to explain which archetypal features the selected heroes possess and how these features are connected to their roles.

When examining the answers to the research questions; the answer to the first research question, "Are archetypes used in MOBA games?" is yes, archetypes are used in MOBA games. Mobile Legends: Bang Bang incorporates archetypes in its in-game narrative. However, the presence of archetypes in MLBB does not imply that archetypes are present in every MOBA game. The reason for choosing research questions instead of hypotheses in this study is that no research was conducted to reach general conclusions. It is not possible to examine all MOBA games in the discipline of digital game studies. Future research analyzing archetypes in more MOBA games will allow for the formation of a general consensus.

The answer to the question, "Are all archetypes found in the hero stories and in-game hero dynamics of Mobile Legends: Bang Bang?" is that all archetypes are present in the in-game narrative. All twelve archetypes are found in the in-game hero stories, dialogues, and narratives of MLBB. In fact, some characters exhibit multiple archetypes, but these characters were analyzed through their dominant archetype.

In the study titled "Digital Game as a Form of Cyberdrama: The Example of Alice in Wonderland" written by Özge Baydaş Sayılgan, the story of Alice in Wonderland was examined according to archetypes in novel, film, and digital game formats, and it was stated that archetype use was found in all media elements (2012). In the study titled "Brand Identity Analysis in the Mobile Game Market: The Case of Tencent Games" by Öztürk and Bülbül, archetypes were used when analyzing the brand identity of the game producer Tencent Games, and it was concluded that the company possesses the Creator archetype (2022). In the study by Savett titled "Virtual Psyche in Play and Tending the Collective Unconscious: An Archetypal Psychology Perspective of Digital Games," the concepts of Carl Jung and James Hillman on archetypes were connected to digital games and the concept of archetypes (2016). As seen in previous studies, archetype use has been addressed in analyses of digital games within the scope of transmedia and in studies of digital game producer brand identities. Numerous studies on archetypes can be found both in digital game studies and other disciplines in the literature.

Archetypes continue to exist as phenomena containing various characteristic traits, emotions, and tendencies inherited from our ancestors. Today, studies on archetypes continue to be conducted in psychology, cinema, literature, marketing, and other disciplines. Especially after the publication of Jung's Red Book, it can be said that studies on archetypes have increased. The fact that the study was designed based on qualitative methods (content analysis and thematic analysis) leaves it open to discussion in terms of validity and reliability. Qualitative methods can contain subjective data as a research method. Therefore, it is important that future studies on archetypes and digital games are supported by quantitative methods in order to reach more objective results.

FUTURE RESEARCH DIRECTIONS

While this study offers valuable insights into the representation of archetypes in *Mobile Legends: Bang Bang* through qualitative content and thematic analysis, it also highlights several promising directions for further research within the field of digital game studies. Although qualitative methods provide a rich and interpretive understanding of narrative structures and symbolic elements, future studies would benefit from the incorporation of mixed-methods research designs to enhance both validity and generalizability. In this context, quantitative approaches—such as player surveys, behavioral data analysis, and experimental designs—can complement qualitative findings by offering measurable and replicable evidence on how players perceive and interact with archetypal characters.

In addition, broadening the scope of analysis beyond *Mobile Legends: Bang Bang* to include a wider selection of MOBA titles could allow researchers to determine whether the integration of all twelve Pearsonian archetypes is unique to this game or indicative of a broader genre-wide trend. Comparative studies involving games developed by different companies and situated in various cultural contexts may contribute to the formulation of a more comprehensive theoretical model of archetypal representation in digital games.

Cross-cultural comparative research also holds significant potential, particularly in understanding how cultural narratives influence the recognition, interpretation, and emotional resonance of specific archetypes. Given the global nature of contemporary digital games, such studies would provide meaningful insight into the localized dynamics of archetypal engagement among diverse player communities.

Finally, longitudinal studies may be instrumental in assessing whether sustained interaction with particular archetypes influences players' behavior, identity construction, or even consumer preferences over time. By integrating psychological frameworks with game studies, future research can not only advance theoretical discourse across disciplines but also offer actionable insights for game designers, narrative developers, and marketing professionals within the mobile gaming industry.

REFERENCES

Akto, S., & Akto, A. (2017). *Methods and Techniques Used in Values Education in Preschool.* E-Oriental Scientific Research Journal., DOI: 10.26791/sarkiat.342143

Baydaş Sayılgan, Ö. (2012). Digital Game as a Form of Cyberdrama: The Example of Alice in Wonderland. Journal of Folklore and Literature, pp. 113–134.

Braun, V., & Clarke, V. (2021). Thematic analysis: A practical guide. *Sage (Atlanta, Ga.).*

Bülbül, H. İ. (2022) About Digital Games, https://dergipark.org.tr/en/download/article-file/2678176

Pearson, C. (1991). *Awakening the heroes within: Twelve archetypes to help us find ourselves and transform our world.* No Title.

Frasca, G. (2001). Rethinking Agency and Immersion: Video Games as a Means of Consciousness-Raising. *Digital Creativity (Exeter)*, *12*(3), 167–174. DOI: 10.1076/digc.12.3.167.3225

Jung, C. G. (1954). *Psychological aspects of the mother archetype. The Collected Works of C. G. Jung; Read, H.,Fordham, M., Adler, G., (journal.) inside.* Routledge.

Jung, C. G. (2019). *Four Archetypes.* Metis Publishing.

Öztürk, B. N., & Bülbül, S. (2022). *A Study on Brand Identity in the Mobile Game Market: The Case of Tencent Games.* Alanya Academic Review Journal.

Piaget, J. (1962). *Play, dreams, and imitation in childhood.* Norton.

Pixune. (2024). What are the different kinds of video game genres? Retrieved January 30, 2025, from https://pixune.com/blog/video-game-genres/

Radoff, J. (2010). Jon Radoff's Internet Wonderland: History of social games. Retrieved January 30, 2025, from https://web.archive.org/web/20100527090108/http://radoff.com/blog/2010/05/24/history-social-games/

Savett, S. M. (2016). *Virtual Psyche in Play and Tending the Collective Unconscious: An Archetypal Psychology Perspective of Digital Games. S. B. Schafer içinde, Exploring the Collective Unconscious in the Age of Digital Media.* IGI Global. DOI: 10.4018/978-1-4666-9891-8.ch006

Statista. (2024). Video gaming worldwide - Statistics & facts. Retrieved April 3, 2025, from https://www.statista.com/topics/1680/gaming/#topicOverview

Tsai, S. P. (2006). Investigating archetype-icon transformation in brand marketing. *Marketing Intelligence & Planning*, *26*(6), 648–663. DOI: 10.1108/02634500610701708

Uzunoğlu, A. (2021). Digital Games and Addiction. https://dergipark.org.tr/en/download/article-file/2085319

Zachrisson, A., & Karancsi, A. H. (2023) MOBAs, the beginning From mod to genre, https://www.diva-portal.org/smash/get/diva2:1768354/FULLTEXT01.pdf

ADDITIONAL READING

Athalia, S., A., (2023) Revealing How Characters Manifest Carl Jung's Archetypes in the Game "Persona 4", Litera Kultura: Journal of Literary and Cultural Studies, pp. 14-19

Conway, S. (2018) Anima ludus, Hockley, L., (Ed.) inside The Routledge International Handbook of Jungian Film Studies, Taylor & Francis Group

Garcia, A., (2023) Archetype and Individuation Process in Alan Wake (2010) Video Game, Journal of Games, Game Art and Gamification, pp. 1-10

Kang, B., & Seo, G. (2023) A study on the design method using Jung's archetype and color psychology for MOBA game characters, Journal of Korea Game Society

Lim, C., & Harrell, F. D. (2015). *Revealing Social Identity Phenomena in Videogames with Archetypal Analysis*. University of Kent.

Özkurt, M. (2023) A Jungian Archetypal analysis of Earnest Cline's Ready Player One: quest for the Axis Mundi (unreleased thesis)

Power, P., & Corchnoy, S. (2024). *The World of Gaming and Jungian Analysis*. Taylor & Francis. DOI: 10.1080/00332925.2024.2350338

Savett, M. S. (2016) Virtual Psyche in Play and Tending the Collective Unconscious: An Archetypal Psychology Perspective of Digital Games, pp. 156-179, Schafer, B., S., (Ed.) inside Exploring the Collective Unconscious in the Age of Digital Media, IGI Global Scientific Publishing

Schafer, B. S. (2012) Articulating the Paradigm Shift: Serious Games for Psychological Healing of the Collective Persona, pp. 352-377, Cruz-Cunha, M., M., (Ed.) inside Handbook of Research on Serious Games as Educational, Business and Research Tools (2 Volumes), IGI Global Scientific Publishing

Stefanska, M., & Mazurkiewicz, B. (2021). *Archetypes of Video Game Players – Do Other Typologies Exist?* IBIMA.

KEY TERMS AND DEFINITIONS

Archetype: The manifestation of a few universal human traits reflected in contemporary identities.

Digital Game Industry: The emerging leading sector of entertainment and one of the fastest-growing industries, surpassing the revenues of many traditional industries today.

Digital Game Studies: An academic field within the social sciences that has gained momentum in light of the digital game industry and technological advancements.

Digital Game: Physical and digital activities that facilitate a brief pause within the life cycle.

In-Game Character: Virtual identities created by game designers.

MOBA: A genre of digital games featuring two opposing teams of five players each, competing on virtual maps, where players simultaneously experience a wide range of positive and negative emotions.

Narrative in Digital Games: Immersive cycles created within a virtual space intended to engage and influence real players.

Chapter 8
YouTube and the Presentation of Privacy

Uğur Arslan
https://orcid.org/0000-0001-6597-0612
Dicle University, Turkey

ABSTRACT

Privacy has been expressed with concepts such as individuals' private space and confidentiality in the historical process. With the opportunities provided by Web 2.0, it transforms communication and makes publishing and reaching masses extremely easy. The features offered by social media platforms such as participation, content creation, publishing and sharing have made the digital world a center of attraction for individuals. Social media platforms, which are offered for "free", provide their economy by storing individuals' private life and privacy information and commercializing the attitudes of individuals that enable them to voluntarily disclose their privacy within the platform. On the platform where more views and subscribers mean monetization, users increasingly destroy their privacy in order to attract the attention of the masses. When YouTube and Privacy literature is examined, it is seen that YouTubers try to become famous by publicizing privacy. Privacy is destroyed for the sake of individuals' self-realization and the goal of becoming famous.

INTRODUCTION

As the most fundamental area of freedom, privacy is the individual's right to have a say about his/her private sphere and to decide what to share and what not to share in the public sphere. In addition to the individual's control of information about himself/herself, privacy also includes what information others have about him/her. Provisions regarding the right to privacy, which is also considered as the protection

DOI: 10.4018/979-8-3373-6192-5.ch008

of personal data, are guaranteed in the laws of state (Lokke, 2020, p. 24-25). In the communication dictionary, "privacy" is defined as follows (Mutlu, 2008, p. 206):

The process of setting an interpersonal boundary that regulates the interaction of a person or group with others. Changing the degree of human openness to others determines the degree of openness of this hypothetical personal boundary to social interaction with others. Privacy is therefore a dynamic process involving the selective control of an individual or a group over its boundary. Privacy is based on a regulatory process that opens and closes the boundaries of one's environment in order to control the degree of contact and relationship with others. Individuals have certain levels of privacy they desire, which are based on mechanisms of boundary control, leading to easily achieved privacy.

Privacy, also referred to as "confidentiality", also stands out as an important phenomenon in the formation of social groups and the strengthening of ties. The fact that individuals decide with whom they will share their secrets and private spaces contributes to the determination of friendship networks. By sharing intimate or private space, best friends are determined and the sense of trust is reinforced through this sharing (Bauman, 2018, p. 38). Altman defines privacy as the control over one's personal space in terms of access to one's self or to another group. Individuals choose the information they will share while interacting with other individuals during the socialization process. With this definition, other dimensions of privacy are revealed by taking into account not only the desire of individuals to be alone, but also the desire to be with other individuals. Individuals do not only aim for privacy, but also tend to share intimate information by socializing. With this feature, privacy can be said to be a dialectical playground between the impulses to be alone and to be with others (Yüksel, 2009, p. 278). Privacy is also defined in terms of its opposite; public space. In the public sphere, which is open to anyone who wants to enter, individuals take on the responsibilities of being seen, watched and heard. In the public sphere, consent is given to the results and the right to object disappears. In this way, private information and publicization decisions are two opposite poles and are expressed separately through their opposition to each other (Bauman, 2018, p. 32). Although privacy is perceived through the privacy of the "body" today, there are four different types of privacy: person, space and information. Privacy of the person means that the individual does not violate the privacy of other individuals, privacy of information means that information characterized as "secret" is not disclosed, and privacy of space draws attention to individuals' homes, which are private spaces. The phenomenon of privacy, which has existed since the beginning of history, has been one of the areas that those in power have been very interested in. In the process in which the rulers monitor individuals with surveillance tools, privacy is recorded with civil registry books in the past and with the storage methods made possible by computer technology today. Although threats to the private life and privacy of individuals are considered together with the "state", developments in information and communication technologies facilitate the obscuring and publicization of private life and privacy. In this period, individuals are concerned about the interception of their phone calls, digital health data, the display of articles or photographs related to their private lives and privacy in mass media, or negative situations that may arise from banking applications. Privacy in the digital environment is becoming a phenomenon that needs to be reconsidered and legally reorganized (Yüksel, 2003, p. 183).

In the pre-internet era, television was one of the mass media that obscured privacy. In popular culture, the most valuable programs on television are measured by ratings. Over time, series actors become the face of the channel they are on. Television series are also the productions in which advertisers invest the most. The most watched series are usually dramas and dramas try to attract the attention of viewers through fictional stories and the display of intimacy. Before digitalization surrounded the world, the dynamics of mass communication and the television industry were formed by dramas fed by the display of privacy in which society found itself (Arık & Arık, 2021, p. 18). The process of commodification of privacy through popular culture products before digitalization is not limited to dramas. Along with Hollywood productions, magazine programs and reality shows are becoming areas that lead to the obscuration of privacy. The private lives of celebrities and reality shows, which give ordinary people the opportunity to become famous and bring cameras into their bedrooms, are met with interest by the viewers. Another output of popular culture, cinema's relationship with privacy is not only in dramas but also in biographical themes. Biographical films are productions in which the lives of public celebrities are narrated. In the biographical movie narrative, information about the private lives of individuals is given and thus the theme is directly related to privacy. By narrating the lives of individuals, private life is publicized and conveyed to the audience in this way. As a result, it is quite usual for the audience to witness a display of intimacy. The movie Bohemian Rhapsody, which tells the life of Freddie Mercury, contains a lot of content about Mercury's private life as well as his music career (Balcı, 2021, p. 81).

Dolgun states that with the emergence of internet technology and globalization, interaction has evolved into a transnational situation, making it possible to monitor personal information and privacy anywhere in the world. Thus, individuals, who have become users in the digitalized world, have become extremely vulnerable to data. What distinguishes the information society from the capitalist market is that ordinary people can also be surveilled. With the activation of communication in the cyber world and the combination of security policies with technology after September 11, surveillance practices continue in an extremely intense manner (Dolgun, 2015, p. 210-211). After 9/11, the increase in surveillance activities globally has led to debates on the private life and privacy of individuals. Closed-circuit televisions in the UK, which has the highest number of security cameras in the world, and chip ID cards in Australia have been met with concern. However, the phenomenon of increased surveillance on privacy has been adopted as a popular theme by global technology companies, which have been steadily building new infrastructures for surveillance and making significant profits (Lyon, 2013, p. 73). In the pre-digital period, it was the Panopticon that enabled everyone to be monitored from a center and brought about modernity. In modernity, the panopticon, which was used to discipline individuals in institutions such as prisons, armies and factories, also ensured the socialization of individuals. Today, surveillance of individuals' privacy is no longer carried out through the Panopticon, but through the Synopticon, where everyone watches everyone else. In this period, individuals both watch everyone and voluntarily make themselves vulnerable to everyone's surveillance (Şişman, 2020, p. 9).

Appealing to the most basic need of individuals for the development and disclosure of the social environment and the interest in the private life and privacy of other individuals, social media platforms have transformed into a digital living space visited by billions of people. This perspective refers to the sociology behind the transformation of social media platforms. However, in order to make a definition, we should not forget the technological infrastructure behind the sociological transformation. Developments such as the development of new communication technologies, convergence and Web 2.0 constitute the background (Kara, 2013, p. 53-54). Crowley and Heyer explain that Web 2.0 technologies democratized fame and entertainment and liberated culture when social media platforms began to diversify (Crowley&Heyer, 2019, p. 396):

Technologies and pundits unabashedly slapped the Web 2.0 label on wikis, blogs, social networking sites, tagging sites and user content sites such as Wikipedia, MySpace, Facebook, YouTube, del.icio.us, Flickr, Digg and Twitter. These technologies supposedly envisioned liberation from traditional media sources or Big Media. They promised the democratization of fame and entertainment, new forms of activism and the possibility for information of all kinds to become open and transparent. Web 2.0 praised the adoption of social technologies as a precursor to a better, freer society and presented the gathering and sharing of information as the mainstay of this revolution.

With billions of users, social media platforms create a technically flawless internet base for surveillance practices and implement policies that legitimize and encourage surveillance and the display of privacy. While the phenomenon of surveillance and the demand for privacy was practiced through coercion in the pre-digital era, today, with the significant influence of social media platforms, it is adopted as a digital culture, where everyone spies on everyone else and voluntarily shares their privacy.

With the widespread use of social media platforms and their becoming the center of individuals' lives, there is no need for any extra effort to record or monitor privacy. The attitudes of individuals displaying privacy on social media platforms are welcomed with interest by the audience and the digital world becomes an environment where private content is voluntarily displayed and consumed. Social media platforms such as YouTube, with their structure and broadcast policies, encourage users to exhibit privacy and reward individuals for exhibiting privacy.

SOCIAL MEDIA AND PRIVACY

Social media platforms, which emerged with the development of Web 2.0 technologies, allow individuals to produce and share content in the digital environment without the need for software knowledge and to come together with other individuals through the platform. Over time, this has increased the mass access to social media platforms and today the number of users on social media platforms has reached billions. Users spend a significant portion of their day on the platform by writing, reading, sharing photos, videos or watching videos, and the prerequisite for their presence on the platforms is that they share information about their private lives and privacy with social media companies. Digital media environments play an important role in the development of celebrity culture. The internet, which has emerged as a result of communication technologies, has become the most effective and fastest medium for the development of celebrity culture. With digitalization, the accessibility of ordinary people to fame becomes easier and the phenomenon of fame becomes the most important and fastest target to be reached. Especially with the emergence and popularization of social media platforms, the culture of fame has gained a completely different momentum in this new environment (Akyazı, 2020, p. 256). Social media platforms are similar to traditional media in good ways. First, social media platforms have become mainstream and the distribution of information is driven by the users themselves. Another similarity is the dependence of social media platforms on advertising. The need for advertising revenues requires both advertisers and users to be satisfied and digital circulation must be constantly active (Crowley&Heyer, 2019, p. 409-410). Users' satisfaction is ensured by the fact that entertainment is the main output of the platforms and information circulates continuously and quickly. The diversification of games, quizzes, character analysis and video/photo sharing within the platform, and the inclusion of news platforms in social media platforms can be exemplified as factors that increase interaction here. In such an environment, the increase in users and continuous data generation will help advertisers to increase their advertisements and consolidate profits by storing big data.

Today, there are dozens of social media platforms in the digital world with a large number of users. While individuals use social media platforms for information, entertainment, socializing, socializing and finding friends, the chat feature of the environment has also turned the platforms into a direct communication channel. According to WeAreSocial's 2022 data, the social media platform with the most users in the world is Facebook with 2.9 billion users. Facebook is followed by YouTube with 2.5 billion users, Whatsapp with 2 billion users, Instagram with 1.5 billion users and Tik-Tok with 1 billion users. Twitter has 436 million users (WeAreSocial, May 25 2023). WeAreSocial 2025 data shows that YouTube has overtaken Facebook. Reaching 2.53 billion people, YouTube is visited by 45.5% of the world's internet users; almost half of them. However, according to 2025 data, 2.28 billion users are active on Facebook (WeAreSocial, Feb 5 2025). Van Dijk classifies social media in terms of media richness and

focus. The individual focus is on blogs and microblogs (Twitter), the category of social networking sites (Facebook, Linkedin, TikTok), and Second Life as virtual social worlds. As a collective focus, social media such as wikis as chat boxes and collaboration platforms, online encyclopedias, YouTube as interest and content and sharing sites, and Pubg as virtual game worlds are described (Van Dijk, 2018, p. 252).

In another respect, these social media offer new areas for multinational media companies in terms of advertising. The involvement of multinational media companies in the digital environment through social media also takes place in order to re-commoditize information. However, digital platforms such as YouTube, Facebook, etc. have important links between advertisers and political actors who want to filter content or circulate new content in this network environment (Castells, 2016, p.133). Therefore, the discourse that social media platforms are "free" feeds social media companies that commodify users' private lives and privacy and aim to recruit more users. The product is entirely social media users, and all digital traces on the platforms are considered as data and commodified. Space for "self-creation", "self-realization", "self-publishing" Social media platforms differ from each other in that they allow for different types of use. The common point of social media platforms is that they are "social" and implement their policies according to this sociability. The emphasis on sociability is more on a form of sociability focused on sharing, group and partnership combined with information and communication. All social media platforms use a business model based on targeted advertising that aims to turn users' personal data into a commodity (Fuchs, 2015, p. 356). People strive to make a good impression in every aspect of their lives. In order to achieve continuity in interpersonal relationships, efforts are made to realize self-presentations at a level that can affect other individuals. In this case, the person makes a self-presentation according to the expectations of the audience and reshapes his/her identity on relationships (Goffman, 2016, p. 28). The rewarding system on platforms that allow individuals to show and share their self-presentations, and practices such as income generation, are designed to ensure the continuity of the show. The structure of social media platforms is designed for sharing information, not keeping it. It is the flow of information that keeps platforms and networks up to date. Networks are formed through information flows, in other words, through users' production and dissemination of information and self-presentations (Papacharissi, 2020, p. 168). In the digital environment, individuals take risks in terms of self-presentation as they determine the amount of information about themselves. Individuals, who choose new identities in the internet world with digitalization, offer their private and private areas, which are considered private and private, to the consumption of other individuals with the feature of anonymity with online communication, unlike traditional communication. All kinds of expressions that cannot be revealed or said in daily life can be said in digital life. Thus, as the world turns into a digital screen, the line between private and public space disappears. While private spaces become public, with digitalization, everything is left open to show and to be seen. In this way, the body, which is not shown, is expressed with a new identity through communication embodied through the computer keyboard. This is where the phrase "create yourself, produce yourself" comes from. The individual reproduces his/her identity with language in digital media (Timisi, 2005, p. 96-97).

The infrastructure based on targeted advertising allows algorithms to work much more effectively with the voluntary participation of users, and everything related to private life and privacy becomes a commodity and circulates in the digital environment. Kara categorizes the appropriate social media platforms according to their self-presentation as follows (Kara, 2013, p. 70-71):

On the other hand, photo and video sharing sites such as YouTube and Flick are examples of platforms where the degree of self-disclosure and self-presentation is low, but media richness is moderate. On these platforms, users make extensive use of visual elements as well as text-based communication. While content is still at the forefront, self-presentation is low. On the other hand, network-based applications such as Facebook and Google+ are examples of sites where the personality traits of the individual sharing the content are as prominent as the content shared. On such platforms, users share content such as texts, videos and photos, as well as personal information such as education level, religious beliefs, political views, family members, entertainment habits and photos. Therefore, even if social presence and media richness are moderate, self-presentation is quite high. Virtual gaming platforms, the most well-known of which is World of Warcraft, are applications where media richness is very high and self-presentation is weak. The reason for the weak self-presentation is the limited possibility of creating a new character in such games. The user chooses between several characters given to them by the game and manages them. In contrast to virtual game platforms, virtual world simulations are applications where self-presentation is high, as they allow for the design of the character according to all personal characteristics. In this grouping, the most well-known example of which is Second Life, emotional as well as physical characteristics can be added to the characters. For this reason, the user has the opportunity to reflect his/her self to the character he/she creates at the highest level.

Social media platforms request information related to private life and privacy such as name, surname, age and e-mail address when making individuals social media users. Users who fulfill these conditions can join the platform "for free". The "participation" offered by social media to individuals increases the production and consumption of privacy-related content. The reason why Facebook and other social media platforms have high market values despite the fact that their main services are free of charge is due to the size of the data accessed by companies and users. As companies create business models based on data, privacy issues arise due to the economization of data. The reason why the service provided on social media platforms is free of charge is that users are products; personal data is capitalized. In other words, users pay for the service they receive with their personal data. Attitudes and behaviors on social media are commercialized by the platforms (Lokke, 2020, p. 71)

The system's content policies that make privacy visible and users' display of privacy in the name of self-presentation, entertainment or self-realization limit private spaces and increase public spaces in the virtual environment. Facebook CEO Mark Zuckerberg, who has adopted the goal of publicizing privacy in social media as his editorial policy, summarizes the relationship between social media and privacy as follows (BBC Turkish, Mar 7 2019):

Over the last 15 years, Facebook and Instagram have helped people connect with friends, communities and areas of interest in a digital version of a town square. But increasingly, people want to connect in the privacy of the digital version of the living room.

Social media platforms have a significant social and personal impact on individuals. Another social and personal impact of social media platforms, which remove the boundary lines in communication, create information overload, increase social pressure and addiction, is that they cause individuals to face dilemmas about privacy and identity disclosure (Van Dijk, 2018, p. 258). With "sociability" on social media, individuals are expected to be proud of their selves and enjoy displaying their selves, and individuals are expected to represent themselves on the platform. In addition, it is experienced that individuals determine with whom they can communicate and show which brand they adopt (Lovink, 2017, p. 44). While individuals are concerned about the features on the platform that make their private life and privacy risky, on the other hand, they try to become popular on the platforms by voluntarily displaying their private life and privacy. The infrastructure of social media platforms is also designed to facilitate individuals' voluntary obscuring of privacy. Privacy-oriented publishing policies are increasing in power, and users are encouraged to exhibit private life and privacy behaviors. In a system where individuals are empowered by their behaviors that demonstrate privacy in the digital environment, privacy today is voluntarily obscured by individuals themselves. It is no longer the panopticon that threatens privacy, but the digital panopticon that legitimizes exposure and disclosure. In the digital panopticon, individuals are both the killer and the victim of privacy (Han, 2020, p. 72). At this point, individuals voluntarily destroy their privacy themselves. Privacy is paid as a price for the world of entertainment and self-realization offered by social media platforms. Everything private is done in the virtual public sphere and open to public consumption. Social media platforms change individuals' understanding of what should be public and what should be private (Bauman&Lyon, 2018, p. 35-36). "Activism" on social platforms can be achieved on the condition that individuals share their personal information.

Individuals tend to share their personal information in order to measure the impact of the virtual identities they create. Social media companies are also aware of the importance of personal information for advertisements and benefit from individuals' behaviors that expose privacy (Van Dijk, 2018, p. 259). In the traditional mass media, the display of the private life of Hollywood stars through magazine programs and the exposure of the privacy of ordinary people trying to become "famous" in reality shows such as Big Brother with panoptic strategies are now added to the privacy-oriented content created by influencers, who are expressed as internet celebrities, in order to increase their popularity. While the disclosure of the self and the display of privacy takes place on television or cinema in traditional mass media, in the era of the digital panopticon, the medium of privacy is social media platforms. Han explains the digital panopticon through the relationship between social media and privacy as follows (Han, 2020, p. 18):

The inhabitants of Bentham's panopticon are isolated from each other for disciplinary purposes and are forbidden to speak to each other. The inhabitants of the digital panopticon, on the other hand, engage in intense communication with each other and voluntarily disclose everything. In this way, they actively cooperate with the digital panopticon. The digital control society makes extensive use of freedom. This is only possible through voluntary self-exposure and self-undressing. It is as if the digital Big Brother has delegated his work to the inhabitants. In this way, the disposal of data is not forced, but a result of a genuine need. Hence the efficiency of the digital panopticon.

Social media platforms, which emerged with digitalization, use "freedom" as a source of motivation for the voluntary exposure of individuals. With expressions such as "publish yourself", "share", "like", "comment", etc., individuals are encouraged to exhibit and disclose their private life and privacy, and the easiest and most entertaining place for this is social media platforms. Users feel that they are free by sharing on social media platforms, in other words, they actually experience a paradox by aiming to be liberated by exhibiting privacy. The fact that social media platforms are capitalist companies and the system aims to make profit by commoditizing the private life and privacy of individuals reinforces the privacy problems in social media. For example, influencers on YouTube or Instagram broadcast by internalizing neoliberal techniques. While broadcasting on different themes, special products are promoted on platforms with slogans such as freedom and creativity. In this way, viewers want to buy the products consumed by influencers and internet celebrities become role models for individuals. Influencers show consumption as a symbol of self-realization and freedom. Thus, the phenomenon of consumption is frequently encouraged by the new and voluntary actors of the system (Han, 2023, p. 13). Users who want to be included in the digital culture on social media platforms, which distract from the problems of everyday life and promise a perfect world, try to achieve happiness by commodifying whatever belongs to identity. In the digital environment, individuals who both surveil while consuming and consume while surveilling reproduce all elements in the digital world while publicizing their private spaces with their own consent. The panoptic show of sovereignty transforms not only the digital environment but also the way of life of the individual in daily life (Akaydın&Koç 2024, p. 126). At this point, differences emerge between the understanding of privacy in daily life and the understanding of privacy in the digital environment, and with social media platforms, the lack of privacy in the public sphere and attitudes of secrecy are becoming strange for individuals.

What makes social media attractive is voyeurism and exhibitionism. In addition, social media platforms spread the culture of fame and nurture narcissistic behaviors. Behaviors that are considered private in daily life, such as sharing semi-nude photos and revealing secrets, are shared on social media platforms with narcissistic feelings (Twenge&Campbell, 2023, p. 69). By encouraging surveillance and exposure, social media platforms reward individuals with strategies such as being visible or earning wages. Thus, every user on social media platforms becomes a data machine. In the digital age, where statistics such as the number of likes, subscribers, views and followers mean pleasure and reputation, individuals voluntarily give up their privacy, which is the most basic area of freedom, for the sake of becoming visible or earning income. In this way, private life and privacy data circulate unlimitedly and privacy disappears in the virtual environment where everything is transparently written, drawn and shared.

A SPACE FOR THE DISPLAY OF PRIVACY: YOUTUBE

While in the past television occupied living rooms, today YouTube is beginning to replace televisions. While individuals turn on televisions and search for content to watch, they now do so through YouTube in the digital world. The YouTube algorithm encourages individuals to consume more video content by showing video after video. Thus, viewing times, which is the main purpose of YouTube, increase (Walker, 2021, p. 227). In addition, television channels accept the rise of YouTube as a result of digitalization by moving their content to YouTube. Not only TV channels, but also almost all representatives of traditional media such as radio and newspapers are trying to be visible by opening channels on YouTube. As a result of these developments, especially in the recent period, TV screens have become like monitors, and individuals are no longer bound to the broadcast streams of traditional media, but have started to watch the content of their choice on platforms such as YouTube, Netflix, etc. by creating their own broadcast streams.

On YouTube, whose motto is "Broadcast Yourself", individuals are both producers and consumers. While users consume video content uploaded from around the world, they can also share videos produced by themselves on the platform. This sharing can be done professionally using a variety of tools or in an amateur way using only a phone. With the widespread use of publishing on YouTube, the platform has also become a source of income. YouTube has started to pay publishers based on the number of views and subscribers, and a new professional group called "YouTuber" or "Influencer" has emerged. The monetization opportunity on the platform increases the number of users.

In order to monetize on YouTube, users are expected to pass certain stages. Making money on the platform depends on consistent content production, being up-to-date, and reaching a certain number of subscribers and views. YouTube summarizes the conditions for generating revenue for content creators through the platform as follows (YouTube, June 19, 2025):

Content must be your own original work. When you use another user's content, you must adapt it to your own style by changing it significantly.

Your content should not repeat itself. Your content should aim to entertain or educate viewers, not just increase views.

Our review team checks that your channel and content comply with our policies. As it's not possible to review every single video on your channel, we look for the following elements:

Main theme

Most watched videos

New videos

Videos that make up the largest portion of watch time

Video metadata (including titles, thumbnails, and descriptions)

The "About" section of the channel

The examples above are only a fraction of the content our review team may consider. Other sections of your channel may also be checked to ensure that every aspect of your channel complies with our policies.

YouTube is one of the most popular social media platforms, being the most searched platform after Google. What differentiates YouTube from other social media platforms is the emergence of internet celebrities, referred to as "YouTubers" or "Influencers", who generate direct income from the platform. In order for content creators to generate revenue from YouTube, they need to continue producing videos consistently and reach a certain number of subscribers and views. This situation pushes content producers to search for more striking or entertaining content that includes privacy in video production in order to get more attention from viewers. Arık states that the platform is an unlimited environment for the display of privacy and the platform structure as follows (Arık, 2013, p. 105-106).

On YouTube, as in reality shows, ordinary people tell their own stories, while a wide range of media content can also be uploaded to the system. Bypassing the media managers, gatekeepers and producers of traditional media, YouTube is essentially a user-generated site; therefore, many unrelated content complements the medium. Every moment of life can be the subject of this site; therefore, an unlimited opportunity to exhibit gives YouTube its power. One of the main goals on this platform is to be watched the most; therefore, interesting strategies are employed to get 'clicks' and exposing oneself through different appearances gains importance.

Influencers' personalities on YouTube are based on sharing selected aspects of the influencers. Video content often shares personal and non-public lives, demanding the surveillance of the masses. Therefore, privacy becomes a commodity that is manipulated and performed in order to advance on the YouTube career path (Abidin 2020, p. 32). The parasocial or social relationship refers to the intimate relationship between media personalities and the audience. In traditional mass media, the parasocial relationship is demonstrated through media performances. The warm language that radio or television programmers establish with the audience is done in order to establish sincere ties. The emotions and thoughts of the masses can be influenced through parasocial relations. Through communication in the studio, the media professional determines when and how audiences will react (Laughey, 2010, p. 139). With the rise of social media platforms, YouTube in particular has become the center of the parasocial relationship. On the one hand, YouTubers serve as role models for their viewers, on the other hand, they gain the trust of the audience by exhibiting privacy through the parasocial relationship they establish and entertain individuals by distracting them from the troubles of daily life. Through the parasocial relationship on YouTube, individuals develop intimacy with people they have never seen or never met. Since the YouTube celebrity's private life and all daily routines are constantly staged, viewers know everything about privacy. On the other hand, through the parasocial relationship created through makeup channels, food channels or travel channels, individuals learn “what is the best” from YouTubers and their attitudes can be determined. In the research on British YouTuber Zoe Sugg, it was found that Sugg became famous by establishing a parasocial relationship with the audience. Sugg's adoption of a content policy of displaying her privacy is appreciated by viewers. Showing her daily routines and offering them for consumption shows that privacy is a stepping stone to fame (Berryman&Kavka, 2017, p. 318). Again, in a study conducted on YouTubers in Turkey, although YouTubers have produced content on different themes, the common point of all of them is that they themselves have obscured their privacy. YouTuber Black Giyen Genç's sharing of his child's daily routines down to diapers, Vlogger Aslı Kıvanç's sharing of information about his private life up to childhood traumas with viewers, and travel channel Gökhan Yıldırım's unannounced footage of someone using the toilet show that YouTubers aim to become famous by destroying privacy. Despite the negative consequences of the display of privacy and the voluntary surveillance process, the aforementioned YouTubers continue to publicize privacy (Arslan, 2025, p. 156-157). Wang, who conducted research in China on the relationship between YouTube and Privacy, reveals that the famous Chinese YouTuber Li Ziqi has rapidly increased her followers due to her emotional connection with the audience when she analyzes the story, performance and video comments of her videos on YouTube. Content creators like Li Ziqi, who produce content on YouTube, especially as vloggers, contribute significantly to the growth of the influencer economy (Wang, 2020, p. 43-44). YouTubers who are aware of the commodity value of privacy on YouTube voluntarily exhibit their privacy more and try to increase their followers by establishing parasocial relationships with viewers. Individuals trust influencers who produce privacy-oriented content and express their demand for more privacy through YouTube comments. Thus, through the “vlogs” created within the platform, although content producers broadcast on different themes, cameras are set up from the bedroom to the bathroom of the house, from the hotel room to restaurants, and all of the activities of the day are shown to meet the viewers' demand for privacy. Privacy, which is a symbol of both freedom and security, is voluntarily destroyed by individuals for purposes such as earning income, self-realization and attracting attention.

Consumer-oriented surveillance on YouTube goes hand in hand with incentives for producers, i.e. users who broadcast and own channels on YouTube. YouTube pays its users according to the number of subscribers and views, and as a result, users live with the need to broadcast continuously in order to increase their target audience and viewership rates. This situation causes users to become YouTube's digital laborers, while at the same time sharing more striking and attention-grabbing content in order to earn more money from YouTube and become famous. The consistent production of content increases the need for engaging new content, leading individuals to compromise more on information, physical and spatial privacy. This is because individuals seek to find attention-grabbing and sensational topics from their environment, especially from themselves, in order to maintain and increase their existing audience. In particular, the number of subscribers and views of some YouTubers exceeding millions, becoming famous, earning significant sums of money as a source of motivation for other YouTube content producers, in order to reach this point, individuals give up their personal privacy more easily and voluntarily participate in surveillance.

CONCLUSION

Social media platforms facilitate masses to communicate with each other through networks, creating a fast, instant and interactive form of communication. With digitalization, individuals decide how and with whom to communicate, especially through social media platforms. In addition, the opportunity to produce and share content offered by Web 2.0 technology eliminates the requirement of knowing software or being a professional at the point of producing and disseminating information. By becoming active on social media platforms, individuals have evolved from merely receiving and consuming information to producing it. Thus, individuals have turned into consumers who produce with the contribution of social media platforms. With slogans such as "Publish Yourself", "What do you think", "What's Happening", social media platforms encourage individuals to engage in attitudes and behaviors that produce more data. The design of social media platforms is also designed to encourage individuals to become users.

The phenomenon of privacy has been one of the most debated issues throughout history, and today it is being reassessed with the social media platforms created by communication technologies. While individuals were forced to be visible through the panopticon system in the pre-modern period, with the emergence of mass media, they were voluntarily encouraged to be visible, especially through television and cinema productions. Drama series, reality shows and magazine programs have gained ratings through the commodification of privacy. The capitalist system has objectified and commodified everything related to private life and privacy through commercialization, sometimes through celebrities and sometimes through ordinary people. The phenomenon of surveillance, conceptualized as "panopticon", has transformed into superpanopticon, synopticon as a result of the equipping of social life with surveillance technologies with the entry of technology into the center of individuals' lives, and with digitalization and the social media platforms it has created, the era of omnipticon, a form of society in which everyone spies on everyone else, has passed. Especially with the social media platforms created by Web 2.0 technologies, individuals have started to voluntarily participate in the surveillance process. Social media platforms have thus become the center of the process of voluntary surveillance. The social media economy revolves around the display of privacy and digital surveillance, and social media companies have become the center of the process of voluntary surveillance.

YouTube, one of the most popular social media platforms with a reach of 2.5 billion people according to the latest data, is one of the social media platforms that compromises the privacy of individuals and turns their surveillance into a commercial commodity. YouTube, which gives individuals the opportunity to become "Influencers" or "YouTubers", own their own channels and earn money by producing content, in return reinforces its profits through the digital labor of individuals. YouTube, which makes a huge profit from the interaction between content producers and viewers, pays content producers according to their subscriber, view and like statistics in order to continue to increase its earnings. In doing so, the YouTube system, which places advertisements on "free" broadcasts, expands its commercial range by commodifying users' data and emotions. Individuals who fall under the spell of digital platforms, especially YouTube, with the fees they receive, demand surveillance of the masses and sometimes try to produce content by compromising the most basic freedom of privacy. YouTubers, who realize that videos with privacy content attract more attention, trivialize privacy, which is one of the most important values of human life, and try to quickly meet the conditions for YouTube to earn income. When we look at the studies evaluating YouTubers in the UK, China and Turkey in terms of privacy, we see that although different themes are broadcasted, privacy is voluntarily publicized to buy the attention of viewers. Emotional bonds with viewers are established through the display of private life, and viewers find YouTubers who produce such content sincere.

YouTubers, who have emerged thanks to the opportunities offered by digital technology, strive to become new digital celebrities, interact with the audience through a parasocial relationship and act with their public private selves in the digital environment. Sometimes the parasocial relationship is established to sell a product to the target audience and sometimes to increase the target audience. The common characteristic of YouTubers is that they use privacy in a deliberately ambiguous way with the motivations of money, fame and self-realization. The vlogging culture created by YouTube is based on individuals exhibiting their entire daily routines, and a new digital celebrity identity has emerged as Vlogger alongside the concept of YouTuber. The system gives the ordinary person the opportunity to become a celebrity, but it does so by buying whatever is related to privacy or identity.

In addition to the fact that YouTube's content and broadcasting policies stipulate the publicization of privacy as a condition, one of the reasons for behaviors that display privacy is YouTubers' illusion of freedom on the platform. Individuals think that they are broadcasting freely on the platform, but the increase in subscribers or views brings risks, not freedom. As with other social media platforms, YouTube presents itself to individuals as a free medium, but it publicizes the private life and privacy of individuals and exploits the digital labor on the other hand. The system based on the exploitation of the individual continues with individuals feeling free.

Social media platforms and their "Digital Celebrities" are popular culture products that legitimize the current system. The tools of the global culture industry are social media platforms and the celebrities are phenomena or influencers. While in traditional mass media, the status of celebrities is measured through ratings, box office or circulation, the status of new celebrities is measured through the number of subscribers, views and likes. YouTubers are role models for viewers, just like the celebrities of the culture industry, and the masses are tried to be directed with content created on different themes. This can sometimes be about the best cosmetic product, places to visit or the best restaurants. The magic of technology transforms viewers into YouTuber candidates and increases the number of consumers producing content day by day. In the past, doctors and lawyers were seen as ideal professions, but today, with the influence of technology, becoming a YouTuber or influencer is the dream of individuals. Although increased surveillance increases the gates of fame and opportunities to earn money, on the other hand, the use of privacy by trivializing it negatively affects the mental health of individuals, and also increases harassment, cyberbullying and social lynch culture.

There is one fact that must be accepted, and that is that fame requires responsibility. While in the past, when traditional mass media was more effective, there were certain criteria and a sense of responsibility regarding fame, today's celebrities do not live this life with a sense of responsibility. As a result, the uncontrolled fame provided by the digital environment leads these people to disaster after a certain period of time. It is a fact that this system gives the opportunity of fame to ordinary citizens and creates short-term fame by producing new new fame. Especially in the new generation, the goal of earning money without producing and realizing digital fame through social media platforms is increasing day by day. Thus, more courageous and destructive steps are easily taken for the sake of realizing this goal. However, one of the problems of this process is that with the significant contribution of social media platforms, publicity triumphs over privacy. Those who are not public are ostracized or marginalized. Today, it has become a surprising phenomenon for any individual not to have a social media account or not to post, "offlineness".

The uncontrolled use of social media platforms and the fact that they have become an indispensable part of individuals' lives make media education compulsory. In order to increase privacy awareness and digital surveillance awareness, it would be beneficial to expand media literacy education and increase studies on digital media literacy. In addition, organizations or projects that will bring together experts and academics on "digital surveillance and privacy" with the society should be put into practice.

REFERENCES

Abidin, C. (2020). L8r H8r: Commoditized privacy, influencer wars, and productive disorder in the influencer industry. In Lind, R. A. (Ed.), *Produsing theory in a digital world 3.0* (pp. 31–48). Peter Lang.

Akaydın Aydın, A., & Koç, N. E. (2024). Examining intimacy through reality shows: An analysis on "Love is Blind". In Kahraman Gökalp, E., & Yıldız, İ. (Eds.), *Dimensions of digital privacy: Dijital alanda araştırmalar ve tartışmalar* (pp. 123–135). Istanbul University Publishing House., DOI: 10.26650/B/SSc5SSc20.2024.030.008

Akyazı, A. (2020). Sosyal medyanın şöhret kültürüne etkisi. *İstanbul Aydın Üniversitesi Dergisi, 12*(3), 251–274.

Arık, E. (2013). The rise of the common man: Social media celebrities. *Communication and Diplomacy*, 97–112.

Arık, E., & Arık, M. B. (2021). Televizyon ve mahremiyet. In Kütükoğlu, E. (Ed.), *Mahremiyetin medyası* (pp. 13–30). Eğitim Yayınevi.

Arslan, U. (2025). *Kendini yayınla: YouTube ve mahremiyet.* Nobel Akademik Yayıncılık.

Bauman, Z. (2018). *44 letters from the fluid modern world.* Habitus Book.

Bauman, Z., & Lyon, D. (2018). *Fluid surveillance.* Ayrıntı Publications.

BBC. (2019, March 7). *Sosyal medya fenomenleri: Influencer'lar nasıl para kazanıyor?* https://www.bbc.com/turkce/haberler-47478637

Berryman, R., & Kavka, M. (2017). "I guess a lot of people see me as a big sister or a friend": The role of intimacy in the celebrification of beauty vloggers. *Journal of Gender Studies, 26*(5), 692–703. DOI: 10.1080/09589236.2017.1288611

Castells, M. (2016). *The power of communication* (Kılıç, E., Trans.). Istanbul Bilgi University Publications.

Crowley, D., & Heyer, P. (2019). *İletişim tarihi: Taş devri sembollerinden sosyal medyaya.* Siyasal Kitabevi.

Dolgun, U. (2015). *Şeffaf hapishane yahut gözetim toplumu.* Ötüken Neşriyat.

Fuchs, C. (2015). *Digital labor and Karl Marx* (Kalaycı, T. E., & Oğuz, S., Trans.). NotaBene Publications.

Goffman, E. (2016). *Günlük yaşamda benliğin sunumu* (Cezar, B., Trans.). Metis Yayınları.

Han, B.-C. (2020a). *Transparency society*. Metis Publications.

Han, B.-C. (2020b). *Psikopolitika: Neoliberalizm ve yeni iktidar teknikleri*. Metis Publications.

Han, B.-C. (2023). *Enfocracy: Crisis of digitalization and democracy*. Ketebe Publications.

Kara, T. (2013). *Sosyal medya endüstrisi*. Beta Basım.

Laughey, D. (2010). *Medya çalışmaları: Teoriler ve yaklaşımlar*. Kalkedon Yayınları.

Lokke, E. (2020). *Privacy: Private life in digital society*. Koç University Publications.

Lovink, G. (2017). *The bottomless well of social media*. Otonom Publishing.

Lyon, D. (2013). *Gözetim çalışmaları*. Kalkedon Publishing.

Mutlu, E. (2008). *Dictionary of communication*. Ayraç Kitabevi.

Papacharissi, Z. (2020). Sensiz ben hiçbirşeyim: Twitter'da benliğin gösterileri. In Aydoğan, F. (Ed.), *Yeni medya kuramları II* (pp. 163–188). Der Publishing.

Timisi, N. (2005). Sanallığın gerçekliği: İnternetin kimlik ve topluluk alanlarına girişi. In Binark, M., & Kılıçbay, B. (Eds.), *İnternet, toplum, kültür* (pp. 89–105). Epos Publishing.

Twenge, J. M., & Campbell, W. K. (2023). *Asrın vebası: Narcissism illeti* (Korkmaz, Ö., Trans.). Kaknüs Publications.

Uğur Balcı, A. (2021). Sinema ve mahremiyet: Sine-gözün alanları. In Kütükoğlu, E. (Ed.), *Mahremiyetin medyası* (pp. 63–88). Eğitim Publishing.

Van Dijk, J. (2018). *Network society*. Epsilon Publishing House.

Walker, C. S. (2021). *YouTubers* (Demir, B. M., Trans.). Lykeion Publishing.

Wang, T. (2020). *Parasocial relationship: An analysis of Li Ziqi and her audiences* [Unpublished master's thesis]. Middle Tennessee State University.

Yüksel, M. (2003). Mahremiyet hakkı ve sosyo-tarihsel gelişimi. *Ankara University SBF Journal*, *64*(1), 181–213.

Yüksel, M. (2009). Philosophical approaches to the right to privacy and individual freedoms. *Ankara University SBF Journal*, *64*(4), 1–24.

Chapter 9
Digital Media Representation of Feminism:
Sentiment Trends and Cultural Influences in the US, UK, and India

T. K. Sateesh Kumar
https://orcid.org/0000-0002-8406-409X
Kristu Jayanti College, India

Vishnu Achutha Menon
https://orcid.org/0000-0003-4028-3685
Institute for Educational and Developmental Studies, India

Lijo P. Thomas
https://orcid.org/0009-0009-7031-5001
Kristu Jayanti College, India

Juby Thomas
https://orcid.org/0000-0003-2167-0620
Kristu Jayanti College, India

ABSTRACT

This study examines how media outlets in the US, UK, and India portray feminism through sentiment analysis and machine learning-based classification models. By assessing sentiment polarity and evaluating model accuracy, the research highlights variations in feminist discourse across different media landscapes. Findings indicate that UK media maintains a more balanced and positive stance, whereas US and Indian media exhibit slight variations influenced by socio-political and cultural

DOI: 10.4018/979-8-3373-6192-5.ch009

factors. The study provides a comparative perspective on feminist representation, offering insights into global media narratives.

INTRODUCTION

The way feminism is portrayed in the media differs across cultural and political settings. News outlets influence public perceptions, either reinforcing traditional beliefs or promoting progressive ideas. Sentiment analysis helps determine whether media discussions on feminism are positive, negative, or neutral, revealing patterns in bias, framing, and ideological influence. This study explores how different media outlets discuss feminism and the extent to which political and cultural factors shape these narratives. Media coverage of feminism reflects the social and political climate of each country. In the UK, discussions often focus on policy and legislative changes, making the discourse more structured. In the US, media sentiment shifts based on political divisions, with feminism being framed differently depending on the media's ideological stance. In India, feminist coverage is shaped by traditional values, cultural expectations, and modern feminist movements, resulting in more varied sentiment scores. A comparative study of these countries provides insight into how feminism is discussed and framed in different media environments. Media influences public opinion, social attitudes, and policy discussions on feminism, yet few studies compare its portrayal across different countries. This research addresses that gap using sentiment analysis and machine learning models to analyze feminist discourse in media from the US, UK, and India.

This study aims to:

- Provide a data-driven perspective on how media portrays feminism.
- Compare sentiment trends across different countries to identify cultural and political influences.
- Assess the effectiveness of machine learning models in classifying media sentiment on feminism.

REVIEW OF LITERATURE

Several recent studies have examined the intersection of digital platforms, sentiment expression, and algorithmic mediation within the Indian and broader global context. Education, economic concerns, the United States, and sports emerged as the most frequently reported and commonly discussed themes in COVID-19-related news across the United Kingdom, India, Japan, and South Korea. Among these countries, the United Kingdom, which experienced the most severe pandemic outcomes based on the dataset, exhibited the highest proportion of negative sentiment within its news coverage on the pandemic (Ghasiya & Okamura, 2021). In a separate study, Ahmed et al. (2023) conducted sentiment analysis and topic modeling on Twitter posts concerning the "Digital India" campaign. This analysis employed a range of machine learning algorithms, including logistic regression, support vector machines, K-nearest neighbors, and decision trees. The results demonstrated that several models, particularly decision trees and logistic regression, were able to achieve a classification accuracy of 95.63% in identifying and interpreting sentiment in social media data. The study further assessed model performance using standard evaluation criteria such as precision, recall, F-score, and overall accuracy.

In another contribution, Padmaja et al. (2014) compiled a sentiment-rich corpus comprising 689 news articles drawn from three major Indian English-language newspapers, spanning a four-day period in 2009. This corpus served as a testbed for examining the efficacy of various sentiment analysis techniques, both supervised machine learning models and unsupervised lexical-based methods. The study also addressed the methodological challenge of distinguishing between the sentiment expressed in opinions (positive or negative) and the sentiment embedded in news events themselves (i.e., whether the news reported was inherently good or bad).

Kashyap and Singh (2021) conducted a controlled study to investigate whether Instagram's algorithmic structures in India exhibit bias by prioritizing majoritarian feminist content over intersectional feminist perspectives. By comparing engagement and growth metrics of two curated Instagram accounts aligned with these ideological positions, the study provided empirical evidence of unequal content visibility. This investigation was supplemented by a critical review of secondary literature, which contextualized findings within broader discussions on data bias, algorithmic discrimination, and the framework of Data Justice. In parallel, Patil et al. (2018) focused on political sentiment analysis on Twitter to better understand public reactions to governmental strategies. Their study utilized a large dataset of Twitter content spanning various modalities—text, images, and videos—pertaining to political discourse. The analysis aimed to trace sentiment flows and thematic variations, with an underlying assumption that such data could offer meaningful perspectives on public response to policy discourse and political developments.

The role of machine learning classifiers in sentiment detection has also been explored extensively. Rani and Kumar (2019) implemented a sentiment analysis system using a support vector machine (SVM) classifier. Their model achieved a classification accuracy of 68% for movie reviews and 82% for Twitter data. Although model performance varied by context, the results were positioned as applicable to multiple domains, including consumer review analysis and the study of social behavior in digital environments. The study further suggested the model's potential use in predicting social disturbances, thereby linking computational methods to sociopolitical applications. In the domain of news analytics, J. Ahmed and Ahmed (2023) proposed a classification approach that categorized news articles into five dominant themes: Crime, Cure and Treatment, Economy, Communal, and Entertainment. Their model for detecting fake news yielded an accuracy of 87%, with the "communal" category identified as the most vulnerable to misinformation. The study developed a sentiment classification model capable of distinguishing between positive and negative news articles with 89% accuracy. These findings contribute to the growing body of literature on misinformation detection and media sentiment classification, particularly within the Indian context.

In the domain of feature selection and classification performance, several studies have investigated the relative effectiveness of different algorithmic approaches. Trivedi et al. (2018) reported that the Relief-F (RF) feature selection method exhibited superior performance when the maximum number of features was retained. Specifically, the method produced higher F-values, lower false positive rates, and faster training times compared to other feature selection techniques, suggesting its suitability for high-dimensional datasets. However, when fewer features were used, the one-R method outperformed RF, indicating that its utility may vary depending on the dimensionality of the dataset. Regarding classification techniques, the Support Vector Machine (SVM) emerged as the most effective, consistently achieving the highest classification accuracy across multiple datasets. Nevertheless, the Bayesian classifier showed comparable performance under certain conditions, suggesting its potential as an alternative, particularly in applications requiring probabilistic classification.

In a related context, Mishra et al. (2016) conducted a sentiment analysis of Twitter data concerning the Digital India campaign. Their findings revealed a diverse distribution of public opinion: approximately 50% of tweets conveyed positive sentiment toward the initiative, 20% expressed negative views, and the remaining 30% were classified as neutral. These results point to a generally favorable perception of the campaign, while also highlighting a substantial segment of critical or undecided users. The study underscores the importance of accounting for sentiment diversity when assessing digital engagement with policy initiatives.

Chandra and Jana (2020) extended this line of inquiry by employing both machine learning classifiers and deep learning models to classify tweets into positive or negative sentiment categories. To address the variability of language and expression on social media platforms, the study applied multiple model architectures, thereby enhancing robustness in capturing sentiment nuances. The classification models developed in the study demonstrated the potential to analyze live Twitter data across a broad range of topics, suggesting their applicability in real-time sentiment monitoring.

Building upon these methodological foundations, Pai and Alathur (2020) explored sentiment and emotional responses associated with a recent social movement, presumably related to women's empowerment. Their study analyzed social media data to extract inferences and patterns that could inform public discourse and policy-making processes. The results indicated that digital platforms serve as valuable spaces for understanding collective sentiment, with implications for shaping policy interventions and social strategies.

Recent advancements in transformer-based architectures have demonstrated significant improvements in multilingual sentiment analysis. The XLM-R (Cross-lingual Language Model - RoBERTa) model, in particular, has achieved state-of-the-art results on several benchmark datasets. On the English SemEval 2017 sentiment analysis dataset, XLM-R outperformed previous models, establishing its efficacy in capturing nuanced sentiment expressions in English. In the context of Hindi sentiment analysis, the XLM-R model employed with zero-shot transfer learning surpassed existing state-of-the-art methods (Kumar & Albuquerque, 2021).

In the field of sentiment analysis involving code-mixed Indian language text, Support Vector Machine (SVM) has emerged as the most frequently employed machine learning classifier, followed by Naive Bayes (NB) and Random Forest (RF) (author, year). These models have been widely applied due to their simplicity and effectiveness in text classification tasks. However, recent studies indicate that neural network-based approaches, particularly Long Short-Term Memory (LSTM) and Bidirectional LSTM (BiLSTM) models, tend to outperform traditional classifiers in terms of both accuracy and F1-measure. This performance improvement can be attributed to the ability of neural models to capture complex contextual and sequential patterns in mixed-language data, which are often missed by conventional algorithms. Regarding data sources, Twitter remains the most extensively utilized platform for collecting code-mixed sentiment data, given its brevity, linguistic variability, and widespread public accessibility. Facebook and user-generated reviews of films or products constitute the next most common sources. These platforms offer rich and diverse datasets that reflect informal language usage and frequent switching between languages, thereby presenting both challenges and opportunities for developing more effective sentiment analysis systems in multilingual contexts (Ahmad et al., 2022). Sentiment analysis techniques have been widely applied to large-scale consumer review datasets to evaluate public opinion. In one such study, a corpus of over four million product reviews was analyzed and classified into positive and negative sentiment categories. The classification process involved a comparative evaluation of three machine learning algorithms: Naive Bayes, Support Vector Machine (SVM), and Decision Tree (Singla et al., 2017). To ensure the reliability and generalizability of the results, the performance of each model was assessed using 10-fold cross-validation. This methodological approach provided a robust framework for identifying the strengths and limitations of each classifier in handling large, user-generated textual data, thereby contributing to ongoing efforts in optimizing sentiment classification for commercial applications.

Mendon et al. (2021) conducted a comprehensive study analyzing Twitter data related to the Kerala floods, classifying sentiments using similarity and polarity indices. The study identified dominant themes and topics of discourse and further examined emotional expressions and the role of influential users in shaping public dialogue. The findings were positioned as relevant for governmental and non-governmental organizations seeking to understand patterns of public engagement and emotional response during natural calamities.

Building on the role of demographic variables in sentiment classification, S. Kumar et al. (2020) investigated the performance of sentiment analysis across gender and age groups. The study reported that data from female users resulted in higher model accuracy—reaching 80% when using a convolutional neural network (CNN)—compared to data from male users. Additionally, the model performed more effectively on data collected from individuals aged 50 and above. These observations suggest that demographic factors influence the linguistic features used in expressing sentiment. The authors proposed that future improvements in model performance could be achieved through more demographically diverse data collection.

In another contribution, Shanmugavadivel et al. (2022) developed a hybrid deep learning approach—specifically a CNN combined with BiLSTM—for sentiment classification of Tamil code-mixed text. Following extensive data preprocessing, which included the removal of emojis, repeated characters, symbols, punctuation marks, and numbers, the CNN+BiLSTM model achieved an accuracy of 0.66. This performance was higher than that of several traditional machine learning algorithms, standalone deep learning architectures, and transfer learning-based models, affirming the value of hybrid configurations in processing morphologically rich and informal linguistic data.

Cross-cultural sentiment dynamics during global crises have also been explored in recent research. Imran et al. (2020) examined emotional responses expressed on Twitter in the context of the COVID-19 pandemic. The study analyzed sentiment and thematic patterns across countries, observing significant cross-cultural variations in how users reacted to governmental policies and pandemic-related developments. These findings underline the role of cultural context in shaping public sentiment and suggest that sentiment analysis tools must be adapted to account for regional linguistic and socio-political differences.

Volkova et al. (2013) investigated gender-based linguistic variations in social media communication across three languages—English, Spanish, and Russian. The study focused on the use of subjective language, emoticons, and hashtags, revealing that sentiment analysis performance can be significantly enhanced by integrating gender-specific features. It was observed that simply including gender as a binary variable was insufficient; rather, substantial improvements in subjectivity and polarity classification were achieved when lexical and gender-dependent sentiment features were combined.

In the Indian context, social media has increasingly become a site of engagement with issues of public safety, particularly concerning women in metropolitan areas. Yadav et al. (2020) examined how experiences of harassment and public nuisance are articulated by women in Indian cities and explored the role of social responsibility in shaping perceptions of safety. Their study highlighted how platforms such as Twitter, Facebook, and Instagram are employed in raising awareness and generating discourse around women's safety. In a related effort, Kaur and Sharma (2020) analyzed Twitter datasets associated with hashtags such as #Women and #Metoo, using machine learning algorithms to classify tweets into positive, negative, or neutral sentiment categories. The models were evaluated using standard metrics, including precision, recall, and F1-score, to determine their effectiveness in capturing the nuances of public discourse on gendered issues.

Further contributions to sentiment classification research include comparative evaluations of supervised machine learning algorithms. K. et al. (2016) conducted an empirical study on sentiment analysis of movie reviews, assessing the performance of multiple supervised learning models. The analysis was supported by experimental results and visual representations, providing a comprehensive comparison across algorithms. The authors suggested that the findings could inform future research efforts applying advanced machine learning techniques in domains beyond film reviews.

In the context of regional language processing, Thavareesan and Mahesan (2019) focused on sentiment analysis of Tamil texts. The study tested five distinct corpora and experimented with various feature representations, including both basic features such as word and punctuation counts and traditional features like Bag-of-Words (BoW) and Term Frequency–Inverse Document Frequency (TF-IDF). Among the approaches evaluated, the supervised learning method employing fastText feature representation achieved the highest accuracy—79%—on the UJ_Corpus_Opinions_Nouns corpus. The results demonstrated the effectiveness of combining feature representation strategies with machine learning methods for analyzing sentiment in morphologically rich languages.

The integration of sentiment analysis into studies of sociopolitical and cultural discourse has expanded considerably in recent years, with applications ranging from war-time communication to gender and financial analytics. Maathuis and Kerkhof (2023) applied a design science research approach to examine the themes and sentiments expressed by Ukrainian Telegram users during the first two months of the war in Ukraine. Their study sought to inform broader strategic, socio-ethical, and technical discussions related to the conflict. Acknowledging the early stage of social media analytics in the context of the war, the authors emphasized the need for robust analytical frameworks capable of capturing real-time public discourse during periods of crisis.

In the Indian context, Hore and Bhattacharya (2019) evaluated public sentiment surrounding the "Beti Bachao Beti Padhao" initiative, launched by the Government of India in 2015 to counter gender discrimination and promote female empowerment. Employing multi-class sentiment classification models, the study analyzed Twitter data to interpret evolving societal attitudes toward the girl child. The performance of four distinct machine learning classifiers was assessed using accuracy metrics and Kappa statistics, highlighting the efficacy of computational methods in tracking social change narratives.

A spatial dimension to sentiment was explored by Scarborough and Helmuth (2021), who investigated the relationship between urban place character and public sentiment toward feminism on Twitter. Their findings indicated that areas characterized by revitalization showed higher support for feminist perspectives, while regional shopping hubs were associated with more negative sentiment. Interestingly, factors such as cultural vibrancy and historical or artistic significance were not found to be significantly related to sentiment trends, suggesting that socio-economic factors may play a stronger role in shaping digital opinion.

In financial domains, sentiment analysis has been employed to improve the predictive performance of bankruptcy models. Makeeva and Sinilshchikova (2020) found that incorporating sentiment variables, especially those derived from negative news related to legal issues, debt, crime, and product quality, substantially enhanced the accuracy of bankruptcy prediction. Conversely, positive news concerning innovation, partnerships, and awards was associated with financial stability. The integration of sentiment indicators into financial modeling represents an advancement in risk assessment methodologies.

Friedman et al. (2019) examined cultural gender biases embedded in language, using word embedding techniques to quantify and correlate these biases with gender inequality metrics. The study revealed that word sets organized around specific themes could capture different dimensions of gender bias and that the strength and direction of these biases corresponded with observed gender gaps in society. This approach illustrates how computational linguistics can be utilized to explore latent cultural structures that contribute to systemic disparities.

In the context of multilingual and code-mixed social media content, deep learning techniques have proven to be particularly effective. Jamatia et al. (2020) evaluated the performance of several deep learning architectures—including BiLSTM-CNN, Double BiLSTM, and attention-based models—for sentiment classification in English-Hindi and English-Bengali code-mixed text. These models demonstrated improvements ranging from 20% to 60% over traditional machine learning methods. Furthermore, contextual models such as BERT outperformed standard classifiers in handling the irregular, informal, and syntactically complex nature of code-mixed social media language.

Recent advancements in sentiment analysis and predictive modeling have explored user behavior and engagement across diverse cultural and digital contexts. Pitroda (2022) developed three predictive models aimed at identifying the most suitable virtual engagement platforms for Indian adolescents and young adults. Using demographic and experiential variables such as age, gender, geographic location, and user satisfaction, the models achieved accuracies of 79%, 90%, and 85%, respectively. In addition to classification, sentiment analysis was conducted on user-generated reviews of these platforms, offering insights into user experiences and potential areas for platform enhancement.

Cultural differences in the interpretation of feminist themes in media have also been explored through sentiment analysis. Huang (2023) conducted a cross-cultural study on audience reactions to the film *Barbie*, comparing responses from Chinese and English-speaking viewers. The findings suggested that Chinese audiences were more emotionally responsive and expressive toward feminist themes, although the discussions often focused on gender roles and cultural preferences rather than engaging directly with feminism as a political ideology, which remains somewhat marginalized in the Chinese context. A positive correlation was observed between favorable sentiment toward feminist ideas and higher movie ratings, indicating the influence of ideological alignment on media evaluation.

In the domain of model performance evaluation for sentiment classification, Radaideh and Dweiri (2023) compared multiple machine learning and deep learning approaches. Among these, the BERT pre-trained model achieved the highest classification accuracy at 94.56%, outperforming traditional models such as Random Forest, which reached 70.82%. Interestingly, while BERT excelled in overall accuracy, the LSTM model exhibited the best performance across recall, precision, and F1-score metrics, suggesting its strength in maintaining balanced classification across different sentiment classes.

The effectiveness of sentiment analysis techniques is closely tied to the choice of algorithm, feature selection, and contextual application. Waila et al. (2012) examined the performance of both supervised and unsupervised approaches, demonstrating that the Naive Bayes algorithm can achieve results comparable to those of Support Vector Machines (SVM) when supported by appropriate feature selection strategies. Additionally, the study introduced the unsupervised SO-PMI-IR algorithm, which enables sentiment classification without the need for pre-labeled training data. The accuracy of this approach was found to be contingent upon the selection of specific linguistic features, such as part-of-speech tags, as well as the aggregation and thresholding methods used in the analysis.

Sentiment trends in global media coverage, particularly during the COVID-19 pandemic, have also been a subject of investigation. Chakraborty and Bose (2020) reported a strong correlation between global news sentiment and the number of COVID-19 cases and deaths. However, this relationship was not uniform across countries and was shaped by socio-political contexts. Italy, in particular, exhibited the strongest correlation between pandemic statistics and media sentiment. The prevailing tone of global news remained predominantly negative, a pattern attributed not only to epidemiological data but also to broader political and social developments. The authors suggested that sustained exposure to such negativity could have enduring effects on public mental health.

The predictive capacity of social media sentiment has been explored in electoral contexts. Jaidka et al. (2019) assessed the potential of Twitter data to forecast election outcomes in South Asia. Their findings indicated that while sentiment analysis and tweet recency significantly improved prediction accuracy in India and Pakistan, similar methodologies were not effective in the Malaysian context. Combining sentiment polarity with tweet volume or social network information enhanced the predictive performance, especially for smaller parties and independent candidates, thereby offering a more granular understanding of political engagement online.

Media studies have also turned to sentiment polarity consistency across news outlets and analytical tools. Castellanos et al. (2021) found general agreement in the polarity of sentiment across various international news agencies, though the magnitude of sentiment differed substantially. The study also evaluated the reliability of multiple sentiment analysis tools, proposing a reproducible metric for comparing global news sentiment and its applications in cross-national media research.

Political polarization in digital spaces has been another area of focus. Dash et al. (2022) analyzed the behavior of Indian influencers engaging with politically contentious issues on Twitter. The study revealed clear partisan alignments, with influencers predominantly supporting either the ruling Bharatiya Janata Party (BJP) or the opposition Indian National Congress (INC). Groups such as journalists and fan accounts exhibited consistent polarization across multiple political events. Polarized influencers, especially those with moderate to high follower counts, were found to receive greater engagement in terms of retweets and follower growth, suggesting that partisanship may function as a strategic engagement mechanism on social media platforms.

The application of sentiment analysis in understanding economic, legal, and social phenomena has gained increasing scholarly attention, particularly through the use of advanced machine learning and natural language processing (NLP) techniques. Basak et al. (2019) explored the link between media sentiment and financial indicators, specifically the British pound exchange rate during the Brexit period. Their findings indicated a long-run relationship and causal connection between sentiment trends and currency fluctuations. The study introduced a Bayesian learning-based method to construct a context-sensitive sentiment lexicon, tailored for analyzing media narratives around Brexit. This machine learning pipeline was proposed as a generalizable framework applicable to other socioeconomic contexts, facilitating the detection of latent associations between text data and economic outcomes.

In another financial context, Shirsat et al. (2019) evaluated the effectiveness of machine learning algorithms in extracting sentiment from news articles at the sentence level. The Support Vector Machine (SVM) classifier achieved an accuracy of 96.46%, while the Naive Bayes model reached 94.16%, demonstrating high levels of precision in identifying sentiment-bearing text. These results reinforce the potential of machine learning approaches in media sentiment mining for financial and economic forecasting.

Jena and Majhi (2023) extended this inquiry by developing a Long Short-Term Memory (LSTM) model to assess the effect of COVID-19-related sentiment on stock markets in both the United States and India. Their model outperformed traditional time-series statistical techniques in predicting stock indices, with comparative analysis across economic sectors and national contexts. The study provided insights into how health-related public sentiment can influence financial behavior and market dynamics in a cross-national setting.

Beyond economic and financial domains, sentiment analysis has also been employed to examine legal and policy-related discourse. Gupta et al. (2023) proposed a two-stage NLP-based framework combining topic modeling and sentiment analysis to extract public reactions to legal documents in India. This framework enabled the identification of dominant legal themes and corresponding public sentiment, marking a novel application of computational techniques to the legal domain in the Indian context. The authors argued that this methodological approach could shape public perception of contentious legal issues through a better understanding of document content.

In the sphere of gender-based violence, sentiment analysis has been applied to examine public discourse on social media. Yuniarossy et al. (2024) employed a Convolutional Neural Network (CNN) model to analyze tweets related to sexual harassment and domestic violence. The CNN model achieved 86% accuracy on the sexual harassment dataset and 82% on the domestic violence dataset (Kekerasan Dalam Rumah Tangga, or KDRT), based on 1001 tweets. Sentiment analysis, supported by word cloud visualizations, indicated that discourse on sexual harassment was generally more positive than that on domestic violence, revealing differences in public engagement with these issues.

Research Questions

1. How do media outlets in the US, UK, and India vary in their sentiment portrayal of feminism, considering political, cultural, and ideological influences?
2. What are the sentiment polarity trends in feminist media coverage across these countries?
3. How well machine learning models predict sentiment related to feminism in different media outlets?

METHODOLOGY

This study employs a sentiment analysis approach combined with machine learning-based classification models to examine how media outlets in the US, UK, and India portray feminism. The methodology involves data collection, preprocessing, sentiment scoring, and machine learning model evaluation to compare sentiment polarity trends across different media landscapes.

Data Collection and Preprocessing: News articles related to feminism were collected from major media outlets in the US, UK, and India. The dataset includes a diverse range of publications to capture varied political, cultural, and ideological perspectives. The articles were gathered using web scraping techniques and publicly available news archives, ensuring a balanced representation of sources across the three countries.Following data collection, text preprocessing was performed to prepare the articles for sentiment analysis. This included tokenization, stop-word removal, lemmatization, and removal of special characters and redundant whitespace. The cleaned text was then processed for sentiment scoring and classification.

Sentiment Analysis and Scoring: Sentiment analysis was conducted to determine the sentiment polarity of the articles, assigning each article a sentiment score ranging from 0 (negative) to 1 (positive). A pre-trained sentiment analysis model was used, employing Natural Language Processing (NLP) techniques to evaluate the textual content. The sentiment scores were aggregated for each media outlet, allowing for a comparative assessment of how different countries' media outlets frame discussions on feminism. The analysis examined variations in sentiment polarity across US, UK, and Indian media, considering political, cultural, and ideological influences.

Machine Learning Classification Model: A supervised machine learning model was developed to classify articles as either positive or negative in their sentiment toward feminism. The model was trained and tested on labeled datasets using the training-validation split method to ensure accuracy. The classification model utilized logistic regression, support vector machines (SVM), and random forest algorithms, with the best-performing model selected based on accuracy metrics. To evaluate the model's performance, a confusion matrix was used, measuring True Positives, True Negatives, False Positives, and False Negatives. Additional performance metrics included:

- Classification accuracy (80%) to assess overall model effectiveness.
- AUC-ROC score (0.7943) to measure the model's ability to distinguish between positive and negative sentiment.
- Log Loss (7.2087) indicating classification confidence.
- Cohen's Kappa and Matthews Correlation Coefficient (MCC) for agreement measurement beyond chance.

Evaluation and Comparative Analysis: The sentiment polarity distribution was analyzed to identify patterns and variations in media sentiment toward feminism across different countries. Statistical comparisons were conducted to assess differences in sentiment scores, highlighting the influence of political discourse, cultural norms, and ideological factors on media representation. The confusion matrix and ROC curve were used to validate the model's predictive ability, ensuring the reliability of sentiment classification across media outlets. The results were analyzed in the context of media biases, linguistic variations, and socio-political factors influencing feminist discourse in the US, UK, and India.

RESULTS DISCUSSION

How do media outlets in the US, UK, and India vary in their sentiment portrayal of feminism, considering political, cultural, and ideological influences?

Table 1. Sentiment polarity across media outlets

Media Outlet	Average Sentiment Score
India Media	0.9497
UK Media	0.9579
US Media 1	0.9487
US Media 2	0.9427

The dataset as explained in Table 1, contains individual sentiment scores ranging from 0.82 to 0.99, suggesting that most articles lean towards neutral to positive sentiment in feminist discussions. UK Media, Exhibits the most balanced sentiment, likely due to policy-driven discourse and feminist activism being integrated into public debates. US Media, shows slight variation, reflecting political polarization and ideological divides in media discourse. Indian Media, displays greater fluctuation in sentiment, influenced by traditional values, cultural norms, and modern feminist movements. This analysis explains RQ1 and infer that, UK media maintains a balanced, policy-driven representation, while US and Indian media exhibit slight variations due to political and cultural influences. The sentiment scores indicate that UK media portrays feminism slightly more positively, whereas US and Indian media have similar patterns but with more variation in sentiment distribution.

UK media leads with the highest polarity score (0.9579), suggesting a more consistent and slightly positive stance. US and Indian media follow similar trends, with sentiment scores around 0.94, showing neutral-to-positive representation. Greater variation in Indian media suggests diverse perspectives on feminism, ranging from conservative to progressive viewpoints. UK media portrays feminism most positively, while Indian media shows greater sentiment fluctuations.

What are the sentiment polarity trends in feminist media coverage across countries?

In the subsequent phase, the researcher explores on confusion matrix to address the RQ2. Figure 1, is the visualization of the confusion matrix.

Figure 1. Confusion matrix

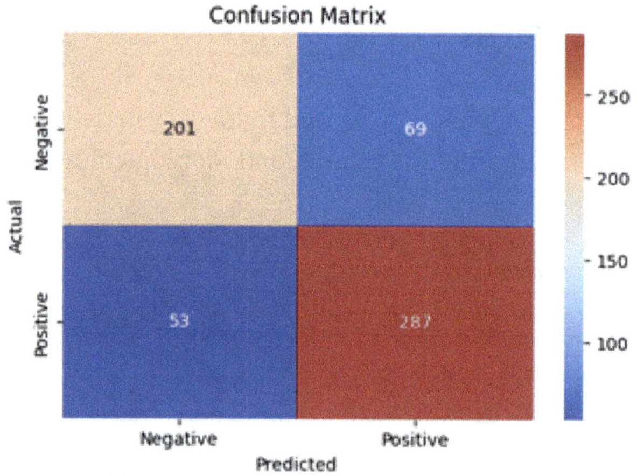

Figure 1, confusion matrix visualizes the performance of a classification model. It shows the counts of True Positive, True Negative, False Positive (Type I error), and False Negative (Type II error) predictions. For instance, the model correctly identified 287 instances as positive (feminist-aligned) and 201 as negative. However, it misclassified 69 negative instances as positive and 53 positive instances as negative. This matrix is crucial for evaluating the model's accuracy and identifying potential biases in how feminist discourse is categorized within the news media across the US, UK, and India, by this the researcher able to 'what are the sentiment polarity trends in feminist media coverage across countries' RQ2.

The errors suggest areas where the model might be struggling to accurately capture nuanced sentiment related to feminism in media coverage. Thus, this prompt for addressing the RQ3.

How well machine learning models predict sentiment related to feminism in different media outlets?

Table 2. Showing model parameters

Metric	Value
Classification Model Accuracy	80%
AUC-ROC Score	0.7943
Log Loss	7.2087
Cohen's Kappa	0.5922
MCC (Matthews Correlation Coefficient)	0.5930

In the table 3, shows classification model achieves 80% accuracy, indicating a strong but improvable ability to classify sentiment. AUC-ROC Score of 0.7943 suggests a moderate predictive power in distinguishing positive and negative sentiments. Log Loss (7.2087) and Cohen's Kappa (0.5922) indicate that sentiment classification is reliable but encounters challenges due to linguistic variations. The classification model performs well (80% accuracy), but moderate confidence suggests challenges in linguistic variations in feminist discourse. This substantiates the RQ3, that how well machine learning models predict sentiment related to feminism in different media outlets.

Figure 2. Showing ROC curve

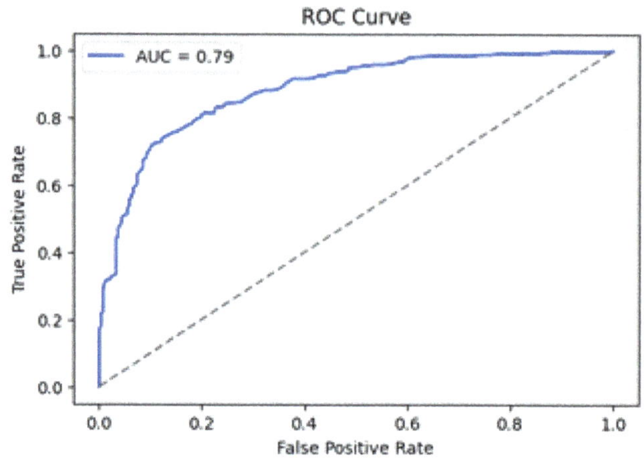

This ROC curve in figure 2, illustrates the performance of a machine learning model designed to predict sentiment related to feminism in media outlets. The curve plots the True Positive Rate (sensitivity) against the False Positive Rate (1-specificity) at various threshold settings. An AUC (Area Under the Curve) of 0.79 suggests the model has a reasonably good ability to distinguish between positive and negative sentiment towards feminism, though there's room for improvement. The closer the curve hugs the top-left corner and the higher the AUC, the better the model's performance in accurately classifying sentiment. The UK media exhibits the most positive and balanced sentiment, whereas US and Indian media show slight variations influenced by cultural and political factors. Machine learning models demonstrate promising accuracy in sentiment classification but can be further improved with deep learning approaches.

SUMMARY AND CONCLUSION

The comparative analysis demonstrates that UK media provides the most balanced and positively inclined portrayal of feminism, while US and Indian media reflect varying degrees of ideological and cultural influences. Although sentiment scores in all three countries remain generally positive, the degree of fluctuation differs, with Indian media showing the widest range. The machine learning model used in this study shows reliable but improvable performance in classifying sentiment, especially given the linguistic and contextual complexities inherent in feminist discourse. Overall, sentiment analysis combined with classification metrics suggests that while current models offer useful insights, further refinement—potentially through advanced deep learning techniques—is necessary to enhance the precision and contextual understanding of feminist representation in global media narratives.

FUTURE RESEARCH DIRECTIONS

The current study of unearth foundation for understanding how digital media portraits feminism across US, UK and India. The study also significant as it dwells on sentiment analysis and machine learning models to prompt for further avenues and Exploration.

1. Deep learning applications – is another future scope of study, that can be explored on Transformer based model such as BERT, and classification models.
2. Cross platform comparative studies can be explored on media outlets national, regionally including social media platform.
3. Temporal sentiment shifts can be explored on a longitudinal studies how the sentiments towards feminism evolves during the significant Socio Political event.
4. Intersectionality and representation can be another analysis such as race, LGBT and class. Also on how these evolved over the different spheres in media narratives.
5. The researcher can also explore and cultural and linguistic adoption specially for developing localised language as a medium and for better interaction with understanding of the sentiments.
6. Sentiment and policy impact can be another area where the media sentiment can be analysed in context of policy making or gathering public opinion.
7. There could be a study on media ownership influence on the structural and significant media outlets on the portrayal of feminist topics addressing potential bias at institutional levels.

REFERENCES

Ahmad, G. I., Singla, J., Ali, A., Reshi, A. A., & Salameh, A. A. (2022). Machine learning techniques for sentiment analysis of code-mixed and switched Indian social media text corpus - A comprehensive review. *International Journal of Advanced Computer Science and Applications, 13*(2). Advance online publication. DOI: 10.14569/IJACSA.2022.0130254

Ahmed, J., & Ahmed, M. (2023). Classification, detection and sentiment analysis using machine learning over next generation communication platforms. *Microprocessors and Microsystems, 98*(104795), 104795. DOI: 10.1016/j.micpro.2023.104795

Ahmed, S. S., Uppalapati, P. J., Ayesha, S., Hussain, S. M., Narasimharao, K., & Silpa, N. (2023). Assessing public sentiment towards digital India through twitter sentiment analysis: A comparative study. *2023 7th International Conference on Intelligent Computing and Control Systems (ICICCS)*, 955–959.

Basak, G. K., Das, P. K., Marjit, S., & Mukherjee, D. (2019). British stock market, Brexit and media sentiments - A big data analysis. SSRN *Electronic Journal*. DOI: 10.2139/ssrn.3432808

Castellanos, E., Xie, H., & Brenner, P. (2021). Global News Sentiment Analysis. In *Proceedings of the 2019 International Conference of The Computational Social Science Society of the Americas* (pp. 121–139). Springer International Publishing.

Chakraborty, A., & Bose, S. (2020). Around the world in 60 days: An exploratory study of impact of COVID-19 on online global news sentiment. *Journal of Computational Social Science, 3*(2), 367–400. DOI: 10.1007/s42001-020-00088-3 PMID: 33102926

Chandra, Y., & Jana, A. (2020). Sentiment analysis using machine learning and deep learning. *2020 7th International Conference on Computing for Sustainable Global Development (INDIACom).*

Dash, S., Mishra, D., Shekhawat, G., & Pal, J. (2022). Divided we rule: Influencer polarization on twitter during political crises in India. *Proceedings of the International AAAI Conference on Web and Social Media, 16*, 135–146. DOI: 10.1609/icwsm.v16i1.19279

Friedman, S., Schmer-Galunder, S., Chen, A., & Rye, J. (2019). Relating word embedding gender biases to gender gaps: A cross-cultural analysis. *Proceedings of the First Workshop on Gender Bias in Natural Language Processing*, 18–24. DOI: 10.18653/v1/W19-3803

Ghasiya, P., & Okamura, K. (2021). Investigating COVID-19 news across four nations: A topic modeling and sentiment analysis approach. *IEEE Access : Practical Innovations, Open Solutions*, *9*, 36645–36656. DOI: 10.1109/ACCESS.2021.3062875 PMID: 34786310

Gupta, I., Chatterjee, I., & Gupta, N. (2023). A two-staged NLP-based framework for assessing the sentiments on Indian supreme court judgments. *International Journal of Information Technology : an Official Journal of Bharati Vidyapeeth's Institute of Computer Applications and Management*, *15*(4), 2273–2282. DOI: 10.1007/s41870-023-01273-z PMID: 37256028

Hore, S., & Bhattacharya, T. (2019). Analyzing social trend towards girl child in India: A machine intelligence-based approach. In *Advances in Intelligent Systems and Computing* (pp. 43–50). Springer Singapore.

Huang, J. (2023). Comparative analysis: The development of Chinese feminism based on east and west Barbie film reviews. *Communications in Humanities Research*, *22*(1), 51–63. DOI: 10.54254/2753-7064/22/20231568

Imran, A. S., Daudpota, S. M., Kastrati, Z., & Batra, R. (2020). Cross-cultural polarity and emotion detection using sentiment analysis and deep learning on COVID-19 related tweets. *IEEE Access : Practical Innovations, Open Solutions*, *8*, 181074–181090. DOI: 10.1109/ACCESS.2020.3027350 PMID: 34812358

Jaidka, K., Ahmed, S., Skoric, M., & Hilbert, M. (2019). Predicting elections from social media: A three-country, three-method comparative study. *Asian Journal of Communication*, *29*(3), 252–273. DOI: 10.1080/01292986.2018.1453849

Jamatia, A., Swamy, S. D., Gambäck, B., Das, A., & Debbarma, S. (2020). Deep Learning based sentiment analysis in a code-mixed English-Hindi and English-Bengali social media corpus. *International Journal of Artificial Intelligence Tools: Architectures, Languages. International Journal of Artificial Intelligence Tools*, *29*(05), 2050014. DOI: 10.1142/S0218213020500141

Jena, P. R., & Majhi, R. (2023). Are Twitter sentiments during COVID-19 pandemic a critical determinant to predict stock market movements? A machine learning approach. *Scientific African*, *19*(e01480), e01480. DOI: 10.1016/j.sciaf.2022.e01480 PMID: 36465525

Kashyap, S., & Singh, A. (2021). Testing Data Feminism in India. *Scholars Journal of Arts Humanities and Social Sciences*, *9*(10), 516–530. DOI: 10.36347/sjahss.2021.v09i10.006

Kaur, C., & Sharma, A. (2020). Social Issues Sentiment Analysis using Python. *2020 5th International Conference on Computing, Communication and Security (ICCCS).*

Kumar, A., & Albuquerque, V. H. C. (2021). Sentiment analysis using XLM-R transformer and zero-shot transfer learning on resource-poor Indian language. *ACM Transactions on Asian and Low-Resource Language Information Processing*, *20*(5), 1–13. DOI: 10.1145/3461764

Kumar, S., Gahalawat, M., Roy, P. P., Dogra, D. P., & Kim, B.-G. (2020). Exploring impact of age and gender on sentiment analysis using Machine Learning. *Electronics (Basel)*, *9*(2), 374. DOI: 10.3390/electronics9020374

Maathuis, C., & Kerkhof, I. (2023). The first two months in the war in Ukraine through topic modeling and sentiment analysis. *Regional Science Policy & Practice*, *15*(1), 56–75. DOI: 10.1111/rsp3.12632

Makeeva, E., & Sinilshchikova, M. (2020). News sentiment in bankruptcy prediction models: Evidence from Russian retail companies. *Korporativnye Finansy*, *14*(4), 7–18. DOI: 10.17323/j.jcfr.2073-0438.14.4.2020.7-18

Mendon, S., Dutta, P., Behl, A., & Lessmann, S. (2021). A hybrid approach of machine learning and lexicons to sentiment analysis: Enhanced insights from twitter data of natural disasters. *Information Systems Frontiers: A Journal of Research and Innovation, 23*(5), 1145–1168. DOI: 10.1007/s10796-021-10107-x

Mishra, P., Rajnish, R., & Kumar, P. (2016). Sentiment analysis of Twitter data: Case study on digital India. *2016 International Conference on Information Technology (InCITe) - The Next Generation IT Summit on the Theme - Internet of Things: Connect Your Worlds*. DOI: 10.1109/INCITE.2016.7857607

Padmaja, S., Fatima, S. S., Bandu, S., Kosala, P., & Abhignya, M. C. (2014). Comparing and evaluating the sentiment on newspaper articles: A preliminary experiment. *2014 Science and Information Conference*. DOI: 10.1109/SAI.2014.6918276

Pai, R. R., & Alathur, S. (2020). Women empowerment through social media: Insights from India. In *ICT Analysis and Applications* (pp. 387–395). Springer Singapore. DOI: 10.1007/978-981-15-0630-7_38

Patil, A. P., Doshi, D., Dalsaniya, D., & Rashmi, B. S. (2018). Applying machine learning techniques for sentiment analysis in the case study of Indian politics. In *Advances in Intelligent Systems and Computing* (pp. 351–358). Springer International Publishing.

Pitroda, H. (2022). Analytical Prediction and Sentimental Analysis of virtual engagement tools in teens and youth of urban and rural areas in India. *2022 1st International Conference on Informatics (ICI)*.

Radaideh, A., & Dweiri, F. (2023). Sentiment analysis predictions in digital media content using NLP techniques. *International Journal of Advanced Computer Science and Applications*, *14*(11). Advance online publication. DOI: 10.14569/IJACSA.2023.0141128

Rani, S., & Kumar, P. (2019). A sentiment analysis system for social media using machine learning techniques: Social enablement. *Digital Scholarship in the Humanities*, *34*(3), 569–581. DOI: 10.1093/llc/fqy037

Scarborough, W., & Helmuth, A. S. (2021). How cultural environments shape online sentiment toward social movements: Place character and support for feminism. In *SocArXiv*. DOI: 10.31235/osf.io/juxqk

Shanmugavadivel, K., Sampath, S. H., Nandhakumar, P., Mahalingam, P., Subramanian, M., Kumaresan, P. K., & Priyadharshini, R. (2022). An analysis of machine learning models for sentiment analysis of Tamil code-mixed data. *Computer Speech & Language*, *76*(101407), 101407. DOI: 10.1016/j.csl.2022.101407

Shirsat, V. S., Jagdale, R. S., & Deshmukh, S. N. (2019). Sentence level sentiment identification and calculation from news articles using machine learning techniques. In *Advances in Intelligent Systems and Computing* (pp. 371–376). Springer Singapore.

Singla, Z., Randhawa, S., & Jain, S. (2017). Sentiment analysis of customer product reviews using machine learning. *2017 International Conference on Intelligent Computing and Control (I2C2)*. DOI: 10.1109/I2C2.2017.8321910

Thavareesan, S., & Mahesan, S. (2019). Sentiment analysis in Tamil texts: A study on machine learning techniques and feature representation. *2019 14th Conference on Industrial and Information Systems (ICIIS)*.

Trivedi, S. K., Dey, S., & Kumar, A. (2018). Capturing user sentiments for online Indian movie reviews: A comparative analysis of different machine-learning models. *The Electronic Library*, *36*(4), 677–695. DOI: 10.1108/EL-04-2017-0075

Volkova, S., Wilson, T., & Yarowsky, D. (2013). Exploring demographic language variations to improve multilingual sentiment analysis in social media. *Proceedings of the 2013 Conference on Empirical Methods in Natural Language Processing*, 1815–1827. DOI: 10.18653/v1/D13-1187

Waila, P., Marisha, Singh, V. K., & Singh, M. K. (2012). Evaluating Machine Learning and Unsupervised Semantic Orientation approaches for sentiment analysis of textual reviews. *2012 IEEE International Conference on Computational Intelligence and Computing Research*. DOI: 10.1109/ICCIC.2012.6510235

Yadav, B. P., Sheshikala, M., Swathi, N., Chythanya, K. R., & Sudarshan, E. (2020). Women wellbeing assessment in Indian metropolises using machine learning models. *IOP Conference Series. Materials Science and Engineering, 981*(2), 022042. DOI: 10.1088/1757-899X/981/2/022042

Yuniarossy, B. A., Hindrayani, K. M., & Damaliana, A. T. (2024). Analisis Sentimen Terhadap Isu Feminisme Di Twitter Menggunakan Model Convolutional Neural Network (CNN). *Jurnal Lebesgue : Jurnal Ilmiah Pendidikan Matematika. Matematika Dan Statistika, 5*(1), 477–491. DOI: 10.46306/lb.v5i1.585

KEY TERMS AND DEFINITION

Balanced Media Portrayal News: Balances media portrayal news coverage that presents topic or movements such as feminism in fair and comprehensive manner without access you by as.

Cultural influences: The social, historical, and ideological factors that shape how media content is produce, interpreted and consumed within the specific National are community across the globe.

Digital Media Representation: The portrayal of concepts, individuals, and moments within online news social media and other digital platform shaping public perception

Feminist Discourse: Language and communication that advocate for gender equality critic partiarchal systems, and highlight women's rights and representation.

Ideological Bias: A systematic preferences or prejudice in media content are movies that are influenced by a specific political social or cultural ideologies which can affect and form public understanding.

Machine Learning Model: Algorithms that enable computers to learn from and make predictions based on data patterns, which are widely used in natural language processing tasks.

Sentiment Analysis: It is a computational technique that detects and classify opinion, attitude, or emotions in text data often categorised as positive, negative or neutral.

Compilation of References

Abdullah, S., Hafid, A., Folke, M., Lindén, M., & Kristoffersson, A. (2023). PPG-Feat: A novel MATLAB toolbox for extracting PPG fiducial points. *Frontiers in Bioengineering and Biotechnology*, *11*, 1199604. DOI: 10.3389/fbioe.2023.1199604 PMID: 37378045

Abidin, C. (2020). L8r H8r: Commoditized privacy, influencer wars, and productive disorder in the influencer industry. In Lind, R. A. (Ed.), *Produsing theory in a digital world 3.0* (pp. 31–48). Peter Lang.

Ahmad, G. I., Singla, J., Ali, A., Reshi, A. A., & Salameh, A. A. (2022). Machine learning techniques for sentiment analysis of code-mixed and switched Indian social media text corpus - A comprehensive review. *International Journal of Advanced Computer Science and Applications*, *13*(2). Advance online publication. DOI: 10.14569/IJACSA.2022.0130254

Ahmed, S. S., Uppalapati, P. J., Ayesha, S., Hussain, S. M., Narasimharao, K., & Silpa, N. (2023). Assessing public sentiment towards digital India through twitter sentiment analysis: A comparative study. *2023 7th International Conference on Intelligent Computing and Control Systems (ICICCS)*, 955–959.

Ahmed, J., & Ahmed, M. (2023). Classification, detection and sentiment analysis using machine learning over next generation communication platforms. *Microprocessors and Microsystems*, *98*(104795), 104795. DOI: 10.1016/j.micpro.2023.104795

Akaydın Aydın, A., & Koç, N. E. (2024). Examining intimacy through reality shows: An analysis on "Love is Blind". In Kahraman Gökalp, E., & Yıldız, İ. (Eds.), *Dimensions of digital privacy: Dijital alanda araştırmalar ve tartışmalar* (pp. 123–135). Istanbul University Publishing House., DOI: 10.26650/B/SSc5SSc20.2024.030.008

Akmeşe Demir, Z. ve Demir Ö. (2023). Dijital medyada içerik üretiminin geleneksel içerik üretimi teknikleri bağlamında değerlendirilmesi. Paper presented and published in *Üsküdar Unıversıty Faculty of Communıcatıon 10th International Communication Days Digital Capitalism and Communication Symposium Proceedings Book*, 16-18 Mayıs, 2023, İstanbul: Üsküdar University Publications, pp. 400 – 408.

Akmeşe, E. (2021). Ateşle Oyun filminde bireyin dönüşümü üzerine arketipsel bir analiz. *İNİF E- Dergi, 6*(2), pp. 325-339.

Akto, S., & Akto, A. (2017). *Methods and Techniques Used in Values Education in Preschool*. E-Oriental Scientific Research Journal., DOI: 10.26791/sarkiat.342143

Akyazı, A. (2020). Sosyal medyanın şöhret kültürüne etkisi. *İstanbul Aydın Üniversitesi Dergisi, 12*(3), 251–274.

Alalwan, A. A., Rana, N. P., Dwivedi, Y. K., & Algharabat, R. (2017). Social media in marketing: A review and analysis of the existing literature. *Telematics and Informatics*, *34*(7), 1177–1190. DOI: 10.1016/j.tele.2017.05.008

Albuquerque, P., Mena, J., & Alharthi, M. (2023). The Impact of Social Media Marketing on Brand Awareness: Evidence from Emerging Markets. *JMR, Journal of Marketing Research*, *48*(2), 123–136.

Aljuhmani, H. Y., Elrehail, H., Bayram, P., & Samarah, T. (2023). Linking social media marketing efforts with customer brand engagement in driving brand loyalty. *Asia Pacific Journal of Marketing and Logistics*, *35*(7), 1719–1738. DOI: 10.1108/APJML-08-2021-0627

Alshamrani, S., Abuhamad, M., Abusnaina, A., & Mohaisen, D. (2020). Investigating Online Toxicity in Users Interactions with the Mainstream Media Channels on YouTube. October 2020. In CIKM (Workshops).

Altunay, A. (2023). *Dijital Oyun Kültürü*. Nobel Bilimsel Eserler.

Amarasekara, I., & Grant, W. J. (2018). Exploring the YouTube science communication gender gap: A sentiment analysis. Public Understanding of Science, 28(1), pp. 68-84. (Original work published 2019)DOI: 10.1177/0963662518786654

Anderson, B. (1991). *Imagined Communities: Reflections on the Origin and Spread of Nationalism*. Verso.

Andrejevic, M. (2021). *Automation and the future of work: From artificial intelligence to algorithmic culture*. Wiley-Blackwell.

Androutsopoulos, J. (2008). Potentials and limitations of discourse-centred online ethnography. *Language@Internet*,5(8).

Angraini, N. (2023). Social media marketing influencer: literature review on promotional strategies using the influence of social media celebrities. ijerfa, 1(4). DOI: 10.55227/ijerfa.v1i4.42

Aramendia-Muneta, M. E., Olarte-Pascual, C., & Hatzithomas, L. (2019). Gender stereotypes in original digital video advertising. *Journal of Gender Studies, 29*(4), 403–419. DOI: 10.1080/09589236.2019.1650255

Arık, E. (2013). The rise of the common man: Social media celebrities. *Communication and Diplomacy*, 97–112.

Arık, E., & Arık, M. B. (2021). Televizyon ve mahremiyet. In Kütükoğlu, E. (Ed.), *Mahremiyetin medyası* (pp. 13–30). Eğitim Yayınevi.

Arsenyan, J., & Mirowska, A. (2021). Almost human? A comparative case study on the social media presence of virtual influencers. *International Journal of Human-Computer Studies, 155*, 102694. Advance online publication. DOI: 10.1016/j.ijhcs.2021.102694

Arslan, U. (2025). *Kendini yayınla: YouTube ve mahremiyet.* Nobel Akademik Yayıncılık.

Aydınlı, S. (2021). Factsheet on the national regulatory and self-regulatory framework against hate speech and disinformation. *South East European Network for Professionalization of Media* (EENPM), Peace Institute, Bianet.

Aytekin, A., & Kuvat, O. (2018). Dizüstü Bilgisayar Seçiminde Değerlendirilen Kriterlerin Önem Düzeylerinin AHP ile Belirlenmesi: 1. ve 2. Sınıf Bilgisayar Mühendisliği Öğrencileri Uygulaması. MANAS Sosyal Araştırmalar Dergisi, 7(4).

Bahador, B., Kerchner, D., Bacon, L., & Menas, A. (2019). *Monitoring hate speech in the US media.* Media and Peacebuilding Project, George Washington University.

Bahunar, M. H., & Roshangar, M. Z. (2024). The Nature of Knowledge in Plato's Philosophy: A Study of Episteme and Doxa. Sprin Journal of Arts. *Humanities and Social Sciences, 3*(6), 19–23. DOI: 10.55559/sjahss.v3i6.353

Baker C., Ging D. & Andreasen, M B. (2024). Recommending Toxicity: The role of algorithmic recommender functions on YouTube Shorts and TikTok in promoting male supremacist influencers. DCU Anti-Bullying Centre Dublin City University, April 2024.

Baloğlu, N., & Öz, H. (2021). Yükseköğretim kurumlarında akademik liderlik ile örgütsel bağlılık arasındaki ilişki. *İnönü Üniversitesi Eğitim Fakültesi Dergisi*, 22(1), pp 410-445.

Balsamo, A. (1996). *Technologies Of The Gendered Body: Reading Cyborg Women*. Duke University Press.

Baltezarević, B., Baltezarević, R., Baltezarević, V. N., Kwiatek, P., & Baltezarević, I. (2021). Stereotypical negative female gender roles in digital games. *Acta Ludologica*, *4*(2), 42–61.

Banks, J. (2013). *Co-creating videogames*. Bloomsbury Academic. DOI: 10.5040/9781472544353

Barfield, W., & Pagallo, U. (2021). *The ethical dimensions of grokking AI*. *Ethics and Information Technology*, *23*(5), 347–360. DOI: 10.1007/eit.2021.14

Basak, G. K., Das, P. K., Marjit, S., & Mukherjee, D. (2019). British stock market, Brexit and media sentiments - A big data analysis. SSRN *Electronic Journal*. DOI: 10.2139/ssrn.3432808

Baudrillard, J. (2011). *Simulacra and Simulation* (Adanır, O., Trans.). Doğu Batı.

Bauman, Z. (2018). *44 letters from the fluid modern world*. Habitus Book.

Bauman, Z., & Lyon, D. (2018). *Fluid surveillance*. Ayrıntı Publications.

Baydaş Sayılgan, Ö. (2012). Digital Game as a Form of Cyberdrama: The Example of Alice in Wonderland. Journal of Folklore and Literature, pp. 113–134.

Baym, N. K. (2015). Personal connections in the digital age. *Polity*.

Bayraktar, E. (2021). *Gender and Representation in Popular Culture and New Media: LGBTI Visibility in Digital Games*. [Unpublished Master's Thesis] Istanbul University Institute of Social Sciences New Media and Communication Management.

Bayraktar, R. (2024). Dijital Okuryazarlık. *Dijital İletişimde Güncel Çalışmalar*, İçinde (Ed). Demir, B. Ç. Konya: Eğitim Yayınevi. pp. 27-35

BBC. (2019, March 7). *Sosyal medya fenomenleri: Influencer'lar nasıl para kazanıyor?* https://www.bbc.com/turkce/haberler-47478637

Beasley, B., & Standley, T. C. (2002). Shirts vs. skins: Clothing as an indicator of gender role stereotyping in video games. *Mass Communication & Society*, *5*(3), 279–293. DOI: 10.1207/S15327825MCS0503_3

Beller, J. (2017). *Cultural capital in the age of digital technology*. Routledge.

Benjamin, R. (2019). *Race after technology: Abolitionist tools for the new Jim code*. Polity Press.

Berryman, R., & Kavka, M. (2017). "I guess a lot of people see me as a big sister or a friend": The role of intimacy in the celebrification of beauty vloggers. *Journal of Gender Studies*, *26*(5), 692–703. DOI: 10.1080/09589236.2017.1288611

Beuving, J., & de Vries, G. C. (2015). *Doing qualitative research: The craft of naturalistic inquiry*. Amsterdam University Press.

Bigo.tv. (2024). *Canlı yayın platformları*. Retrieved from:https://blog.bigo.tv/en-iyi-uygulamalar-en/canli-yayin-platformlari/, Date of Access: 02.01.2024.

Bigo.tv. (2025). *En popüler canlı yayın uygulamaları nelerdir?* Retrieved from: https://www.tamindir.com/liste/canli-yayin-uygulamalari/, Date of Access:13.01.2024.

Binark, M., & Çomu, T. (2013). Yeni medya ortamlarında nefret söylemi. In Çınar, M. (Ed.), *Medya ve nefret söylemi: Kavramlar, mecralar, tartışmalar* (pp. 199–216). Hrant Dink Vakfı Yayınları.

Black, M. (2016). Cyber ethnography: A critical tool for the Department of Defense? *Comparative Strategy*, *35*(2), 103–113. DOI: 10.1080/01495933.2016.1176456

Blodgett, B. M., & Salter, A. (2014). #1ReasonWhy: Game communities and the invisible woman.

Bolat, N. (2023). Dijital oyunlarda kültürel görsel kodlarla kültürün yeniden üretimi: Uruz Er kişinin dönüşü. *Middle Black Sea Journal of Communication Studies*, *8*(2), 165–178. DOI: 10.56202/mbsjcs.1361429

Boyalı, U., & Aktaş, C. (2023). Dijital oyun ve sosyal etkileşim. *TAM Akademi Dergisi*, *2*(2), 226–242. DOI: 10.58239/tamde.2023.04.005.x

Boyle, K. (2001). Hate speech, *The United States versus the rest of the world. Maine Law Review*, *53*, 487.

Bragança, L., Mota, R., & Fantini, E. (2016). Twine game narrative and discussion about LGBTQ representation. *In Proceedings of SBGames* (pp. 937–946).

Braidotti, R. (2019). Posthuman, very human: Memoirs and ambitions of a posthumanist, *Cogito - The Posthuman*. Issue: 95-96, pp. 53-97.

Braidotti, R. (2017). *Nomadic Subjects, Embodiment and Gender Difference in Contemporary Feminist Theory* (Karakaş, Ö., Trans.). Kolektif.

Braun, V., & Clarke, V. (2021). Thematic analysis: A practical guide. *Sage (Atlanta, Ga.)*.

Brenner-Levoy, J. (2023). Virtually masculine: Queer men's experiences with harassment in online video games. *Sociology of Sport Journal*, *40*(4), 385–398. DOI: 10.1123/ssj.2022-0170

Brooks, R., Christidis, R., Carah, N., Kelly, B., Martino, F., & Backholer, K. (2022). Turning users into 'unofficial brand ambassadors': Marketing of unhealthy food and non-alcoholic beverages on tiktok. *BMJ Global Health*, *7*(6), e009112. DOI: 10.1136/bmjgh-2022-009112 PMID: 35879104

Bryson, J. J. (2019). The epistemic role of artificial intelligence in the construction of knowledge*. *Journal of Philosophy of Science*, *45*(3), 325–341. DOI: 10.1017/jps.2019.11

Bülbül, H. İ. (2022) About Digital Games, https://dergipark.org.tr/en/download/article-file/2678176

Burgess, J., Green, J., & Rebane, G. (2020). Agency and Controversy in the YouTube Community. In Friese, H., Nolden, M., Rebane, G., & Schreiter, M. (Eds.), *Handbuch Soziale Praktiken und Digitale Alltagswelten*. Springer VS., DOI: 10.1007/978-3-658-08357-1_10

Burgess, M. C. R., Stermer, S. P., & Burgess, S. R. (2007). Sex, lies, and video games: The portrayal of male and female characters on video game covers. *Sex Roles*, *57*(5–6), 419–433. DOI: 10.1007/s11199-007-9250-0

Butt, M. A. (2019). "I never use headsets": Women, wariness, and hypervigilance for the inevitability of online harassment in gaming culture. *AoIR Selected Papers of Internet Research*.

Byun, K. J., & Ahn, S. J. G. (2023). A Systematic Review of Virtual Influencers: Similarities and Differences between Human and Virtual Influencers in Interactive Advertising. *Journal of Interactive Advertising*, *23*(4), 293–306. DOI: 10.1080/15252019.2023.2236102

Caillois, R. (2001). *Man, play, and games* (Barash, M., Trans.). University of Illinois Press. (Original work published 1958)

Cairns, P., & Cox, A. (2008). *Research Methods for Human-Computer Interaction*. Cambridge University Press. DOI: 10.1017/CBO9780511814570

Çakar, Ü. (2021). Popüler kültür ve dijital oyunlar: Twitch platformu üzerine nitel bir araştırma. *SAÜ İletişim*, *1*(1), 26–40.

Çakıcı, Z. (2025). Tiktok as a political communication medium: An examination of the United Nations. *İletişim Kuram ve Araştırma Dergisi* (69), 136-156. DOI: 10.47998/ikad.1580671

Çakıcı, Z. (2024). Cyberstalking practices among youth in Türkiye: Motivational drivers, digital avenues, and perceptual paradigms. *Türkiye İletişim Araştırmaları Dergisi*, (46), 1–22. DOI: 10.17829/turcom.1488278

Çakıcı, Z., & Aslıbay, E. (2025). The utilization of social media by far-right political parties: A study on Victory Party. In Vieira, A. T., Joaquim, A. F., & Duarte, A. (Eds.), *Digital populism and the use of neo-propaganda and fake news*. IGI Global., DOI: 10.4018/979-8-3693-9999-6.ch009

Çakın, Ö. ve Bolat, N. (2018). Sosyal Medya Reklamcılığı ve Dijital Mecra Etkileşimleri (Ed). V. Çakmak & S. Çavuş, içinde *Dijital Kültür ve İletişim*, Konya: Literatürk Yayınevi

Çakın, Ö., & Yaman, D. (2022). Dijital Oyunlar- Fijital Deneyim Alanları. (Ed). M. N. Erdem, in *Gamevertising Dijital Çağda Oyunlaştırma ve Reklam* (pp. 118-134). İstanbul: Eğitim Yayınevi.

Cambronero-Saiz, B., Cristófol-Rodríguez, C., & Segarra-Saavedra, J. (2023). Content analysis from a gender perspective of comments received by Spanish science youtubers. *Media and Communication, 11*(1), 252–263. DOI: 10.17645/mac.v11i1.5971

Castaño-Pulgarín, S. A., Suárez-Betancur, N., Vega, L. M. T., & López, H. M. H. (2021). Internet, social media and online hate speech: Systematic review. *Aggression and Violent Behavior, 58*, 101608. DOI: 10.1016/j.avb.2021.101608

Castellanos, E., Xie, H., & Brenner, P. (2021). Global News Sentiment Analysis. In *Proceedings of the 2019 International Conference of The Computational Social Science Society of the Americas* (pp. 121–139). Springer International Publishing.

Castells, M. (2009). *The Rise of the Network Society*. Wiley-Blackwell. DOI: 10.1002/9781444319514

Castells, M. (2016). *The power of communication* (Kılıç, E., Trans.). Istanbul Bilgi University Publications.

Çayır, K. (2010). Ayrımcılığın sosyolojisi ve Türkiye toplumu. In Çavdar, A., & Yıldırım, A. B. (Eds.), *Nefret suçları ve nefret söylemi* (pp. 45–54). Uluslararası Hrant Dink Vakfı Yayınları.

Chakraborty, A., & Bose, S. (2020). Around the world in 60 days: An exploratory study of impact of COVID-19 on online global news sentiment. *Journal of Computational Social Science, 3*(2), 367–400. DOI: 10.1007/s42001-020-00088-3 PMID: 33102926

Chandra, Y., & Jana, A. (2020). Sentiment analysis using machine learning and deep learning. *2020 7th International Conference on Computing for Sustainable Global Development (INDIACom).*

Chang, E. Y. (2017). Queergaming. In Studies, Q. G. (Ed.), *B. Ruberg & A* (pp. 15–23). Shaw., DOI: 10.3138/jrpc.9.1.003

Chee, F. M. (2015). Online games and digital ethnography. In Mason, R. M., & Peng, H. A. (Eds.), *International encyclopedia of digital communication and society* (pp. 1–6). John Wiley & Sons. DOI: 10.1002/9781118767771.wbiedcs086

Chetty, N., & Alathur, S. (2018). Hate speech review in the context of online social networks. *Aggression and Violent Behavior, 40*, 108–118. DOI: 10.1016/j.avb.2018.05.003

Cheung, M. L., Pires, G. D., & Rosenberger, P. J.III. (2020). Developing a conceptual model for examining social media marketing effects on brand awareness and brand image. *International Journal of Economics and Business Research, 21*(2), 243–261. DOI: 10.1504/IJEBR.2020.10027618

Clement, J. (2025). *Number of video game users worldwide from 2019 to 2029.* Statista.

Cohen-Almagor, R. (2011). Fighting hate and bigotry on the Internet. *Policy and Internet, 3*(3), 1–26. DOI: 10.2202/1944-2866.1059

Columbia University Mailman School of Public Health. (2025). Content Analysis Method Research of Columbia University. https://www.publichealth.columbia.edu/research/population-health-methods/content-analysis

Condis, M. (2021). Playing at racism: White supremacist recruitment in online video game culture. In Nilsen, S. D., & Turner, S. E. (Eds.), *White supremacy and the American media* (pp. 246–274). Routledge. DOI: 10.4324/9781003215172-17

Conn, M. (2015). Gaming's untapped queer potential as art. *QED: A Journal in GLBTQ Worldmaking*, 2(2), 1–5.

Consalvo, M. (2008). Crunched by passion: Women game developers and workplace challenges. In Yasmin, B., Kafai, C. H., Denner, J., & Sun, J. Y. (Eds.), *Beyond Barbie and Mortal Kombat: New perspectives on gender and gaming* (pp. 177–193). MIT Press. DOI: 10.7551/mitpress/7477.003.0017

Consalvo, M. (2012). Confronting toxic gamer culture: A challenge for feminist game studies scholars. *Ada: A Journal of Gender, New Media, and Technology,* 1. Retrieved from: https://adanewmedia.org/supplements/ada/issue1/Consalvo_Final.pdf.doi:10.7264/N33X84KH

Cooper, S. (2002). *Technoculture and Critical Theory*. Routledge.

Costa, S., da Silva, B. M., & Tavares, M. (2023). Online hate speech in video games communities: A counter project. In Ullman, S., & Tomalin, M. (Eds.), *Counterspeech: Multidisciplinary perspectives on countering dangerous speech* (pp. 123–146). Taylor & Francis. DOI: 10.4324/9781003377078-9

Costa, S., Tavares, M., da Silva, B. M., Isca, B., & Cerol, F. (2020). Hate speech in video games and online gaming communities — *State of the art. Revista Comunicando, 9*(1), 261–278.

Cote, A. C. (2016). I can defend myself. *Games and Culture, 12*(2), 136–155. DOI: 10.1177/1555412015587603

Couldry, N., & Mejias, U. A. (2019). *The costs of connection: How data is colonizing human life and appropriating it for capitalism.* Stanford University Press.

Cresci, (2018) Available at https://www.bbc.com/news/newsbeat-45474286

Creswell, J. W., & Poth, C. N. (2018). *Qualitative inquiry and research design: Choosing among five approaches* (4th ed.). Sage Publications.

Cross, L., Kaye, L. K., Savostijanovs, J., McLatchie, N., Johnston, M., Whiteman, L., Mooney, R., & Atherton, G. (2024). Gendered violence and sexualized representations in video games: (Lack of) effect on gender-related attitudes. *New Media & Society, 26*(3), 1648–1669. DOI: 10.1177/14614448221075736

Crowley, D., & Heyer, P. (2019). *İletişim tarihi: Taş devri sembollerinden sosyal medyaya.* Siyasal Kitabevi.

Cunningham, S., & Craig, D. (2019). *Social Media Entertainment: The New Intersection of Hollywood and Silicon Valley.* NYU Press.

Dash, S., Mishra, D., Shekhawat, G., & Pal, J. (2022). Divided we rule: Influencer polarization on twitter during political crises in India. *Proceedings of the International AAAI Conference on Web and Social Media, 16*, 135–146. DOI: 10.1609/icwsm.v16i1.19279

Dastin, J. (2023). Bridging the gap: Epistemology and the understanding of AI systems. *Philosophy of Technology Journal, 28*(2), 142–160. DOI: 10.1017/ptj.2023.08

Data Reportal, & Meltwater, & We Are Social. (February 5, 2025). Number of internet and social media users worldwide as of February 2025 (in billions) [Graph]. In Statista. Retrieved February 14, 2025, from https://www.statista.com/statistics/617136/digital-population-worldwide/

Dean, B. (2024). YouTube Stats: How Many People Use YouTube? In Backlinko. Retrieved from February 14, 2025, from https://backlinko.com/youtube-users

Dehkhoda, S., & Gunica, J. (2022). *Analyzing Toxicity in YouTube Comments with the Help of Machine Learning. Department of Computer and Systems Sciences.* Stockholm University.

Deleuze, G., & Guattari, F. (1993). *Kapitalizm ve şizofreni 2: Bin yayla* (Akay, A., Trans.). Bağlam Publications.

Delgado, R. (1982). Words that wound: A tort action for racial insults, epithets, and name-calling. *Harvard Civil Rights-Civil Liberties Law Review, 17*, 133–181.

Demirel, S., Çakıcı, Z., & Bulur, N. (2025). Exploring reflections of the 2023 Kahramanmaraş earthquake on X: A computational study on Türkiye and Syria. *Akademik İncelemeler Dergisi, 20*(1), 143–171. DOI: 10.17550/akademikincelemeler.1593038

Demir, V. I. (2017). Evaluation of Kardelen Fincancı, Nezaket Ekici and Tunç Ali Çam's works on the concepts of Deleuze and Spinoza, *Turkish Online Journal of Design. Art and Communication, 7*(3), 427–437. DOI: 10.7456/10703100/005

Deng, F., Tuo, M., Chen, S., & Zhang, Z. (2024). Born for marketing? The effects of virtual versus human influencers on brand endorsement effectiveness: The role of advertising recognition. *Journal of Retailing and Consumer Services, 80*, 103904. Advance online publication. DOI: 10.1016/j.jretconser.2024.103904

Derrida, J. (1976). *Of grammatology*. Johns Hopkins University Press.

Di Cicco, R., Neri, A., & Pino, G. (2024). Emotional communicative style and anthropomorphism in virtual influencers: An experimental study on Instagram. *Journal of Business Research, 172*, 114379. DOI: 10.1016/j.jbusres.2024.114379

Dietz, T. L. (1998). An examination of violence and gender role portrayals in video games: Implications for gender socialization and aggressive behavior. *Sex Roles, 38*(5–6), 425–442. DOI: 10.1023/A:1018709905920

Dill, K., Gentile, D., Richter, W., & Dill, J. (2005). Violence, sex, race and age in popular videogames. In Cole, E., & Daniel, J. (Eds.), *Featuring females: Feminist analyses of media* (pp. 115–130). American Psychological Association. DOI: 10.1037/11213-008

Dinh, T., & Lee, Y. (2021). "i want to be as trendy as influencers" – how "fear of missing out" leads to buying intention for products endorsed by social media influencers. *Journal of Research in Interactive Marketing, 16*(3), 346–364. DOI: 10.1108/JRIM-04-2021-0127

Dixon, J. C., Singleton, R. A.Jr, & Straits, B. C. (2016). *The process of social research.* Oxford University Press.

Dogarawa, A. B. (2005). *The Role of Cooperative Societies in Economic Development. University Library of Munich.* MPRA Paper., DOI: 10.2139/ssrn.1622149

Doğruyol, B., & Olgaç, A. (2018). Gelecek Zaman Perspektifi Ölçüm ve Kavramsallaştırmalarına Yeni Bir Bakış. *Psikoloji Çalışmaları, 38*(2), 201–217. DOI: 10.26650/SP2018-0011

Dolgun, U. (2015). *Şeffaf hapishane yahut gözetim toplumu.* Ötüken Neşriyat.

Döring, N., & Mohseni, M. R. (2019b). Fail videos and related video comments on YouTube: A case of sexualization of women and gendered hate speech? *Communication Research Reports, 36*(3), 254–264. DOI: 10.1080/08824096.2019.1634533

Döring, N., & Mohseni, R. (2017). Do female Youtubers receive more hateful comments? Results of three content analyses. Conference: CYPSY22 - 22nd Annual CyberPsychology, CyberTherapy & Social Networking ConferenceAt: Wolverhampton, England. June 2017. DOI: DOI: 10.13140/RG.2.2.29229.46561

Döring, N., & Mohseni, R. (2019a). Male dominance and sexism on YouTube: Results of Three Content Analyses. *Feminist Media Studies, 19*(4), 512–524. DOI: 10.1080/14680777.2018.1467945

Downs, E., & Smith, S. L. (2010). Keeping abreast of hypersexuality: A video game character content analysis. *Sex Roles, 62*(11–12), 721–733. DOI: 10.1007/s11199-009-9637-1

Drenten, J., & Brooks, G. (2020). Celebrity 2.0: Lil Miquela and the rise of a virtual star system. *Feminist Media Studies*, *20*(8), 1319–1323. DOI: 10.1080/14680777.2020.1830927

Duncum, P. (2011). Youth on YouTube: Prosumers in a peer-to-peer participatory culture. *The International Journal of Art Education*, *9*(2), 24–39.

Dynel, M. (2014). Participation framework underlying YouTube interaction. *Journal of Pragmatics*, *73*, 37–52. DOI: 10.1016/j.pragma.2014.04.001

Eagleton, T. (2011). *Ideology* (Özcan, M., Trans.). Ayrıntı Publications.

Elliot, R. (2024). Gamers spend more time on social video than games. Midia Research Blog. 5, Dec. 2024. Retrieved from: https://www.midiaresearch.com/blog/gamers-spend-more-time-watching-twitch-and-youtube-than-playing-games-are-publishers-leaving-engagement-and-revenue-on-the-table

Ellison, N. B., Steinfield, C., & Lampe, C. (2007). The benefits of Facebook "friends": Social capital and college students' use of online social network sites. *Journal of Computer-Mediated Communication*, *12*(4), 1143–1168. DOI: 10.1111/j.1083-6101.2007.00367.x

Elnur, A. (2022). From cyberfeminism to technofeminism: Developments in feminist technology studies. *Eurasian Journal of International Studies*, *10*(32), 321–339. DOI: 10.33692/avrasyad.1176864

Eubanks, V. (2018). *Automating inequality: How high-tech tools profile, police, and punish the poor*. St. Martin's Press.

European Commission Against Racism and Intolerance. (2015). ECRI General Policy Recommendation No. 15 on combating hate speech.

Everett, A., & Watkins, S. C. (2008). The power of play: The portrayal and performance of race in video games. In Tekinbaş, K. S. (Ed.), *The ecology of games: Connecting youth, games, and learning* (pp. 141–164). MIT Press.

Facebook. (2025). Hate speech. Meta Transparency Center. https://transparency.meta.com/reports/community-standards-enforcement/hate-speech/instagram/

Fleck, A. (2025). State of Play: Female Gamers Around the World. Statisca, Video Gaming Industry Blog. Published on March 7, 2025. April 2, 2025. Retrieved from: https://www.statista.com/chart/34067/femal-pc-and-console-gamers/

Floridi, L. (2021). *The Ethics of Artificial İntelligence*. Oxford University Press.

Foucault, M. (1975). *Discipline and Punish: The Birth of the Prison*. Vintage Books.

Foucault, M. (1977). *Language, Counter-Memory, Practice: Selected Essays and Interviews*. Cornell University Press.

Foucault, M. (2005). *The Political Function of the Intellectual* (2nd ed.). (Ergüden, I., Akınhay, O., & Keskin, F., Trans.). Ayrıntı Publications.

Fox, J., & Tang, W. Y. (2016). Women's experiences with general and sexual harassment in online video games: Rumination, organizational responsiveness, withdrawal, and coping strategies. *New Media & Society*, *19*(8), 1290–1307. DOI: 10.1177/1461444816635778

Franke, C., Groeppel-Klein, A., & Müller, K. (2023). Consumers' responses to virtual influencers as advertising endorsers: Novel and effective or uncanny and deceiving? *Journal of Advertising*, *52*(4), 523–539. DOI: 10.1080/00913367.2022.2154721

Frasca, G. (2001). Rethinking Agency and Immersion: Video Games as a Means of Consciousness-Raising. *Digital Creativity (Exeter)*, *12*(3), 167–174. DOI: 10.1076/digc.12.3.167.3225

Fricker, M. (2007). *Epistemic injustice: Power and the ethics of knowing*. Oxford University Press. DOI: 10.1093/acprof:oso/9780198237907.001.0001

Friedman, S., Schmer-Galunder, S., Chen, A., & Rye, J. (2019). Relating word embedding gender biases to gender gaps: A cross-cultural analysis. *Proceedings of the First Workshop on Gender Bias in Natural Language Processing*, 18–24. DOI: 10.18653/v1/W19-3803

Fuchs, C. (2015). *Digital labor and Karl Marx* (Kalaycı, T. E., & Oğuz, S., Trans.). NotaBene Publications.

Gaming Turkey. (2022). Turkey game market report 2022. https://www.turkiyeoyunsektoruraporu.com/en/turkey-game-market-report-2022/

Gao, G., Min, A., & Shih, P. C. (2017). Gendered design bias. *Proceedings of the 29th Australian Conference on Computer-Human Interaction*. https://doi.org/DOI: 10.1145/3152771.3152804

Garcia, A. C., Standlee, A. I., Bechoff, J., & Cui, Y. (2009). Ethnographic approaches to the internet and computer-mediated communication. *Journal of Contemporary Ethnography*, *38*(1), 52–84. DOI: 10.1177/0891241607310839

Gee, J. P. (2003). What Video Games Have to Teach Us About Learning and Literacy. [CIE]. *Computers in Entertainment*, *1*(1), 20–20. DOI: 10.1145/950566.950595

Gelber, K., & McNamara, L. (2016). Evidencing the harms of hate speech. *Social Identities*, *22*(3), 324–341. DOI: 10.1080/13504630.2015.1128810

Ghasiya, P., & Okamura, K. (2021). Investigating COVID-19 news across four nations: A topic modeling and sentiment analysis approach. *IEEE Access : Practical Innovations, Open Solutions*, *9*, 36645–36656. DOI: 10.1109/ACCESS.2021.3062875 PMID: 34786310

Ghazali, E., Mutum, D., & Lun, N. (2023). Expectations and beyond: The nexus of ai instrumentality and brand credibility in voice assistant retention using extended expectation-confirmation model. *Journal of Consumer Behaviour*, *23*(2), 655–675. DOI: 10.1002/cb.2228

Gillin, L. E., & Signorella, M. L. (2023). Attitudes toward sexual orientation and gender identity in online multiplayer gaming spaces. *Psychological Reports*. PMID: 36688329

Glaubke, C. R., Miller, P., Parker, M. A., & Espejo, E. (2001). *Fair play? Violence, gender and race in video games*. Children Now.

Global Media Insight. (2025). YouTube Statistics 2025 (Demographics, Users By Country & More). Global Media Insight. February 14, 2025, Retrieved from: https://www.globalmediainsight.com/blog/youtube-users-statistics/#:~:text=Monthly%20Active%20Users%20on%20YouTube,-Monthly%20active%20users&text=YouTube%20has%20more%20than%202.70,population%2C%2052%25%20access%20YouTube

Goel, P. and Garg, A. (2025), "Virtual personalities, real bonds: anthropomorphised virtual influencers' impact on trust and engagement", Journal of Consumer Marketing, Vol. ahead-of-print No. ahead-of-print. DOI: 10.1108/JCM-05-2024-6915

Goffman, E. (2016). *Günlük yaşamda benliğin sunumu* (Cezar, B., Trans.). Metis Yayınları.

Gökerik, M. (2024). Consumer cynicism in influencer marketing: an impact analysis on purchase intention and brand loyalty. İnsan Ve Toplum Bilimleri Araştırmaları Dergisi, 13(1), 404-421. DOI: 10.15869/itobiad.1422438

Grand View Research. (2024). *Virtual Influencer Market Size, Share & Trends Analysis Report*. https://www.grandviewresearch.com/industry-analysis/virtual-influencer-market-report

Gray, K. L. (2011). Intersecting oppressions and online communities: Examining the experiences of women of color in Xbox Live. *Information Communication and Society*, *15*(3), 411–428. DOI: 10.1080/1369118X.2011.642401

Gray, K. L. (2012). Deviant bodies, stigmatized identities, and racist acts: Examining the experiences of African-American gamers in Xbox Live. *New Review of Hypermedia and Multimedia, 18*(4), 261–276. DOI: 10.1080/13614568.2012.746740

Gray, K. L., Voorhees, G., & Vossen, E. (2018). *Feminism in play*. Palgrave Macmillan. DOI: 10.1007/978-3-319-90539-6

Gupta, I., Chatterjee, I., & Gupta, N. (2023). A two-staged NLP-based framework for assessing the sentiments on Indian supreme court judgments. *International Journal of Information Technology : an Official Journal of Bharati Vidyapeeth's Institute of Computer Applications and Management, 15*(4), 2273–2282. DOI: 10.1007/s41870-023-01273-z PMID: 37256028

Gür. (2019) Available at https://vogue.com.tr/moda-haber/calvin-klein-lgbtq-toplulugundan-ozur-diledi

Güregen, E. S. & Karaöz, Ç. (2022). Kadın Oyuncular, Cinsiyetçi Tektipleştirme ve Toksisite: İntearktif Sözlükler Üzerine Bir Araştırma. A chapter of "Dijital Oyunlar 2.0: Kimlik". Nobel Yayınevi, Aralık 2022

Gutuleac, R., Baima, G., Rizzo, C., & Bresciani, S. (2024). Will virtual influencers overcome the uncanny valley? The moderating role of social cues. *Psychology and Marketing, 41*(7), 1419–1431. DOI: 10.1002/mar.21989

Güzel, E. (2020). Sosyal Medya Sosyolojisi L. Eraslan (Ed), *Dijital Toplum, Kamusal ve Özel Alan: Mahremiyet ve İlişkilerinin Dönüşümü*, Anadolu Üniversitesi Yayınları, pp. 62-86.

Halitoğlu, Ş. N., & Akpınar, B. (2022). Okul yöneticilerinin liderlik stilleri ile öğretmenlerin stres algısı arasındaki ilişki. *Elektronik Sosyal Bilimler Dergisi, 21*(82), 661–673. DOI: 10.17755/esosder.1028315

Hamari, J., Koivisto, J., & Sarsa, H. (2014). *Does gamification work? A literature review of empirical studies on gamification*. 47th Hawaii international conference on system sciences, pp. 3025-3034. DOI: 10.1109/HICSS.2014.377

Hamilton, W. A., Garretson, O., & Kerne, A. (2014). Streaming on Twitch: Fostering participatory communities of play. *Proceedings of the SIGCHI Conference on Human Factors in Computing Systems*, pp. 1315-1324. DOI: 10.1145/2556288.2557048

Han, C., Seering, J., Kumar, D., Hancock, J. T., & Durumeric, Z. (2023). Hate raids on Twitch: Echoes of the past, new modalities, and implications for platform governance. *Proceedings of the ACM on Human-Computer Interaction,* 7(CSCW1), 1–28. DOI: 10.1145/3579609

Han, B.-C. (2020a). *Transparency society*. Metis Publications.

Han, B.-C. (2020b). *Psikopolitika: Neoliberalizm ve yeni iktidar teknikleri*. Metis Publications.

Han, B.-C. (2023). *Enfocracy: Crisis of digitalization and democracy*. Ketebe Publications.

Haq, M. D., Tseng, T.-H., Cheng, H.-L., & Chiu, C.-M. (2024). An empirical analysis of eWOM valence effects: Integrating stimulus-organism-response, trust transfer theory, and theory of planned behavior perspectives. *Journal of Retailing and Consumer Services*, *81*, 104026. DOI: 10.1016/j.jretconser.2024.104026

Haraway, D. J. (2006). *The Cyborg Manifesto: Science, Technology and Socialist Feminism in the Late Twentieth Century*. Agora Library.

Haraway, D. J. (2010). *Another Place* (Pusar, G., Trans.). Metis Publications.

Harrington, N. (2023, February 9). The epistemology of AI. Project Q. https://projectqsydney.com/the-epistemology-of-ai/

Heaton, B. (2024, December 2). ‘Brain rot’ named Oxford Word of the Year 2024. Oxford University Press. https://corp.oup.com/news/brain-rot-named-oxford-word-of-the-year-2024/

Heidegger, M. (1977). *The question concerning technology and other essays*. Harper & Row.

Hine, C. (2000). *Virtual ethnography*. Sage Publications. DOI: 10.4135/9780857020277

Hofeditz, L., Nissen, A., Schütte, R., & Mirbabaie, M. (2022) Trust me, I’m an influencer!-A comparison of perceived trust in human and virtual influencers [Paper presentation]. https://aisel.aisnet.org/ecis2022_rip/27

Hofeditz, Lennart; Nissen, Anika; Schütte, Reinhard; and Mirbabaie, Milad, “Trust Me, I’m an Influencer! - A Comparison of Perceived Trust in Human and Virtual Influencers” (2022). ECIS 2022 Research-in-Progress Papers. 27.

HonoraryReporter. (2023) Available at https://honoraryreporters.korea.net/board/detail.do?pageidx=1&board_no=11587&tpln=1&articlecate=1&searchtp=all&searchtxt=taiba#:~:text=Oh%20Rozy%20(%EC%98%A4%20%EB%A1%9C%EC%A7%80)%20is,of%20Sidus%20Studio%20X%2C%20Mr

Hore, S., & Bhattacharya, T. (2019). Analyzing social trend towards girl child in India: A machine intelligence-based approach. In *Advances in Intelligent Systems and Computing* (pp. 43–50). Springer Singapore.

Howard, P. N. (2002). Network ethnography and the hypermedia organization: New media, new organizations, new methods. *New Media & Society*, *4*(4), 550–574. DOI: 10.1177/14614440232146681 3

Huang, J. (2023). Comparative analysis: The development of Chinese feminism based on east and west Barbie film reviews. *Communications in Humanities Research*, *22*(1), 51–63. DOI: 10.54254/2753-7064/22/20231568

Hu, H., Zhang, D., & Wang, C. (2019). Impact of social media influencers' endorsement on application adoption: A trust transfer perspective. *Social Behavior and Personality*, *47*(11), 1–12. DOI: 10.2224/sbp.8518

Huizinga, J. (1950). *Homo Ludens: A Study of the Play-Element in Culture*. Beacon Press.

Imran, A. S., Daudpota, S. M., Kastrati, Z., & Batra, R. (2020). Cross-cultural polarity and emotion detection using sentiment analysis and deep learning on COVID-19 related tweets. *IEEE Access : Practical Innovations, Open Solutions*, *8*, 181074–181090. DOI: 10.1109/ACCESS.2020.3027350 PMID: 34812358

İnan, İ. (2020). Awareness of ignorance. *SATS*, *20*(2), 141–173. DOI: 10.1515/sats-2020-2004

Influencer Marketing Hub. (2025). Influencer Marketing Benchmark Report 2025. *Available at* https://influencermarketinghub.com/influencer-marketing-benchmark-report/

Instagram. (2025). Hate speech. Meta Transparency Center. https://transparency.meta.com/reports/community-standards-enforcement/hate-speech/instagram/

Jaidka, K., Ahmed, S., Skoric, M., & Hilbert, M. (2019). Predicting elections from social media: A three-country, three-method comparative study. *Asian Journal of Communication*, *29*(3), 252–273. DOI: 10.1080/01292986.2018.1453849

Jamatia, A., Swamy, S. D., Gambäck, B., Das, A., & Debbarma, S. (2020). Deep Learning based sentiment analysis in a code-mixed English-Hindi and English-Bengali social media corpus. *International Journal of Artificial Intelligence Tools: Architectures, Languages. International Journal of Artificial Intelligence Tools*, *29*(05), 2050014. DOI: 10.1142/S0218213020500141

Jansz, J., & Martis, R. G. (2007). The Lara phenomenon: Powerful female characters in video games. *Sex Roles*, *56*(3–4), 141–148. DOI: 10.1007/s11199-006-9158-0

Jasanoff, S. (2020). The ethics of in/visibility: Artificial intelligence and the social construction of knowledge. *Harvard International Review*, *42*(2), 58–62.

Jena, P. R., & Majhi, R. (2023). Are Twitter sentiments during COVID-19 pandemic a critical determinant to predict stock market movements? A machine learning approach. *Scientific African*, *19*(e01480), e01480. DOI: 10.1016/j.sciaf.2022.e01480 PMID: 36465525

Jenkins, H. (2006). *Convergence culture: Where old and new media collide*. NYU Press.

Jensen, K. B. (2012). Media reception. In Jensen, K. B. (Ed.), *The handbook of media and communication research* (pp. 171–185). Routledge.

Jenson, J., & Castell, S. (2015). Online games, gender and feminism, In *The International Encyclopedia of Digital Communication and Society*, (Eds.) R. Mansell & P. H. Ang pp. 1-5. DOI: 10.1002/9781118767771.wbiedcs116

Jerald, J. (2015). *The VR Book: Human-Centered Design for Virtual Reality*. Association for Computing Machinery. DOI: 10.1145/2792790

Jhawar, A., Kumar, P., & Varshney, S. (2023). The emergence of virtual influencers: A shift in the influencer marketing paradigm. *Young Consumers*, *24*(4), 468–484. DOI: 10.1108/YC-05-2022-1529

Johnson, M., & Woodcock, J. (2018). The impacts of live streaming and Twitch.tv on the video game industry. *Media Culture & Society*, *41*(5), 670–688. DOI: 10.1177/0163443718818363

Jung, C. G. (1954). *Psychological aspects of the mother archetype. The Collected Works of C. G. Jung; Read, H.,Fordham, M., Adler, G., (journal.) inside*. Routledge.

Jung, C. G. (2019). *Four Archetypes*. Metis Publishing.

Juul, J. (2013). *The art of failure: An essay on the pain of playing video games*. MIT Press.

Kahneman, D. (2012). *Thinking, Fast and Slow*. Penguin, Farrar, Straus and Giroux.

Kan, D. (2012). Yeni medya aracı bilgisayar oyunlarında toplumsal cinsiyetin inşası. *Turkish Online Journal of Design Art and Communication*, *2*(4), 52–60. DOI: 10.7456/10204100/009

Kara, U. Y. (2013). Computer Games, New Media and Identity: Theoretical Quest/ Computer Games, New Media and Identity: A Theoretical Research. [Unpublished Master's Thesis]. Hacettepe University Institute of Social Sciences.

Kara, T. (2013). *Sosyal medya endüstrisi*. Beta Basım.

Kashyap, S., & Singh, A. (2021). Testing Data Feminism in India. *Scholars Journal of Arts Humanities and Social Sciences*, *9*(10), 516–530. DOI: 10.36347/sjahss.2021.v09i10.006

Kaur, C., & Sharma, A. (2020). Social Issues Sentiment Analysis using Python. *2020 5th International Conference on Computing, Communication and Security (ICCCS).*

Keogh, B. (2014). Across worlds and bodies: Criticism in the age of video games. *Journal of Games Criticism*, *1*(1), 1–26.

Keum, B. T., & Hearns, M. (2022). Online gaming and racism: Impact on psychological distress among Black, Asian, and Latinx emerging adults. *Games and Culture*, *17*(3), 445–460. DOI: 10.1177/15554120211039082

Khandaker, J. (2019). *Girl Gamers and Toxicity*. University of Houston. Master Thesis. The Faculty of the Department of Sociology.

Khan, M. I., Raihan, A. F., & Hussain, M. (2023). Interactive marketing in the digital era: Effects on customer loyalty and engagement. *International Journal of Business and Social Science*, *14*(1), 12–20.

Kholkina, V., Chesnokova, E., & Zelenskaya, E. (2025). Virtual or human? The impact of the influencer type on Gen Z consumer outcomes. *Journal of Product and Brand Management*, *34*(1), 104–118. DOI: 10.1108/JPBM-12-2023-4885

Kılıç, N. P. (2020). Reconstruction of memory in digital games: The case of Nusrat. *Moment Journal*, 7(2), pp. 265 286. DOI: 10.17572/mj2020.2.265286

Kim, Y. (2022). Human consciousness and prosthetic temporality: On the way to new technological humanities. *New Techno Humanities.*, *2*(1), 41–46. DOI: 10.1016/j.techum.2022.10.001

King, C. M., & McCashin, D. (2022). Commenting and connecting: A thematic analysis of responses to YouTube vlogs about borderline personality disorder. *Internet Interventions : the Application of Information Technology in Mental and Behavioural Health*, *28*, 100509. Advance online publication. DOI: 10.1016/j.invent.2022.100540 PMID: 35493438

Kishonna, G., McPherson, T., Gillian, R., & Anderson, R. (2024). Video Games and Race. In *Handbook of Children and Screens*, (Eds.) D. A. Christakis & L. Hale, Springer, pp. 291 – 296. Doi: DOI: 10.1007/978-3-031-69362-5_40

Koehler, D., Fiebig, V., & Jugl, I. (2023). From gaming to hating: Extreme-right ideological indoctrination and mobilization for violence of children on online gaming platforms. *Political Psychology*, *44*(2), 419–434. DOI: 10.1111/pops.12855

Konoplıannykova, M. (2024). Influence marketing in social media. SF, 154(2), 118-144. DOI: 10.31617/1.2024(154)07

Kotan, S. (2024). *Dünyayı ardında bırak filmi özelinde sinemada dijital kıyamet anlatısı. İletişim Bilimlerinde Yenilikçi Araştırmalar I, İçinde* (Küçük Durur, E., Yılmaz, A., & Cinisli, Z., Eds.). Gazi Kitabevi.

Kou, Y., & Gui, X. (2023). Harmful Design in the Metaverse and How to Mitigate it: A Case Study of User-Generated Virtual Worlds on Roblox. In *Designing Interactive Systems Conference (DIS'23)*, July 10–14, 2023, Pittsburgh, PA, USA. ACM, New York, NY, USA, 14 pages. DOI: 10.1145/3563657.3595960

Kowert, R., & Quandt, T. (2016). *The Video Game Debate: Unravelling the Physical, Social, and Psychological Effects of Video Games*. Routledge.

Kozinets, R. V. (2010). *Netnography: Doing ethnographic research online*. Sage Publications.

Kraut, R. E., Kiesler, S., Boneva, B., Cummings, J., Helgeson, V., & Crawford, A. (2002). Internet paradox revisited. *The Journal of Social Issues*, *58*(1), 49–74. DOI: 10.1111/1540-4560.00248

Kumar, A., & Albuquerque, V. H. C. (2021). Sentiment analysis using XLM-R transformer and zero-shot transfer learning on resource-poor Indian language. *ACM Transactions on Asian and Low-Resource Language Information Processing*, *20*(5), 1–13. DOI: 10.1145/3461764

Kumar, S., Gahalawat, M., Roy, P. P., Dogra, D. P., & Kim, B.-G. (2020). Exploring impact of age and gender on sentiment analysis using Machine Learning. *Electronics (Basel)*, *9*(2), 374. DOI: 10.3390/electronics9020374

Kumar, S., Kwan, E., Weststar, J., & Coppins, T. (2021). *Developer Satisfaction Survey 2021 Diversity in the Game Industry Report*. International Game Developers Association.

Kurbalija, J. (2024b, April 13). The role of knowledge in the cyber-age of globalisation – Diplo Resource. Richard Falk, Diplo. https://www.diplomacy.edu/resource/the-role-of-knowledge-in-the-cyber-age-of-globalisation/

Kuss, D. J., & Griffiths, M. D. (2012). Internet gaming addiction: A systematic review of empirical research. *International Journal of Mental Health and Addiction*, *10*(2), 278–296. DOI: 10.1007/s11469-011-9318-5

Kuznekoff, J. H., & Rose, L. M. (2012). Communication in multiplayer gaming: Examining player responses to gender cues. *New Media & Society*, *15*(4), 541–556. DOI: 10.1177/1461444812458271

Lages, J. (2022). AI, agency, and the role of critical literacy in human-machine interaction. *Journal of Philosophy and Technology*, *34*(1), 89–104. DOI: 10.1007/jpt.2022.07

Lange, P. G. (2007, March). Commenting on comments: Investigating responses to antagonism on YouTube. In Society for Applied anthropology conference, 31(1), pp. 163-190.

Laughey, D. (2010). *Medya çalışmaları: Teoriler ve yaklaşımlar*. Kalkedon Yayınları.

Leonard, D. J. (2006). Not a hater, just keepin' it real: The importance of race- and gender-based game studies. *Games and Culture*, *1*(1), 83–88. DOI: 10.1177/1555412005281910

Leung, F., Gu, F., Li, Y., Zhang, J., & Palmatier, R. (2022). Influencer marketing effectiveness. *Journal of Marketing*, *86*(6), 93–115. DOI: 10.1177/00222429221102889

Lim, X. J., Radzol, A. R. M., Cheah, J.-H., & Wong, M. W. (2017). The impact of social media influencers on purchase intention and the mediation effect of customer attitude. *Asian Journal of Business Research*, *7*(2), 35. DOI: 10.14707/ajbr.170035

Lokke, E. (2020). *Privacy: Private life in digital society*. Koç University Publications.

Lovink, G. (2017). *The bottomless well of social media*. Otonom Publishing.

Lynch, T., Tompkins, J. E., van Driel, I. I., & Fritz, N. (2016). Sexy, strong, and secondary: A content analysis of female characters in video games across 31 years. *Journal of Communication*, *66*(4), 564–584. DOI: 10.1111/jcom.12237

Lyon, D. (2013). *Gözetim çalışmaları*. Kalkedon Publishing.

Maathuis, C., & Kerkhof, I. (2023). The first two months in the war in Ukraine through topic modeling and sentiment analysis. *Regional Science Policy & Practice*, *15*(1), 56–75. DOI: 10.1111/rsp3.12632

Makeeva, E., & Sinilshchikova, M. (2020). News sentiment in bankruptcy prediction models: Evidence from Russian retail companies. *Korporativnye Finansy*, *14*(4), 7–18. DOI: 10.17323/j.jcfr.2073-0438.14.4.2020.7-18

Martins, N., Williams, D. C., Harrison, K., & Ratan, R. A. (2009). A content analysis of female body imagery in video games. *Sex Roles*, *61*(11–12), 824–836. DOI: 10.1007/s11199-009-9682-9

Marwick, A. E., & Miller, R. (2014). Online harassment, defamation, and hateful speech: A primer of the legal landscape. *Fordham Center on Law and Information Policy Report.*

Massey, C. R. (1992). Hate speech, cultural diversity, and the foundational paradigms of free expression. *UCLA Law Review. University of California, Los Angeles. School of Law*, *40*, 103–177.

Matsuda, M. J. (1989). Pragmatism modified and the false consciousness problem. *Southern California Law Review*, *63*, 1763–1802.

Mayfield, M., & Mayfield, J. (2023). Notes from the editors: spotlight on social media. International Journal of Business Communication, 60(2), 371-374. DOI: 10.1177/23294884221148615

McLean, L., & Griffiths, M. D. (2013). The psychological effects of video games on young people. *Aloma: Revista de Psicologia. Ciències de l'Educació i de l'Esport Blanquerna*, *31*(1), 119–133.

McLean, L., & Griffiths, M. D. (2018). Female gamers' experience of online harassment and social support in online gaming: A qualitative study. *International Journal of Mental Health and Addiction*, *17*(4), 970–994. DOI: 10.1007/s11469-018-9962-0

Medin, D. L., & Bang, M. (2014). *Who's asking? Native science, Western science, and science education*. MIT Press. DOI: 10.7551/mitpress/9755.001.0001

Meisner, C. (2023). Networked responses to networked harassment? Creators' coordinated management of "hate raids" on Twitch. *Social Media + Society*, *9*(2), 20563051231179696. DOI: 10.1177/20563051231179696

Mendon, S., Dutta, P., Behl, A., & Lessmann, S. (2021). A hybrid approach of machine learning and lexicons to sentiment analysis: Enhanced insights from twitter data of natural disasters. *Information Systems Frontiers: A Journal of Research and Innovation, 23*(5), 1145–1168. DOI: 10.1007/s10796-021-10107-x

Meriç, E. (2025). Pandemi döneminde dijital sağlık iletişimi: T.C. Sağlık Bakanlığı COVID-19 kamu spotları üzerine stratejik bir inceleme. *Kronotop İletişim Dergisi*, *2*(1), 77–106.

Meriç, E., Başer, B., & Tandaçgüneş, N. (2021). Kuşaklararası mobil oyun oynama pratikleri üzerine nitel bir inceleme. In Uğurlu, Ö. A., & Kuş, Ö. A. (Eds.), *Oyunların dijital hali* (pp. 77–118). Urzeni Yayınevi.

Militsi, A. (2021). Undoing Gender Interpellations In Role-Playing Videogame Spaces: The Case Of Cyberpunk 2077 As A Case Of Resistance From A Feminist Post-Constructionist Perspective. Umeå University. Umeå Center for Gender Studies. Magister Thesis in Gender Studies.

Miller, M. K., & Summers, A. (2007). Gender differences in video game characters' roles, appearances, and attire as portrayed in video game magazines. *Sex Roles*, *57*(9–10), 733–742. DOI: 10.1007/s11199-007-9307-0

Mishra, P., Rajnish, R., & Kumar, P. (2016). Sentiment analysis of Twitter data: Case study on digital India. *2016 International Conference on Information Technology (InCITe) - The Next Generation IT Summit on the Theme - Internet of Things: Connect Your Worlds*. DOI: 10.1109/INCITE.2016.7857607

Moreno, L., Demo, G., Rocha, T., & Scussel, F. (2021). Take a ride on credibility: The role of brand personality in users' loyalty to virtual brands in the sharing economy. *Internext*, *16*(2), 221–237. DOI: 10.18568/internext.v16i2.670

Mortensen, T. E. (2018). Anger, fear, and games: The long event of #GamerGate. *Games and Culture*, *13*(8), 787–806. DOI: 10.1177/1555412016640408

Mou, Y., & Peng, W. (2009). Gender and Racial Stereotypes in Popular Video Games. In *Handbook of Research on Effective Electronic Gaming in Education*, (Ed.) R. E. Ferdig, IGI Global, pp. 922–937. https://doi.org/DOI: 10.4018/978-1-59904-808-6.ch053

Mouritzen, S. L. T., Penttinen, V., & Pedersen, S. (2024). Virtual influencer marketing: The good, the bad and the unreal. *European Journal of Marketing*, *58*(2), 410–440. DOI: 10.1108/EJM-12-2022-0915

Muda, M., & Hamzah, M. (2021). Should i suggest this youtube clip? the impact of ugc source credibility on ewom and purchase intention. *Journal of Research in Interactive Marketing*, *15*(3), 441–459. DOI: 10.1108/JRIM-04-2020-0072

Munnukka, J., Uusitalo, O., & Toivonen, H. (2016). Credibility of a peer endorser and advertising effectiveness. *Journal of Consumer Marketing*, *33*(3), 182–192. DOI: 10.1108/JCM-11-2014-1221

Munro, E. (2013). *Feminism: A Fourth Wave?* The Political Studies Association.

MusicIndustry123. (2025). How Twitch Transformed the Streaming Landscape: A Deep Dive, https://vocal.media/education/how-twitch-transformed-the-streaming-landscape-a-deep-dive, Date of Access: 14.01.2025.

Mutlu, E. (2008). *Dictionary of communication*. Ayraç Kitabevi.

Nakamura, L. (2019). Gender and race online. In Graham, M., & Dutton, W. H. (Eds.), *Society and the internet: How networks of information and communication are changing our lives* (pp. 126–146). Oxford University Press. DOI: 10.1093/oso/9780198843498.003.0008

Nardi, B., & Harris, J. (2006). Strangers and friends: Collaborative play in World of Warcraft. *Proceedings of the 2006 ACM Conference on Computer Supported Cooperative Work*, 149-158. DOI: 10.1145/1180875.1180898

Newzoo. (2022). *Newzoo Global Games Market Report 2022 | Free Version,* https://newzoo.com/resources?type=trendreports&tag=all. Date of Access: 08.02.2025.

Nissenbaum, H. (2001). How computer systems embody values. *Computer*, *34*(3), 120–119. DOI: 10.1109/2.910905

Noble, S. U. (2018). *Algorithms of oppression: How search engines reinforce racism.* NYU Press. DOI: 10.18574/nyu/9781479833641.001.0001

O'Neil, C. (2016). *Weapons of Math Destruction: How Big Data Increases Inequality and Threatens Democracy.* Crown Publishing Group.

Obadimu, A., Mead, E. L., Hussain, M., & Agarwal, N. (2019). Identifying toxicity within YouTube video comment. In Thomson, R., Bisgin, H., Dancy, C., & Hyder, A. (Eds.), Lecture Notes in Computer Science: Vol. 11549. *Social, Cultural, And Behavioral Modeling* (pp. 207–217). Springer., DOI: 10.1007/978-3-030-21741-9_22

Okmeydan, S. B. (2020). Dijital Yayın Platformlarının Sosyal Medya Analizi: Netflix, Blutv ve Puhutv Youtube Kanalı Örneği. Proceedings Book- Internatıonal Asian Congress on Contemporary Scıences-Iv.

Oliveira, A. B. da S., & Chimenti, P. (2021). "Humanized robots": A proposition of categories to understand virtual influencers. *AJIS. Australasian Journal of Information Systems*, *25*. Advance online publication. DOI: 10.3127/ajis.v25i0.3223

Önder. (2020) Available at https://www.marketingturkiye.com.tr/haberler/michael-jordandan-shudu-grama-yolculuk-influencer-olmak/

Ong, A. K. S., Prasetyo, Y. T., Robas, K. P. E., Persada, S. F., Nadlifatin, R., Matillano, J. S. A., Macababbad, D. C. B., Pabustan, J. R., & Taningco, K. A. C. (2023). Determination of factors influencing the behavioral intention to play "Mobile Legends: Bang-Bang" during the COVID-19 pandemic: Integrating UTAUT2 and system usability scale for a sustainable e-sport business. *Sustainability (Basel)*, *15*(4), 3170. DOI: 10.3390/su15043170

Ortiz, S. M. (2019). “You can say I got desensitized to it”: How men of color cope with everyday racism in online gaming. *Sociological Perspectives, 62*(4), 572–588. DOI: 10.1177/0731121419837588

Özdemir, O., Kolfal, B., Messinger, P. R., & Rizvi, S. (2023). Human or virtual: How influencer type shapes brand attitudes. *Computers in Human Behavior, 145*, 107771. DOI: 10.1016/j.chb.2023.107771

Öztekin, H., & Öztekin, A. (2020). Dijital oyunlarda nefret söylemi ve ayrımcı dil: Agar.io örneği. *Turkish Studies -. Social Sciences, 15*(1), 533–558.

Öztekin, H., & Öztekin, A. (2020). Hate speech and discriminatory language in digital games: The case of Agar, *Turkish Studies-. Social Sciences, 15*(1), 533–558. DOI: 10.29228/TurkishStudies.39019

Öztürk, B. N., & Bülbül, S. (2022). *A Study on Brand Identity in the Mobile Game Market: The Case of Tencent Games*. Alanya Academic Review Journal.

Paaßen, B., Thekla, M., & Stratemeyer, M. (2017). What Is a True Gamer? The Male Gamer Stereotype and the Marginalization of Women in Video Game Culture. *Sex Roles, 76*(7), 421–435. DOI: 10.1007/s11199-016-0678-y

Padmaja, S., Fatima, S. S., Bandu, S., Kosala, P., & Abhignya, M. C. (2014). Comparing and evaluating the sentiment on newspaper articles: A preliminary experiment. *2014 Science and Information Conference*. DOI: 10.1109/SAI.2014.6918276

Pai, R. R., & Alathur, S. (2020). Women empowerment through social media: Insights from India. In *ICT Analysis and Applications* (pp. 387–395). Springer Singapore. DOI: 10.1007/978-981-15-0630-7_38

Pankowski, R. (2007). *How to understand and confront hate speech* (Vol. 3). United for Intercultural Action.

Pan, S., Qin, Z., & Zhang, Y. (2024). More Realistic, More Better? How Anthropomorphic Images of Virtual Influencers Impact the Purchase Intentions of Consumers. *Journal of Theoretical and Applied Electronic Commerce Research, 19*(4), 3229–3252. DOI: 10.3390/jtaer19040157

Papacharissi, Z. (2020). Sensiz ben hiçbirşeyim: Twitter’da benliğin gösterileri. In Aydoğan, F. (Ed.), *Yeni medya kuramları II* (pp. 163–188). Der Publishing.

Parekh, B. (2012). Is there a case for banning hate speech? *In The content and context of hate speech: Rethinking regulation and responses* (pp. 22–23). DOI: 10.1017/CBO9781139042871.006

Park, C. S., Liu, Q., & Kaye, B. K. (2021). Analysis of ageism, sexism, and ableism in user comments on YouTube videos about climate activist Greta Thunberg. *Social Media + Society*, *7*(3), 1–14. DOI: 10.1177/20563051211036059

Pearson, C. (1991). *Awakening the heroes within: Twelve archetypes to help us find ourselves and transform our world*. No Title.

Perez, A., & Martins, A. M. (2024). Exploring the Relationship between Social Media Marketing and SEO Outcomes. *Journal of Digital Marketing*, *29*(1), 45–60.

Petrova E., & Gross N. (2017 June). 4 Reasons People Watch Gaming Content on YouTube: On Video, Gaming. Consumer Insights and Gaming. *Consumer Insights Report*. Think With Google.

Piaget, J. (1962). *Play, dreams, and imitation in childhood*. Norton.

Pinski, M., Haas, M., & Benlian, A. (2024). Building Metaknowledge in AI Literacy – The Effect of Gamified vs. Text-based Learning on AI Literacy Metaknowledge. Proceedings of the . . . *Annual Hawaii International Conference on System Sciences/ Proceedings of the Annual Hawaii International Conference on System Sciences*. DOI: 10.24251/HICSS.2024.619

Pitroda, H. (2022). Analytical Prediction and Sentimental Analysis of virtual engagement tools in teens and youth of urban and rural areas in India. *2022 1st International Conference on Informatics (ICI)*.

Pixune. (2024). What are the different kinds of video game genres? Retrieved January 30, 2025, from https://pixune.com/blog/video-game-genres/

Plant, S. (1998). *Zeros And Ones*. Fourth Estate.

Postill, J., & Pink, S. (2012). Social media ethnography: The digital researcher in a messy web. *Media International Australia, Incorporating Culture & Policy*, *145*(1), 123–134. DOI: 10.1177/1329878X1214500114

Powell, A., & Williams-Johnson, D. (2023). "You dumb cracker b*tch": The legitimizing of white supremacy during a Twitch ban of HasanAbi. *New Media & Society*. Advance online publication.

Pramesti, K. & Alversia, Y. (2023). The influence of attitude toward user generated content (ugc) in tiktok on purchase intention., 630-639. DOI: 10.2991/978-94-6463-234-7_66

Pulos, A. (2013). Confronting heteronormativity in online games: A critical discourse analysis of LGBTQ sexuality in World of Warcraft. *Games and Culture*, *8*(2), 77–97. DOI: 10.1177/1555412013478688

Putnam, R. D. (2000). *Bowling Alone: The Collapse and Revival of American Community*. Simon and Schuster.

Qu, Y., & Baek, E. (2024). Let virtual creatures stay virtual: Tactics to increase trust in virtual influencers. *Journal of Research in Interactive Marketing*, *18*(1), 91–108. DOI: 10.1108/JRIM-09-2022-0280

Radaideh, A., & Dweiri, F. (2023). Sentiment analysis predictions in digital media content using NLP techniques. *International Journal of Advanced Computer Science and Applications*, *14*(11). Advance online publication. DOI: 10.14569/IJACSA.2023.0141128

Radoff, J. (2010). Jon Radoff's Internet Wonderland: History of social games. Retrieved January 30, 2025, from https://web.archive.org/web/20100527090108/http://radoff.com/blog/2010/05/24/history-social-games/

Rakes, Z. T. (2016). *My Avatar, My Self: A Posthuman Examination Of Video Games And Cyborg Bodies*. [Unpublished Master's Thesis]. Marshall University.

Raneri, P. C., Montag, C., Rozgonjuk, D., Satel, J., & Pontes, H. M. (2022). The role of microtransactions in Internet Gaming Disorder and Gambling Disorder: A preregistered systematic review. *Addictive Behaviors Reports*, *15*, 100415. DOI: 10.1016/j.abrep.2022.100415 PMID: 35434248

Rani, S., & Kumar, P. (2019). A sentiment analysis system for social media using machine learning techniques: Social enablement. *Digital Scholarship in the Humanities*, *34*(3), 569–581. DOI: 10.1093/llc/fqy037

Rheingold, H. (2000). *The Virtual Community: Homesteading on the Electronic Frontier*. MIT Press. DOI: 10.7551/mitpress/7105.001.0001

Rosenstein, (2018) Available at https://www.harpersbazaar.com/beauty/makeup/a16810663/shudu-gram-fenty-model-fake/

Ruberg, B., & Shaw, A. (Eds.). (2017). *Queer Game Studies*. University of Minnesota Press.

Rutinika. (2024). "Dijital Topluluklar Nedir?" https://rutinika.com/dijital-topluluklar-nedir/, Date of Access: 10.01.2024.

Ruvalcaba, O., Shulze, J., Kim, A., Berzenski, S. R., & Otten, M. P. (2018). Women's experiences in eSports: Gendered differences in peer and spectator feedback during competitive video game play. *Journal of Sport and Social Issues*, *42*(4), 295–311. DOI: 10.1177/0193723518773287

Sade-Beck, L. (2004). Internet ethnography: Online and offline. *International Journal of Qualitative Methods*, *3*(2), 45–51. DOI: 10.1177/160940690400300204

Sahaf, M. F., & Nazir, A. (2024). Influentiality of social media influencers on purchase intention of consumers: A regional perspective. *International Journal of Media and Communication Research*, *5*(1), 1–20. DOI: 10.25299/ijmcr.v5i1.14924

Şahin, M. (2016). Geleneksel Medyanın Yeni Rakibi Yeni Medya ve Canlı Yayınlar. *Yeni Medya*, *1*(1), 50–63.

Salen, K., & Zimmerman, E. (2004). *Rules of play: Game design fundamentals.* MIT Press.

Sands, S., Campbell, C. L., Plangger, K., & Ferraro, C. (2022). Unreal influence: Leveraging AI in influencer marketing. *European Journal of Marketing*, *56*(6), 1721–1747. DOI: 10.1108/EJM-12-2019-0949

Saritepeci, M. (2021). Multiple Screen Addiction Scale: Validity and reliability study. *Instructional Technology and Lifelong Learning*, *2*(1), 1–17. DOI: 10.52911/itall.796758

Savett, S. M. (2016). *Virtual Psyche in Play and Tending the Collective Unconscious: An Archetypal Psychology Perspective of Digital Games. S. B. Schafer içinde, Exploring the Collective Unconscious in the Age of Digital Media.* IGI Global. DOI: 10.4018/978-1-4666-9891-8.ch006

Sayar, T. E. (2022). *Dijital Oyunlar ve Kimlik*. Eğitim Yayınevi.

Scarborough, W., & Helmuth, A. S. (2021). How cultural environments shape online sentiment toward social movements: Place character and support for feminism. In *SocArXiv*. DOI: 10.31235/osf.io/juxqk

Scholz, T. M. (2020). Deciphering the World of eSports. *International Journal on Media Management*, *22*(1), 1–12. DOI: 10.1080/14241277.2020.1757808

Sellars, A. (2016). Defining hate speech. Berkman Klein Center Research Publication, No. 2016-20; Boston University School of Law, *Public Law Research Paper*, 16–48.

Sepetci, T. (2017). Digital Games, Digital Players: Counter Hegemony Practices and Social Interaction. [Unpublished Doctoral Thesis]. Akdeniz University Social Sciences Institute.

Shankar, V., Inman, J. J., Mantrala, M., Kelley, E., & Rizley, R. (2011). Innovations in Shopper Marketing: Current Insights and Future Research Issues. *Journal of Retailing*, *87*(1), S29–S42. DOI: 10.1016/j.jretai.2011.04.007

Shanmugavadivel, K., Sampath, S. H., Nandhakumar, P., Mahalingam, P., Subramanian, M., Kumaresan, P. K., & Priyadharshini, R. (2022). An analysis of machine learning models for sentiment analysis of Tamil code-mixed data. *Computer Speech & Language*, *76*(101407), 101407. DOI: 10.1016/j.csl.2022.101407

Shaw, A. (2012). Talking to gaymers: Questioning identity, community and media representation. *Westminster Papers in Communication and Culture*, *9*(1), 67–89.

Shaw, A. (2015). *Gaming at the Edge: Sexuality and Gender at the Margins of Game Culture*. University of Minnesota Press. DOI: 10.5749/minnesota/9780816693153.001.0001

Shen, Z. (2021). A persuasive ewom model for increasing consumer engagement on social media: Evidence from irish fashion micro-influencers. *Journal of Research in Interactive Marketing*, *15*(2), 181–199. DOI: 10.1108/JRIM-10-2019-0161

Shepherd, T., Harvey, A., Jordan, T., Srauy, S., & Miltner, K. (2015). Histories of hating. *Social Media + Society*, *1*(2), 2056305115603997. Advance online publication. DOI: 10.1177/2056305115603997

Simondon, G. (1989). *Individuation in Light of Notions of Form and Information*. University of Minnesota Press.

Sims, C. (2014). Video game culture, contentious masculinities, and reproducing racialized social class divisions in Middle School. *Signs (Chicago, Ill.)*, *39*(4), 848–857. DOI: 10.1086/675539

Singla, Z., Randhawa, S., & Jain, S. (2017). Sentiment analysis of customer product reviews using machine learning. *2017 International Conference on Intelligent Computing and Control (I2C2)*. DOI: 10.1109/I2C2.2017.8321910

Šisler, V. (2008). Digital Arabs: Representation in video games. *European Journal of Cultural Studies*, *11*(2), 203–220.

Sjöblom, M., & Hamari, J. (2017). Why do people watch others play video games? An empirical study on the motivations of Twitch users. *Computers in Human Behavior*, *75*, 985–996. DOI: 10.1016/j.chb.2016.10.019

Sloman, A. (1979). Epistemology and Artificial Intelligence. Expert Systems in the Microelectronic Age. https://cogaffarchive.org/sloman-epist-ai.pdf

Smith, D. (2020). *Critical AI literacy: A call for ethical understanding in artificial intelligence*. *Journal of Digital Ethics*, *4*(3), 56–72. DOI: 10.1007/jde.2020.12

Smith, L. (2019). Economic cooperation and communal dynamics. *Journal of Applied Econometrics*, *39*(3), 112–130.

Sofuoğlu. (2021) Available at https://www.indyturk.com/node/366471/ya%C5%9Fam/sosyal-medyan%C4%B1n-y%C3%BCkselen-trendi-sanal-fenomenlik

Soh, H., Reid, L. N., & King, K. W. (2009). Measuring Trust In Advertising. *Journal of Advertising, 38*(2), 83–104. DOI: 10.2753/JOA0091-3367380206

Sookkaew, J., & Saephoo, P. (2021). "Digital influencer": Development and co-existence with digital social groups. *International Journal of Advanced Computer Science and Applications, 12*(12), 243–252. DOI: 10.14569/IJACSA.2021.0121243

Srivastava, A., Mukaria, B., & Arora, M. (2024). Influencer marketing: A citation and co-citation analysis within business and management domains. *International Academic Publishing House, 44*, 149–161. DOI: 10.52756/ijerr.2024.v44spl.013

Statisca (2024). Distribution of video gamers in the United States from 2006 to 2023, by gender. https://www.statista.com/statistics/232383/gender-split-of-us-computer-and-video-gamers/

Statista. (2024). Video gaming worldwide - Statistics & facts. Retrieved April 3, 2025, from https://www.statista.com/topics/1680/gaming/#topicOverview

Steele, C. M., & Aronson, J. (1995). Stereotype threat and the intellectual test performance of African Americans. *Journal of Personality and Social Psychology, 69*(5), 797–811. DOI: 10.1037/0022-3514.69.5.797 PMID: 7473032

Steinkuehler, C., & Williams, D. (2006). Where everybody knows your (screen) name: Online games as "third places". *Journal of Computer-Mediated Communication, 11*(4), 885–909. DOI: 10.1111/j.1083-6101.2006.00300.x

Stermer, S. P., & Burkley, M. (2015). SeX-Box: Exposure to sexist video games predicts benevolent sexism. *Psychology of Popular Media Culture, 4*(1), 47–55. DOI: 10.1037/a0028397

Stiegler, B. (2010). *For a New Critique of Political Economy*. Polity Press.

Stiegler, B. (2018). *The Neganthropocene*. Open Humanities Press.

Stiegler, B. (2019). *The Age of Disruption: Technology and Madness in Computational Capitalism*. Polity Press.

Sweeney, L. (2013). *Discrimination in online ad delivery*. ACM Digital Library., DOI: 10.1145/2460276.2460278

Takahashi, D. (2021, June 14). How Riot Games will ensure that Valorant's esports stars include women. VentureBeat. Retrieved from: https://venturebeat.com/games/how-riot-games-wants-to-ensure-that-valorants-esports-stars-include-women/#:~:text=But%20Valorant%20is% 20different% 20from,in%20an%20interview%20with%20GamesBeat.

Taylor, T. (2019). *Watch Me Play: Twitch and the Rise of Game Live Streaming*. Princeton University Press., DOI: 10.1515/9780691184975

Thavareesan, S., & Mahesan, S. (2019). Sentiment analysis in Tamil texts: A study on machine learning techniques and feature representation. *2019 14th Conference on Industrial and Information Systems (ICIIS)*.

Thomas, S. (2022). *Metaknowledge and AI: Understanding Systems Beneath the Surface. *AI in Context*, *19*(2), 67–85. DOI: 10.1007/aic.2022.02

Thomas, V. L., & Fowler, K. (2021). Close Encounters of the AI Kind: Use of AI Influencers As Brand Endorsers. *Journal of Advertising*, *50*(1), 11–25. DOI: 10.1080/00913367.2020.1810595

TikTok. (2025). Countering hate speech and behavior. https://www.tiktok.com/safety/en/countering-hate

Timisi, N. (2005). Sanallığın gerçekliği: İnternetin kimlik ve topluluk alanlarına girişi. In Binark, M., & Kılıçbay, B. (Eds.), *İnternet, toplum, kültür* (pp. 89–105). Epos Publishing.

Toffler, A. (2022). *The Third Wave: The Classic Study of Tomorrow*. Bantam.

Topics, E. (2025). How Many Gamers Are There? (New 2025 Statistics). by Fabio Duarte. Exploding Topics Blog. March 28, 2025. Retrieved from: https://explodingtopics.com/blog/number-of-gamers

Trivedi, S. K., Dey, S., & Kumar, A. (2018). Capturing user sentiments for online Indian movie reviews: A comparative analysis of different machine-learning models. *The Electronic Library*, *36*(4), 677–695. DOI: 10.1108/EL-04-2017-0075

Tsai, S. P. (2006). Investigating archetype-icon transformation in brand marketing. *Marketing Intelligence & Planning*, *26*(6), 648–663. DOI: 10.1108/02634500610701708

Tufekci, Z. (2015). Algorithms in our midst: The hidden politics of AI and machine learning. *Information Communication and Society*, *18*(7), 787–804. DOI: 10.1080/1369118X.2015.1008966

Turkle, S. (1995). *Life on the Screen: Identity in the Age of the Internet*. Simon & Schuster.

Turkle, S. (2011). *Alone together: Why We Expect More from Technology and Less from Each Other*. Basic Books.

Twenge, J. M., & Campbell, W. K. (2023). *Asrın vebası: Narcissism illeti* (Korkmaz, Ö., Trans.). Kaknüs Publications.

Ülker, Y., & Tosun, N. (2021). Mağaza imajının ikon marka algısına yansıması. [Turkish Review of Communication Studies]. *Türkiye İletişim Araştırmaları Dergisi, 38*(38), 205–221. DOI: 10.17829/turcom.805829

United Nations (2020). United Nations Strategy And Plan Of Action On Hate Speech.

Uzunoğlu, A. (2021). Digital Games and Addiction. https://dergipark.org.tr/en/download/article-file/2085319

Van Dijk, J. (2018). *Network society*. Epsilon Publishing House.

Vervaeke, J. (2025, March 18). AI and the Meaning Crisis | Redefining Human Flourishing [Video]. YouTube. https://www.youtube.com/watch?v=C2Jws87yA1Y

Vizcaíno-Verdú, A., De-Casas-Moreno, P., & Tirocchi, S. (2023). Online prosumer convergence: Listening, creating and sharing music on YouTube and TikTok. *Communicatio Socialis, 36*(1), 151–166. DOI: 10.15581/003.36.1.151-166

Volkova, S., Wilson, T., & Yarowsky, D. (2013). Exploring demographic language variations to improve multilingual sentiment analysis in social media. *Proceedings of the 2013 Conference on Empirical Methods in Natural Language Processing*, 1815–1827. DOI: 10.18653/v1/D13-1187

Waila, P., Marisha, Singh, V. K., & Singh, M. K. (2012). Evaluating Machine Learning and Unsupervised Semantic Orientation approaches for sentiment analysis of textual reviews. *2012 IEEE International Conference on Computational Intelligence and Computing Research*. DOI: 10.1109/ICCIC.2012.6510235

Wajcman, J. (2004). *El Tecnofeminismo*. Universitat de València.

Wajcman, J. (2006). Technocapitalism meets technofeminism: Women and technology in a wireless world. labour and industry. *Journal Of The Social And Economic Relations Of Work, 16*(3), 7–20.

Wajcman, J. (2007). From women and technology to gendered technoscience. *Information Communication and Society, 10*(3), 287–298. DOI: 10.1080/13691180701409770

Wajcman, J. (2010). Feminist theories of technology. *Cambridge Journal of Economics, 34*(1), 143–152. DOI: 10.1093/cje/ben057

Waldron, J. (2012). *The harm in hate speech.* Harvard University Press. DOI: 10.4159/harvard.9780674065086

Walker, C. S. (2021). *YouTubers* (Demir, B. M., Trans.). Lykeion Publishing.

Wallenius, M., Rimpelä, A., Punamäki, R. L., & Lintonen, T. (2009). Digital game playing motives among adolescents: Relations to parent–child communication, school performance, sleeping habits, and perceived health. *Journal of Applied Developmental Psychology, 30*(4), 463–474. DOI: 10.1016/j.appdev.2008.12.021

Wang, T. (2020). *Parasocial relationship: An analysis of Li Ziqi and her audiences* [Unpublished master's thesis]. Middle Tennessee State University.

Ward, K. D. (1997). Free speech and the development of liberal virtues: An examination of the controversies involving flag-burning and hate speech. *University of Miami Law Review, 52*, 733–788.

Ward, L. M., & Grower, P. (2020). Media and the development of gender role stereotypes. *Annual Review of Developmental Psychology, 2*(1), 177–199. DOI: 10.1146/annurev-devpsych-051120-010630

We Are Social. 2025 https://www.guvenliweb.org.tr/dosya/95AwI.pdf

Wei, L. (2024). User-generated-content behaviours shape brand loyalty: A self-determination theory perspective. Journal of Education. *Humanities and Social Sciences, 27*, 287–292. DOI: 10.54097/mzf86j96

Welch, T. (2018). The Affectively Necessary Labor Of Queer Mods. Game Studies, 18(3). Retrieved from: https://gamestudies.org/1803/articles/welch

Wells, G., Romhányi, Á., & Steinkuehler, C. (2025). Hate speech and hate-based harassment in online games. *Frontiers in Psychology, 15*, 1422422. DOI: 10.3389/fpsyg.2024.1422422 PMID: 40046807

Wijkstra, M., Rogers, K., Mandryk, R. L., Veltkamp, R. C., & Frommel, J. (2024). How to tame a toxic player? A systematic literature review on intervention systems for toxic behaviors in online video games. Proceedings of the ACM on Human-Computer Interaction, 8(CHI PLAY), 1-32.

Williams, D. (2006). Virtual cultivation: Online worlds, offline perceptions. *Journal of Communication, 56*(1), 69–87. DOI: 10.1111/j.1460-2466.2006.00004.x

Williams, D., Ducheneaut, N., Xiong, L., Zhang, Y., Yee, N., & Nickell, E. (2006). From tree house to barracks: The social life of guilds in World of Warcraft. *Games and Culture, 1*(4), 338–361. DOI: 10.1177/1555412006292616

Williams, D., Martins, N., Consalvo, M., & Ivory, J. D. (2009). The virtual census: Representations of gender, race and age in video games. *New Media & Society, 11*(5), 815–834. DOI: 10.1177/1461444809105354

Winfield, A. F. T. (2018). Ethics, autonomy, and artificial intelligence. In van den Hoven, M. (Ed.), *The ethics of artificial intelligence and robotics* (pp. 217–234). Springer., DOI: 10.1007/978-3-030-01789-2_14

Winner, L. (1986). *The whale and the reactor: A search for limits in an age of high technology*. University of Chicago Press.

Wolf, M. (2016). *Tales of Literacy for the 21st Century*. Oxford University Press.

Wotanis, L. L., & McMillan, L. (2014). Performing Gender on YouTube. *Feminist Media Studies, 14*(6), 912–928. DOI: 10.1080/14680777.2014.882373

Wullach, T., Adler, A., & Minkov, E. (2021). Fight fire with fire: Fine-tuning hate detectors using large samples of generated hate speech. *arXiv,* 1–6.

Xie-Carson, L., Magor, T., Benckendorff, P., & Hughes, K. (2023). All hype or the real deal? Investigating user engagement with virtual influencers in tourism. *Tourism Management, 99*, 104779. Advance online publication. DOI: 10.1016/j.tourman.2023.104779

Yadav, B. P., Sheshikala, M., Swathi, N., Chythanya, K. R., & Sudarshan, E. (2020). Women wellbeing assessment in Indian metropolises using machine learning models. *IOP Conference Series. Materials Science and Engineering, 981*(2), 022042. DOI: 10.1088/1757-899X/981/2/022042

Yao, M. Z., Mahood, C., & Linz, D. (2010). Sexual priming, gender stereotyping, and likelihood to sexually harass: Examining the cognitive effects of playing a sexually-explicit video game. *Sex Roles, 62*(1–2), 77–88. DOI: 10.1007/s11199-009-9695-4 PMID: 20098511

Yee, N. (2018, June 14). Beyond 50/50: Breaking down the percentage of female gamers by genre. Quantic Foundry. https://quanticfoundry.com/2017/01/19/female-gamers-by-genre/

YouTube. (2025). Hate speech & harassment policy. https://www.youtube.com/howyoutubeworks/our-commitments/standing-up-to-hate/

Yuan, J. E. (2025). Making virtual celebrity: Platformization and intermediation in digital cultural production. *International Journal of Cultural Studies, 28*(1), 316–331. DOI: 10.1177/13678779241230564

Yüksel, M. (2003). Mahremiyet hakkı ve sosyo-tarihsel gelişimi. *Ankara University SBF Journal*, *64*(1), 181–213.

Yüksel, M. (2009). Philosophical approaches to the right to privacy and individual freedoms. *Ankara University SBF Journal*, *64*(4), 1–24.

Yuniarossy, B. A., Hindrayani, K. M., & Damaliana, A. T. (2024). Analisis Sentimen Terhadap Isu Feminisme Di Twitter Menggunakan Model Convolutional Neural Network (CNN). *Jurnal Lebesgue : Jurnal Ilmiah Pendidikan Matematika. Matematika Dan Statistika*, *5*(1), 477–491. DOI: 10.46306/lb.v5i1.585

Yurdigül, A., & Yurdigül, Y. (2019). Information society and television news. (Ed). Sarı, Ü. & Aytekin, M., in *International Communication Studies*. İstanbul: Kriter Yayınevi, pp.193-200.

Zachrisson, A., & Karancsi, A. H. (2023) MOBAs, the beginning From mod to genre, https://www.diva-portal.org/smash/get/diva2:1768354/FULLTEXT01.pdf

Zeng, X., McKenna, B., Richter, S., & Cai, W. (2019). How social media can afford engagement processes., 272-279. DOI: 10.1007/978-3-030-11395-7_23

Zheng, S. (2023). An empirical study on the effects of information characteristics in influencer marketing on consumers' purchase intention. *Advances in Economics and Management Research*, *8*(1), 179. DOI: 10.56028/aemr.8.1.179.2023

Zuboff, S. (2019). The Age of Surveillance Capitalism. Public Affairs. Liddell, H. G., & Scott, R. (1940). A Greek English Lexicon. Clarendon Press. via Perseus Project.

About The Contributors

M. Nur Erdem completed her undergraduate and graduate studies in Public Relations and Publicity at Kocaeli University. In 2014, she got her PhD degree with her thesis titled “A Digital Literacy Education Model Proposal in the Context of Consumption-Based Consciousness Industry and Advertising”. Erdem has many national and international books, articles and papers in the fields of digital advertising, digital culture, game-vertising and advertising narrative. She is currently working as a faculty member at Ondokuz Mayıs University, Faculty of Communication, Department of Communication and Design. She is also a member of ATIKA (Akıllı Toplum İçin Kadın Akademisyenler - Female Academics for a Smart Society) initiative, which was established with the aim of providing a network for female postgraduate students. She also lectures and conducts scientific research at Ondokuz Mayıs University, Department of Neuromarketing.

Özgün Arda Kuş graduated from Maltepe University, Department of Public Relations and Advertising, with a full scholarship, and also pursued a double major in Psychology. He completed his Master's degree in the Department of Sales and Marketing at Okan University, Business Administration Department. He completed his Ph.D. education in the Department of Public Relations and Advertising at Istanbul University with a thesis titled “Digital Games as an Interactive Communication Space; A study on the effects of playing motivations on digital game addiction.” He is currently continuing his academic studies as an Assistant Professor at the Department of Public Relations and Advertising at Uskūdar University Faculty of Communication. He has participated in various international and national certificate programs in the fields of marketing and psychology. He has authored the internationally published book “The Concept of Mobile Marketing, A Study for Istanbul and Generation Y,” the nationally published book “Relationships Among Game, Digital Game, Addiction, and Motivation Concepts,” and has served as editor for the compilation books “Digital Forms of Games 1,2 and 3” co-edited with Ozge

Ugurlu Akbas. He has also presented papers at international scientific conferences and contributed chapters and articles to various books. The areas of research and interest for Ozgün Arda Kus include: digital games, alienation, self, mobile marketing, consumer behaviors and generations, mood disorders, and behavioral addictions. He is a full member of the Turkish Psychological Association.

***

Vishnu Achutha Menon is an assistant professor at the Institute for Educational and Developmental Studies in Noida. His research interests span various fields, including film studies, new media, Virtual Reality (VR), Augmented Reality (AR), Artificial Intelligence (AI), data journalism and visualization, educational media, immersive technology, interactive media, media psychology, digital ethnography, smart education, digital pedagogy, verbal and nonverbal communication, South Asian performances, Natyasastra, and Ethnomusicology. He has published journal articles in Economic and Political Weekly, IEEE Proceedings, Springer Lecture Note Series, International Journal of Emerging Technologies in Learning (iJET), Studies in Media and Communication, Journal of Media and Communication, Journal of Arts, among others. Vishnu has contributed book chapters to publishers such as IGI Global, Wiley, CRC Press, and Emerald. He has also written book reviews for Asian Theatre Journal, Space and Culture, Urban India, and others. He specializes in mixed methods in social sciences and humanities research.

Özgül Dağlı had finished her Bachelors Degree in Anadolu University Communication Arts Department in Eskişehir, year 1999. She has completed her M.A and PHD in the same University, Public Relations and Advertising Department. Dağlı has studied on the Usage of Metaphors in Television Advertising and her PHd thesis title was "The Usage of Metaphors in Advertising". Dağlı, has started her profession as an academician in Anadolu University and she is working as a Professor in Uskudar University. Özgül Dağlı received her associate professor title in 2018 and her professorship on 25.05.2023. Since then, she has been the head of the Advertising department at Üsküdar University Faculty of Communication. Dağlı's academic field of studies are; Advertising, copywriting, creative processes in advertising, neuromarketing, process of brand building, consumer behavior and the role of senses and experiences in consumer buying processes.

Serhat Erdem, born in 1982 in Kırıkkale, completed his high school education at Samsun Ondokuz Mayıs High School. In 2004, he earned his bachelor's degree from Atatürk University, Faculty of Communication, Department of Radio, Television, and Cinema. In 2005, he began his academic career as a Research Assistant in the Department of Cinema and Television at Atatürk University's Faculty of Fine Arts. Erdem completed his master's degree in 2009 at Atatürk University, Institute of Social Sciences, Department of Journalism, with a thesis titled "An Analysis of the Transformations Caused by Matte Painting Applications in Cinema." In 2010, he began his doctoral studies at Istanbul University, Institute of Social Sciences, Department of Radio, Television, and Cinema. He received the title of Doctor in 2015 after successfully completing his dissertation titled "The Use of Visual Effects in the Reconstruction of Reality: Spatial Construction in the Spartacus Television Series." Between 2005 and 2022, Erdem served as an Assistant Professor in the Department of Cinema and Television at Atatürk University's Faculty of Fine Arts. In 2022, he earned the title of Associate Professor in the field of Visual Communication Design. Since February 2022, he has continued his academic work in the Department of Radio, Television, and Cinema at Atatürk University's Faculty of Communication.

Feride Zeynep Güder works as an associate professor at Uskudar University. After completing a BA in English Language & Teaching at Atatürk University (1994) and an MA in English Language & Literature at İstanbul Kültür University (2004), she completed her Ph.D. in journalism at İstanbul University (2012). With an emphasis on digital humanities, she specializes in communication studies. She gives lectures on "Critical AI Literacy," "City and Memory," "Cross-Cultural Communication," "Digital Media and Translation," "Digital Culture," "Discourse Analysis," "Literature Society and Culture," "Media and Truth," "Media and Ideology," "Memory and Culture in New Media Ecology," "Political Communication," "Postmodernism," and "Techno-Culture and Critical Reading." She received the "Best Presentation Paper Award" at the international CIM conference in the USA (2013). Later, she received awards for being the best presenter at the International Conference in Barcelona (2020). She is the author of two books: "Voyeuristic Gaze" and "The Language of Persuasion and Media." She published Scopus-indexed book chapters. In addition to digital media studies, her academic trajectory follows a wide span: critical epistemology, critical AI literacy, digital humanities, meta-cognitive strategies and AI, and political epistemology.

Esra Pelin Guregen Dereboyu graduated in 2018 from Marmara University's Faculty of Communication with a double major in Public Relations and Promotion, and Radio, Television and Cinema, and a minor in Journalism. She went on to complete her master's degree in Public Relations at Marmara University with a thesis entitled "Impression Management of Multinational Corporations: A Study of Multinational Enterprises Operating in Turkey." In 2024, she earned her PhD in the Department of Public Relations and Promotion at Istanbul University with the dissertation "From the Construction of Consumer Culture to Postmodern

Times: Examining the Role of Social Media in the Relationship between Love and Consumption in Web 2.0." Between 2019 and 2022, she served as a Research Assistant in the Department of Public Relations and Advertising at Istanbul Esenyurt University's Faculty of Arts and Social Sciences. From 2022 to 2024, she continued her role as Research Assistant in the Department of New Media and Communication at Fenerbahçe University's Faculty of Communication, where, as of 2024, she holds the position of Assistant Professor. Her scholarly work focuses on digital communication, artificial intelligence, communication psychology, consumer behavior, and cultural studies.

Esin Selin Karaoz holds a double major in Visual Communication Design and New Media from Beykent University. She completed her master's thesis titled "The Impact of Narrative in Mobile Games on the Gaming Experience" in the New Media and Communication Management program at Istanbul University. Currently, she is pursuing her PhD in the Department of Communication Studies at Kadir Has University, focusing on online games and intercultural communication. She works as a Research Assistant in the Department of Visual Communication Design at Istanbul Bilgi University. She has various academic publications on game culture, game narrative and digital communication. Her research examines digital game and online communities, toxicity, and cultural representations through netnographic and qualitative methods. Her academic interests include game studies, cultural studies, intercultural communication, and new media.

Damla Karşu Cesur received her bachelor's degree in Advertising from Kadir Has University in 2012 and her masters degree in Public Relations and Advertising from Sakarya University in 2015. She completed her PhD in Advertising at Marmara University in 2021. She is currently serving as an Assistant Professor at Kocaeli University. Her research interests includes advertising, social media marketing, consumer behavior and advertising research.

Meltem Merve Urfali was born in Amasya. After completing high school, she graduated from the Public Relations and Promotion Department of the Faculty of Communication at Ondokuz Mayıs University in 2020. In 2021, she was accepted into the Master's Program in Media and Communication Sciences at the Graduate School of Ondokuz Mayıs University. Urfalı completed her education in 2024 with her master's thesis titled "The Construction of Gender in Digital Games from a Technofeminist Perspective." In 2024, Urfalı was admitted to the Radio, Television, and Cinema Master's Program at Ondokuz Mayıs University and is currently pursuing her second master's degree. Her areas of interest and research include gender, feminism, queer theory, digital activism, digital games, body politics, and feminist film narratives.

Asena Irmak Yavuz was born in 2000 in Antalya, Turkey. She completed her primary and secondary education in Bodrum. In 2018, she was admitted to SWPS University of Social Sciences and Humanities in Warsaw, Poland, to pursue undergraduate studies in psychology. After residing in Warsaw for two years, she returned to Turkey due to the COVID-19 pandemic and discontinued her studies. In 2021, she enrolled in the undergraduate program in New Media and Communication at Üsküdar University, where she is currently continuing her education.

Index

A

B

C

D

F

G

H

M

N

O

P

S

T

V

W

Y

www.ingramcontent.com/pod-product-compliance
Lightning Source LLC
LaVergne TN
LVHW081526300926
849161LV00006B/1317